THE CAMBRIDGE COMPANION TO
CONSTANT

Benjamin Constant is now widely regarded as a founding father of modern liberalism. *The Cambridge Companion to Constant* presents a collection of interpretive essays on the major aspects of his life and work by a panel of international scholars. Separate sections are devoted to Constant as a political theorist and actor, his work as a social analyst and literary critic, and his accomplishments as a historian of religion. Themes covered range from Constant's views on modern liberty, progress, terror, and individualism, to his ideas on slavery and empire, literature, women, and the nature and importance of religion. *The Cambridge Companion to Constant* is a convenient and accessible guide to Constant and the most up-to-date scholarship on him.

Helena Rosenblatt is Professor of History at Hunter College and the Graduate Center of the City University of New York. She received her M.A. and Ph.D. from Columbia University. She is the author of *Rousseau and Geneva: From the First Discourse to the Social Contract 1749–1762* and *Liberal Values: Benjamin Constant and the Politics of Religion*. She has written numerous articles for journals such as *Modern Intellectual History*, *French Historical Studies*, *History of European Ideas*, *French Politics, Society and Culture*, and *Daedalus*. A member of the editorial board of *Modern Intellectual History*, she has also been a Fellow at the National Humanities Center.

Continued after the Index

The Cambridge Companion to
CONSTANT

Edited by

Helena Rosenblatt
Hunter College and the Graduate Center, CUNY

CAMBRIDGE
UNIVERSITY PRESS

CAMBRIDGE UNIVERSITY PRESS
Cambridge, New York, Melbourne, Madrid, Cape Town, Singapore, São Paulo, Delhi

Cambridge University Press
32 Avenue of the Americas, New York, NY 10013–2473, USA

www.cambridge.org
Information on this title: www.cambridge.org/9780521672436

First published 2009

Printed in the United States of America

A catalog record for this publication is available from the British Library

Library of Congress Cataloging in Publication data
The Cambridge companion to Constant / edited by Helena Rosenblatt.
   p.   cm. – (Cambridge companions to philosophy)
ISBN 978-0-521-67243-6 (pbk.) – ISBN 978-0-521-85646-1 (hardback)
   1. Constant, Benjamin, 1767–1830.   2. France – Intellectual life – 19th century.
3. France – Politics and government – 1789–1815.   4. France – Politics and
government – 1814–1830.   5. Intellectuals – France – Biography.   6. Novelists,
Swiss – 19th century – Biography.   7. Liberalism – France – History.   I. Rosenblatt,
Helena, 1961–   II. Title.   III. Series.
DC255.C7C36   2009
944.06092–dc22   2008044606
[B]

ISBN 978-0-521-85646-1 hardback
ISBN 978-0-521-67243-6 paperback

CONTENTS

PREFACE

Interest in the thought of Benjamin Constant has been growing steadily on both sides of the Atlantic. Long recognized as the author of the literary masterpiece *Adolphe*, Constant is best known today for his political thought and, in particular, for his 1819 lecture "On the Liberty of the Moderns Compared with That of the Ancients." A steady stream of paperback editions of his major political works is appearing in both French and English (also in Italian and soon in Spanish). College textbooks more and more frequently include references to him, and anthologies increasingly contain selections from him. Along with a growing body of scholarship, this renewed interest in Constant is serving to confirm his stature as a founding father of modern liberalism. In fact, many people today regard Constant as *the* most important liberal thinker between Montesquieu and Tocqueville.

As is often the case with great thinkers and historical personalities, Constant's reputation suffered a decline after his death, but it began to recover during the late nineteenth century and then rose dramatically in the second half of the twentieth century. Karl Marx read Constant carefully, but dismissed him, along with liberals in general, as a mere spokesperson of bourgeois class interests. Thereafter, Constant's political thought was largely forgotten, as public interest turned to his autobiographical writings and his psychological novel, *Adolphe*. Eventually, however, the reaction against Marxism and the concomitant growth of interest in the origins of liberalism stimulated new research into Constant's political thought. The collapse of Soviet Communism and the related sea change in French intellectual politics reinforced the trend. In recent years, together with Tocqueville, Constant has emerged as a truly great thinker, whose subtle and sophisticated defense of individual rights and freedoms are particularly relevant to modern men and women. Indeed, political theorists on both sides of the Atlantic, and as diverse as Isaiah Berlin, Marcel Gauchet, Tzvetan Todorov, and Stephen Holmes, have taken inspiration from Constant's work. They have read Constant in order to gain insights into subjects as varied as the meaning and significance of the French Revolution, the promises and problems of liberal democracy, the roots of totalitarianism, the psychological malaise of modern man, and the dynamics of gender relations. In a significant recent turn of events, two distinguished American jurists, Supreme Court judge Stephen Breyer and Harvard law professor Charles Fried, have taken direct inspiration from Constant in their interpretations of the American Constitution and the meaning of liberty.

Although Constant's definition of modern liberty continues to attract the attention of political theorists and public intellectuals, others are now exploring new and different dimensions of his work. The *Œuvres complètes de Benjamin Constant*, begun in 1988 and led by an international team of experts, is contributing to this trend. The editorial committee has projected a total of fifty-four volumes divided into two series, one devoted to Constant's correspondence and the other to his published and unpublished works. This ongoing publishing event (twenty volumes of which have appeared so far) is facilitating new approaches to him. The Institut and Association Benjamin Constant, established in 1979 in Lausanne, Switzerland, lends its support by collaborating on the *Œuvres complètes*, by sponsoring publications such as the *Annales Benjamin Constant*, and by organizing regular conferences.

The Cambridge Companion to Constant is both a reflection of and a contribution to this ongoing Constant revival. Its aim is to introduce interested readers to Constant and to the secondary literature about him. Constant made seminal contributions to diverse fields, from literature, psychology, and political theory to the history of religion. A consequence of this is that scholarship has been scattered in different scholarly disciplines. The resulting problem of accessibility is compounded by the fact that much of this recent scholarship is in languages other than English. One of the aims of this *Cambridge Companion* is to gather into one English-language volume some of the most exemplary recent scholarship from around the world on the various dimensions of Constant's œuvre. Another is to combat simplistic interpretations of Constant's life and thought by bringing to the foreground its nuances, depth, and even tensions and ambiguities.

OVERVIEW OF THE VOLUME

Dennis Wood's biographical sketch reminds us that Constant's metamorphosis into a successful French politician and renowned political theorist was far from foreseeable at the outset. He had rather inauspicious beginnings – a foreign birth, a highly erratic upbringing, and a complicated family life – and he encountered many hurdles along the way. And yet he managed to carve out for himself a successful career under the wildly fluctuating political circumstances of Revolutionary and post-Revolutionary France. Wood attributes his ability to overcome these obstacles to a steadfast commitment to his political principles and his lifelong attachment to liberalism.

The first, and most substantial, section of this volume is devoted to Constant as political theorist and actor. It begins with a much-celebrated essay by Marcel Gauchet, reproduced here for the first time in English and in slightly abbreviated form. When it originally appeared in 1980, this essay helped to propel the Constant revival. Gauchet, who has since become one of France's most prominent contemporary philosophers, believes Constant's brilliance to lie in the many insights he offers into the contradictions of modernity and the dangers of democracy. Gauchet admires Constant for his prescience in combining certain conservative, essentially monarchical, principles with progressive, emancipatory ones.

The second essay in this section is by the American political theorist Stephen Holmes. In 1984, Holmes's *Benjamin Constant and the Making of Modern Liberalism* also helped to rekindle interest in Constant, especially in the Anglophone world. In his essay for this volume, Holmes offers a fresh reading of Constant, focusing on his forceful denunciation, more than two hundred years ago, of a government's use of informants, secret denunciations, and military tribunals. Holmes finds Constant's steadfast defense of legal procedures and transparency in a time of war particularly relevant to the current political climate in the United States. Constant understood that modern liberty is closely related to, and indeed dependent on, judicial guarantees. Citizens must feel safe under a system of laws in order to be free.

In the following essay, British scholar Jeremy Jennings focuses squarely on Constant's famous distinction between modern and ancient liberty. He surveys the recent scholarly interpretations of this distinction and, through a careful reading of Constant's principal political works, shows the often underappreciated nuances of Constant's analysis.

The next three essays locate Constant within the liberal debates of his own time, highlighting his originality and distinctiveness. Stefano De Luca discusses Constant's pronouncements on the Terror, evaluating the strengths and weaknesses of his arguments, and how they evolved over time. As Constant grappled with the thought of Rousseau, and seized on the modern/ancient liberty distinction, his argument became more sophisticated and characteristically liberal. Jennifer Pitts's essay broaches a new topic in Constant scholarship, namely, his views on empire and slavery. She notes that although Constant was an outspoken opponent of both imperial expansion and the slave trade, his pronouncements on slavery reveal some not insignificant tensions and ambiguities. In the final essay in this section, Robert Alexander describes Constant's career as a Restoration politician. Liberals have often been portrayed as uninterested in politics, or at least as downgrading the value of political engagement. By contrast, Alexander shows Constant's deep commitment to political *practice*, emphasizing his crucial role as a pragmatic strategist and grassroots organizer for the Liberal Opposition.

The second section of this volume considers Constant as a psychologist and analyst of society. Interdisciplinary perspectives, informed by psychology, literature, and history, are offered on both Constant's own emotional state and his analytical skills. One of the many particularities of Constant is not just that he led an interesting and full life, but that he reflected so deeply on it and wrote so copiously about it. Steven Vincent broaches the topic of Constant's relationships with women. Traditionally, Constant's many love affairs either have been dismissed as irrelevant or have exposed him to ridicule and disdain. Instead, Vincent illustrates how very interesting and varied Constant's relationships with women were and how important they were to his emotional and intellectual development.

Vincent shows that Constant's reflections about love and intimacy informed his thinking about morals and politics.

Gerald Izenberg argues that from the very beginning of his political career, Constant displayed deep ambivalence toward the self-interested motivations that he simultaneously saw as the foundation of modern liberty. Constant spent a lot of time thinking about the needs of "individuality" – what Izenberg refers to as the "Romantic self." Patrick Coleman highlights the close connections that exist between Constant's literary and political works, once again refuting any reduction of his thought to the mere protection of private interests. He examines the distinctive meaning Constant attached to "literature" and how Constant's literary productions related to his broader commitments. The final essay in this section, by Etienne Hofmann, analyzes the key concept of "perfectibility" in Constant's thought. It is a notion that spanned multiple disciplines, including literature, moral philosophy, and history. As Hofmann explains, the concept also had definite political resonances that Constant was keen to exploit.

The *final section of this volume* turns to a long-neglected, but now recognized as central, aspect of Constant's œuvre: his thoughts on religion. It is a well-known fact that Constant began research on a history of religion at the age of eighteen and continued working on it throughout his life, until he finally published it as the five-volume *De la religion considérée dans sa sources, ses formes et ses développements* (1824–31). In the meantime, he wrote other pieces on religion, some of which he published and some of which he did not. It is also known that Constant himself regarded his research into religion as his most important undertaking and, as Tzvetan Todorov reminds us, it was for *De la religion* that he most wished to be remembered. Against those who have dismissed this book as somehow irrelevant and outdated, Todorov insists that it continues to convey a valuable and enduring message: far from disappearing over time, Constant shows why religion is here to stay. Moreover, Todorov believes that Constant's approach to religion, pathbreaking for its time, makes him one of the founders of religious anthropology.

The essays by Laurence Dickey and Bryan Garsten show how wrong it is to compartmentalize Constant's writings on religion. They highlight the fact that Constant's liberalism was always imbued with religious values and that his view of liberal politics depended on such values. Garsten argues that despite Constant's advocacy of state neutrality in religious matters, he favored a particular kind of religion, namely, a privatized, sentimental, and anticlerical religion close to the liberal Protestantism of his lifelong partner, Madame de Staël. Dickey shows Constant to have been heir to a long tradition of "philosophical theism," which guided his thinking throughout his life.

Finally, as a conclusion to the volume, my own piece surveys Constant's posthumous reputation, emphasizing the very different reception his ideas encountered in France and America, and how perceptions of Constant evolved over time.

ACKNOWLEDGMENTS

I am delighted to recognize the friends and colleagues who have helped bring about *The Cambridge Companion to Constant*. First and foremost is Cheryl Welch, who encouraged me to undertake this project and who offered invaluable advice and guidance along the way. The contributors to this volume have been a pleasure to work with, and I thank them all. I was very fortunate to have Ed Parsons as editor, and I have much appreciated the enthusiasm and professionalism with which he has guided me through the whole process.

A generous grant from the Florence Gould Foundation made it possible to include three essays originally submitted in French and one in Italian. I was very pleased and honored when Art Goldhammer agreed to translate them for us, and I thank him for his outstanding work here.

The Institut Benjamin Constant, with its incomparable Anne Hofmann, has been unfailingly helpful to me. Anne has cheerfully answered questions, tracked down citations, proofread texts, and been a wonderful general sounding board. She is a main reason why the Institut Benjamin Constant is such a wonderful resource, and I am most grateful to her.

Finally, I thank my colleagues in the Hunter College History Department, and especially my chair, Barbara Welter, for encouragement and help of all kinds. Last, but not least, the steadfast support and good humor of my husband sustain me always.

CONTRIBUTORS

ROBERT ALEXANDER is Professor of History at the University of Victoria, Canada. He is the author of *Bonapartism and Revolutionary Tradition in France* (1991), *Napoleon* (2001), and *Re-Writing the French Revolutionary Tradition* (2003). He is currently working on a history of nineteenth-century European politics entitled "Europe's Uncertain Path."

PATRICK COLEMAN is Professor of French and Francophone Studies at the University of California, Los Angeles. He is the author of *Rousseau's Political Imagination: Rule and Representation in the "Lettre à d'Alembert"* (1984), *The Limits of Sympathy: Gabrielle Roy's The Tin Flute* (1993), and *Reparative Realism: Mourning and Modernity in the French Novel 1730–1830* (1998). He is also the editor of Constant's *Adolphe* (2001).

STEFANO DE LUCA teaches the history of political thought at the University La Sapienza of Rome and is a researcher at the University Suor Orsola Benincasa of Naples. He is the author of *Il pensiero politico di Benjamin Constant* (1993) and *Alle origini del liberalismo contemporaneo. Il pensiero di Benjamin Constant tra il Termidoro e l'Impero* (2003). He is at present bringing out an Italian edition of Constant's *Principles of Politics.*

LAURENCE DICKEY is Professor Emeritus at the University of Wisconsin–Madison. He is the author of *Hegel: Religion, Economics, and the Politics of Spirit* (1987) and a contributor to the *Cambridge Companion to Hegel* (1993). He is also the editor of *Hegel's Political Writings* (1999) and *Adam Smith's "The Wealth of Nations"* (1993).

BRYAN GARSTEN is Associate Professor of Political Science at Yale University. He is the author of *Saving Persuasion: A Defense of Rhetoric and Judgment* (2006). Currently, he is writing about representative government and its relation to religion.

MARCEL GAUCHET is Director of Research at the Ecole des hautes études en sciences sociales in Paris and the editor of *Le Débat* and coeditor of *La Pensée politique*. His publications include *The Disenchantment of the World* (French 1985, English translation 1997), *La révolution des droits de l'homme* (1989), *La révolution des pouvoirs* (1995), *La religion dans la démocratie* (2001), *La démocratie contre elle-même* (2002), and *La condition historique* (2003). In 1980, he edited Constant's *Ecrits politiques*.

ETIENNE HOFMANN teaches the history of historiography at the University of Lausanne, Switzerland. He is the author of *Les "Principes de politique" de Benjamin Constant: la genèse d'une œuvre et l'évolution de la pensée de leur auteur, 1789–1806* (2 vols.) (1980) and *Catalogue raisonné de l'œuvre manuscrite de Benjamin Constant* (1992). He is the coeditor, with Tzvetan Todorov, of Constant's *De la religion, considérée dans sa source, ses formes et ses développements* (1999). He is also a member of the editorial board of Constant's *Œuvres complètes* and the *Annales Benjamin Constant*.

STEPHEN HOLMES is Walter E. Meyer Professor of Law at New York University. He is the author of *Benjamin Constant and the Making of Modern Liberalism* (1984, French translation 1994), *Anatomy of Antiliberalism* (1993), *Passions and Constraints: The Theory of Liberal Democracy* (1995), and *The Matador's Cape: America's Reckless Response to Terror* (2007).

GERALD IZENBERG is Professor of History at Washington University, and the author of *The Existentialist Critique of Freud: The Crisis of Autonomy* (1976), *Impossible Individuality: Romanticism, Revolution and the Origin of Modern Selfhood* (1992), and *Modernism and Masculinity: Mann, Wedekind and Kandinsky through World War One* (2000). A contributor to the *Cambridge Companion to Freud* (1992), he is additionally a psychoanalyst and was formerly president of the St. Louis Psychoanalytic Society.

JEREMY JENNINGS is Professor of Political Theory at Queen Mary, University of London. His publications include *Georges Sorel* (1985), *Syndicalism in France* (1990), *Intellectuals in Twentieth-Century France* (1993), and (with Iseult Honohan) *Republicanism in Theory and Practice* (2006). With Aurelian Craiutu, he has recently published *Tocqueville on America after 1840: Letters and Other Writings* (2009).

JENNIFER PITTS is Associate Professor of Political Science at the University of Chicago. She is the author of *A Turn to Empire: The Rise of Imperialism* (2005, French translation 2008) and the editor and translator of Alexis de Tocqueville's *Writings on Empire and Slavery* (2001). She is currently working on a book about European conceptions of the international legal community and of legal relations with non-European states in the eighteenth and nineteenth centuries.

HELENA ROSENBLATT is Professor of History at Hunter College and The Graduate Center, CUNY. She is the author of *Rousseau and Geneva: From the First Discourse to the Social Contract 1749–1762* (1997) and *Liberal Values: Benjamin Constant and the Politics of Religion* (2008).

TZVETAN TODOROV is Director of Research at the Centre national de recherches scientifiques (CNRS) in Paris. His publications include *The Conquest of America* (1982), *Frail Happiness: An Essay on Rousseau* (1985), *On Human Diversity* (1993), *Imperfect Garden: The Legacy of Humanism* (1998), and *A Passion for Democracy: The Life, the Women He Loved and the Thought of Benjamin Constant* (1999). He is also the coeditor, with Etienne Hofmann, of Benjamin Constant's *De la religion*.

K. STEVEN VINCENT is Professor of History at North Carolina State University. He is the author of *Pierre-Joseph Proudhon and the Rise of French Republican Socialism* (1984) and *Between Marxism and Anarchism: Benoît Malon and French Reformist Socialism* (1992), and the coeditor of *The Human Tradition in Modern France* (2000).

DENNIS WOOD is Emeritus Professor of French Literature at the University of Birmingham (UK) and the author of *Benjamin Constant: A Biography* (1993) as well as *Benjamin Constant: Adolphe* (1987). He is also a member of the editorial board of Constant's *Œuvres complètes*.

ABBREVIATIONS

ABC   *Annales Benjamin Constant*, 1980. Lausanne:
                Institut Benjamin Constant/Geneva: Slatkine.
AML   Benjamin Constant, "The Liberty of the Ancients
                Compared with That of the Moderns," in *PW*.
DLR   Benjamin Constant, *De la religion, considérée
                dans sa source, ses formes et ses développements*.
                Edited by Tzvetan Todorov and Etienne Hofmann.
                Arles, France: Actes Sud, 1999.
EP   Benjamin Constant, *Ecrits politiques*. Edited by
                Marcel Gauchet. Paris: Gallimard, 1997.
Mélanges   Benjamin Constant, *Mélanges de littérature et de
                politique*, in *EP*, 623–755.
OCBC/*Œuvres*   Benjamin Constant, *Œuvres complètes*. Edited by
                Paul Delbouille, Kurt Kloocke, *et al.* Tübingen:
                Max Niemeyer Verlag, 1993–. Série I, *Œuvres*.
OCBC/CG   Benjamin Constant, *Œuvres complètes*. Edited by
                C. P. Courtney, Paul Delbouille, *et al.* Tübingen:
                Max Niemeyer Verlag, 1993–. Série II, *Correspon-
                dance générale*.
Œuvres   Benjamin Constant, *Œuvres*. Edited by Alfred
                Roulin. Paris: Gallimard, 1957 (Bibliothèque de la
                Pléiade).
PoP (1806)   Benjamin Constant, *Principles of Politics Applica-
                ble to All Governments*. Edited by Etienne Hof-
                mann. Translated by Dennis O'Keeffe. Indianapo-
                lis, IN: Liberty Fund, 2003.
PoP (1815)   Benjamin Constant, *Principles of Politics Applica-
                ble to All Representative Governments*, in *PW*.

PW   Benjamin Constant, *Political Writings*. Edited and
            translated by Biancamaria Fontana. Cambridge:
            Cambridge University Press, 1988.
SCU   Benjamin Constant, *The Spirit of Conquest and
            Usurpation and Their Relation to European Civi-
            lization*, in *PW*.

CHRONOLOGY[1]

1767   Benjamin Constant is born in Lausanne on October 25. His mother dies on November 10. He is raised by his grandmothers and then, from 1772 on, by a series of tutors.

1783   Constant is briefly enrolled at the University of Erlangen (February 1782–May 1783) and then at the University of Edinburgh, where he spends almost two years studying hard and participating in student life.

1785   Constant visits Paris and stays with the Suards (May–August), where he is introduced to intellectual celebrities.

1787   He meets Isabelle de Charrière.

1788   At the behest of his father, Constant goes to Brunswick to take up a position as chamberlain. There he meets and marries Minna von Cramm. The couple is divorced in 1793. In January of the same year, Constant meets Charlotte von Hardenberg, who eventually becomes his second wife (in 1808).

1794   On September 19, Constant meets Germaine de Staël.

1795   In May, Constant accompanies Madame de Staël to Paris, where he throws himself into politics.

---

[1] In composing this chronology, I have found particularly useful those in *EP*, *OCBC*, and Kurt Kloocke, *Benjamin Constant: une biographie intellectuelle* (Geneva: Droz, 1984).

1796   Constant publishes his first major pamphlet, *De la force du gouvernement actuel de la France et de la nécessité de s'y rallier.*

1797   In March, he publishes *Des réactions politiques*, followed by *Des effets de la Terreur* at the end of May.

On June 8, Albertine de Staël, the presumed daughter of Constant and Madame de Staël, is born.

On November 5, the Directory designates Constant president of the Administration of Luzarches.

1798   He works on a translation of Godwin and publishes *Essai sur la contre-révolution d'Angleterre en 1660.*

1799   On December 24, Constant is nominated to the Tribunate, where he immediately makes his opposition to the regime clear. He is placed under police surveillance.

1802   On January 17, Constant is expelled from the Tribunate along with other prominent opponents of Napoleon.

1803   Constant begins his first journal, *Amélie et Germaine.*

Madame de Staël is exiled by Napoleon and Constant accompanies her to Germany.

1804   He begins a new journal.

1805   Constant is deeply saddened by the deaths of Julie Talma and Isabelle de Charrière.

1806   He begins to write his *Principles of Politics.*

1807   Visiting Lausanne, Constant frequents a pietist sect called the Ames intérieures.

He works on an adaptation of Schiller, *Wallstein,* which is published in 1808.

1808   Constant secretly marries Charlotte von Hardenberg.

1811–13   On an extended trip to Germany, he works on his book
            on religion.

1812   Constant writes *Ma vie* (*Le cahier rouge*).

            He is made a corresponding member of the Royal Society
            of Sciences of Göttingen.

1813   On October 17–19, Napoleon is defeated at the Battle of
            Leipzig.

            On November 6, Constant meets Bernadotte in Hanover.
            Later that month, Constant writes *De l'esprit de conquête
            et de l'usurpation*.

1814   Constant arrives in Paris on April 15, where he prepares a
            new edition of *De l'esprit de conquête et de l'usurpation*.

            He publishes *Réflexions sur les constitutions, la distri-
            bution des pouvoirs et les garanties dans une monarchie
            constitutionnelle* on May 24.

            On July 6, he publishes *De la liberté des brochures, des
            pamphlets et des journaux considérés sous le rapport de
            l'intérêt du gouvernement*.

            On August 18, he publishes *Observations sur le discours
            de S.E. le Ministre de l'Intérieur en faveur du projet de loi
            sur la liberté de la presse*.

            Constant falls in love with the legendary beauty, Juliette
            Récamier, who does not return his affections.

1815   On February 2, Constant publishes *De la responsabilité
            des ministres*.

            On March 5, news of Napoleon's landing in Golfe-Juan
            reaches Paris.

On March 11 and 19, Constant publishes violent articles against Napoleon in the *Journal de Paris* and *Journal des débats*.

On March 23, Constant leaves Paris; he returns on March 27.

On April 14, 15, and 18–19, Constant meets Napoleon and agrees to work with him.

On April 20, Constant is made Conseiller d'Etat.

A version of the *Principles of Politics* is published on May 29.

On June 18, Napoleon is defeated at the Battle of Waterloo. Four days later, he abdicates.

On July 19, Constant receives a royal order to leave France. The order is revoked five days later, after Constant explains his behavior in his *Mémoire apologétique*.

On October 31, Constant nevertheless leaves Paris for Brussels.

1816   On January 27, Constant and Charlotte travel to London, where they stay until the end of July.

In the spring, Constant publishes *Adolphe*.

In September, he returns to Paris.

In answer to Chateaubriand's *De la monarchie selon la charte*, Constant publishes *De la doctrine politique qui peut réunir les partis en France*.

1817   Constant revives the *Mercure de France*.

Elected deputy from Sarthe, he becomes an important participant in debates.

On July 14, Madame de Staël dies in Paris.

In September, Constant fails to get elected to the Chamber.

1818   The *Minerve française* is launched by Constant and others.

Constant fails, once again, to get elected.

In February, he delivers his first lecture on religion at the Athénée royal.

1818   Constant publishes his *Collection complète des ouvrages publiés sur le gouvernement représentatif [. . .] formant une espèce de Cours de politique constitutionnelle.*

1819   In February, Constant delivers at the Athénée royal his famous lecture "De la liberté des anciens comparée à celle des modernes."

On March 25, he is elected to the Chamber. He is very active there.

On June 15, Constant and friends found the daily newspaper the *Renommée.*

In September, Constant's *Mémoires sur les Cent-Jours* begin to appear in the *Minerve.*

1820   The Duc de Berry is assassinated on February 13. Constant plays an important role in the debates that follow.

1820–22   Constant delivers major speeches on the freedom of the press and on the slave trade.

1821   Constant makes more than thirty-five speeches in the Chamber.

1822   Constant makes more than thirty speeches in the Chamber.

In January, Constant publishes the first part of *Commentaire sur l'ouvrage de Filangieri;* the second part comes out in 1824.

On November 3, he loses the election in la Sarthe.

1824   On February 26, Constant is elected from Paris. He grows in stature, eventually becoming the recognized leader of the liberal opposition.

The first volume of *De la religion* comes out at the end of May.

Louis XVIII dies on September 16.

Constant is seriously ill in October–December.

1825   In April, Constant's article "Christianisme. (Causes humaines qui, indépendamment de sa [*sic*] source divine, ont concouru à son établissement)" comes out in the *Encyclopédie moderne.*

In September, Constant publishes the *Appel aux nations chrétiennes en faveur des Grecs*, and in October, the second volume of *De la religion* comes out.

On December 3, Constant delivers his lecture "Coup d'œil sur la tendance générale des esprits dans le XIXème siècle" at the Athénée royal.

1826   Constant publishes an important review of Charles Dunoyer's *L'industrie et la morale considérées dans leur rapport avec la liberté.*

He publishes an article on the "Développement progressif des idées religieuses" in the *Encyclopédie progressive.*

1827   Volume 3 of *De la religion* comes out.

Constant delivers important speeches on freedom of the press.

1827–28 The *Discours de M. Benjamin Constant à la Chambre des Députés* are published.

1829   Constant publishes his *Mélanges de littérature et de politique.*

He writes many articles for the *Courrier français.*

His "Réflexions sur la tragédie" appear in the *Revue de Paris*.

1830   On July 25, the Four Ordinances are issued, triggering "The Glorious Days" of July 27, 28, and 29.

On November 19, Constant delivers his last speech in the Chamber. He makes his last appearance there on November 26.

On December 8, Constant dies.

On December 12, Constant is given a state funeral. The services take place at the Protestant church of the rue Saint-Antoine, and the burial at the Père-Lachaise cemetery.

Introduction

1 Benjamin Constant: Life and Work

A year before his death, Benjamin Constant confided to his readers in the preface to the *Mélanges de littérature et de politique* (1829):

> For forty years I have defended the same principle: freedom in all things, in religion, philosophy, literature, industry and politics. And by freedom I mean the triumph of the individual both over an authority that would wish to govern by despotic means and over the masses who claim the right to make a minority subservient to a majority.[1]

In this often-quoted statement lies the key to Constant's literary and political success in his own age and his continuing relevance for our own. The period in which he lived – the end of the *ancien régime*, the Revolution and Terror, the Napoleonic Empire, and the Restoration – had frequently been inimical to personal freedom in France and elsewhere. It was Constant's good fortune to have precisely the character, intellect, and pugnacity to be able to challenge this state of affairs untiringly, as well as to discern its source and potential for future misery. Reading Constant's elegant prose, with its irony, pointed epigrams, and concision, one is often reminded of the Roman historian Tacitus. The parallel indeed does not end there, for in both writers there is an awareness of the opposing extremes of *libertas* and *dominatio*. Events in the world since Constant's death in 1830 have only emphasized how perceptive Constant was to fear the growth of the omniscient and omnicompetent state and to champion the individual's right to privacy. Even in genuinely democratic states, the inner

---

[1] Reproduced in *Œuvres*, 833. All translations are my own unless otherwise indicated.

sanctum of a citizen's private thoughts and beliefs can sometimes appear to be under siege, especially in our modern age of increasing electronic sophistication. In many countries, however, citizens risk a great deal if they speak their mind, and they may even be obliged to demonstrate publicly their admiration for what they hold privately to be an abhorrent regime. Constant himself was familiar with a state apparatus of secret police and informers – that of Napoleon. "Nothing is gained by submission, except that heavier burdens are laid on those who appear to have willing shoulders,"[2] wrote Tacitus, lending his voice to barbarian Britons chafing under the yoke of imperial Rome. Such independence of mind takes courage – something that Constant had in good measure – as well as a degree of foolhardiness, but it also has its price, which in the case of Constant was long years of exclusion from French political life and the inability to publish.

What were the circumstances that formed such a lifelong attachment to the notion of personal liberty in Constant? He was not himself born under a tyranny; indeed, his background was one of affluence and security. His father, Louis-Arnold-*Juste* de Constant de Rebecque (1726–1812), came from a Swiss Protestant aristocratic family of French Huguenot origin and was a well-read and intelligent army officer in the service of Holland.[3] Benjamin-Henri Constant de Rebecque was born in Lausanne on October 25, 1767. The family boasted at least one writer, Juste de Constant's brother Samuel de Constant, who was a novelist. The political circumstances of Lausanne and the Pays de Vaud were, however, not ideal. Since the sixteenth century Lausanne had been ruled by the German-speaking oligarchy of Berne, whose representative in Lausanne was the Bailli or Bailiff resident in the castle. In his unfinished autobiography *Ma vie*, Constant remarks ruefully apropos of a young Bernese aristocrat with whom he had once shared a coach journey: "My father loathed that government and had brought me up to feel the same way. Neither he nor I knew then that all old governments are gentle because they are old and all new governments are harsh because they

---

[2] Cornelius Tacitus, *De Vita Iulii Agricolae* [*The Life of Julius Agricola*], chapter XV ("Nihil profici patientia nisi ut graviora tamquam ex facili tolerantibus imperentur"), ed. H. Furneaux, rev. J. G. C. Anderson (Oxford: Clarendon Press, 1939), 12.

[3] On the facts of Constant's life, see Dennis Wood, *Benjamin Constant: A Biography* (London and New York: Routledge, 1993).

are new."[4] From his earliest years Constant had a mildly despotic government close at hand that he could detest, in the form of the Bernese nobility.

However, there was a more pressing and immediate form of servitude – that of his father Juste de Constant – against which Benjamin was to struggle with limited success for more than forty years. Benjamin's mother, Henriette-Pauline *née* de Chandieu-Villars (1742–67), died on November 10, 1767, sixteen days after his birth. As Juste was frequently away in Holland, where he served in a Bernese regiment, Benjamin was brought up largely by others. To the loss of his mother can be added the further misfortune of having a capricious, irascible, and generally impossible father who now conceived the extraordinary notion of having his only child Benjamin brought up by a peasant girl, Marianne Magnin, by whom he was eventually to have two other children and whom he married in secret – a fact of which Benjamin was unaware until his mature years. Benjamin disliked the woman who was to become his stepmother. As if this were not bad enough – an absent father and a detested governess – he was then put in the care of a series of violent or incompetent male tutors. All of these episodes are described with comic relish in *Ma vie*: the brutal German who beat him, the tutor who left his charge alone in a Brussels brothel while he took his pleasures, and the earnest English clergyman Nathaniel May whom Benjamin and his father secretly mocked. And yet Benjamin somehow acquired a solid foundation in Latin and Greek, to which German and English were subsequently added. In 1782 he was enrolled as a student at Erlangen University in southern Germany, where all courses were taught in Latin. After becoming involved in a duel – the first of several in his life – it seems, over a woman at the Court of the Margrave of Ansbach-Bayreuth, Benjamin was obliged to return home, whereupon his father had the good sense to send him to the University of Edinburgh.

The education that Constant received in Scotland between 1783 and 1785 and the friendship of companions who were later to distinguish themselves in different fields – James, later Sir James Mackintosh (1765–1832), historian and philosopher; Malcolm Laing (1762–1818), historian; and John Wilde, later professor of civil law at Edinburgh – were undoubtedly a decisive factor in his life. It was at

---

[4] *Ma vie (Le cahier rouge)*, in *OCBC/Œuvres*, III, 1, 353–54.

the Edinburgh Speculative Society that Constant first participated
in debates on political and historical subjects, and it was at the
university that he attended lectures on the religion and myth in the
ancient world. After eighteen months Constant left for Brussels,
where he began to write a book about the history of religions, an
intellectual interest that would occupy him on and off for the rest
of his life. In Brussels he also had an affair with a married woman,
Marie-Charlotte Johannot, the first of very many relationships with
women. Taken to Paris by his father in the winter of 1786–87, Constant frequented the literary salon of the writer Jean-Baptiste Suard
(1733–1817) and met a woman, Isabelle de Charrière (1740–1805),
a novelist of some note, who was to become not only a loyal – if
critical – friend but also an inspiration to pursue work worthy of
his intellect. At the same time Constant's behavior in Paris became
so wayward that, fearing his father's rebukes, the young man took
the extreme course of running away to England, where he spent the
months of June to September 1787 living off his father's banker and
off friends while he wandered around the kingdom on horseback,
meandering from London to Edinburgh and back.

Constant's father now intervened decisively and, having concluded that Benjamin needed some form of employment, sent him to
the court of the Duke of Brunswick in 1788, where he was assigned
the largely ceremonial post of Gentleman of the Bedchamber. The
six years of tedium and frustration that Constant experienced in
north Germany (March 2, 1788–August 8, 1794) were relieved by
the brilliant and often very witty correspondence he maintained
with Isabelle de Charrière, which reflects both the young man's
enthusiasm for the Revolution in France and her skepticism about
it. These Brunswick years were also made bearable by Constant's
friendship with Jakob Mauvillon (1743–94), a bilingual polymath of
French Huguenot descent and a Freemason whose interest in politics
and religion matched Constant's own. On May 8, 1789, perhaps out
of boredom or pity, Constant made a disastrous marriage to a lady-in-
waiting at the ducal court, *Wilhelmine* Luise Johanne von Cramm
(1758–1823), known as Minna von Cramm. Her public infidelity to
him later with a Russian prince was matched by his own friendship
with Georgine *Charlotte* Auguste *née* von Hardenberg (1769–1845),
wife of Baron Wilhelm von Marenholtz (1752–1808). In the end it was
the very public dispute between Constant and Minna preceding their

divorce that led to Constant's withdrawal from the Brunswick court and return to Switzerland in August 1794. In September that year, he met Anne-Louise-*Germaine* de Staël (1766–1817), daughter of Louis XVI's director-general of finances, Jacques Necker (1732–1804), and became entirely captivated by her personality, intellect, and conversation. At the end of the year they became lovers. Madame de Staël was politically a moderate with royalist leanings; Constant's own enthusiasm for the new regime in France, the Directory, and his wish to be involved in political life now took him to Paris, where Germaine de Staël's influence and the connections he made at her Paris salon proved invaluable. In late June 1795 he published the first of many political texts in Jean-Baptiste Suard's journal *Nouvelles politiques*, *Lettres à un député de la Convention*, attacking the convention and defending his republican ideal. He worked with a member of the convention, the novelist Jean-Baptiste Louvet, known as Louvet de Couvray (1760–97), and in April 1796 produced a pamphlet, entitled *De la force du gouvernement actuel et de la nécessité de s'y rallier*, defending the status quo in France. By now, Constant saw clearly that his future lay in that country and in June 1796 applied to become a French citizen by virtue of his distant French Huguenot ancestry. Although his relationship with Isabelle de Charrière had become tense on account of his liaison with Madame de Staël, in Paris he found a new friend in the staunchly republican Julie Talma (1756–1805), estranged wife of the great actor Talma (1763–1826).

Constant's support for the Directory was based on his desire to hold on to the positive things that the Revolution had achieved while avoiding a return to either Jacobin Terror or the *ancien régime* monarchy. In the years 1795–99 this moderate position involved some personal risk. In 1797 he was involved in the setting up of a political society, the Club de Salm, and on March 30, 1797, took on his first political role as chairman of the municipality of Luzarches, near Chantilly, on the northern outskirts of Paris. Yet despite his efforts to establish his position clearly, Constant was frequently criticized on the one hand for being a Swiss aristocrat who was too close to the Necker family of Madame de Staël and on the other for lending his support to a government that had been set up by the regicides of 1793. When in 1797 he defended the Directory's *coup d'état* of 18 Fructidor (September 4, 1797) against moderates and royalists, which was reminiscent of the Terror and resulted in many deaths and deportations, Constant's position was seen as decisively on the Left. But two years later he both supported the decisive *coup d'état* of 18 Brumaire (November 9, 1799) that brought Napoleon Bonaparte to power *and* wrote, the following day, to Emmanuel-Joseph Siéyès (1748–1836), whom he greatly admired, expressing his concern that liberty would perhaps need to be defended against the successful general.[5] As so often, Constant found himself on both sides of an argument at once, a situation that rarely made for clear and decisive action, not least in his troubled relationships with women. And so he sought a position in Bonaparte's Tribunate from which he could oppose the First Consul's new legislative program. On December 24, 1799, Constant was elected as a member of the Tribunate and on January 5, 1800, he made a speech stressing the need for the Tribunate to be independent of the government, as if the tribunes were members of His Majesty's Loyal Opposition in England and not expected to offer only the very minimum of opposition to the First Consul's plans. Bonaparte's anger at what he saw as Constant's perfidy lasted many years. He felt that Constant not only was ungrateful to him for having been made a tribune at all, but was also being encouraged in his obstinate behavior by Germaine de Staël.[6]

During Constant's period in the Tribunate, when he attempted – unsuccessfully – to impose some legal limits on Bonaparte's exercise of power, there was an important and dramatic episode in his emotional life: his passionate affair with Anna Lindsay *née* O'Dwyer (1764–1820), the daughter of an Irish innkeeper at Calais. In late November 1800 Constant was introduced to Anna by their mutual friend Julie Talma and within a short time they became lovers. The intensity of their feelings is reflected in their letters, written in both English and French. For a while Constant believed that their relationship would last a lifetime, but by January 1801 his letters betrayed the first signs of impatience. Anna resented his continuing friendship with Germaine de Staël; Constant for his part was always suspicious of a relationship in which Anna might become possessive. The affair continued for several more months, with Anna being obliged reluctantly to return to her resentful aristocratic "protector," Auguste, marquis de Lamoignon (1765–1845). There can be little doubt that

---

[5] Letter of November 10, 1799, in *OCBC/CG*, III (1795–1799), 455.
[6] *OCBC/CG*, IV (1800–1802), 42, notes 1 and 2.

Anna was to serve, in part at least, as a model for Ellénore in *Adolphe*, and there are strong parallels between the celebrated description of Ellénore in Chapter 2 of that novel and the passionate, impetuous, and possessive nature of Anna. Throughout the affair Constant continued to work tirelessly, criticizing draft laws in his speeches at the Tribunate, with the result that by January 1802 he was viewed by Bonaparte as an unwelcome troublemaker and found himself on the list of tribunes excluded from office. As long as the consular regime lasted he could play no further role in French politics. He wrote to Napoleon Bonaparte on April 15, 1803, to defend his actions and those of Madame de Staël and stated that "henceforth literary work will be my occupation. I will try to achieve some success in the career which remains open to me."[7]

During the 1790s, under the Directory, Constant's pamphlets had already attracted attention and interest. Under the First Consul's rule, however, all publications were closely controlled and the official French government newspaper, *Le Moniteur*, had its drafts read and corrected by Napoleon Bonaparte himself. France was rapidly evolving toward a new form of monarchy, and there was little likelihood that Constant would be able to publish political works in such circumstances. He continued to divide his time between Paris and Madame de Staël's chateau at Coppet, on Lake Geneva, and to meditate on constitutional theory, work which was to culminate in *Principes de politique applicables à tous les gouvernements*.[8] Constant's lifelong interest in religion and religious feeling which had its origins in the 1780s, was given considerable stimulus when in October 1803 Bonaparte ordered Germaine de Staël to leave France, and Constant chose to accompany her into exile. The couple made their way across Germany to Weimar, reaching the city on December 14, 1803. Amid the literary activity, philosophical speculation, and scholarly research that characterized Weimar at this period, Constant's investigations into religious sentiment throughout the world and throughout history were to intensify, although many years would pass and endless redrafting would take place before it became

---

[7] *OCBC/CG*], V (1800–1805, 92.
[8] See Étienne Hofmann, *Les 'Principes de Politique' de Benjamin Constant (1806)*, 2 vols, vol. 1, *La Genèse d'une œuvre et l'évolution de la pensée de leur auteur 1789–1806* (Geneva: Droz, 1980).

De la religion (1824–31). After three months of unremitting intellectual activity and meetings with Goethe and Schiller, all of which are
noted in his journal, Constant returned alone to Switzerland, only
to discover shortly after his arrival on April 7, 1804, that Germaine
de Staël's father Jacques Necker had died. Although his relationship
with Madame de Staël had since long lost its passion, Constant felt
deep affection for her and, knowing the extent of her grief and despair
when she learned of the death of a father whom she had always
venerated, he set off back to Weimar to tell her the news himself.
Constant's sympathy for Germaine did not diminish his wish to be
free and to end his relationship with her. Such feelings alternated
with their very opposite, a desire to settle the matter once and for
all by, of all things, marrying Germaine. Indeed if a possible model
for Ellénore in *Adolphe* was the tempestuous Anna Lindsay, it is
equally clear that the changing emotions and shifting allegiances of
Constant himself are not dissimilar to those of the chronically indecisive Adolphe. Intensive research and writing about ancient religions offered Constant a distraction from such emotional concerns,
and inspiration came too in his friendship with Charles de Villers
(1765–1815), a friend of Madame de Staël and a bilingual scholar
somewhat in the mold of Jakob Mauvillon, who was a specialist in
German philosophy and religious thought.[9]

Thus Constant's life continued, alternating between long hours
spent on his study of religion and frustration with the ties that bound
him to Germaine de Staël, until in October 1806 there came a radical change in his emotional life. During his time at the court of the
Duke of Brunswick in the 1790s, Constant had formed a close friendship with Charlotte *née* von Hardenberg, wife of Baron Wilhelm von
Marenholtz at that time. He had last seen Charlotte in May 1793,
and they had not corresponded since the end of 1795. Charlotte and
her husband had divorced in 1794, and in 1798 she had remarried,
to a penniless French royalist, the Vicomte Alexandre Du Tertre.
After moving to Paris in 1803, Charlotte had heard that Constant
was lonely and in a precarious financial situation. She had written
to him and offered him half of what she possessed – and this even
though she was still married to Du Tertre. Constant, touched by her

---

[9] On this friendship, see Kurt Klooke et al., eds., *Madame de Staël, Charles de Villers,
Benjamin Constant: Correspondance* (Frankfurt am Main: Peter Lang, 1993).

generosity, went to Paris to find her, but she had in the meantime left for Geneva with her husband. They corresponded once again somewhat sporadically. Charlotte was aware of her own intellectual inferiority to Constant and believed Madame de Staël to be far better suited to him in that respect. Constant himself, however, had tired of Germaine, and Charlotte's kind, affectionate, if rather dull, nature now appealed to him more. On October 19, 1806, they finally met in Paris, and the following day they became lovers for the first time.[10] This event released in Constant a new stream of artistic creativity. He noted in his journal on October 30: "Began a novel which will be our story. Any other work would be impossible for me."[11] This novel would retrace the events of the preceding twenty years. Although the original manuscript has never been found, the unfinished autobiographical *Cécile* probably originated in this first account of the vicissitudes of Constant's relationship with Charlotte from their first meeting in Brunswick. Also, from this story grew, it would seem, an "episode about Ellénore" written around November 10, 1806, out of which the novel *Adolphe* may have developed.[12]

The course of Constant's relationship with Charlotte was to be no smoother than that of his relationships with other women. He felt protective toward her and grateful for her devotion to him, but greatly missed the wit and brilliance of Germaine de Staël. Even as the process of annulling Charlotte's marriage to Du Tertre went ahead in the archbishopric of Paris, Constant was unable to commit himself entirely to either woman, and when Madame de Staël was exiled by Napoleon in April 1807, Constant followed her to Coppet. There were frequent occasions during that summer when Germaine's anger at the relationship with Charlotte overflowed, and Constant's despair and bewilderment led him briefly to turn for consolation to a mystical Pietistic sect in Lausanne, the *Mystiques* or *Ames intérieures*, as *Cécile* records, which was led by his first cousin Charles, Chevalier de Langalerie (1751–1835).[13] Madame de Staël's

---

[10] *Journaux intimes (1804–1807)* in *OCBC/Œuvres*, VI, journal entries for October 19 and 20, 1806, 466–7.
[11] *Journaux intimes*, 471, 473.
[12] Both of these texts are in *OCBC/Œuvres*, III, 2.
[13] See Frank Bowman, "L'épisode quiétiste dans *Cécile*," in *Benjamin Constant: Actes du Congrès Benjamin Constant (Lausanne, octobre 1967)* (Geneva: Droz, 1968), 97–108.

departure for Vienna and Charlotte's serious illness in Besançon, caused by the continuing uncertainty of her situation, brought some stability to Constant, who finally married Charlotte on June 5, 1808, in a Protestant religious ceremony. Yet, almost unbelievably, this was not the end of Constant's relationship with Madame de Staël, and for the next three years he migrated between the two women – despite an apparent attempt by the despairing Charlotte to poison herself in Lyon on June 9, 1809. Despite the emotional turmoil he was living through, Constant published, to some critical acclaim, a French translation of Schiller's play *Wallenstein* in 1809 and continued working on drafts of his study of religion.

Gambling had long been an irresistible temptation for Constant, and at the end of 1810 he lost so massively at the Paris gaming tables that he was obliged to sell his house in France, *Les Herbages*, his furniture, and his library. Having bid what both believed to be a final farewell to Germaine de Staël in Lausanne in May 1811, he left with Charlotte for Germany, more and more obsessed with his recent studies of polytheism, the belief in many gods. In November 1811 the couple settled in the quiet university town of Göttingen, not far from Charlotte's family estate at Hardenberg, and for the next three years Constant immersed himself in his reading. His father Juste, with whom relations had, in recent years, been very difficult because of long-running, acrimonious financial disputes, died on February 12, 1812, and it may be that at about this time Constant worked on an account of his boyhood and adolescence, *Ma vie*, also known as *Le Cahier rouge*, which is frequently comical and which he left unfinished. In this work the erratic behavior of Juste figures largely.[14] While eastern Europe was the scene of warfare and carnage leading to the eventual overthrow of Napoleon, and while Germaine de Staël was fleeing to Vienna, Moscow, St. Petersburg, and finally Stockholm, Constant remained engrossed in his studies, remarking in a letter apropos the destruction of Moscow: "A city of 500,000 inhabitants can be blown up without a Göttingen professor lifting his eyes from his book."[15] However, with the downfall of Napoleon

---

[14] *Ma vie [Le Cahier rouge]*, 295–358.
[15] Letter to Claude Hochet, October 5, 1812, in *Benjamin Constant et Madame de Staël, Lettres à un ami. Cent onze lettres inédites à Claude Hochet*, ed. Jean Mistler (Neuchâtel: A la Baconnière, [1949]), 225.

came the first real possibility, in many years, for Constant to play a role in French politics once again, and his journal entries at this point took on a febrile note of hope. On November 3, 1813, Constant traveled to Hanover to dine with Jean-Baptiste Bernadotte (1763–1844), Crown Prince of Sweden, and to offer his service to this potential new constitutional monarch and leader of France. He also began, in late November 1813, one of his finest pieces of writing, *De l'esprit de conquête et de l'usurpation*, published at the end of January 1814. In this writing Constant returns to the relationship between citizens and their rulers in the modern world and attacks a concept of society most dangerously popularized in the previous century by Jean-Jacques Rousseau in *Du Contrat social* (1762) in the notion of the general will. In such a society every member of the community has a right to interfere in the life of every other citizen, a state of affairs characterized in classical antiquity by Sparta, where the individual's sense of personal identity was systematically crushed. In *De l'esprit de conquête*, Constant argues passionately that such an arrangement has no place in the modern world. The world of the ancients was one of tyrannical rule based on military conquest and enslavement: the modern world is fundamentally different, and Napoleon's warlike regime and personal rule are a pernicious anachronism. What characterizes the modern world is commerce, for which the prerequisites are peace and individual freedom. In this extraordinary text Constant analyzes with prophetic insight the workings of what we would now call the totalitarian regime. Paradoxically, it was Constant's period in the political wilderness since 1802 that had allowed his liberalism to develop and his political principles to mature.

Bernadotte's hopes of power were short lived. After the fall of Paris the Allies saw to it that the Bourbon Louis XVIII was proclaimed king of France in April 1814. Nevertheless, Constant, eager for a role on the changed political scene, returned to Paris the same month and began publishing articles and pamphlets, especially on the subject of the freedom of the press that the new government was intent on curbing. Then at the end of August 1814, at the age of forty-six and after some years of relative calm in his emotional life, Constant fell head over heels in love with Juliette Récamier (1777–1849), whose beauty had been immortalized by the painters Jacques-Louis David (1748–1825) in 1800 and by François-Pascal-Simon Gérard (1770–1837) in 1805. His passion for Madame Récamier lasted for over a year, during which he suffered agonies of unreciprocated desire.[16] In March 1815 Napoleon escaped from captivity on Elba and returned triumphantly to France. Constant's long years of dogged opposition to military dictatorship had earned him considerable credit, which he now threw away on Napoleon's arrival in Paris. A leading representative of liberalism was needed by Napoleon to lend the revived empire a fig leaf of respectability: looking for a post of some kind in the new order, Constant obligingly stepped forward, and after an interview with the Emperor on April 14, 1815, he was appointed *conseiller d'État*. Constant set about drafting the *Acte additionnel* to the constitution of the empire, which was meant to ensure no return to the despotism of earlier years. It was a serious misjudgment on Constant's part for two reasons: first, his faith in a reformed Napoleon was not shared by everyone and made him appear to be an opportunistic turncoat; and second, the *Grande Armée* was shortly to be defeated on June 18, 1815, at Waterloo and the Emperor was sent into his final exile on the island of St. Helena. Constant was fortunate indeed to avoid being exiled himself by the restored King Louis XVIII, and on October 31, he left Paris for Brussels, before moving on to London with Charlotte, where he spent the months of January to September 1816.

Despite the recent revival of interest in Constant's liberalism and in his writings on religion, it is fair to say that his fame with the general public today still rests largely on his novel *Adolphe*, the first edition of which was published in May 1816 during his stay in London. This poignant story of the consequences of a love affair between the young intellectual Adolphe and an older woman, Ellénore, analyzes in detail the shifting emotions of a man who has "fallen out of love," but who cannot bring himself to end the relationship for fear of hurting the woman who still loves him. The elegance and concision of Constant's style is remarkable, as are the psychological insights and pithy aphorisms that the short work contains. Of Constant's three "personal" works – as opposed to his political writings or works on religion – *Adolphe* is more completely "fictional" than *Ma vie* (*Le Cahier rouge*) and *Cécile*, and yet it seems to distil many experiences and relationships, most notably Constant's difficulties

---

[16] This is reflected in his desperate letters to her in Benjamin Constant, *Lettres à Madame Récamier (1807–1830)*, ed. Éphraïm Harpaz (Paris: Klincksieck, 1977).

with his father Juste, his friendship with Isabelle de Charrière, and his many liaisons with women, most notably with Germaine de Staël, Anna Lindsay, and Charlotte von Hardenberg. The central situation of the novel – a man who has tired of a woman and yet who cannot bring himself to leave her – is, as we have seen, one with which Constant was very familiar and that, according to the Freudian critic Han Verhoeff, may have had its roots in the early loss of his mother.[17] Whether this was so or not, it is a well-documented fact that before the novel appeared in print Constant had read the manuscript aloud at various society gatherings in London, and the enormous emotion that it released not only in his audience but also in the author himself suggests that it plunged its roots very deep indeed into his psyche.[18]

On his return to Paris, Constant launched himself with renewed enthusiasm into the world of Restoration politics, publishing pamphlets and also reviving the fortunes of the journal *Le Mercure de France*, which became a vehicle for introducing his liberal worldview to a wider audience. So successful was Constant in this enterprise that the government closed it down in December 1817, whereupon he set up, with the help of like-minded friends, the weekly *La Minerve française* in order to defend the freedom of the individual and to oppose the reactionary and oppressive tendencies of the Right.[19] At the same time he had lost none of his interest in religion, and gave a series of lectures on the subject at the Athénée Royal in 1818.[20] After unsuccessful attempts to obtain a parliamentary seat, he was finally elected to represent the Sarthe region of Normandy on March 25, 1819, and went on not only to participate actively with his renowned sardonic wit and impassioned eloquence in debates in the Chamber but also to found a daily newspaper *La Renommée*. His extraordinarily vivid account of Napoleon's Hundred Days in 1815, the *Mémoires sur les Cent-Jours*, which was published in the *Minerve* between September 1819 and March 1820, made this

---

[17] Han Verhoeff, *'Adolphe' et Constant: une étude psychocritique* (Paris: Klincksieck, 1976).

[18] See Harold Nicolson, *Benjamin Constant* (London: Constable, 1949), 243–44.

[19] Éphraïm Harpaz, *L'École libérale sous la Restauration, le 'Mercure' et la 'Minerve', 1817–1820* (Geneva: Droz, 1968).

[20] Kurt Kloocke, *Benjamin Constant: une biographie intellectuelle* (Geneva: Droz, 1984), 353.

another highwater mark of Constant's career as a political writer.[21] However the assassination of the Duc de Berry on 13 February 1820 by a fanatical republican saddler, Louis-Pierre Louvel, ushered in an era of suspicion and repression. The newspaper *La Renommée* was closed down, and laws were brought in which Constant sought with all his energies to oppose, particularly on the slave trade. Indeed, his physical and moral courage came to the fore when his life was at risk during a visit to Saumur on October 7–8, 1820, an incident that caused him to write a public letter of complaint to the minister for war.[22]

Constant was now becoming increasingly infirm. In 1818 he sustained a fall that had damaged his leg. In March 1821 he hurt the same leg and was effectively crippled. He lost his parliamentary seat in November 1822,[23] was fined as the result of government plots against him, and withdrew from public life to devote himself once again to his still unpublished work on religion. Constant had become convinced of the universality and importance of religious sentiment in human history, despite the variety of superficial manifestations it had assumed and the persistent attempts by different priestly castes to dominate what was essentially a personal phenomenon. He judged Christianity in its Protestant form to be the purest manifestation of this religious feeling. In July 1823 *De la religion* (1824–31) was announced as forthcoming in a publisher's prospectus. However the first of five volumes did not appear until 1824, and in the meantime, Constant continued his researches on the subject. He was reelected to Parliament by Parisian electors on February 26, 1824, and, despite a serious illness at the end of 1824, was tirelessly active both in the Chamber as part of the small liberal minority and in writing for the press. Freedom of expression remained central to his liberalism, and he enthusiastically espoused the cause of Greek independence from the Ottoman Turks, publishing in September 1825 an *Appel aux nations chrétiennes en faveur des Grecs*. In November 1827, after a tour of Alsace and a stay at the spa of Baden-Baden, Constant was chosen by the electors of both Paris and the Bas-Rhin, the Lower

---

[21] *Mémoires sur les Cent-Jours*, in *OCBC/Œuvres*, XIV.
[22] *Lettre à Monsieur le marquis de Latour-Maubourg* (Paris: Béchet, 1820).
[23] On Constant's time as *député* for the Sarthe in the French parliament, see *Benjamin Constant et Goyet de la Sarthe: Correspondance, 1818–1822*, ed. Éphraïm Harpaz (Geneva: Droz, 1973).

Rhine department, to be their representative. Constant chose to represent the Bas-Rhin, and in the declining years of his life the focus of his activity was very much on this part of France. His impressive speeches in the Chamber, with their frequently cutting irony, were published by subscription in two volumes in 1827–28,[24] and yet despite his exceptional gifts as a writer and orator he failed in his attempt to become a member of the French Academy in 1828. The following year, and with another attempt at the Academy in mind, Constant published a miscellany of articles, some revised and some hitherto unpublished, under the title *Mélanges de littérature et de politique*, in which the whole range of his thoughts on many subjects was displayed.[25] Once again, in November 1830, his candidature for the Academy was to be unsuccessful.

Although there was every sign that his health was failing, Constant worked on securing reelection for Strasbourg in June 1830. It was at this point that King Charles X and his minister, the Duc de Polignac (1780–1847), made the mistake of choosing to ignore the result of the elections in which Polignac's ministry had been decisively defeated and a liberal majority returned. They issued the Four Ordinances on July 25, 1830, to alter the Charter of 1814, by which France had become – technically at least – a constitutional monarchy. These ordinances dissolved the new chamber, called fresh elections, in which only the richest part of the electorate could vote, and imposed new restrictions on the press. This was a step too far, and widespread discontent now turned into revolt in the *Trois Glorieuses* or Three Glorious Days of the July Revolution, July 27–29, 1830, which resulted in many deaths on the streets of Paris, the abdication of the stubbornly intransigent Bourbon King Charles X, and his replacement on August 1, 1830, by his cousin the Duke of Orleans, King Louis-Philippe. Although Constant took no direct part in the events, he did draw up with Count Sébastiani (1772–1851) a declaration in favor of Louis-Philippe on July 30, 1830. It was a change that seemed to offer the possibility of reforms in line with Constant's own liberal ideals, and he took up his place in the Chamber after being reelected as deputy for Strasbourg in October 1830.

[24] *Discours de M. Benjamin Constant à la Chambre des Députés* (Paris: Ambroise Dupont, 1827–28).
[25] *Mélanges de littérature et de politique* (Paris: Pichon et Didier, 1829).

He gave advice to the new government and continued to defend freedom of thought and expression. But a double disappointment soon followed: a proposal of his concerning the regulation of printing and bookselling was overwhelmingly rejected by the Chamber, and on November 18, 1830, despite having the support of Chateaubriand, he failed once again in his candidature to the French Academy. This blow struck him as his physical decline and extreme frailty became manifest. Despite frequent hydrotherapy at the Tivoli Baths in Paris, his health was growing worse. Yet he worked almost until the last, and he was still correcting the proofs of *De la religion* when he died on December 8, 1830. His funeral on December 12, 1830, became a state occasion, the streets were lined with huge crowds, and his body was interred amid eulogies at the Père Lachaise cemetery.

Until the latter half of the twentieth century, it was Constant's diaries, autobiographical writings, and above all his novel *Adolphe* that attracted the attention of writers and commentators. Indeed it was not until long after his death that *Ma vie (Le Cahier rouge)*, *Cécile*, and the *Journaux intimes* were published. Distinguished critics such as Paul Bourget (1852–1935),[26] Charles Du Bos (1882–1939),[27] and Georges Poulet (1902–91)[28] published essays examining the relationship between Constant's lived experience and his various accounts of it.[29] *Adolphe* was brought to a still wider audience when it was adapted for the cinema in 2002 by the French director Benoît Jacquot, encouraged by the actress Isabelle Adjani, who played the role of Ellénore.[30] Constant's status as a founding father of liberalism in Europe, already highlighted by Sir Isaiah Berlin in the 1960s,[31] was given greater luster by the collapse of the Soviet Empire, and numerous political writers and social scientists – for example,

---

[26] Paul Bourget, *Essais de psychologie contemporaine (1883–1886)* (Paris: Plon-Nourrit, 1901).

[27] Charles Du Bos, *Approximations (I–VI)*, (192?–1932), reprinted by Éditions des Syrtes (2000), and *Grandeur et Misère de Benjamin Constant* (Paris: Corrêa, 1946).

[28] Georges Poulet, *Benjamin Constant par lui-même* (Paris: Du Seuil, 1968).

[29] On the critical reception of *Adolphe*, see Paul Delbouille, *Genèse, structure et destin d''Adolphe'* (Paris: Les Belles Lettres, 1971).

[30] *Adolphe de Benjamin Constant* (2002), film directed by Benoît Jacquot, with Isabelle Adjani as Ellénore and Stanislas Merhar as Adolphe.

[31] Isaiah Berlin, *Four Essays on Liberty* (London: Oxford University Press, 1969).

Stephen Holmes,[32] Tzvetan Todorov,[33] and Lucien Jaume[34] – have highlighted Constant's concern about preventing the individual from being subordinated to the collective and have rediscovered in his work a powerful restatement of the citizen's inviolable right to personal freedom. In Sir Isaiah Berlin's celebrated phrase, he remains "the most eloquent of all defenders of freedom and privacy."[35]

---

[32] Stephen Holmes, *Benjamin Constant and the Making of Modern Liberalism* (New Haven: Yale University Press, 1984).

[33] Tzvetan Todorov, *Benjamin Constant. La passion démocratique* (Paris: Hachette Littératures, 1997).

[34] Lucien Jaume, *La liberté et la loi. Les origines philosophiques du libéralisme* (Paris: Fayard, 2000).

[35] Berlin, 126.

I. The Political Thinker and Actor

2 Liberalism's Lucid Illusion*

Translated by Arthur Goldhammer

The Constant I propose to exhume here numbers among those authors who drew the most profound lessons from the Revolution's failure to achieve a stable political form, among the most acute analysts of the democratic transition. When we read Constant, he emerges as one of the very rare writers capable of enlightening us about the great and deeply mysterious transformation from which modern society arose. He can do this because he methodically took stock of where he stood in relation to that transformation. He was also a politician whose options in the crucial years 1814 and 1815 were as inconsistent as his choices were unfortunate – but *that* Constant may be left to would-be prosecutors; he does not interest us here. Let us take seriously, however, the man who more than anyone else strove to characterize the distinctive features of "liberty among the moderns" and who, in seeking a theoretical answer to the key question that stumped the revolutionary will – what does the representative principle actually imply about the organization of power? – had the exceptionally good fortune to foresee the turn that history would actually take. Although circumstances conspired against him and led him to choose the wrong path for himself, he was nevertheless remarkably prescient about the course of history and was able to specify in theory the conditions under which a regime according a proper place to civil liberties did in fact establish itself. It is for this reason that he is worth reading today, as one

---

* This essay was first published as "Benjamin Constant: L'Illusion lucide du libé-ralisme," in *De la liberté chez les Modernes. Ecrits politiques*, ed. Marcel Gauchet (Paris: Livres de Poche, 1980). It has here been abridged by Helena Rosenblatt and translated by Arthur Goldhammer.

of the best guides we have for understanding what difficulties had to be overcome before something so simple and easy in principle, yet so difficult to coordinate and operate in practice, could come to pass: namely, a government of human beings, based solely on human will. [...]

REVOLUTION: SOVEREIGN PEOPLE AND SUBJUGATED PEOPLE

The Revolution's swerve toward tyranny was central to Constant's thought. For him as for many other contemporary observers, that swerve was compounded by Napoleon's despotism, which he saw as a close cousin of Jacobin dictatorship. As radically different as these two forms of tyranny were, both stemmed ultimately from the same source and obeyed the same political logic; they were merely two faces of a usurpation that the principle of popular sovereignty made possible. The excesses and reversals of the revolutionary process oblige us to consider the ways in which that principle can be perverted: when the legitimacy conferred by heredity and guaranteed by divinity is abolished, the human community regains full power over itself; yet the power that has theoretically been recovered and mastered turns out to be more elusive than ever. With terrifying ease what has been reappropriated in principle slips away in fact. No power over man is more likely to escape man's control altogether than the power that is supposed to emanate solely from his own decisions. In the place of the sovereign people emerges a power with limitless pretensions, a power that presents itself as the embodiment of the will of all and therefore claims the right to impose itself on all. It is a power arbitrary in its very essence and in practice exempt from the law, because it is the will of the people that makes the law, and this power embodies or expresses the people: its will is law. It is, finally, a *confiscated* power, whose proclaimed generality conceals the seizure of authority by a group or individual bent on imposing a particular ambition of its or his own. This can come about in any number of quite different ways. An assembly may claim that it is one with the people who elected it and simply substitute itself for the people. Or an individual may declare himself or herself to be the sole repository and instrument of the general will and simply deny the people any ability to govern in its own name without his or her assistance. ("Everything for the people, nothing by the people," as the saying goes.) Representatives and represented may falsely be identified (as in Jacobinism), or authority may irrevocably be delegated (as in Bonapartism); yet for the person subjected to an authority that is all the more merciless for being turned against the society from which it is supposed to emanate, the result is the same. [...]

A sovereign people is a people more in danger of alienating its sovereignty than any other. Indeed, there is no way to compare the alienation of power implicit in a monarchy that is "modified by time," "softened by habit," and "surrounded by intermediate bodies that support and limit it,"[1] with the radical dispossession that becomes possible when the people are free to choose their own government. In the latter case the executive agent makes off with every vestige of social power, regardless of whether it proclaims itself "the people" or ostentatiously divorces itself from the people, the better to embody the people's supposed will. Hereditary monarchical power, which is imposed on society from without and sustained by a formal tradition that justifies but at the same time restrains its actions, was never able to claim so sweeping or unlimited a right to intervene against its own subjects. [...] In the triumph of the democratic principle is a paradox with which we are still grappling today: namely, that this triumph opens the way not only to liberty but also to a new kind of tyranny unprecedented in its scope.

What exactly are the avenues by which this perversion of popular sovereignty proceeds? Must it be seen as inevitable? If not, how can it be prevented? The Revolution made these questions unavoidable. So did the reaction against the Revolution, which raised similar questions about the viability of a republican organization in France in the early nineteenth century. Between the dictatorship of public safety and Bonaparte's usurpation came the spectacle of the Thermidorian republic, which was hardly of a nature to encourage optimism either: there, weakness vied with arbitrariness, the *coup d'état* became a normal means of government, instability reigned, and the apparatus of state was riven by internal conflicts. The choice seemed to be between anarchic impotence on the one hand and unrestrained power on the other. Was there no other alternative? [...]

---

[1] *SCU*, 88.

In justice to Constant, one should begin by acknowledging that the number of people in France prepared to concede in 1802 that a republican regime "based solely on temporary election" had a chance of surviving was no doubt quite small. Here I am speaking not of people whose commitment to republicanism was merely sentimental, but of sophisticated minds capable of responding rationally to the difficulties that would have to be faced. Had not the Revolution's successive deviations driven home a striking and irrefutable lesson? In the first place, the idea that all citizens might take an equal share in managing public affairs in "an association of thirty million people" seemed downright chimerical. Had not Rousseau himself acknowledged that political liberty could truly be established only in a community of limited size? Furthermore, how could the rule of law be established beyond challenge when those to whom the law applied participated in its elaboration? A few years later Joseph de Maistre would offer a striking rejoinder to this argument: "The essence of a fundamental law is that no one has the right to abolish it. But how can the law stand above all, if someone has made it? Agreement among the people is impossible, and if it were, an agreement is not a Law and is not binding on anyone, unless there is some higher authority to guarantee it."[2]

Finally, the spectacle of Napoleon's arbitrary usurpation, following the incoherence of the representative regimes of the revolutionary period, cruelly unmasked as fiction the belief that men were capable of entering into a contract with one another to create a sovereign authority reflecting their common will. As Bonald would later ask, "What are we to think of the profound ignorance or audacious presumption of the men who said, 'Let us gather together and invent a society'?"[3] In reality, power "pre-exists society," since power constitutes society, and a society without power or law of any kind could never be constituted."[4] That which is a precondition of every institution cannot be instituted. Collective order must in this sense be called *natural*, that is, "different from man's will, because it precedes his actions and is therefore independent of

[2] Joseph de Maistre, *Essai sur le principe générateur des constitutions politiques* (Paris: Société typographique 1814), 2.
[3] Louis de Bonald, *Essai analytique sur les lois naturelles de l'ordre social* (Paris, 1800), 149.
[4] *Essai analytique*, 95.

man."[5] In de Maistre's words, "the origin of sovereignty must always appear outside the sphere of human power, so that the men who seem to participate in it directly are nevertheless merely circumstantial."[6] Yet Burke, writing in the early stages of the Revolution, had in a way already expressed the essence of these critiques, having noted in particular the indispensable superiority of the law as well as the necessary exteriority of power:

Society requires not only that the passions of individuals should be subjected, but that even in the mass and body as well as in the individuals, the inclinations of men should frequently be thwarted, their will controlled, and their passions brought into subjection. This can only be done by a *power out of themselves*; and not, in the exercise of its function, subject to that will and to those passions which it is its office to bridle and subdue.[7]

[...] Constant's originality was in a sense to take note of the essential points of this conservative opposition to the Revolution and incorporate some of them while rejecting the main thrust of the criticism. Like Burke, for instance, he conceded that "the leveling of equality is terrifying, with the pressure of despotism." "Under abusive governments," he wrote, "heredity can be useful. Where rights have disappeared, privileges are an asylum and a defense. Despite its drawbacks, heredity is preferable to the absence of any neutral power."[8] Yet he vigorously rejected any idea of the inevitability of servitude, which modern efforts at emancipation had allegedly neglected: "We are not condemned to believe that men require a master. We see no reason to despair of liberty."[9]

He also rejected the argument that the geographic and demographic size of a country like France would make a republican constitution impossible. The book that he set out to write sometime around 1802 was meant to reaffirm the notion that a "large country" was not in itself an obstacle to establishing a fully elected regime.

---

[5] Ibid., 151–52.

[6] *Essai sur le principe générateur des constitutions*, 44.

[7] *Reflections on the Revolutions in France*, ed. J. C. D. Clark (Stanford: Stanford University Press, 2001), 219.

[8] *Fragments d'un ouvrage abandonné sur la possibilité d'une constitution républicaine dans un grand pays*, ed. Henri Grange (Paris: Aubier, 1991), 118. In Gauchet's text, Constant's word "pressure" is rendered as "passion." It has been corrected here.

[9] *Fragments*, 242.

But did the civil unrest attendant on the Revolution not suggest that republican government and disorder were inextricably intertwined? To see that this was not the case, one only had to look outside of France: "America offers us an example of wise and tranquil government without hereditary institutions."[10] What was remarkable about Constant's approach, however, was that he endeavored systematically to incorporate elements derived from the old monarchical vision of power into a system based on representation. Tacitly, he drew the conclusion that a constitution based entirely on election must overcome the serious but not crippling flaws revealed by the initial uncertainty as to the definition of authority. To do this, the state edifice required an institution capable of fostering the qualities of eminence, permanence, and independence that had once been associated with the person of the monarch. [...]

Whatever the ills of democracy – despotism or anarchy, usurpations of sovereignty, or difficulty with fixing the form of authority – the origin was always the same, Constant argued: namely, ambiguity in the relation between the governing and the governed, which the terms of the elective principle left completely undefined. This principle assumed a theoretical identity of the two: those who governed either did nothing but carry out the will of the governed, or else the governed somehow governed themselves through their representatives, though it was impossible to say precisely how this relationship worked. But as the revolutionary experience had abundantly demonstrated, it was in this realm of ambiguous abstraction, shrouded in obscurity, that either the governed were methodically dispossessed of their power or their inability to govern was revealed. Either a faction or an individual took control of the general will for its own purposes, or else no clear expression of that general will established itself unambiguously, thus leading to conflict, recourse to force, and a general climate of arbitrariness.

To put it another way, the fundamental problem of a "constitution based solely on temporary election" was that the immanence of the principle of the general will created illusions of unity and totality. Power, which under the monarchy had been exercised by one person or a few people outside of society, had been brought back into society and enshrined as the power of all. Yet, in fact, it was still exercised

---

[10] Ibid., 117.

by a few, and the evil was compounded by the fact that those who wielded power, being entitled to hide behind the claim of unanimity, were in a position to claim initially that their power had no limits and later that it would brook no opposition or contradiction. [...] Hence the first priority was to dispel the obscurity surrounding this exercise of power, which encouraged misrepresentation or failure, and to shed as bright and revealing a light as possible on the nature of the relationship between power and society. The goal was twofold: first, to prevent power from substituting itself for society, and second, to prevent society from appropriating all power to itself. In short, the goal was to regulate the difference between power and society in such a way as to avoid both the encroachments of authority and the dissolution of authority. [...]

This, in my view, is the pivot around which all of Constant's thought is organized. The comparison of the liberty of the ancients with the liberty of the moderns; the critique of the notion of popular sovereignty; theoretical individualism; the doctrine of limitations on the actions of authority; and the idea of neutral power – all these fundamental themes aim at the same target. All contribute to one basic goal: to fix that which the democratic principle of social power leaves frighteningly undetermined, namely, the relationship between the actual agent of power and the society in the name of which, for which, but also on which that power is exercised.

To that end Constant adopts two distinct approaches: one theoretical (the critique of popular sovereignty) and the other historical. Indeed, his major idea is that modernity was oddly unconscious of itself, of its novelty and originality in relation to earlier forms of society. The collective consciousness remained strangely backward relative to the profound transformations that laid the groundwork for political liberty. As a result of this (and of a certain vagueness in the principles that define the way in which the general will is supposed to operate), the Revolution had revived and imposed archaic, not to say completely anachronistic, models.

A major source of revolutionary despotism lay in the complete misunderstanding of the norms of the new social organization, along with a tendency to invoke the patterns of the past, exemplified by the misguided attempt to impose the framework of ancient democracy on a society that was in fact driven by needs and ideals literally antithetical to those of the republics of Greece and Rome. That is why Constant felt the need to draw out the true characteristics of civilization in its current state of development by way of comparison with the ancient world. Constant's predilection for the comparative method was sustained by an acute awareness of the distinctiveness of modern Europe. [...]

Confusion as to the times and possibilities was thus the result of both misguided imitation of antiquity and perpetuation of the authoritarian patterns of the recent past. Both led to a pathological increase of the government's power over society when what was needed was precisely the opposite: the emancipation of society and its individual members, whom history had brought to the fore, breaking down old constraints in the process. The resulting confusion had obscured the fundamental distinction of the hour between the "principles of social authority" and the "principles of liberty." The habit of concealing the present beneath the ossified forms of an obsessive heritage would remain the polemical target of all of Constant's writing, which tirelessly denounced the contradiction between the old and the new. [...]

The new republic's misfortune was to project itself into the past, into a history where in fact it had no equivalent. It failed to recognize how utterly it differed from earlier incarnations of popular power as well as from all previous systems of authority. Hence it offered no prospect of true liberty in the novel sense we have adopted here – civil liberty and individual liberty – because it possessed no awareness of the distance separating us from our predecessors and made no conscious decision to be modern. The decision to be modern could not be taken for granted – and, I might add, it still cannot be taken for granted two centuries later. The difficulty that Constant perceived at the dawning of the democratic age remains with us to a remarkable degree: the vital present is always in danger of being swallowed up by a dead past that cannot be dispelled.

FROM COLLECTIVE AUTHORITY TO INDIVIDUAL RIGHTS

[...] Succinctly stated, the revolutionary enterprise was remarkably blind to the *individualism* of the society that it brought into being. On the one hand stood the values of equality and identity among individuals, which undermined hereditary superiorities and led to an insistence that power should emanate from the free choice of each individual. On the other hand, however, stood the contradictory reaffirmation of the primacy of the whole over the parts, of the necessary "sacrifice of the individual to the collectivity," a reaffirmation that was at once violent and unreal, to which an emancipatory movement insufficiently aware of its underlying tendency was led by the invincible power of an unmastered past.

What is remarkable about Constant's diagnosis is that it can be applied to nearly all subsequent excursions into totalitarianism. To be sure, it does not provide a complete interpretation of these lapses, but it does identify one essential element: the veering away from what is supposed to be a radical democratic process, whose purpose is ostensibly to bestow full sovereignty on individuals or even to reduce society to a free association of independent individuals, toward a system of regimentation, or even of fusion of individuals into a "mass" alleged to be fully represented by its leaders. The resulting system of unification–incorporation can only be understood as a resurgence of the fundamental principle of the society that preceded the individualist revolution, namely, the primacy of the whole over its individual parts, exemplified with particular clarity by regimes such as the ancient republics, in which collective liberty was coupled with subjugation of the individual to the collectivity. [. . .]

What was the crucial and tragically misunderstood change that severed the tie between modern society and the societies that preceded it? None other than the supplanting of "great public interests" by what Constant calls "private affections," the withdrawal into the "obscure" sphere of "private relations," and the retreat into the realm of pleasures to which individual freedom gives access – or, to put it another way, *the acquisition of the right to live without consciousness of the fact that we are living in society*, with the implicit assumption that society nevertheless remains perfectly intact even though its individual members have ceased to be conscious participants in its institution, whether by direct involvement in sovereign decision making or by conscious submission to the law that both enacts and symbolizes the superiority of the collective principle. [. . .] If there was indeed a revolution, it was in its deepest sense a revolution in the process by which society is constituted and reproduced. If individuals were indeed emancipated, it was as a result of the abrogation or elimination of the intimate obligation they felt to obey or to participate through deliberation in the creation and restoration of the community. Now they were free to think only of their own affairs and to forget about the common welfare. [...]

At the root of modern individualism, which Constant accepted along with all its political consequences, was thus a fundamental confidence that the social bond could constitute itself. Faith was placed in a faculty said to be inherent in "the natural constitution of man" (who, said Paine, was so made for society that it is almost impossible to extract him from it"): a faculty to forge indissoluble bonds with his fellow man without conscious effort, a capacity to relate. With this faith it became possible to trust individuals to set their own course and free them from an obligation on which Rousseau, for one, had stubbornly insisted: namely, the obligation to surrender consciously, completely, and exclusively to the duties of citizenship, so that from the conjunction of separate individual wills to exist in society there might arise the permanent explicit bond without which no body politic is truly viable. One might even venture to characterize this Rousseauian view as the idea that there can be no individualism without a certain "sociologism," by which I mean some minimal recognition of the specific nature of the social bond and some at least tacit awareness of the fact that its creation is independent of individual consciousness and will.

In this respect, the diagnosis that Constant proposed in the wake of the Revolution remains irrefutable for two reasons, and in some respects it might even be said to possess a peculiarly recurrent validity. First, what distinguishes today's society from all past societies has to do with this right of individuals to banish consciousness of the existence of society from their minds, whether as subjects or citizens. In other words, once the reign of the individual has begun, two spheres are indelibly marked out: a civil sphere, constituted by relations established at the initiative of individual agents when they use their freedom to own property, to forge alliances, to express themselves, or to worship; and a political sphere, constituted *exclusively* by certain specific requirements of collective life. The essence of any regime of liberty is to define and secure the boundary between these two spheres. [...] By contrast, modern despotism exhibits several distinctive features: one is the intrusion of political norms on the civil or individual sphere; [... another] is the enforced inclusion of all individuals in the realm of the political. [...] Constant was utterly convinced that in the social state toward which the human race was beginning to move, the civil sphere would increasingly be forced to take care of itself and assert its autonomous creative power.

DEMOCRATIC POWER AND STATE GROWTH

Now this is obviously the crux of the matter: [...] The relation between state and society has been stood on its head just as Constant imagined; the individual has been emancipated; civil society has emerged as a separate and autonomous sphere. Yet at the same time public power has continued to grow; the functions of the state have continued to expand; and the state's influence over civil society has become both more powerful and more subtle. Is this due to some exogenous factor? To the weight of tradition? Or, as one is quickly tempted to argue, to some reactionary and parasitic countermovement? No. It is rather the result of a parallel and related process stemming from a common source. The undeniable secession and self-constitution of the civil sphere, which Constant believed would logically be obliged to limit the prerogatives and mandates of the social power, has in fact gone hand in hand with a strengthening of the influence and extension of the competence of the political apparatus. In other words, the actual dynamics of modern society has ensured not only the coexistence but the association, the mutual support, of two aspects of social existence that liberal political science took to be incompatible: the grip of the state tightened even as the zone of individual independence widened.

This paradox calls our attention to the fundamental illusion of liberalism. What is remarkable about this illusion is that it is linked to, if not incorporated within, an accurate perception of the upheaval in human relations that actually took place. There can be no doubt that the symbolic order that attributed the existence of society to the will that society should exist (a will of which power, or more precisely the "physical unity" of power, was the material form) did indeed collapse. Nor can there be any doubt about the emancipation of some considerable part of human life from the political. What might have been expected to follow from this was a limitation of the prerogatives of government to keeping the peace domestically and guaranteeing security against attack from abroad. What occurred instead, however, was an extraordinary expansion of the administrative apparatus. Not only did this apparatus grow in sheer physical size; its role in the regulation, organization, and definition of social life also increased dramatically. Thus despite liberalism's authentic insight, this huge blind spot remained. Why? What was it about the quite accurate perception of the separation of civil from political society on which modernity was founded that ultimately functioned as a smoke screen?

The answer, to use the terms in which Constant posed the problem, is that it is misleading to speak of "limitation of sovereignty" or "social power" in describing the new relationship between the state and the sphere of individual existence. It is misleading to speak as if there were a certain sum of power and authority to be divided, so that an increase on one side would have to be compensated by a decrease on the other. In fact, social sovereignty, though radically severed from a henceforth autonomous communal existence, nevertheless remained intact, undivided, and "absolute." To be sure, the social power was no longer employed to constrain its subjects and thus make them aware of the existence of an infinitely superior will, which held them together; more than ever, however, its use was justified in terms of society's total power over itself. A further point, moreover, is closely related to what has been said thus far. The relation between state and society cannot be thought of as a simple division of labor, in which the state simply takes on those tasks that cannot be performed as efficiently by society. The roles of state and society are not merely parallel or complementary. Their relation is rather the product of the social body's reflection on its own existence. What is enigmatic about this relationship is that it depends on the isolation of power from society and on its separation from a shared identity. [...]

Why, in examining the (as it were) textbook case of the French Revolution and its aftermath, is it so strategically important to be clear about this irresistible expansion of popular sovereignty from below? Because it is essential if we are to understand what was happening throughout Europe at the top, namely, an inexorable increase in governmental power, though without the violence, arbitrariness, or tyranny of the past. The reason for this was that on the European side of the Atlantic, the deeply entrenched apparatus of monarchy prevented the democratic principle from developing on the local level, in the immediate and multiple forms of local self-government. Instead, it was channeled almost irresistibly into an administrative

and centralized form. This difference between the United States and
Europe is well known and well studied: on the one hand we find
extension of state control, subtle and widespread penetration of
social life, and ever greater "unity, ubiquity, and omnipotence" of
social power, while on the other hand popular sovereignty established itself at every level.

This, to borrow Tocqueville's well-known formulation, is nothing more or less than the assertion that the people are "the initial
and final cause of everything," from which "everything emanates
and to which everything returns." This is what lies behind the concentration and deepening of public authority. Instead of establishing
itself at the base, however, through close and persistent participation
in the drafting and enforcement of the law, this popular sovereignty
materialized in a refracted form at the top, as the administrative state
vastly expanded its control over collective life down to the most
minute details. This was done without arbitrariness, harassment,
coercion, or terroristic invasion of the private sphere; nor was any
direct constraint *imposed*. The "immense tutelary power" that was
just then emerging was as "regular, provident, and mild" as it was
"absolute and minute." It wanted nothing but the satisfaction and
happiness of its subjects, so long as it was "the sole agent and arbi-
ter." It aspired to *substitute* its own entirely benevolent authority
for the spontaneous decisions of individuals, and to do so without
conflict or inconvenience, in such a way as to secure for itself the
power to shape and define the transformation of social relations and
private desires into collective action.

This fundamental tendency of the state to peacefully substitute
itself for society was entirely due to the progress and evolution
of popular sovereignty. It served as the instrument whereby society for the first time seized control of itself, and it also became
the symbol of that process and served to legitimate it, as democratic revolution opened the way to unlimited power over the community. [...]

Turning now from Constant to the intellectual movement on
which he drew, still looking for the cause of liberalism's initial blindness to the ineluctable growth of public power under a regime of
individual liberty, we find that one overarching factor played a decisive role: namely, blindness as to the ultimate function of power,
blindness that stemmed from a right and proper understanding of

the disappearance of the state's former function as society's explicit symbolic underpinning. Paine said that society could subsist without government and that the time when people looked to government to exert its superior will so that society might exist belonged to the past. In saying this, he put his finger on a major social transformation: people no longer looked to the political as the cause of the social. Yet at the same time he missed something even more crucial: although society was no longer conceived as a product of *overt* government action, the foundational role of government, though now *covert*, nevertheless remained essential. The state was no longer the striking, imperious, central element of the edifice, the keystone of an ultimate order linking the living to both the dead and the unborn. Yet even though the state was no longer the crucible of identity, the visible incarnation of an ultimate will, so that society was now free to assert its autonomy, government continued to serve in a completely different way as society's symbolic underpinning, the source of its collective identity and cohesiveness, whose actions enabled individuals to feel that they lived together in a shared world of common meanings over which they exercised a measure of control.

Indeed, the state now began to exercise this crucial function more broadly than ever before, but it dissimulated its activity, hiding its constitutive role behind an increase in its actual responsibilities. Its symbolic function was covered up by a thick layer of practical activities, in such a way that it was relegated to the social unconscious. The social still originated in the political, but no longer as an express act of political will; it became a matter of unconscious institution. The existence of society still depended on the operation of the state, but it no longer insisted on knowing how this came to be, and the formal will of the state ceased to be necessary.

The political authorities acquired this new type of efficacy by assuming a place outside society from which to administer it, from which to guide and direct all social activity while allowing the actors some initial degree of latitude. Power was applied later. It sought to understand mechanisms and motives, and if it sought influence, it was always to shape the future. Now the method was to organize in detail rather than to compel crudely; to lay down minute rules rather than issue sweeping edicts; to incite rather than prohibit. For Burke, the imperative of imperatives had to originate within the human realm and make itself universal, so as to engrave in men's souls an indelible belief that the "law is not subject to the will of those, who by an obligation above them, and infinitely superior, are bound to submit their will to that law."[11] Otherwise one falls back into the old culture of domination, with all its paradoxes: there exists a supreme law above every individual, to which everyone must submit. This formulation grants the state total symbolic control over society, but in practice its control is very limited. With the advent of the modern democratic state, however, the terms of the political equation are inverted: explicit subordination and subjugation disappear, but effective control is enhanced to a fantastic degree. Society is left helpless before a power that claims to emanate from it, for it is tacitly understood that it must constitute itself without the help of the authority to which power is delegated. In reality, however, this apparent (and effective) autonomization of society allows the state to set itself up outside society, to break the organic bonds that had linked it to the human community, and to devote all its energy not merely to *maintaining* society but to *developing* it from a position of radical exteriority. [...]

NECESSITY OF THE POLITICAL AND NEUTRALITY OF POWER

This structural contradiction between the manifest logic of social institutions and the hidden logic of the institution of society itself proved to be a central difficulty in the attempt to establish a republican regime in a large country, and recognizing this fact brings us back to Constant. Indeed, his notable originality lay in the fact that he did not limit himself to a naïve liberal brief in favor of individual action as opposed to state intervention. Indeed, he anticipated and in some ways described *the need for a government* that would be more than a mere representative of individual interests, a government that could command the respect without which political organization fails of its essential purpose. He was not among those who believed that society was sufficient unto itself and could, if need be, do without government. Indeed, he was well aware of his originality as perhaps the only political thinker of his time to grasp the idea that a government must be something more than a faithful reflection of the will

[11] *Reflections*, 261.

of its citizens and that it must not be limited to carrying out the decisions of the majority. He intuited the notion that while society must ultimately constitute the state, it cannot do so by itself and that the role, structure, and design of the state must be such as to enable it to fulfill the elusive but crucial function of constituting society. As early as 1802 he concluded that there could be no viable republic unless, in addition to the usual and well-known ways in which society proceeds, by way of provisional election, to create and establish a state, the constitution also provided for the establishment of an independent government capable of providing society with the kind of self-understanding essential to the formation of its political identity.

We must, he argued, "rely on methods other than election and create a power other than the legislative and the executive," that is, "an authority independent of both the people and the executive."[12] Thus he stumbled on the paradox of democratic government: if the government is to provide a valid representation of society, it must free itself in certain ways from the influence of social agents. There was nothing original about Constant's point of departure. His was one among many contributions to the intense constitutional debate that had always surrounded the upheavals of the Thermidorian period. What is more, he was in the somewhat odd position of arriving on the scene after the battle had ended, at a time when the argument about the causes of chronic institutional stability had been resolved once and for all by the advent of dictatorship. How should one "halt the Revolution," stabilize the republic, and reconcile a regime of freedom with regular governmental operations and a solid base of authority? Constant went on talking about a subject about which everyone had been talking but which, by the time he began to write, was to be relegated to the past soon enough that his work was doomed to remain unpublished. What is more, his answer drew to some degree on the work of earlier writers, some of whom may have inspired him personally, above all Sieyès. And leave aside Madame de Staël, with whom he collaborated too closely to permit attribution of responsibility for specific ideas. Nevertheless, Constant's answer was still fundamentally new, if only in the sharpness of its formulation. After reviewing recent political events, he wrote:

[12] *Fragments*, 279, 377.

All the faults thus far described stem from a single cause. In a constitution where the only political powers are the power that makes the law and the power that executes it, when those powers are divided, there is no one to reestablish harmony between them; and when they are united, there is no one to impede the trespasses that their union encourages. It is this defect that must be repaired, and in order to repair it, a third power must be created, one that is neutral between the legislative power and the executive power.[13]

In other words, power must be able to strike at power: "The power that preserves," Constant puts it, "is in a sense the power to judge the other powers."[14] What is required is a power beyond those powers that normally emanate from election and that can be wielded against them, to turn them back:

The purpose of the preservative power is to defend government against division among the governing and to defend the governed against oppression by the government.... To that end, two powers are essential: the power to dissolve legislative assemblies, and the power to remove from office those in whom executive power has been vested.[15]

Indeed, there are perils other than dissension or collusion of the elected powers against which preventive measures should be taken, such as concentration of authority "sometimes in the hands of the executive power, other times in the hands of the legislative. In the former case, law that is meant to cover only specific objectives extends everywhere. Arbitrariness and tyranny are without limits.... In the latter, you have despotism."[16] In any event, there is a need for a higher tribunal as the substantive embodiment of society's control over the powers it has delegated. This is the essence of the neutral power as Constant conceives it: the fact that suffrage is the source of power is not enough to guarantee republican liberty, which requires in addition that society exercise power over those powers that represent it.

The preservative power cannot fulfill this function if it, like the legislative and executive powers, is elected for a fixed period. If it stands on the same footing as they do, from what does it derive its legitimacy? It must be exempt from the influence of the electorate

[13] Ibid., 373.
[14] Ibid., 390.
[15] Ibid., 387.
[16] Ibid., 373.

and "independent of the people." Yet Constant, reasoning in his 1802 work entirely on the basis of republican premises, does not imagine any means of selection other than the people's ballot. He envisions only a complex filtering process and election for life, with conditions of age, wealth, number, and ineligibility for any other political function intended to make this "oligarchy," as he calls it, an absolutely independent agency "disinterested," as it were, in anything outside its official purview. The essential fact is that once this body is constituted, it is to be radically exempt from outside control. It is to be an isolated body, entirely autonomous and external to all other agencies of government. A second essential fact is that this independent power is never to be applied directly to the society: "The preservative power," Constant wrote, "has nothing to do with individuals."[17] It deals only with the other powers, the legislative and the executive, not to guide their action in any positive sense (for its prerogatives include only the "right to call the attention of the executive power to the requirements of individuals"), but solely to impede and sanction them by sending the people's representatives back to face the voters. It is to play no role whatsoever in shaping public opinion, choosing the representatives of the nation, or designating the agents of government. Its one and only prerogative is "discretionary authority over the other powers"[18] when it detects deficiencies stemming from discord between them or arbitrary trespasses made possible by their collusion. It makes a principle of reaffirming the wishes of the voters, yet can at any time call upon the electorate to express its will against the authorities in power. In other words, it seeks to ensure that society and its representatives are in harmony, that their views coincide; yet it can do so paradoxically because it is itself independent of society and exempt from its control. In order to enforce respect for the collective will, it must be free of it.

Clearly, this intellectual construct aims at something far more ambitious than a simple solution to a difficult problem of constitutional mechanics. It marks the beginning of an effort to explore the ultimate nature of power, its true raison d'être and authentic functions. For Constant, society needs to exercise full control over itself, but in reality a power that emanates from society and receives

[17] Ibid., 401.
[18] Ibid., 417.

its mandate escapes its influence. Yet the principles of representation and popular sovereignty remain inviolable. From these premises Constant derives the need for a preservative power, which does not act on society or shape the collective process in any way but which offers the community a way to imagine, regaining possession of itself by turning against the powers derived from it. Through this preservative power society posits itself effectively and symbolically as the ultimate master of its fate and reasserts its full sovereignty while allowing the mechanisms of suffrage and delegation to operate freely. What Constant understood with his unique insight was that alongside or above the powers generated by men and recognized by them as authoritative, it was essential to conceive and establish another locus of power external to human will, which society could then invoke to constitute itself as a self-conscious collectivity.

If the social has a character all its own, so does the political: in power there is an element that is beyond the creation of men. Thus a regime that is organized in such a way as to welcome the initiatives of individual wills must also contrive somehow to recognize and represent the fact that some aspects of political order are not within the power of citizens to decide. The political order is in some respects prior to the will of citizens. There are ways in which it is constitutionally autonomous: Constant's neutral power is an example of this in that its members serve for life, are not subject to periodic replacement, and are presumed to exhibit absolute independence of judgment and complete detachment from the rest of the society. To put it another way, no democratic regime is viable unless the mechanism by which power is derived from society is somehow reconciled with a system in which power is always already separate from society, in which the source of power is always independent of and prior to society. Society does not possess the freedom to determine its own course where there is no possibility of appealing the decisions of elected authorities to a supreme yet strictly circumscribed higher authority. If democratic sovereignty is truly to exist, therefore, power must be limited; it must to some extent be taken from the hands of the people and irrevocably withdrawn from the common run of mankind.

In historical terms, this means that democracies could not establish themselves on a firm foundation until they learned to incorporate the external and prior dimensions of power, which their conservative adversaries criticized them, not without justice, for failing to understand. Bonald, for example, observed that "power always exists before society, since it is power that constitutes society." And Burke remarked that there was no way to maintain men in society without a "power out of themselves."[19] The problem is that there are many ways of recognizing the priority and exteriority of power. Such recognition is not only compatible with the democratic principle, according to which society enjoys full power to determine its own direction, but in fact indispensable to the full exercise of democratic power. It was Constant's distinctive genius to have grasped this fact, and through his insight we become eyewitnesses to the decisive shift from a set of principles intended to *preserve* society to a new system intended to allow society to *express* its wishes.

Continuing with our historical analysis, we see that democracies were able to solve the problems attending their birth and achieve stability only by incorporating a monarchical element, only by tolerating a secret continuity with the deposed royal power, whose role in the inception of the very idea of democratic society needs to be examined. Constant himself perceived the issue clearly: as early as 1802 he acknowledged that his idea of a neutral power had its source in monarchy. Despite his republican preferences, monarchy in itself did not disturb him unduly so long as the monarch's constitutional prerogatives were strictly limited to the exercise of the neutral power, which he deemed essential in any case. His support for the restored monarchy, which went hand in hand with his militant insistence on the rights of the nation's representatives, was perfectly consistent with the beliefs he had always espoused. As early as his *Fragments*, he had inquired about the viability of a purely elective system and remarked that

one of the greatest advantages of monarchy is that the power to remove a government from office is in a sense placed in the hands of the king. A zealous proponent of this form of government (M. Clermont-Tonnerre) observed that the monarchical power contains two powers, the executive, which is invested with positive prerogatives, and the royal, which is based on illusions derived from religion and tradition. The royal power is in a sense a neutral power between the people and the executive power per se, which is always delegated to ministers. The power to remove the officials

[19] *Reflections,* 261.

to whom executive power has been entrusted is vested in this neutral power, and because this power is fixed within limits, its sting is drawn and it becomes less dangerous when circumstances require that it be created, or, rather, seized, in a moment of emergency.[20]

Thus within the old monarchical powers Constant found two powers combined in one: a power of *action* and a power of *representation*. To have a liberal monarchy, it was enough to separate the two and subject the executive power, delegated to ministers, to the control of representative assemblies. (This was what had been done in England, which of course remained a model for Constant: there, the royal power was neutral, in fact, if not in law.) Yet even if the monarchical framework were eliminated, a republicanized form of the neutral power of representation would still be needed, and it would need the power to remove governments from office, thus offering society a recourse against the powers established by democratic suffrage.

The question that must be asked is the following: the idea of these two mutually exclusive forms or images of power – one that acts on society and one that is the incarnation of the authority of society itself – did this idea not form within the monarchical power itself? It is an idea adequate to the affirmation of sovereign power, to the concentration in the person of the monarch (or what Bonald calls "the physical unity of power") of absolute power over human affairs. The very nature of this power requires that the person who wields it be cut off from society and that his action be circumscribed within strictly defined limits. He must never act directly but only through delegated authority: this is the essence of his power. Was it not in this way that monarchical absolutism consolidated its image as the central locus from which all human affairs could be embraced, penetrated, and possessed, thereby creating out of whole cloth and introducing into this world the democratic perspective of man's total power over the organization of human life? Was it not in the guise of a king, as the head of a state whose Christian roots and national contours gave him unprecedented sway over his subjects, that man's unlimited sovereignty over human society first took shape on this earth? The democratic revolution merely reappropriated this infinite power of the social over society itself, now bestowing it on

[20] Ibid., 398.

society as a whole rather than on one man. Yet in order to exercise this total sovereignty, democracy needed to preserve something of the figure onto which it had originally projected the limitlessness of social power: namely, the reference to an "abstract" neutral power. This neutral power was vacant in a human sense, for even though held by a person, he was "not truly a person," as Constant observed. Indeed, "heredity creates a kind of neutrality." The king occupied his place not as an individual but as the representative of a dynasty. Hence his place was that special kind of void created by the very perfection of the surrounding plenitude: "The king can do no wrong." The definition of the king's place as a distinct locus of power thus enabled modern society to reflect on itself, to exert full control over itself, to create itself out of nothing via the mediation of a state that liberated, dispossessed, and subsumed it. Constant missed the tendency toward bureaucratic control that accompanied the democratic appropriation of monarchical power. In that he was a victim of the liberal's inveterate optimism. Yet he succeeded better than anyone else in exposing the "neutral" point in the refraction of social power, the essential yet unseen foundation of all democracy on which a free society erects itself, along with an all-powerful state by means of which that society endlessly seeks to secure its liberty against itself. "The preservative power, as we understand it, is therefore not a stationary power, which would induce immobility in social organization, nor a conservative power, which would exert itself on behalf of some body of opinion. . . . It does not consecrate any opinion."[21] Twenty-five years later, he put this vision in a more programmatic form: "With respect to opinion, belief, and knowledge, the government shall remain entirely neutral, because the government, being composed of men of the same nature as those they govern, has no more access than they do to incontrovertible opinion, certain belief, or infallible knowledge."[22]

The question is this: How can a government bearing the mark of partiality in its convictions portray itself as the representative of the whole community's determination to shape its own future? The state's doctrinal reticence is imposed by the force it is charged with representing, a force that, though infinite, is always gradual and

---

[21] Ibid., 417.
[22] Preface to *Mélanges*, 626.

mild. Here, intellectual neutrality is not tantamount to impotence
but rather the prerequisite of power: therein lies the mystery of the
democratic state, which stands apart in order to encompass all the
more fully. Even as Constant was writing, however, a new note was
beginning to be heard, a note to which he responded critically in the
final years of his life, though he had no inkling of the future that lay
in store for the ideas of a sect that he regarded as "fortunately obscure
and weak" and really rather ridiculous – a sect with pretensions to
what he called "industrial papism":

In all dissidence of opinion or diversity of effort, this sect sees anarchy. It
is frightened that men do not all think the same, or, rather, that they do
not all think as this sect's leaders would have them think. And in order to
put an end to this scandalous variety, it invokes a spiritual power, which,
by means that it prudently refrains from revealing, would restore this most
precious unity, or so it claims.[23]

The Saint-Simonians to whom Constant here refers had only just
begun their efforts to regenerate the world and "transport it from
a transitory to a definitive state." What their innocent efforts only
dimly portended we have come to know from direct and bitter experience. Intellectual neutrality on the one hand, spiritual power on
the other: what is enigmatic about the origins of totalitarianism is
that these two phenomena emerged at the same time and progressed
at the same pace. As a lucid analyst of the "great crisis that has been
gathering for two centuries and working itself out over the last forty
years," Constant recognized that the constitution of a democratic
power involved a relative willingness to allow society to determine
its own direction; yet this same aloofness made room for, and in
a sense encouraged, the very different project of restoring ultimate
intellectual unity, of bringing society into harmony with its own
fulfilled meaning, and of making an end to history. This was all
the more true because, as the state advanced into neutrality, it also
developed in complexity, and the ambition to achieve the true purpose of human existence once and for all acquired an instrument
potent enough for such an ambitious undertaking. Just as the historical process seemed to be taking a definitive turn in favor of the
liberal cause, the stage was being set for an about-face, for a repetition

---

[23] "De M. Dunoyer et de quelques-uns de ses ouvrages," in *EP*, 674.

on a scale incomparably more vast of the mad attempt to reconcile, in the incandescence of the revolutionary present, society's ancient form – unity under a power that willed it so – with the new future-directed political order. On this point, Constant's diagnosis of the causes of the relatively modest state terrorism that he was obliged to witness needs only to be extended and systematized: totalitarianism is in essence the resurgence of an old and precisely identifiable paradigm, that of power as cause, within the new paradigm according to which man exercises full power over the social order. What is striking in this is that the growth of the new seems fated to revive the obscure ideal of the past. It is as if the liberal transition can never be completed, as if, as we hurtle ever more rapidly into the unimaginable future, we are doomed never to free ourselves from the hoary phantom of a world that no longer exists.

3 The Liberty to Denounce: Ancient and Modern

What is wrong, legally and morally, with a two-track judicial system, where most suspects are tried in ordinary courts but where individuals who are alleged to be especially dangerous are hauled before extraordinary civilian tribunals or "military commissions" with radically reduced procedural guarantees? Benjamin Constant asked and answered this question, with exemplary clarity, two hundred years ago: "It means declaring men convicted ahead of time, even when they are only accused." No infallible external signs distinguish the guilty from the innocent. This is why legal procedures must not be casually circumvented, for they remain "the best methods available for ascertaining the facts." That political authorities that claim to be curtailing due-process rights for the sake of "public safety" are guilty of "absurdity," if not outright mendacity, was another one of his lifelong convictions. Even more remarkably, he explained in persuasive detail how the system of criminal justice is inevitably perverted when it is assigned the task not of punishing past crimes but of preventing future ones. "The pretext of preventing future crimes," he argues, is wholly incompatible with a free society for the simple reason that "the possibility of committing a criminal act is an inherent feature of individual liberty."[1]

As these remarkable passages suggest, Constant's lucid writings on judicial power remain eerily relevant to twenty-first-century concerns. The present chapter focuses on a theme closely related to

---

[1] *PoP* (1806), 74–77, 153–57. Although citations in this essay refer to *PoP* (1806) and AML, I have frequently altered the translations. All other translations from the French are my own.

those just mentioned and one that speaks equally directly to legal and political difficulties of the present.

I

Among the multiple sources, literary and experiential, from which Constant distilled his concept of modern liberty, a fertile passage in *The Spirit of the Laws* stands out: "Political liberty in a citizen is that tranquility of spirit which comes from the opinion each one has of his security, and in order for him to have this liberty the government must be such that one citizen cannot fear another citizen."[2] In Montesquieu's vocabulary, political liberty is not essentially about participatory rights such as the right to examine the state budget, the right to vote for representatives, or the right to hold elected officials accountable for their public actions. In the passage cited, at least, political liberty is associated with a socially diffuse peace of mind, based on the citizens' universally shared confidence that they have nothing to fear from each other. This leaves open the question: How should a government be organized, and how should political officials behave, so that no citizen need fear another? That periodic elections to a representative assembly might contribute to this end is obviously not excluded by Montesquieu's Anglocentric exploration of the underlying meaning of political liberty.

A coherent and effective government may prevent citizens from employing force or fraud to harm each other grievously. But what will prevent the temporary wielders of governmental power from misapplying public means to serve their own illicit private ends? Checks and balances provide one answer; periodic elections another. To pursue the question of political accountability would lead us directly into the expanses and intricacies of Constant's constitutional theory. Although that remains an important and challenging pursuit, my focus here is narrower and deeper.

All citizens, inside and outside government, are capable of treating their compatriots unjustly. Constitutional and procedural limits on the power of government officials are justified, in the first instance, because they create disincentives designed to deter the

---

[2] Montesquieu, *The Spirit of the Laws*, ed. and trans. A. M. Cohler, B. C. Miller, and H. S. Stone (Cambridge: Cambridge University Press, 1989), 157.

misbehavior of public officials. They are additionally justified, however, because they make it more difficult for private parties to attack
each other using the instrumentalities of public power. If the government's capacity to punish private citizens is highly discretionary,
that is to say, unbound by strict procedural formalities, it will be relatively easy for tightly knit nongovernmental factions to "capture"
the punitive authority of the state and to use it to attack and even
destroy their rivals.

That Constant was deeply concerned with this grim possibility
is clear from his lifelong interest in the pathologies of "ténébreuses
délations,"[3] that is, the danger posed to personal autonomy (or modern freedom) by malicious and especially anonymous informants.
Constant was not the first or only liberal theorist to focus on the
problem of unreliable hearsay evidence being smuggled into the
judicial system for illicit private purposes.[4] But the insistence with
which he returns to the theme throughout his career suggests the
seriousness with which he viewed the issue.[5] There is no greater
crime against liberty, he repeatedly argued, than for a man to be "judged according to secret information, transmitted, so to speak, clan-
destinely to his judges" and "without the accused being allowed to
refute it."[6]

The following passage on "the freedom to denounce," drawn from
his *Commentaire sur l'ouvrage de Filangieri* (1822–24), is typical. I
cite at length to convey the flavor of Constant's approach:

The liberty to denounce [someone to the police] has disadvantages that can
be exceedingly serious. Hatred, envy, all the base or spiteful passions, will
take advantage of this liberty. Innocence will be subjected to slander; the
most irreproachable citizens will find themselves at the mercy of a hidden
enemy... when men resort to partly odious measures, it is rarely because
of zeal or disinterestedness, and out of one hundred denunciations, it is

[3] *Discours de M. Benjamin Constant à la Chambre de Députés*, vol. 2 (Paris:
Ambroise Dupont, 1828), 158 (July 22, 1822); he already discussed this issue in
Des suites de la contre-révolution de 1660 en Angleterre (Paris: F. Buisson, 1799),
90–94.
[4] Cf. Montesquieu, *The Spirit of the Laws*, book XII, chap. 24, 208.
[5] *Discours de M. Benjamin Constant à la Chambre de Députés*, vol. 1, 199; vol. 2,
169–78.
[6] "Lettre à M. Odillon-Barrot sur l'affaire de Wilfrid Regnault condamné à mort
(1818)," in *Cours de politique constitutionnelle*, vol. 2 (Paris: Librairie de Guillaumin, 1872), 398; see also 409–11.

probable that hardly one will have been dictated by the love of justice or the hatred of crime . . . The magistrate who, on the basis of a secret denunciation, has the denounced man put in chains, commits an unjust and inexcusable act.[7]

High evidentiary standards for arrest, conviction, and punishment are designed not only to tie the hands of potential tyrants, in other words, but also to prevent witness malice, deliberate disinformation furnished by private parties, from poisoning the system of criminal justice and hijacking ostensibly impartial authority for blatantly partial ends.

The threat posed by informers to civic tranquility was evident in France throughout Constant's active political life, starting with the Revolution. According to François Furet and Denis Richet, "seen as ignominious during the Old Regime, informing became a virtue and a duty because one was now in a republic."[8] Something similar could be said about France both under Napoleon and during the first years of the Restoration.

The possibility of witness malice in particular forces us to reconceptualize the relationship between political authority and civil society. In a Hobbesian framework, at least, state-building is understood as the replacement of horizontal threats posed by individuals and groups to each other with a single vertical threat posed by the state to private individuals and substate groups. By drawing attention to informing, Constant helps scramble this simplistic account, dispelling the myth that civil society, after a coherent government has been established, is suddenly transformed from a dangerous into an innocent realm. He shows us, on the contrary, how "vertical" state-building, far from repressing the "horizontal" use of force and fraud between citizens, can provide an additional weapon by means of which private parties can pursue the destruction of personal and factional enemies. The "Terror," in the late eighteenth-century sense, was not merely a top-down affair but was instead a highly participatory public–private joint venture.

What makes the private use of public power especially interesting for students of Constant is the light it sheds on his distinction

---

[7] *Commentaire sur l'ouvrage de Filangieri* (Paris: Les Belles Lettres, 2004), 238.
[8] François Furet and Denis Richet, *La Révolution française* (Paris: Hachette, 1973), 211.

between ancient and modern liberty. To understand the connection, we need to reexamine briefly that famous contrast.

II

Human interests and desires are being constantly reshaped by opportunities that the organization of society makes available at any given time and place. People can will only what is in their perceived interest, and their interests, in turn, are by-products of historical transformations wholly beyond their control.[9] The inhabitants of ancient Greek republics, for example, felt neither the attraction of nor the need for the kind of freedom typical of modern Europe. They desired another kind of freedom: "Their social organization led them to desire an entirely different freedom from the one which this system grants to us."[10] Not only what they were able to achieve but what they wanted to achieve was a product of their international environment and institutional setup, as well as reflecting the culturally entrenched dos and don'ts of life eked out in a small, slaveholding, warrior republic.

Whatever "freedom" includes, in Constant's stylized contrast, it apparently excludes the freedom to choose the kind of freedom one desires. The goals that human beings passionately or unthinkingly pursue are not freely selected but imposed on them by a kind of inescapable fate, depending on when and where these particular people happen to live. (An important exception to this deterministic principle is discussed later.)

What sort of freedom was desired, according to Constant, by the inhabitants of ancient republics?[11] The answer that commentators conventionally give involves a version of "positive liberty." Ancient citizens, in their collective capacity, were able to exercise directly and personally, and not through elected representatives, many parts of sovereignty. They deliberated in the public square about war and

---

[9] *Du polythéisme romain considéré dans ses rapports avec la philosophie grecque et la religion chrétienne*, vol. 2 (Paris: Béchet Aîné, 1833), 168.

[10] "The Liberty of the Ancients Compared with That of the Moderns [AML]," 310.

[11] Constant employed the stylized concepts of "the ancient city" and "the ancient citizen," which may be worth recalling, not as historically accurate descriptive terms, but instead as ideal types that usefully draw attention to some significant characteristics of certain classical republics and their politically active members.

peace, ratified treaties of alliance with foreign powers, passed legislation, pronounced verdicts, and oversaw the actions of the executive
officials – forcing these officials to appear before the assembled people, condemning or absolving them, and so forth.

This paraphrase is correct so far as it goes; but it does not go very
far. Above all, it misleadingly downplays the vividly negative nature
of ancient freedom conveyed by Constant's own account. Ancient
liberty, for Constant, is *freedom from* before it is *freedom to.*

The brutally violent, competitive, and dangerous world outside
each city's walls goes a long way toward explaining the kind of
liberty cherished by the inhabitants of ancient republics. Because
ancient republics were small and constantly interfering with each
others' quest for security, prestige, power, and wealth, they were
driven, by the imperatives of honor and survival, not only to build
forbidding protective walls but also to maintain their entire male
citizen populations trained and ready for combat. Bellicosity was not
a cause but an effect of their external vulnerability: "Thus driven
by necessity against one another, they fought or threatened each
other constantly. Those who had no ambition to be conquerors could
still not lay down their weapons, lest they should themselves be
conquered. All had to buy their security, their independence, their
whole existence at the price of war."[12] The inhabitants of ancient
republics could not separate their viscerally prized freedom from
their coordinated effort in wartime because if they were defeated in
combat and allowed to survive, they would be callously sold into
merciless slavery. Citizens who had no interest in being conquerors
could not put down their weapons. If they singly repudiated the
collective martial ethos, they would singly suffer civic and civilized
if not physical death.

Ancient liberty sounds positive when Constant describes it as "an
active and constant participation in collective power."[13] But its negative dimension bursts dramatically into view when he describes it
as freedom from enslavement, not metaphorical but brutally real.
Ancient citizens did not simply make a virtue of necessity. Instead,
historical necessity compelled them to enshrine the warrior's virtues
at the pinnacle of their hierarchy of values. War was the unrelenting

---

[12] AML, 312.
[13] Ibid., 316.

interest and the habitual occupation of the free cities of antiquity. Their warrior culture was perfectly adapted to the despoiling of neighbors; but it was also the price that ancient citizens paid for fending off the wrath and greed of citizen-soldiers from rival republics.

The liberty valued in ancient republics was radically incompatible with equality. It could not, by its nature, be universalized. For some men to be free, others had to be enslaved. The inequality between freemen and slaves that characterized the ancient republics was a necessary by-product of their need to maintain collective readiness for war.[14] Citizens could concentrate on training for combat only if the economy was placed in the hands of noncitizens, including metics as well as slaves. This is how Constant, a passionate opponent of the ongoing nineteenth-century slave trade, thought about the cruelly selective liberty of the ancient republics. Citizens could maintain their freedom from military conquest by rival cities only by subjecting slaves to the arbitrary will of a master class. Give me a citizen-soldier, and I will give you a slave-driver with a hardened conscience.

Active participation in collective decision making itself was a direct result of the ceaseless involvement of ancient republics in defensive and acquisitive wars. Ancient citizen-soldiers had to find some profitable use of their spare time between wars, and the low prestige of economic activity, associated with slavery, meant that their only option was political life. When he comes to describing the peacetime participation of ancient citizens in their republics, however, Constant does not place much emphasis on voting. What he stresses, instead, is collective involvement in punishing, banishing, and putting fellow citizens to death.

In ancient republics, each citizen took part in the exercise of national sovereignty. But why did the ancient citizen experience the exercise of political rights as "a vivid and repeated pleasure"?[15] Constant's answer is somewhat disconcerting: "As a member of the collective body, he interrogated, dismissed, condemned, beggared, exiled, or sentenced to death his magistrates and superiors."[16] Constant's most important literary source, in this case, is no doubt the

[14] Cf. *The Spirit of the Laws*, book IV, chap. 8.
[15] AML, 316.
[16] Ibid., 312.

famous chapter in the *Discorsi* in which Machiavelli explains how public trials, where the poor can bring criminal charges against the rich, help stabilize republics by giving vent to ill feelings that might otherwise explode in revolutionary violence.[17]

The institution that most fully expressed the total subordination of personal autonomy to group existence was ostracism. The banishment of a citizen by secret ballot without any reason being required or given (and without any defense being allowed) was a practice found even in Athens, the one ancient republic that otherwise shared something in common with those modern states most widely understood to be free, namely, the United States and Great Britain: "Ostracism in Athens rested upon the assumption that society had complete authority over its members."[18] Because of his family background and personal experience, Constant knew a great deal about exile and expatriation. This may be why he repeatedly used ostracism to symbolize the supremacy of society over the individual.[19] A common practice in small republics in antiquity and the Middle Ages, banishment was ostensibly incompatible with the morality and social structure of modern Europe: "Ostracism, that legal arbitrariness, extolled by all the legislators of the age; ostracism, which appears to us, and rightly so, a revolting iniquity, proves that the individual was much more subservient to the supremacy of the social body in Athens, than he is in any of the free states of Europe today."[20] Admittedly, innocent asylum-seekers continued to flee from the unfree states of modern Europe. Constant's personal familiarity with the varieties of nonvoluntary expatriation no doubt explains the gusto with which he describes ancient ostracism from the viewpoint of its victims. The citizen-judges in ancient republics might have felt excitingly influential, but anyone on the receiving end of ancient liberty had a different experience: "As a subject of the collective body he could himself be deprived of his status, stripped of his privileges,

---

[17] Niccolò Machiavelli, *Discourses on Livy (1513–19)*, trans. Harvey C. Mansfield and Nathan Tarcov (Chicago and London: The University of Chicago Press, 1996), book I, chap. 7; for Constant's discussion, see *Commentaire sur l'ouvrage de Filangieri*, 241.

[18] AML, 321.

[19] That Constant did not consistently view the penal transportation of lower-class criminals as a revolting iniquity is made clear in part III, chap. 13, of the *Commentaire sur l'ouvrage de Filangieri*.

[20] AML, 316.

banished, put to death, by the discretionary will of the whole to which he belonged."

It should be mentioned that political banishment in antiquity was by most measures a more draconian penalty than political banishment in modern Europe. This was largely due to the greatly increased circulation of money characteristic of the modern international economy. In earlier periods, iron trumped gold. Men with weapons could dominate men with money, because wealth was concentrated in fixed assets such as land and could therefore be seized by force. The relative power of force and wealth shifted with the development of modern commercial societies and especially the spread of liquid assets: "Commerce makes the action of arbitrary power over our existence more oppressive than in the past, because it changes the nature of property, which becomes, in virtue of this change, almost impossible to seize."[21] According to Constant, in modern Europe, "Individuals carry their treasures far away; they take with them all the enjoyments of private life."[22] The chance for the wealthy to transfer considerable liquid assets abroad and out of reach of the banishing authority cushioned to some extent the experience of exile, at least for certain social classes.

III

Elsewhere in "The Liberty of the Ancients Compared with That of the Moderns," Constant refers to the events of 1789 and immediately thereafter as "our happy Revolution."[23] He praises the Revolution precisely because it resulted in the permanent dismantling of a system of legal inequality. In other works, he describes it as a great crisis that had been prepared for two centuries, by the diffusion of property and enlightenment, and that suddenly exploded in 1789 due to various short-term factors such as the monarchy's daunting fiscal deficit.[24] Having overthrown the monarchy, the

---

[21] Ibid., 324. Similarly, "commerce confers a new quality on property, circulation. Without circulation, property is merely a usufruct; political authority can always affect usufruct, because it can prevent its enjoyment; but circulation creates an invisible and invincible obstacle to the action of social power" (pp. 324–25).

[22] AML, 325.

[23] Ibid., 309.

[24] *Mélanges de littérature et de politique*, vol. 1 (Bruxelles: Imprimerie-Libraire Romantique, 1829), iii.

leaders of the Revolution were intoxicated by their victory and soon began to overestimate their capacity to change the country. Having read books about how republics, as opposed to monarchies, should be governed, they started introducing institutional reforms that could possibly not be stably maintained in a modern country: "They wished to exercise public power as they had learnt from their guides it had once been exercised in free states."[25]

But exactly what role did ideas or ideology play in producing the cruel excesses of Revolutionary France? According to Constant, the Terror resulted, at least in part, from the confusion of two ideas that should have been kept distinct. This is how he introduces his discussion of ancient and modern liberty: "The confusion of these two kinds of liberty has been amongst us, in the all too famous days of our revolution, the cause of many an evil."[26] The cause of the Terror was not simply the idea of ancient liberty, but rather the confusion of old-style republican liberty, typical of small city-states, with "a liberty suited to modern times."[27]

The most important source of this incompatibility is self-evident. Modern times is characterized above all by "the tendency towards equality"[28] and especially by a moral revulsion against slavery. The most progressive minds of antiquity thought that slavery was perfectly moral, while not even the most reactionary minds of modern France would imagine resurrecting the odious institution: "The most absurd men of today cannot, despite themselves, regress to the point where the most enlightened men of earlier centuries had arrived."[29] Any attempt to resurrect ancient liberty in modern France was doomed, therefore, if only because ancient liberty, by its very nature, cannot be universalized, while the only liberty that can survive in the modern world must be susceptible to universalization.

As a result, the people of France did not want what their Revolutionary leaders wanted them to want. They wished to say "monsieur" instead of "citizen," to eat fish on Friday, to go to church, to marry foreigners, and so forth. For such perfectly natural desires, a number of unlucky Frenchmen fell victim to the Terror: "France was exhausted by useless experiments, the authors of which, irritated by

---

[25] AML, 320.
[26] Ibid., 309.
[27] Ibid., 323.
[28] *Mélanges de littérature et de politique*, vol. 2, 142.
[29] Ibid., 136.

their poor success, sought to force her to enjoy the good she did not want, and denied her the good which she did want."[30] Frustrated by the recalcitrance of pre-revolutionary habits to rapid change under the supervision of officials, the revolutionaries became violent, trying to achieve by compulsion and intimidation what they could not achieve by persuasion. Far from being excessively "rational," Robespierre inflicted cruel punishments not in reasonable proportion to the gravity of the offense but for acts that ordinary people viewed as excusable or even morally obligatory.[31]

The sensibility of modern Frenchmen had been produced by centuries of social evolution. It could not be erased or replaced by political fiat in a few short months. Because they govern choice, desires themselves cannot be chosen, at least not in the same way as other objects of desire. This is an important insight because most Frenchmen in 1792–94 wanted a different kind of freedom than the one being offered by the Jacobins. The power concentrated in the Committee of Public Safety was able to torment the individual but was unable to destroy the individual's need for independence. The attachment to personal autonomy was a long-gestation product of modern history, not an ephemeral fashion that could be erased by cutting off a few heads.

Despite themselves, some of the leading proponents of the Terror occasionally revealed the yawning gap between revolutionary pretensions and the ingrained constraints of public morality at the time. Constant's most amusing example of this pattern is the following: "Saint-Just delivered all his speeches in short sentences, suitable for keeping tired souls awake. And while he pretended that the nation was capable of making the most painful sacrifices, he acknowledged by his very style that it was incapable even of paying attention."[32] Because the vast majority of Frenchmen did not really want, and were not capable of sustaining, the kind of liberty being offered, the revolutionary project, however well intentioned, was doomed to fail: "The restored edifice of the ancients collapsed, notwithstanding many efforts and many heroic acts which call for our admiration."[33]

---

[30] AML, 309.
[31] Des suites de la contre-révolution de 1660 en Angleterre, 56–57.
[32] PoP (1806), 362.
[33] AML, 320.

According to Constant, "men invested with authority display a constant inclination to wrap themselves in mystery."[34] Premodern rulers typically used religion to bolster their legitimacy, claiming that the laws must be obeyed because they were handed down by God or the gods.[35] France's Revolutionary rulers adopted a similar strategy, claiming to rule in the name of the only occult power that could still be persuasively invoked in modern times, namely, the will of the sovereign people. Thus, Constant regularly refers to the Jacobins as "those who act in the name of all."[36] This is perhaps the signal contribution of the revolutionary generation to modern political development: the decoration of oppression with the symbols and rhetoric of freedom. When the Committee of Public Safety oppressed an individual, it did not claim to be doing so under divine authority. It oppressed the people, instead, in the name of the people. Even more strikingly, "It is in the name of liberty that we were given prisons, scaffolds, and innumerable vexations."[37] Modern tyranny, as opposed to traditional autocracy, enacts a "parody of liberty."[38] Constant describes this Revolutionary reorganizing of despotic power with his striking phrase: "The triumph of tyrannical force is to compel slaves to proclaim themselves free."[39]

In some passages of the 1819 lecture, Constant appears to back off from the idea that the Jacobins *confused* ancient and modern liberty, arguing that they saw the distinction clearly enough but simply misunderstood the trade-offs involved. They thought that restrictions on individual rights would be amply compensated for by participation in the social power: "They believed that everything should give way before collective will, and that all restrictions on individual rights would be amply compensated by participation in social power."[40] But the sacrifice of personal autonomy for a share in political power was a much better deal in a small ancient republic

---

[34] *Cours de politique constitutionnelle*, vol. 1, 75.

[35] See for one discussion among many well known to Constant, Rousseau, *Contrat social*, book II, chap. 7.

[36] *Cours de politique constitutionnelle*, vol. 1, 279.

[37] Ibid., vol. 2, 217; cf. *Recueil d'articles: Le Mercure, La Minerve et La Renommée*, vol. 1 (Geneva: Droz, 1972), 291; and *PoP* (1806), 57–58, 384–85.

[38] *PoP* (1806), 110.

[39] *Discours de M. Benjamin Constant à la Chambre de Députés*, vol. 2, 60 (speech of February 9, 1822).

[40] AML, 320.

than in a large modern state. The Jacobin project was doomed by the size and population of modern republics. Political participation might still be valuable; but it was no longer so extraordinarily valuable that it would be worthwhile to abandon personal autonomy to possess it.

IV

What about modern liberty? The liberty compatible with modern times, in Constant's account, has two distinct and mutually reinforcing dimensions. These two dimensions of modern freedom must not be confused, but rather clearly distinguished and then strategically combined.

The first facet of modern freedom is what we might call due process or the rule of law: "the right to be subjected only to the laws, and to be neither arrested, detained, put to death or maltreated in any way by the arbitrary will of one or more individuals."[41] Due process of law serves the human interest in predictability and helps foster that "peace of mind" or sense of personal security that Montesquieu identified with political liberty.

Constant consistently identifies modern liberty with the personal experience of security: "Individual rights include the certainty that one will not be treated arbitrarily . . . that is to say, the guarantee that one will neither be arrested, nor detained, nor tried, except according to law and following due process."[42] Above all, modern citizens, living under a free government, can be banished (or imprisoned or put to death) only according to rules that are known in advance and with a reasonable chance to disprove in a public hearing the factual premises behind the decision to punish.

In a sense, modern liberty is the antonym of ancient ostracism. As Constant explained, "No one has the right to exile a citizen, if he is not condemned by a regular tribunal, according to a formal law which attaches the penalty of exile to the action of which he is guilty."[43] What is impermissible about ancient ostracism is its arbitrariness, including the impossibility for the individual being

---

[41] Ibid., 310.
[42] *PoP* (1806), 151.
[43] AML, 321–22.

ostracized to put up a vigorous legal defense. What the practice of
ostracism symbolizes, once more, is a shared belief that society has
total authority over individual citizens.

Far from being freedom from society, in other words, modern freedom is freedom to remain a member of one's own society if one so
wishes: "No one has the right to tear the citizen from his country,
the owner away from his possessions, the merchant away from his
trade, the husband from his wife, the father from his children, the
writer from his studious meditations, the old man from his accustomed way of life." Formulated differently, modern freedom is the
opposite of independence. If we wished to describe it in negative
terms, we might call it freedom from expulsion and exile. Once
again, "All political exile is political abuse. All exile pronounced by
an assembly for alleged reasons of public safety is a crime which the
assembly itself commits against public safety, which resides only in
respect for the laws, in the observance of forms, and in the maintenance of safeguards."[44] Notice here that modern ostracism is not
a crime against the individual alone, but also a crime "against the
public welfare." Whether or not the individual is free from arbitrary
banishment determines whether or not the country as a whole can
be called free.

Private citizens, in a free country, cannot be arbitrarily banished,
but they have the right to come and go without asking permission or
giving reasons for their actions. Government officials, by contrast,
must give reasons for their actions. Above all, they have to demonstrate the accuracy of the factual premises of their decisions to use
coercive force. This striking asymmetry is an essential feature of
modern freedom. Public officials have to justify their actions, while
private citizens do not. This brings us back to ostracism.

Under Napoleon, the rulers of post-Revolutionary France lost
interest in most republican institutions, but they felt a strange
affection for one set of ancient practices, namely, "those which
allow them to banish, to exile, or to despoil." Constant makes the
point anecdotally: "I remember that in 1802, they slipped into the
law on special tribunals an article which introduced into France
Greek ostracism."[45] The bill was eventually withdrawn, but its

[44] Ibid., 322.
[45] Ibid., 321.

mere consideration revealed volumes about the continued hostility toward modern liberty characterizing Napoleonic France.

The first dimension of modern liberty is the subjective certainty that one will not be punished on the arbitrary say-so of another citizen, in or out of public office. Without this tranquility of spirit, personal autonomy is of little value, or rather, no individual will feel genuinely independent. Individual independence, in other words, can exist only in a well-organized legal system. This elementary paradox of liberal thought might be called *the dependence of independence*. Far from being a natural state, personal autonomy is an improbable and always fragile achievement of political coordination.

The paradox cuts even deeper, however. This becomes clear in Constant's discussion of the second dimension of modern liberty, namely, the political right to examine and criticize the government and to vote politically responsible officials out of office. Modern liberty would be essentially incomplete and unstable if it were identified exclusively with personal autonomy. Constant formulates this point in the most memorable sentence of his famous lecture: "The danger of modern liberty is that, absorbed in the enjoyment of our private independence, and in the pursuit of our particular interests, we should surrender our right to share in political power too easily." The danger of renouncing one's right to participate in the exercise of political power is obvious. Aspiring abusers of authority will fill the vacuum and, having concentrated all power in their hands, will proceed to destroy personal autonomy as well.

Modern liberty depends on a delicate balance between the privacy of individual citizens and the secrecy of government actions. When the boundary shifts, when privacy radically contracts, and when secrecy inordinately expands, modern liberty is destroyed. This is true for a simple reason. Modern liberty hinges essentially on the somewhat idealized but not altogether utopian notion that the government works for the citizens, not the other way round. A government that spies invasively on its subjects while hiding itself jealously from its subject's prying eyes is not a free government in Constant's sense, because it is blatantly not acting as a servant of the people.

Constant is completely clear that citizens in a free state should treat public officials in the same way that any principal would treat its agents. Unless they are negligent, corrupt, or incompetent, the rich will examine with attention and severity those employed to look after their affairs. Citizens should do no less. To successfully monitor the government's fulfillment of its duty to govern in the public interest, citizens must invest significantly in their own political knowledge: "In order to judge the management of these proxies, the landowners, if they are prudent, keep themselves well-informed about affairs, the management of which they entrust to them."[46] Democracy is rooted in distrust. Above all, citizens must never take at his word a ruler who loudly proclaims that he is acting in their name.

Personal autonomy is unsustainable unless modern citizens exercise "an active and constant surveillance over their representatives."[47] At first, Constant's argument for adding the right to share in political power to his portrait of modern liberty seems largely instrumental. In ancient republics, full-time political participation was valued greatly because personal autonomy was valued very little. The opposite logic prevails in the free states of modern times. Political participation, now exercised on a part-time basis, should be valued highly because personal autonomy is the highest good and personal autonomy would be destroyed if political participation were allowed to wither. To embrace private rights while rejecting political rights is like building a house without a foundation, for all other rights will be taken away in the absence of the right to examine and criticize one's government. On this account, personal autonomy is valuable in itself, while political participation is valuable only as a means to an end.

To fill out our picture of Constant's theory of modern liberty, however, we need to mention the opposite causal relation, namely, the dependence of effective political participation on the survival and flourishing of personal autonomy. Here lies one of the principal lessons he drew from the French Revolution. If the authorities could persuade gullible citizens to sacrifice their personal autonomy for a share in political power, they would soon take away that share in political power as well: "To ask the peoples of our day to sacrifice, like those of the past, the whole of their individual liberty to political liberty, is the surest means of detaching them from the former and,

---

[46] Ibid., 326.
[47] Ibid., 326.

once this result has been achieved, it would be only too easy to deprive them of the latter."[48]

To summarize thus far, modern liberty is a complicated and interlocking system in which two clearly distinct forms of freedom provide each other with mutual support.

But this is not Constant's last word on the subject. Indeed, he concludes his 1819 lecture with a very different account of political participation, not as an instrument for preserving personal autonomy from the depredations of unmonitored authority, but as a vehicle for the moral education of citizens. The right to vote gives citizens an incentive to invest in their own political education. To deny citizens the suffrage on the grounds that they do not possess the knowledge to exercise it wisely is to misunderstand the relationship between capacity and opportunity. People do not develop the capacities that they know they will never have a chance to exercise. French citizens may seem incapable of serving on juries, for example, but this is only a transient appearance. An institution such as the jury trial or the right to vote, if it is intrinsically good, will soon become beneficent and suitable, "because the nation acquires, through the institution itself, a capacity that it previously lacked."[49]

That institutions do not simply restrain rulers but can also mobilize the dormant talents of citizens and bring them to bear on common problems is an essential insight of Constant's positive constitutionalism. The right to vote, he says, calls citizens to "contribute by their votes to the exercise of power," guaranteeing them "a right of control and supervision by expressing their opinions." Here we come back to Constant's idea that human desires are products of social organization. But here, at least implicitly, he modifies his deterministic claim that human beings cannot choose the kind of freedom they desire. Constitution makers, by guaranteeing political rights, can stimulate citizens to educate themselves politically and "give them both the desire and the right to discharge these."[50] The constitution maker can shrewdly circumvent *l'empire des circonstances* by manipulating the circumstances, by providing most

---

[48] Ibid., 323.
[49] "Réflexions sur les constitutions," in *Cours de politique*, vol. 1, 235; see p. 238 for Constant's discussion of the jury system as a stimulus to the moral education of the French.
[50] AML, 328.

citizens with the opportunity to share in political power. He can create the desire to share in political power, that is, can lead modern citizens to see the exercise of their political rights as in intrinsic, not merely instrumental, part of modern freedom.

My paraphrase thus far, although essentially accurate, has underplayed the rhetorically overwrought character of the last section of *Ancient and Modern Liberty*. What Constant suddenly begins to argue, in an unexpected volte-face, is that political participation should be valued not as a guarantee of happiness but as a pathway to something higher: "Political liberty is the most powerful, the most effective means of self-development that heaven has given us."[51] The right to vote and criticize the government will elevate "the largest possible number of citizens to the highest moral position."[52] But assigning all citizens the task of examining their own most sacred interests, political liberty enlarges their spirits and ennobles their thoughts, giving their nation a grandeur that it hitherto lacked. Political rights will draw citizens of all classes and professions from their workplaces, leading them to make intelligent choices, to resist energetically all abuse, to see through the mendacity of rulers, to stand up courageously to threats, and to resist nobly the sweet seductions of the powerful. The profound and sincere patriotism that results will animate the countryside, vivify the towns, and so forth.

So why exactly did the usually disillusioned Constant choose to hype the positive consequences of political rights in this egregious way?

V

Constant's suggestion that people want only the kind of liberty that suits their social circumstances would, if taken literally, make nonsense of the failed Revolutionary attempt to resurrect ancient liberty in modern times. Constant's grand moral imperative, also repeated under Napoleon and the Restoration, was as follows: Obey the spirit of the age! This advice would have been redundant, of course, if it were automatically obeyed. In fact, it makes sense for Constant to urge his contemporaries to adjust their goals to modern times because they habitually, or at least occasionally, refuse to do so. His

[51] Ibid., 327.
[52] Ibid., 328.

own polemical stance, in other words, reveals the residual allure of anachronistic desires and the weak control exerted over the political imagination by the spirit of the age. The freedom of the human mind apparently includes the freedom to desire a kind of freedom that is neither suitable to nor sustainable in the social world in which one lives.

European history after Constant's death certainly did not confirm his predictions that commerce would replace war and that the weakening of national sentiment and "the communication amongst peoples"[53] had made all Europeans into compatriots incapable of mutually destructive homicidal collectivism. So why does war and nationalism flourish despite their ostensible incompatibility with the so-called spirit of the modern age?

Perhaps bellicose nationalism represents an escape from one of the most psychologically troubling aspects of modern civilization, namely, the chronic uncertainty of individuals who have been bereft by secularization of those occult powers that, in earlier times, had steadied and guided their reason. Constant frequently refers to modern times as "the epoch of legal conventions," by which he means that it is the first period in human history when legal conventions have existed alone, without being mixed with and sustained by prejudices and superstitious venerations. "It is only today that man, having reached the point where he no longer recognizes occult powers... wants to consult only his reason and only acknowledges conventions that result from interaction with the reasoning of his neighbors."[54] Modern times is the age of skepticism, uncertainty, and self-doubt. The only basis for belief is adversarial process or free and open debate among fallible individuals. This is why the right of the accused to dispute the evidence of the prosecution in open court is the foundation stone of modern liberty.

But uncertainty and self-doubt are also subjectively painful to some extent. One of Constant's lifelong concerns, and one of the main reasons why he viewed with some skepticism the psychological premises of the political economy he had studied in Scotland, was the incoherence and ephemeral nature of human desires, what he sometimes referred to as the "inconsistencies" of the mind or

---

[53] Ibid., 316.
[54] *De la perfectibilité de l'espèce humaine* (Lausanne: Editions l'Age d'Homme, 1967), 63–64.

contradictions of the heart. As he once wrote, "Each individual contains within himself a coalition, that is, a civil war."[55] Human beings typically want and do not want the same thing at the same time.[56] They cannot achieve happiness or maximize individual welfare by satisfying their desires, therefore, because their desires are fatally inconsistent.[57]

Constant valued both art and religion, among other reasons, because they helped people detach themselves from the roiling instability and chaotic incoherence of their inner lives. That he did not want politics to serve the same function goes without saying. The Terror had taught him the devastating consequences of politicizing the impulse to self-transcendence. This is why he valued "the forms" over "the essence" in politics but preferred "the essence" to "the forms" in religion and art. But the very ferocity and relentlessness with which Constant opposed all attempts to channel the self-transcending impulse into politics inadvertently reveals the ferocity and relentlessness of those attempts. Social circumstances may instruct people to treasure personal *happiness* and private *enjoyments*. But deep psychological drives, triggered by social distress and enflamed by revolutionary rhetoric, may lead people to abandon what they know for what they only imagine.

VI

The spare account of modern political rights that Constant gave earlier in the lecture is what makes Constant's claims, at the end of *Ancient and Modern Liberty*, about the morally elevating potential of political participation in modern states seems so astonishing. Here is the contrast he first draws: "The share which in antiquity everyone held in national sovereignty was by no means an abstract presumption as it is in our own day. The will of each individual had real influence: the exercise of this will was a vivid and repeated pleasure." Modern voters, in a mass electorate, rightly feel that they do not have any personal effect on the outcome of an election:

[55] "Lettre à la citoyenne Nassau, née Chandieu (1 February 1796)," *Journal intime de Benjamin Constant et lettres à sa famille et à ses amis*, ed. D. Melegari (Paris: Paul Ollendorff, 1895), 250.

[56] "Cécile," in *Œuvres*, 179.

[57] "Réflexions sur la tragédie," in *Œuvres*, 921–22.

"Lost in the multitude, the individual can almost never perceive the influence he exercises."[58] The influence of the modern citizen is completely lost in a multitude of equal and superior influences: "His sovereignty is restricted and almost always suspended."[59] This brings us back to our fundamental theme.

The palpable ineffectualness of the modern elector contrasts embarrassingly with the perverse effectualness of the modern informant. Putting a ballot in the ballot box has much less influence on the course of events than sending an anonymous letter of denunciation to the police. Sending a fellow citizen to his doom is one of the few ways in which modern citizens living in mass societies can replicate the ancient feeling of being a big fish in a small pond. "The most obscure republican of Sparta or Rome had power. The same is not true of the simple citizen of Britain or of the United States."[60] This diagnosis is correct, unless the modern citizen happens to be an informer. His denunciation "confirms in his own eyes his own role in collective life" and thereby offers him a distant echo of ancient liberty. About informers one might even say that "the will of each individual had real influence."[61]

What we have stumbled on here, under Constant's guidance, may well be an important psychological dimension of the totalitarian temptation. How exactly does a modern tyrant persuade, rather than constrain, his slaves to proclaim themselves free? One way is to provide a palpable psychological benefit. The kinds of modern tyranny that display a façade of liberty may also be tapping into the premodern desire to feel personally effective while "participating," however secretly, in collective decision making.[62] The centrality to classical republicanism of the banishment of despised individuals, which may itself contain a distant echo of the even more primitive practice of human sacrifice, suggests the residual appeal of ancient liberty in modern society. The power to banish on a whim was one of the things that made ancient liberty "a vivid and repeated pleasure."[63]

---

[58] AML, 316.
[59] Ibid., 312.
[60] Ibid., 314.
[61] Ibid., 316.
[62] The pervasive use of civilian informants by the communist regimes of Eastern Europe may be a good example.
[63] AML, 316.

There was no way that modern political rights, permitting "an active and constant surveillance over their representatives,"[64] could provide such a palpable gratification.

Modern denunciation, under conditions of oppression, is a privatized version of ostracism, the exercise of power without responsibility. The informer has privatized a fragment of sovereign power. Malicious denunciation triggers punishment without requiring that a reason be given and allowing no form of legal defense: "That the denunciation is a lie matters little to them."[65] Not all modern citizens are satisfied that their "sovereignty" is narrowly restrained and almost always suspended. To overcome their feelings of helplessness and passivity, they anachronistically desire the same liberty to use public authority to injure the people they hate, a liberty that was so thoroughly enjoyed by the ancients. This is the fundamental reason why nostalgia for ancient liberty can provide aid and comfort to modern tyranny. The modern informant presumably takes personal satisfaction in the direct effect his informing has had and finds in this awareness of his personal importance "ample compensation."

How can we explain Constant's curious decision to end his 1819 lecture with the extravagant claim that "political liberty is the most powerful, the most effective means of self-development that heaven has given us"?[66] The question presses itself on us because of Constant's earlier insistence that the voter's power, in modern times, is invariably "an abstract presumption."[67] If so, then how can political participation, in modern times, also be a pathway to moral elevation? This chapter has explored one possible answer. Constant's concluding apotheosis of political participation represents an inadvertent admission that, distressingly enough, modern societies produce a need for individual influence that modern republics, for all their virtues, cannot satisfy as well as modern tyrannies.

---

[64] Ibid., 326.
[65] *Recueil d'articles 1820–1824* (from an article of July 12, 1823), 320.
[66] AML, 327.
[67] Ibid., 316.

4 Constant's Idea of Modern Liberty

The modern revival of interest in republicanism (most notably associated with the names of Quentin Skinner and Philip Pettit) has unambiguously placed Benjamin Constant among the defenders of negative liberty. This is hardly surprising. In his famous lecture on the "Two Concepts of Liberty,"[1] Isaiah Berlin, placing Constant along with John Stuart Mill among "the fathers of liberalism," contended that "no one saw the conflict between the two types of liberty, or expressed it more clearly, than Benjamin Constant."[2] In a later introduction to his *Four Essays on Liberty* Berlin further asserted that Constant "prized negative liberty beyond any modern writer."[3] On this view, Constant demanded "a maximum degree of non-interference compatible with the minimum demands of social life." Recent scholarship on Constant (echoing Berlin's own claim that his attachment to negative liberty had been misunderstood) has sought to provide a more nuanced description of Constant's understanding of liberty. Laurence Jacobs, for example, has forcefully argued that we are wrong to believe that Constant's rejection of popular participation led him "to advocate privacy and a conception of freedom as freedom from politics."[4]

The revised interpretation of Constant's attachment to liberty draws on two principal pieces of evidence. The first, with good reason, concentrates on the most famous of all Constant's writings, his

---

[1] Isaiah Berlin, "Two Concepts of Liberty," in *Four Essays on Liberty* (Oxford: Oxford University Press, 1969), 118–72.
[2] Berlin, 161–65.
[3] "Introduction," in *Four Essays on Liberty,* xlvi.
[4] Laurence Jacobs, "'Le Moment Libéral': The Distinctive Character of Restoration Liberalism," *Historical Journal,* 31 (1988), 486.

classic speech of 1819 exploring the contrast between the liberty of
the ancients and that of the moderns.[5] Toward the end of that eloquent and powerful address, and having seemingly proclaimed the
dangerous inappropriateness of ancient liberty to the modern, commercial age, Constant surprises his contemporary readers (and presumably his original audience) by concluding that "far from renouncing either of the two sorts of freedom which I have described to you, it
is necessary, as I have shown, to learn to combine the two together."[6]
The grounds for this claim are that if the principal danger of ancient
liberty arises from the fact that we might attach too little importance to individual rights and pleasures, then the principal danger of
modern liberty derives from an undue focus on private enjoyment
that leads us to "surrender our right to share in political power too
easily." This however is not simply because political liberty – the
liberty of the ancients – acts as an indispensable guarantee of what
Constant unhesitatingly called "true modern liberty." Rather, it is
because political liberty "is the most powerful, the most effective
means of self-development that heaven has given us." By calling on
all citizens to attend to their "most sacred interests," political liberty "enlarges their spirit, ennobles their thoughts, and establishes
among them a kind of intellectual equality which forms the glory
and power of a people."[7] Accordingly, Constant finished his speech
with a veritable Rousseauian flourish. The work of the legislator
was not over when peace had been bought to the people. Institutions
must achieve the moral education of all citizens.

The second body of evidence highlights ambiguities in Constant's
conception of the impact of commerce on society. As is well known,
Constant believed that we had finally reached the age of commerce.
It was this that had turned slavery, war, and despotism into anachro-
nisms. In line with thinkers such as Montesquieu and Hume before
him, Constant believed that commerce not only provided for our
material needs and satisfied our physical desires, but also encouraged our sense of individual independence. If this meant that we were
now predominantly interested in our own enterprises and projects,

---

[5] "The Liberty of the Ancients Compared with That of the Moderns [AML]," in *PW*,
307–28.
[6] Ibid., 327.
[7] Ibid.

Constant was also confident that commerce provided the basis for "milder and surer means" to engage with our fellows. Yet it has been suggested that Constant came increasingly to doubt that commerce alone could provide the glue that would hold society together. According to James Mitchell Lee,[8] "in the last decade of his life, if not well before, [Constant] grew weary of utilitarianism and its French expression in the industrial doctrine of Say, Dunoyer and Charles Comte." The pursuit of self-interest would produce social atomization and disintegration, thus necessitating moral and political constraints designed to hold in check our own destructive tendencies. Among the instruments of restraint were to be found the institutions of representative government and a vigorous public opinion.

This dimension of Constant's argument has been best explored in a series of recent articles by Helena Rosenblatt.[9] She has in particular drawn our attention to the importance of Constant's lifelong fascination with religion. Here we might focus on the preface to *De la religion*, for it is arguably in this text (published in 1824) that Constant most strongly challenges the intrinsic worth of "self-interest rightly understood" as a guide to our actions.[10] Casting his mind back over the last twenty years Constant saw a depressing catalog of what he described as human indifference, servility, calculation, prudence, and "moral arithmetic": in short, men had abandoned their most noble and elevated sentiments and had followed the dictates of self-interest rightly understood. The natural effect of this, Constant continued, was to drive men within themselves, for them to be consumed by a narrow egoism, and thus for us all to become isolated one from another. "When everyone is isolated," Constant concluded, "there is only dust. When the storm arrives, the dust is *de la fange.*" In these circumstances liberty could be no more enjoyed than it could be established or preserved.

---

[8] James Mitchell Lee, "*Doux Commerce*, Social Organization, and Modern Liberty in the Thought of Benjamin Constant," *ABC*, 26 (2002), 117–49.

[9] Helena Rosenblatt, "Commerce et religion dans le libéralisme de Benjamin Constant," *Commentaire*, 26, 102 (Summer 2003), 415–26, and "Re-Evaluating Benjamin Constant's Liberalism: Industrialism, Saint-Simonianism and the Restoration Years," *History of European Ideas*, 30 (2004), 23–37. See also Beatrice C. Fink, "Benjamin Constant on Equality," *Journal of the History of Ideas*, 33 (1972), 307–14.

[10] *DLR*, 25–34.

Thus Constant distinguished between two broad moral systems: one where well-being was our goal and self-interest our guide; another where we were driven by a sense of self-abnegation and personal sacrifice. For Constant, the latter constituted the essence of what he regarded as an indestructible and indefinable inner religious sentiment. Not only did this inform our capacity for disinterested actions – thereby making us worthy of our freedom – but it also gave us a glimpse of our capacity to attain a level of human perfection. That Constant believed in the reality of the latter as an unfolding and progressive movement of humankind toward a condition of moral and intellectual maturity is beyond dispute.[11] Our progress toward that end could be impeded, and sometimes temporarily reversed, but it could never be thwarted, not even by the most barbarous of tyrants. By the same token, however, it demonstrated conclusively that in a modern society, commerce alone was not a sufficient guarantee of the existence of liberty and that liberty itself was grounded on and was sustained by religious sentiment.[12]

On this evidence we are right to be suspicious of a simple and straightforward categorization of Constant as an advocate of negative liberty, of liberty as the absence of restraint, and wrong not to recognize his deep, and seemingly long-standing, desire to link the realization of liberty to the active involvement of citizens in political life and to the moral progress of society as a whole. Seen thus, Constant might indeed be better viewed as illustrating what Jean-Fabien Spitz has analyzed as the falsity of the dilemma between negative and positive liberty rather than as one of the key protagonists in a debate that has occupied such a central place in political theory since Isaiah Berlin's inaugural lecture in the autumn of 1958.[13]

We are then entitled to conclude, as Stephen Holmes has rightly observed,[14] that according to Constant, modern society faced not one but two dangers: to overpoliticization (of the kind experienced

---

[11] See his "De la perfectibilité de l'espèce humaine" and "Du développement progressif des idées religieuses," in Benjamin Constant, De la liberté chez les Modernes, ed. Marcel Gauchet (Paris: Pluriel, 1980), 580–95, 523–42.

[12] It is interesting to note that for Constant the abolition of slavery was attributable to three factors: commerce, religion, and the intellectual and moral progress of the human race.

[13] Jean-Fabien Spitz, La Liberté politique: Essai de généalogie conceptuelle (Paris: Presses Universitaires de France, 1995).

[14] Stephen Holmes, Benjamin Constant and the Making of Modern Liberalism (New Haven: Yale University Press, 1984), 20.

during the French Revolution) had to be added overprivatization (of the kind experienced under Napoleon Bonaparte). Yet none of this, as the same author also avows, diminishes the importance of Constant's basic and most important insight: namely, that we are wrong to appeal to the ancients for either our model of society or our understanding of freedom. To do so was dangerous and inappropriate as well as being deeply inimical to the prospects for liberty. As Holmes concludes, "Though Constant had no illusions about modern freedom, he also saw no alternative to it. . . . Radically communal alternatives seemed less attractive still."[15] Constant himself could not have made this any clearer. "Since we live in modern times," he declared to his audience at the *Athénée Royale*, "I want a liberty suited to modern times; and since we live under monarchies, I humbly beg these monarchies not to borrow from the ancient republics the means to oppress us." Political liberty, while indispensable, could only ever be the guarantee and not the substance of individual liberty. "To ask," Constant continued, "the peoples of our day to sacrifice, like those of the past, the whole of their individual liberty to political liberty, is the surest means of detaching them from the former and, once this result has been achieved, it would be only too easy to deprive them of the latter."[16] Given this, we should not be surprised that the greater part of Constant's efforts was devoted to an analysis of the character of modern liberty and the conditions under which it was obtained.

Before turning to these questions let me clarify the broad interpretative framework within which I intend to examine these aspects of Constant's work. I take his well-known statement, found in the preface to Constant's *Mélanges de littérature et de politique*, to the effect that "for forty years I have defended the same principle: liberty in everything. . . and by liberty I mean the triumph of individuality" to contain a substantial element of rhetorical hyperbole.[17] As Steven Vincent has indicated, this "suggests a constancy of political position that the evidence does not support."[18] I likewise accept the conclusion reached by Etienne Hofmann, and by Kurt Kloocke before

---

[15] Ibid., 14.
[16] AML, 323.
[17] Constant, "Préface" to *Mélanges de littérature et de politique*, reprinted in *De la liberté chez les Modernes*, 519.
[18] K. Steven Vincent, "Benjamin Constant, the French Revolution and the Origins of French Romantic Liberalism," *French Historical Studies*, 23 (2000), 607–37.

him, that the political thought of Constant reached full maturity around 1806, if not slightly before.[19] After this date, although he adapted his views to the circumstances (sometimes to dramatic effect), I take it that the fundamentals of Constant's political position remained largely unchanged. It is therefore on this body of writing that I will concentrate.

It was Constant's opinion that the principles of politics transcended and existed independently of specific constitutions, be they monarchical or republican. He saw that the French Revolution had subverted the most fundamental of these principles: namely, that no form of sovereignty, even in the guise of the sovereignty of the people, should be allowed to exercise unlimited authority over individual existence. Rousseau, Constant contended, had overlooked this truth and had therefore established "the most formidable support for all kinds of despotism." As he eloquently expressed it, "When you establish that the sovereignty of the people is unlimited, you create and you toss at random into society a degree of power which is too large in itself, and which is bound to constitute an evil, in whatever hands it is placed."[20] The mistake had been to relocate this power from the monarch to the people rather than to destroy it, with the result that the individual had been left with no protection and had been made subject to terror and tyranny.

Underpinning this argument about the proper nature of sovereignty and extent of legitimate political authority were two ideas of central importance to Constant's defense of liberty. The first was stated by Constant in the following terms (and in terms that would later find an echo in the writings of John Stuart Mill): "There is a part of human existence which necessarily remains individual and independent, and by right beyond all political jurisdiction."[21] When summarized in the form of the "true principles of freedom," this entailed the following conclusions: "That society has no right to be unjust towards a single one of its members, that the whole society minus one is not authorised to obstruct the latter in his opinions,

---

[19] Etienne Hofmann, Les "Principes de politique" de Benjamin Constant (Geneva: Droz, 1980), 16–21, and Kurt Kloocke, Benjamin Constant, Une biographie intellectuelle (Geneva: Droz, 1984), 139.

[20] PoP (1815), 176.

[21] PoP (1806), 31. This phrase was repeated by Constant in his Commentaire sur l'ouvrage de Filangieri (Paris: Les Belles lettres, 2004), 59.

nor in those actions which are not harmful, in the use of his property or the exercise of his labour, save in those cases where that use or that exercise would obstruct another individual possessing the same rights."[22] All governments that failed to respect this boundary were illegitimate. This was complemented by the insight that "variety is life: uniformity death."[23] Secondly, individuals were the possessors of rights independently of all social and political authority. Stated in an abridged form, these would "consist in the option to do anything which does not hurt others...in the right not to be obliged to profess any belief of which one is not convinced...in the right to make public one's thought...finally in the certainty of not being arbitrarily treated."[24]

Neither of the preceding conclusions were timeless ideals. They had, for example, been unknown to the ancients, largely because the latter had not seen the need to differentiate the private individual from the public citizen. But they were appropriate to the modern age, especially in times of political turmoil and uncertainty, where they provided an invaluable safeguard and protection from the unwelcome intrusions of a potentially arbitrary and oppressive state. They could also shield a minority from a majority intent on abusing its power by overstepping the bounds of its legitimate authority. As everyone would sooner or later find themselves in the minority, Constant concluded, to defend its rights was "to defend the rights of all."

This willingness to use the language of rights in order to defend clearly delineated spheres of individual liberty also serves to explain Constant's frequently repeated antipathy to Benthamite utilitarianism. In brief, Constant wanted to disconnect the idea of right from that of utility, believing Bentham's principle not only to be vague and liable to contradictory application but also likely to reduce morality to a matter of calculation. "To wish to make right subject to utility," Constant concluded, "is like making the eternal laws of arithmetic subject to our everyday interests." Consequently, it provided no sure and certain grounds for the maintenance and enjoyment of individual liberty. All manner of different orders and prohibitions could be

[22] *PoP* (1806), 384.
[23] *SCU*, 7.
[24] *PoP* (1806), 39.

justified on utilitarian grounds and it had been this same logic that had recently "turned France into one vast prison."[25]

Yet Constant did not defend individual liberty solely by reference to rights or by describing a boundary beyond which the authority of government did not extend. He also cast a deeply skeptical eye over all arguments designed to justify an extension of government activity. Specifically, he questioned the veracity of three propositions relating to government. It was wrong to believe that government was "indubitably more enlightened than the governed." It was not true that if government made a mistake, its errors were "less disastrous than those of individuals." Thirdly, we should realize that the harm caused by government action frequently outweighed the good it was intended to achieve. As Constant observed, "There is no despotism in the world, however inept its plans and oppressive its measures, which does not know how to plead some abstract purpose of a plausible and desirable kind." Individuals also made mistakes and failed to attain their desired ends, but these errors had less serious consequences and could more easily and quickly be rectified. Guided by interest and experience, the individual could "freely set himself straight." This was no minor matter. If governments took away from men the "right" to be wrong, "they will no longer have any individual freedom."[26]

This in turn begged the question of the proper functions of government. This important issue was best explored by Constant in his commentaries on William Godwin[27] and Gaetano Filangieri.[28] Constant was deeply impressed by Godwin's *Enquiry Concerning Political Justice*, believing that no author had better demonstrated the damaging effects of too much government for both individuals

---

[25] Ibid., 30–42, 47–49.
[26] Ibid., 47–59. Constant developed these arguments in a chapter entitled "Des erreurs en législation," in his *Commentaire sur Filangieri*, 61–72. They were even more forcibly expressed in the conclusion to this text (pp. 316–32).
[27] Constant, "De Godwin et de son ouvrage sur la justice politique," in *De la liberté chez les Modernes*, 563–70, and *OCBC/Œuvres*, II, 2.
[28] Constant, *Commentaire sur Filangieri*. On Constant and Filangieri, see Clorinda Donato, "Benjamin Constant and the Italian Enlightenment in the *Commentaire sur l'ouvrage de Filangieri*: Notes for an Intercultural Reading," *Historical Reflections/Réflexions Historiques*, 28 (2003), 439–54, and Antonio Trampus, "Filangieri et Constant: constitutionnalisme des Lumières et constitutionnalisme libéral," *ABC*, 30 (2006), 51–70.

and society at large. However, he disagreed fundamentally with Godwin's central assertion that government was always an absolute evil. In Constant's view, it was only when government stepped beyond the confines of its proper sphere that it became an evil, causing "incalculable" harm, but at this point government had turned itself into a form of usurpation. From Godwin's first error stemmed a second: in all areas of its activity government should do as little as possible. Constant countered by suggesting that within its proper sphere government should be "all powerful." His overall conclusion was therefore as follows: "Liberty gains enormously from the fact that [government] is severely restricted to its legitimate boundaries; but it gains nothing, indeed it loses, if within this boundary [government] is weak."[29] Constant's underlying point was that government had been "created by the needs of society" and thus it was wrong to categorize all its functions as being illegitimate. Principally, government had been set up to prevent individuals from harming each other and, although the scale of this function might vary according to circumstance, Godwin was wrong to believe that one day, and for the good of the human race, government would cease to exist.

The precise implications of this position were more fully disclosed in the *Commentaire sur l'ouvrage de Filangieri*, a text where Constant, through a detailed examination of Filangieri's muchcommented on and widely read *Scienza della legislazione*, sought to expose what he saw as the fallacies of the legislative absolutism he associated with the eighteenth-century Enlightenment. According to Constant, the philosophers of the eighteenth century had been primarily concerned to ascertain the proper use of authority. Only rarely did they comprehend that it was better to trust to liberty, to individual interest, and to those activities permitted by the exercise of our own faculties and the absence of constraints. Consequently, writers such as Filangieri (Constant also cited Rousseau and Mably) sought to confer on the legislator "an empire almost without bounds over human existence." The law was to be designed in such a way as to regulate our every movement. The result, Constant affirmed, would be an inevitable slide toward tyranny and a return to slavery. Constant implied that this might well always have been the case – recognizing that "reforms that came from above were always

29 "De Godwin," 567.

deceptive" was "a very important truth" – but it was especially so in the modern age of commerce where our goal was "repose, and with repose comfort, and, as the source of comfort, industry."

In such a situation legislation need have only two objectives: to prevent internal disorder and to repel foreign invasion. Repression and defense were the only legitimate and necessary functions of the law, Constant announced. Beyond this, "all was luxury and disastrous luxury at that." The proper functions of government were therefore, in Constant's precise words, "purely negative." Government should suppress evil and let the good operate for itself. For that reason, its slogan should be "*Laissez faire et laissez passer*" and the law maker had to learn when to abstain and when to remain silent. So too the people, when offered legislative improvements, had to respond by demanding constitutional guarantees of their freedoms. If this were done, if individuals could rely on the silence and the neutrality of the law, and if they lived in a condition of liberty and security, then, in Constant's opinion, something akin to what we would now describe as a spontaneous order would emerge. "When the division of property is not constrained and when industry does not meet any obstacles," Constant wrote, "wealth distributes itself and is shared out in a perfect equilibrium."[30]

Perhaps the most obvious point to be made is that for Constant war was inimical to liberty. Viewed from the perspective of the age of commerce, war was an anachronism and one that was now shorn of the positive virtues previously associated with it in antiquity. More than this, however, at a domestic level it encouraged all the worst excesses of government. "This politics of war," Constant wrote, "casts into society a mass of men whose outlook is different from that of the nation and whose habits form a dangerous contrast with the patterns of civil life, with the institutions of justice, with respect for the rights of all, with those principles of peaceful and ordered freedom which must be equally inviolable under all forms of government."[31] In short, the military spirit had no time for law, for discussion, for disagreement, for delay. It favored regulation, regimentation, obedience, coercion, and subordination. These doleful domestic consequences were further accentuated only when the

[30] *Commentaire sur Filangieri*, 53.
[31] *PoP* (1806), 282.

warlike spirit manifested itself through invasion and conquest. In antiquity, Constant argued, the conqueror demanded only submission; today they required the spiritual mutilation and prostration of the vanquished. Masters, Constant announced, cannot impose freedom and to attempt to do so, as the French Revolution had sought to do, was only to invent a pretext for the imposition of an illegitimate and tyrannical slavery.

These then were the general conditions under which modern liberty could be said to flourish. Sovereignty (however popular) should be limited. The legislative authority of government should be restricted to its proper sphere. The state should confine its functions to those of defense and the preservation of law and order. A principle of noninterference should be applied whenever the actions of individuals did not obstruct the actions of others. The rights of individuals to live, think, and work as they pleased were not only to be acknowledged but also protected by constitutional guarantees and legal safeguards. All else was tyranny and despotism.

What, however, were the specific forms and content of modern liberty? Unsurprisingly, Constant went to great lengths to specify these in detail. Here our starting point might be a consideration of Constant's reflections on private property. Constant was unambiguously of the opinion that the right to property, in contrast to the other rights he enumerated, was a social convention. Stated simply, society had discovered that a recognition of the right to property was the best way to secure the distribution and quiet enjoyment of goods to its members. But this did not make the right to property any the less inviolable or sacred. It had to therefore be accorded every possible protection. If not, profoundly damaging political and economic consequences would follow.[32]

At this juncture we should take note that Constant had a clear preference for landed as opposed to commercial or industrial property. The latter was less orderly, more artificial, and less stable than the former. It was for this reason that a political system capable of maintaining liberty and providing good governance – one with a limited franchise – was to be constructed on the advantages of landed property. It alone gave people the leisure and permanence required to exercise political rights. Equally, Constant was adamant

[32] Ibid., 167–68.

that property would cease to perform these beneficial functions if it became a privilege, the preserve of a self-perpetuating elite. It was therefore vitally important and necessary that property should circulate among the members of society and that all the propertyless could aspire to be property owners. Accordingly the exclusion of certain groups or persons from the category of citizen could never be absolute.[33]

Property also had certain commercial merits that were advantageous to the flourishing of liberty. It encouraged emulation and prosperity. It allowed for the division of labor, which itself, according to Constant, was "the basis of the perfecting of all the arts and sciences." Business property in particular assured "the independence of individuals." For these reasons Constant opposed measures to impose the equalization of property ownership. He spoke, for example, of a "crass and forced equality." If therefore he denied the utility of the agrarian laws so beloved by radicals during the Revolution, he also directed his fire against restrictions on the right to make a will. France's Napoleonic inheritance laws were a particular object of censure among French liberals at this time, and Constant was no exception. Laws against primogeniture, he argued, were simply superfluous as they were an attempt "to force what would happen naturally." However, what had followed as a result of their introduction was what always followed when government "arbitrarily restrains men's freedom." People tried to evade the law and from this "followed innumerable obstacles to the transfer, disposal, and transmission of property." Constant's conclusion was that the rightful authority of government over the inheritance of property was "extremely limited." Government should guarantee its transmission and then "leave it alone," even if this meant tolerating the occasional abuse and injustice. To do otherwise would be for the government to enter on "an endless course of action."[34]

Similar principles informed Constant's views on the important issue of taxation. Starting from his recognition that government had proper functions to perform, he did not dispute that the state in justice could ask individuals to make a contribution toward these costs. However, in all matters relating to taxation he believed that the

[33] Ibid., 165–66, 168–71, 185–86, 190–92.
[34] Ibid., 196–99. See also *Commentaire sur Filangieri*, 151–67.

governed had the right to expect that government would remain true to certain principles and practices designed to leave the individual as free and as unhindered as possible. This was a position that Constant could not have stated in clearer terms. "Any tax, of whatever kind," he wrote, "always has a more or less pernicious influence; it is a necessary evil, but like all necessary evils it must be made as negligible as possible. The more means are left for the use of private industry, the more a state prospers. Taxation, for the simple reason that it subtracts some portion of those means from that industry is inevitably damaging."[35] In short, money was best employed when it stayed in the hands of individuals and thus pointless or excessive taxation could never be justified. Indeed, such taxation was a form of theft and the one that was the more culpable and cowardly for being perpetrated by the rich on the poor and by an armed government against unarmed individuals. It encouraged the corruption of government, the subversion of justice, the decline of morals, and more generally, the loss of individual liberty. The latter was particularly so when taxation entailed the harassment and coercion of individual citizens. This occurred when the collection of taxes required undue intrusion and persecution, when indirect taxation fell on basic necessities, when tax fell on capital rather than income, and when it restricted productive activity (as with taxes on patents). Constant also took particular exception to the raising of taxation through government lotteries, believing that they corrupted individuals by offering the possibility of riches that did not derive from "industry, work, and prudence" and that lotteries lacked all fiscal logic. The overall point was that unfair and burdensome taxation first impoverished individuals and then society as a whole.[36]

Individuals therefore had a right to expect that government would raise in taxation only what was strictly necessary for the performance of its duties and that they would also have the right either to approve or to reject taxation. As for the principles of good and sound taxation, Constant derived these directly from those enunciated by Adam Smith in *The Wealth of Nations*. The governed, Constant wrote, may demand that "taxes fall equally on all, proportionately to their wealth, that they leave nothing uncertain nor arbitrary as

---

[35] Ibid., 271.
[36] Ibid., 203–24, and *Commentaire sur Filangieri*, 204–24.

to their incidence or mode of collection, that they are wholly cost-efficient, and finally that their basis is reasonably stable."[37]

The influence of Smith on Constant was only more evident when he came to consider the appropriate level of government intervention in relation to economic activity. Again, Constant stated his position unambiguously. "For industrial nations," he wrote, "it suffices to leave each individual perfectly free in the deployment of his capital and his labour. He will discern better than any government the best use he can make of them."[38] In sum, unless economic activity was injurious to others, government possessed no legitimate jurisdiction over it. Wherever possible, government should, therefore, simply "stay out of it" and recognize the truth of the maxim that "outputs always tend to move to the level of needs, without government getting involved." Government intervention distorted the equilibrium of production. Consequently, Constant rejected all attempts by government either to protect industry or to prohibit competition, believing that such policies not only took away all the advantages of the division of labor but also caused the "entire nation" to suffer "a loss of freedom." This was so because they forced individuals either to use their money or to deploy their labor in ways that they would otherwise not choose to do. By reducing individuals to the level of a "simple machine," such restrictions and subsidies narrowed their intellectual faculties. They also took away our freedom as consumers. Overall they prevented the attainment of national wealth. More than this, once government had conferred on itself the right to intervene, we had entered on a slippery slope with no foreseeable end. Government, Constant wrote, "runs after its money like some gambler."[39]

The extent to which Constant had moved beyond eighteenth-century mercantilist and physiocratic doctrines was best illustrated when he addressed these issues in his commentary on the work of Filangieri. Specifically, Constant came down in favor of removing restrictions on the export of grain, believing that competition and free trade rather than prohibition were in the long term the best ways to overcome shortages and famine.[40] Similarly, Constant argued

---

[37] Ibid., 207.
[38] Ibid., 234–35.
[39] Ibid., 225–59.
[40] *Commentaire sur Filangieri*, 168–80.

against restraints on emigration. To argue otherwise, he affirmed, was "to consider man as a passive agent in the hands of authority." It was also to fail to see that the moderns had a different relationship to their homeland than the ancients. For the latter, to be expatriated was to be deprived of everything they held dear, while for the moderns their homeland was no more than the place where they sought to realize the various forms of happiness appropriate to their individual interests and tastes. "When these are taken away from us at home," Constant wrote, "we set off to find them abroad and governments have neither the right nor the power to deny us this faculty."[41]

Finally, Constant set himself against artificial measures designed to increase domestic population such as laws enforcing marriage or prohibiting celibacy. "It was certainly not because of these positive laws," Constant wrote, "that the population flourished, but on account of other circumstances, all of which can be expressed in one word: freedom." It was Constant's contention therefore that to secure an increase in population it was sufficient to give individuals peace, prosperity, and security and our natural inclinations would do the rest.[42] It should be noted that Constant opposed the recommendations of Thomas Malthus designed to limit population growth, believing again that individual self-interest, rather than government legislation, was the best means to resolve such questions.[43] Constant's overall point was that the writers of the eighteenth century, and Filangieri in particular, had not liberated themselves from the view that government was capable of rectifying all the ills of society. Filangieri, Constant suggested, might have realized that this was an error but he had never dared say so.[44]

It is hard not to draw the conclusion that this defense of freedom of commerce provided the bedrock of Constant's better-known defense of civil freedom. But this was not Constant's own opinion. "I could be wrong in my claims about freedom of production and trade," he wrote, "without my principles of religious, intellectual and personal freedom being weakened by this."[45] This, however,

---

[41] Ibid., 145–50.
[42] Ibid., 119–28.
[43] Ibid., 129–44.
[44] Ibid., 31, 184, 189.
[45] PoP (1806), 228.

seemed something of a strategic concession on his part, as Constant was fully aware that "all questions of this kind are interlinked." The point appears to be that Constant did not wish any mistakes he made about economics to diminish the significance or validity of anything he might say about liberty more generally. He was, after all, examining the principles of politics rather than writing a treatise on commercial economy.

As we are aware, it was Constant's view that under Napoleon Bonaparte France had fallen victim to a form of government he described as usurpation. Usurpation, like war, was an anachronism, but Constant also believed that he was describing something that was new. It was not the same as despotism. It should not be confused with monarchy. Rather it was a novel form of government displaying its own destructive pathologies. Specifically, Constant ended his powerful indictment of usurpation by drawing attention to what, in his opinion, was its most decisive innovation, an innovation that served to differentiate it from earlier forms of despotism.[46] Usurpation parodied and counterfeited liberty. It demanded the assent and approbation of its subjects. Despotism, he wrote, "rules by means of silence, and leaves man with the right to be silent; usurpation condemns him to speak; it pursues him to the intimate sanctuary of his thoughts and, forcing him to lie to his own conscience, denies him the last consolation of the oppressed."[47]

It was this idea of an inner sanctuary as the last bastion against oppression – Constant spoke of it as an "impregnable shelter" – that informed much of his writings on personal freedom. For example, it underpinned his views on freedom of expression and freedom of the press. To restrain either was to curtail our intellectual freedom, with dire consequences as the example of societal decline and stagnation in China showed. Without freedom of the press, Constant affirmed, all other freedoms were illusory, the protection promised by laws being only a chimera. It alone could bring the abuses of government to public attention. It educated government and public opinion alike. The latter Constant described as "a kind of moral sense which develops only in tranquillity." Its existence

[46] *SCU*, 95–97.
[47] Ibid., 96–97.

was incompatible with arbitrary power. It constituted "the life of States."[48]

Constant's preoccupation with the idea of an inner sanctuary is no better exemplified than in his extensive writings on religion. As Helena Rosenblatt has affirmed, "Constant's *De la religion* is a veritable celebration of freedom of conscience and of religious pluralism."[49] The same applies to the other numerous occasions when Constant published or spoke about the Christian religion. The guiding idea was that of all our passions, religious sentiment was the most pure. Everything that was noble and most beautiful in us derived from it. Through it we broke out of the narrow circle of our interests and opened ourselves up to others in a spirit of generosity and sympathy. Yet, as Constant repeatedly avowed, religion had been distorted and denatured. "Man," Constant wrote, "has been pursued into this last refuge, this intimate sanctuary of his existence. In the hands of government, religion has been transformed into a menacing institution." It had been distorted into an instrument of oppression and into a social institution designed to fulfill a utilitarian purpose. For Constant the conclusion was obvious. Whenever government interfered in matters relating to religion, it did harm, and it should therefore leave it alone. There should be no state religion. Neither the spirit of inquiry nor the proliferation of sects was antithetical to the flourishing of religion. Indeed, they ensured that religion kept its vitality and did not descend into ossified dogma. The maxim therefore was to be religious freedom and toleration.[50]

The same principles applied equally to public education. "Enlightenment," Constant wrote, "shines only at the behest of freedom."

---

[48] *PoP* (1806), 101–24, 370–71. On this concept, see Mona Ozouf, "'Public Opinion' at the End of the Old Regime," *Journal of Modern History*, 60 (September 1988), S1–21.

[49] Helena Rosenblatt, "Re-Evaluating Benjamin Constant's Liberalism: Industrialism, Saint-Simonianism and the Restoration Years," *History of European Ideas*, 30 (2004), 36.

[50] Most of the preceding text is taken from *PoP* (1806), 129–46. However, similar views can be found elsewhere, most notably in the *Commentaire sur Filangieri*, 290–315, and in articles published in such journals as *Le Mercure*, *La Minerve*, *La Renommée*, and the *Courrier Français*: see Ephraim Harpaz, ed., *Benjamin Constant: Recueil d'articles*, 2 vols. (Geneva: Droz, 1972); *Recueil d'articles 1825–1829* (Paris: Champion, 1992); *Receuil d'articles 1829–30* (Paris: Champion, 1992).

To entrust the provision of education to government was a gross error and, among other mistaken assumptions, supposed that government had the right and duty to uphold a fixed body of doctrine. As with religion, when government sought to propagate truth or morality through education they both became stunted and stultified and education itself became the plaything of rival factions, each determined to disseminate their own exaggerated doctrines. So at most government should be concerned to provide what Constant termed "limited instruction." Government could appoint and pay teachers but it must not manage or direct education itself. For the rest we had to trust the good intentions of parents toward their children. "In education, as elsewhere," Constant observed, "government should be watchful and protective, but always neutral. Let it remove obstacles and make smooth the roads. We can leave it to individuals to walk them successfully."[51] Indeed, the latter remark chimes in nicely with Constant's overall conclusion. Having examined all the areas where government, exceeding its legitimate competence, intervened in public affairs on grounds of utility, Constant wrote, we have found "that in all these, had people been left to themselves, less bad and more good would have resulted."[52]

Moving from the ancient form of liberty to the modern was not, in Constant's view, without its losses. Our pleasures were less vivid and immediate. We were incapable of lasting emotion. Our enthusiasm was tempered by reflection and experience. Nevertheless, we could not "turn free men into Spartans." This was the important truth that had been overlooked by those at the end of the previous century who had believed themselves "charged with the regeneration of the human race." These reformers, Constant argued, chose to exercise public power in the manner they supposed that it had been exercised in antiquity. They believed "that everything should give way before collective authority and that all restrictions of individual rights would be compensated by participation in the social power."[53] The French, a "people grown old in pleasure," were accordingly made subject to a multitude of despotic laws. It was in the name of liberty,

---

[51] *PoP* (1806), 295–315.
[52] Ibid., 321.
[53] *SCU*, 108.

Constant writes, that "we were given prisons, scaffolds, countless prosecutions."

Constant's next move was, therefore, to try to sketch out a form of government that would be legitimate and where liberty could not be counterfeited. This he attempted most systematically in his *Principles of Politics Applicable to All Representative Governments*, first published in 1815, and in a second text, later republished by Edouard Laboulaye, *Réflexions sur les constitutions et sur les garanties*.[54] At the heart of his answer was the conviction that the task would be accomplished not by attacking the holders of power but rather by attacking power itself, by placing guaranteed restrictions on the possible abuse of power, and by limiting not a particular form of sovereignty but sovereignty itself. No monarch, Constant wrote, even if his claim to legitimacy derives from "the assent of the people," possessed "a power without limits." More precisely, the limitation of sovereignty could be made into a reality "through the distribution and balance of powers."[55] Constant's approach, as can be surmised, follows on from that adopted by Montesquieu. We should, therefore, not be surprised that as Constant sought to give an institutional form to these basic principles, he turned unfailingly toward England as an example.

The particular strength of a constitutional monarchy, Constant argued, was not that it was separated into three branches, as Montesquieu had believed, but that it was separated into five branches: royal power, executive power, the power that represents permanence (i.e., the hereditary assembly), the power that represents opinion (i.e., the elected assembly), and judicial power. The key, innovative distinction here was between "royal power," which Constant described as a "neutral power," and "executive power," which he described as an active power. "The royal power," Constant wrote, "is in the middle, yet above the four others, a superior and at the same time intermediate authority, with no interest in disturbing the balance, but on the contrary having a strong interest in maintaining it."[56] Accordingly, Constant accredited the English monarch with the function

---

[54] Constant, *Cours de politique constitutionnelle* (Paris: Guillaumin, 1872), 167–382.
[55] *PoP* (1815), 175–83.
[56] Ibid., 185.

of not only preserving the constitution itself but also acting as the guarantor of all political liberties.

Constant perceived several distinct advantages to this system of government, all of which, he believed, aided the preservation of liberty. The first of these was an "animated sentiment of public life." Through the watchfulness of parliamentary representatives and the openness of their debates, there would be engendered "a spirit of examination, an habitual interest in the maintenance of the constitution of the State, a constant participation in public affairs."[57] Beyond this, Constant identified four other major guarantees of liberty within a system of constitutional monarchy drawing on the English model. The first derived from one aspect of the separation of powers: namely, the independence of the judiciary and the existence of proper judicial procedures, including the jury system. The second guarantee derived from freedom of the press. On purely prudential grounds, liberty of the press, operating within the law, was indispensable for the preservation of liberty. Third, Constant believed that constitutional monarchy provided the means of reducing the role of the army to that of its one, proper function: repelling foreign invaders. Internal dissent and lawlessness could be dealt with by "salaried officers."

The final guarantee sprang from the independence of municipal and local authorities. In this we touch on one of the central themes of French liberalism: namely, the preservation of local independence and liberties as a means of restricting the power of despotic, central government. This argument, in effect, was an updated supplement to Montesquieu's defense of the rights of the provincial nobility. The French liberals as a whole became preoccupied by what they saw as the systematic destruction of all intermediary powers and the consequent subjection of an undifferentiated and amorphous population at the hands of a highly organized, centralized bureaucratic power. Constant, for example, spoke of "individuals, lost in an unnatural isolation, strangers to the place of their birth, without any contact with the past, living only in a hurried present, scattered like atoms on a vast plain."[58] While Alexis de Tocqueville is the best-known exponent of this argument, it is important to realize that he was by

[57] Ibid., 239.
[58] Ibid., 255.

no means the first to diagnose the nature of this new threat to liberty. "[J]ust as in individual life that part which in no way threatens the social interest must remain free," Constant remarked, "similarly in the life of groups, all that does not damage the whole collectivity must enjoy the same liberty."[59]

Toward the end of the *Principles of Politics Applicable to All Representative Governments* Constant made the following acute observation: all of the constitutions that had been given to France had guaranteed the liberty of the individual, but all of them had violated this liberty. Declarations of principles, in other words, were not enough. Positive safeguards, powerful enough to protect the interests of the oppressed, were required. This was so, he went on, because "political institutions are simply contracts; and it is in the nature of contracts to establish fixed limits."[60] Thus, arbitrariness was incompatible with the existence of any government considered as a set of political institutions: it undermined their very foundations.

This was the message that Constant believed that Napoleon Bonaparte, on his return from Elba in 1814, was ready to hear. He was mistaken.[61] With Louis XVIII's homecoming from exile, he quickly adapted the fundamentals of his thought to the new circumstances of the restored monarchy, defending the strict observance of the *Charte* as the best means in the circumstances to preserve liberty and to protect France against counterrevolution. "What could we want more," he wrote in February 1820, "than what the *Charte* promises and guarantees us if its terms are honoured?"[62]

In the years that followed Constant continued to restate his defense of modern liberty. He did so, for example, in a speech to the *Athénée Royale* in December 1825, entitled "La Tendance générale des esprits dans le dix-neuvième siècle,"[63] and again in a long review of Charles Dunoyer's *L'Industrie et la morale considerées dans leur rapport avec la liberté.*[64] What is intriguing about the latter text is that we catch a glimpse of what Constant imagined might be a new

---

[59] Ibid., 254.
[60] Ibid., 291.
[61] See Constant, *Mémoires sur les cents jours* (Paris: Pichon et Didier, 1829).
[62] Constant, "Du Plan de la faction contre-révolutionnaire," in Harpaz, *Recueil d'articles*, vol. I, 1155.
[63] *Revue encyclopédique*, XXVIII (1825), 661–74.
[64] Ibid., XXIX (1826), 416–35.

form of despotism. As we have seen, Constant, like Montesquieu before him, was broadly optimistic about the effects of commerce on society. In this review article he reaffirmed this but (in a distinct echo of the theme to be found in the final paragraphs of his famous speech of 1819) recognized that the pursuit of individual enjoyment and physical pleasure ran the risk of diminishing our nobler, more civic-minded sentiments.

Yet Constant suggested that this tendency should not be exaggerated. Rather, in a postscript to the review he turned his fire against what he termed "*un papisme industriel*" and which he clearly associated with the new doctrine of Saint-Simonianism.[65] In contrast to the *individualisme* developed by Dunoyer, this "new sect" saw all diversity of thought and activity as an expression of anarchy. Terrified that not all people thought the same (or the same as their leaders), they invoked a spiritual power designed to reconstitute a broken unity. Under the guise of coordinating our thoughts and actions, they sought, in Constant's opinion, "to organize tyranny." Constant's response was to suggest that this supposed "moral anarchy" was nothing other than "the natural, desirable, happy state of a society in which each person, according to his own understanding, tastes, intellectual disposition, believes or examines, preserves or improves, in a word, makes a free and independent use of his faculties." Constant was in little doubt that it was toward this end that society was moving. Nevertheless, in these few remarks on Saint-Simonianism he had identified what would become a growing threat to liberty and the breeding ground for a new type of despotism.[66]

At this point in the argument it has become almost traditional to quote the opening page of Constant's *Mélanges*, where, as we have seen, he proclaimed the consistency of his attachment to certain principles of liberty. A different ending might take the following form: It was Constant's view that we were not bound by any duty to obey an unjust law. There were limits to obedience. The corollary to this, however, was that in times of revolution and despotism "enlightened men" had duties toward their fellow human beings. They should act out of prudence and morality and recognize that

---

[65] Ibid., 432.

[66] It was Constant's fellow liberal, Elie Halévy, who later insisted on the connection between Saint-Simonianism and Bonapartist "Caesarism": see Elie Halévy, *L'Ere des tyrannies* (Paris: Gallimard, 1938), 213, 219.

fanaticism was incompatible with freedom. Constant himself tried to remain true to these principles, although his political judgment was by no means flawless. He was in particular deceived by Napoleon Bonaparte in 1814, believing that the returning Emperor had been converted to the cause of constitutional government and liberty. This was the conclusion that Constant drew from this experience. "Liberty," he wrote, "will emerge from [the] future, however stormy it may now look. Then, after twenty years of defending the rights of man, the safety of the individual and of land, freedom of thought, and the abolition of arbitrary power, I shall dare to congratulate myself for joining, before the victory, those institutions which sanction all these rights. I shall have accomplished my life's work."[67]

[67] *PoP* (1815), 305.

5 Benjamin Constant and the Terror

Translated by Arthur Goldhammer

THE TERROR AND ITS LEGACY

September 5, 1793, was a day of revolutionary agitation and violence in Paris. The sans-culottes invaded the seat of the Convention
demanding bread for the people and the guillotine for the enemies
of the Revolution. There was nothing exceptional about the event,
however. For several months Paris had been periodically rocked by
popular uprisings led by more or less obscure agitators and always
culminating in the same demands: for more food, price controls,
stabilization of the *assignat*, punishment of traitors and moderates,
and surveillance of suspects. A mixture of economic demands and
political obsessions (of a repressive type) proceeded systematically
from the streets, dominated by the sans-culottes and *enragés*, to the
Convention, the seat of legal power.

Faced with this situation, which was aggravated by the insurrection in the Vendée and by the war, the Convention, led by the Jacobins, had already adopted a series of emergency measures. In March
it had instituted the Revolutionary Tribunal to judge "suspects,"
as well as the "committees of surveillance" to identify them. In
April it had created the Committee of Public Safety, which deliberated in secret and was authorized to order immediate execution
of its decisions. Also in April it had dispatched representatives to
the army and invested them with unlimited powers, and in the following months it decreed ceilings on grain and wheat prices (the
famous "*maximum*"), fixed the value of the *assignat*, and established
a tax on large fortunes. Taken together, these "political" measures
already amounted to a dictatorial regime of violence and fear, as the

Girondins complained in vain. In a sense, all that remained was the official sanction.

That sanction came on September 5, which is why this day is important. The sans-culottes having announced their demands before the Convention and having received the backing of a delegation of Jacobins, the Committee of Public Safety, seeking to satisfy the militants, decreed "Terror... the order of the day." This blunt declaration inaugurated the most dramatic phase of the French Revolution. From that moment on, the Terror became a "system of government" and became once and for all a part of the political vocabulary and imagination of the contemporary world. As the Terror proceeded and became increasingly organized, its deeper meaning was revealed by the law of June 10, 1794, which called on the Revolutionary Tribunal to judge "enemies of the people," transforming judicial trials into political ones and denying all guarantees to the accused. Taken together, these institutions enabled the Committee of Public Safety to organize a ruthlessly efficient repressive machine, which in the space of ten months resulted in half a million arrests, sixteen thousand and six hundred executions, and tens of thousands slaughtered in the Vendée (including mass drownings in the Loire).[1]

A mechanism of this type, which fed itself by constantly creating new "enemies" in a potentially endless spiral of violence, could not last too long. In fact, on July 27, 1794 (the ninth of Thermidor, Year III, according to the revolutionary calendar), a conspiracy hatched by Robespierrist henchmen in the provinces put an end to the Jacobin regime and, with it, the Terror. Parisians of all classes exploded with joy at the liberation, symbolized by the irrepressible spread of dancing around the city. But the trauma had been too great, and even though the Convention had declared "justice the order of the day," the Terror was like a ghost that would continue to obsess the political and social life of the Republic from that day forward. The Thermidorian period – by which I mean the time from the fall of Robespierre to the accession of Napoleon, including the Directory – was

---

[1] The dates of the executions are analyzed in a statistical study by Donald Greer, *The Incidence of the Terror during the French Revolution: A Statistical Interpretation* (Cambridge, MA: Harvard University Press, 1935), and incorporated in the summary given by François Furet in his article entitled "Terror" in the *Critical Dictionary of the French Revolution*, trans. Arthur Goldhammer (Cambridge, MA: Harvard University Press, 1990).

marked throughout by the crushing weight of memory and remorse. The effort of the Thermidorians to return the revolutionary current to its original channel, flowing toward a regime of liberal rights and constitutional legality, failed, and one of the principal reasons for that failure was the terrible experience of the Terror, which permanently destroyed the faith of the French in the political class of the Revolution and, to some extent, in the very idea of 1789.

The great hopes that the Revolution had raised seemed irrevocably compromised. During the Thermidorian period, counterrevolutionary forces found themselves in a vulnerable position and sought both political and intellectual reinforcements, while revolutionary forces, though continuing to hold the reins of power, knew doubt, crises of conscience, and division. But this is also a time of extraordinary historical and political interest.[2] It is interesting, first, because it offers a sort of condensed recapitulation of the revolutionary drama, in which all the protagonists (Feuillants, Girondins, Jacobins, Thermidorians, moderate and reactionary monarchists) returned to the stage one last time as the Thermidorians tried to "end the Revolution" by translating the principles of 1789 into a stable political-constitutional regime. Second, because a deeply interesting debate developed in these years about the nature and significance of the Revolution, a debate that not only opposed the leading theorists of the Revolution and Counterrevolution but also pitted proponents of the Revolution against one another, thus setting the political and ideological stage for the years to come.

Young Benjamin Constant, who came to Paris in the spring of 1795, was one of the leading participants in this debate. As eminent historians of the Revolution such as Georges Lefebvre and François Furet have made clear, Constant was the Thermidorian intellectual par excellence, in the sense that he more than anyone else worked to separate the Revolution from the Terror, to "save" 1789 from 1793. His brilliant and polemical writings would provoke the reflections of Joseph de Maistre and Adrien de Lezay-Marnésia and give rise to a debate of fundamental importance on the Terror and its relation to the Revolution.

---

[2] Perhaps the best study of the complexity of Thermidor, which shows how reductive it is to think of the period in terms of "reaction," is Bronislaw Baczko's *Comment sortir de la Terreur. Thermidor et la Révolution* (Paris: Gallimard, 1989).

THE DIRECTORIAL DEBATE ON THE TERROR

To understand the importance of this debate, which took place in the first years of the Directory, 1795–97, we must recall not only the deep scars that the Terror left behind but also the symbolic significance it retained throughout the nineteenth and much of the twentieth century. By linking the principles of 1789 and the republican regime to an unprecedented reign of violence, the Terror not only obsessed the leading figures of the Thermidorian period, frightening liberals and providing the enemies of the Revolution with powerful arguments, but also infused political debate in nineteenth-century France with revolutionary passions. As François Furet rightly observed, at least a century would pass before the republican idea could be freed in France from its unfortunate association with the Terror.

The Bolshevik Revolution would restore the explosive content of the argument, however, owing to the many parallels in slogans, institutions, and modes of action that Lenin himself sought to establish between the Bolsheviks and the Jacobins. Thus the Terror and the Jacobins were restored to life in the twentieth century as subjects of a related historical debate in which the hopes and fears of the present were projected onto them. Scholars who justified the Terror in the name of historical necessity saw it as the prefiguration of another revolutionary dictatorship, the Bolshevik, which was seen as historically necessary for the realization of a classless society. By contrast, scholars who refused to justify the Terror – distinguishing between the good revolution of 1789 and the bad one of 1793 – did so in the name of individual rights, thus setting the principles of 1789 not only against those of 1793 but also against those of 1917. The debate about the Terror therefore carried all the weight and drama of the twentieth-century political and ideological conflict between liberal democracy and totalitarianism (in this case, communist totalitarianism).

In light of all this, the taut debate between Constant and Lezay-Marnésia – with Maistre and Burke lurking in the background – is important for two reasons: First, it became the model for all subsequent discussion of the Terror, anticipating the main argumentative strategies. Second, the participants were ideally situated and took quite similar political positions. Indeed, the opinions of Constant and Lezay concerning the nature, causes, and results of the

Revolution are substantially the same. Both belonged to the same part of the political spectrum: both supported the Directory and fought to establish it on a stable footing. Yet these very similarities make their opposing interpretations of the Terror all the more significant: their divergence on this issue anticipates European political divisions after the 1840s, when the ideological dividing line no longer passed between revolutionaries and counterrevolutionaries but rather pitted the various heirs of the French Revolution against one another.

THE COUNTERREVOLUTIONARY JUSTIFICATION OF THE TERROR: JOSEPH DE MAISTRE

Although Edmund Burke had described the French Revolution in 1790 as the "the most astonishing [event] that has hitherto happened in the world,"[3] contemporaries quickly recognized that the Terror was more astonishing and extraordinary still. Whatever participants and onlookers may have felt, the Terror posed a challenge to the conscience of contemporaries, particularly those who supported the idea of 1789. No one doubted that the scaffold had been raised in the name of the Revolution. This posed the following problem: What was the relation between the Terror and the Revolution? Was there a connection between the principles of 1789 and the appalling violence of 1793–94?

Burke's work might be seen as an answer to this question before the fact. In his *Reflections on the Revolution in France*, the great Irish writer argued that the principles of the Revolution – abstract and metaphysical, devoid of any connection with the historical and social reality of France – would plunge the country into chaos, violence, and dictatorship. It goes without saying that this analysis, formulated in 1790, came to seem prophetic after the Terror. But that was not all. If it had been possible to "predict" the Terror when the Revolution was still in its early stages and the Republic was not yet on the horizon, then this was irrefutable proof that the Terror stemmed directly from the principles of 1789. Here was the proof that there was no substantial difference between 1789 and

---

[3] Edmund Burke, *Reflections on the Revolution in France (1790)*, ed. J. C. D. Clarke (Stanford, CA: Stanford University Press, 2001), 154.

1793, between *monarchiens* and Feuillants, between Girondins and Jacobins. A similar notion lay at the heart of the thinking of all the enemies of the Revolution, and for good reason. In fact, Burke's *Reflections*, though the work of a liberal conservative supportive of constitutional government and the parliamentary regime, almost immediately became the manifesto of the Counterrevolution.

Joseph de Maistre belongs to this tradition. He began his *Considérations sur la France* as a response to Constant, who in 1796 had published his first pamphlet, a ringing defense of the Directory entitled *De la force du gouvernement actuel*.[4] Attacking the nostalgia for the monarchy that seemed to be steadily gaining ground in French public opinion (especially among moderates), Constant had argued that a counterrevolution, far from signifying a return to order and tranquility, would be nothing other than "a new revolution," with all the violence and anarchy this would entail.[5] Maistre no doubt found it very irritating (and very dangerous) that the argument of prudence and moderation had been co-opted by supporters of the Revolution. And in his *Considérations*, which appeared anonymously in Switzerland in 1797, he argued the opposite thesis with all the rhetorical force of which he was capable: the Counterrevolution, he said, would not be "a *contrary* revolution, but *the contrary of* revolution."[6]

Maistre did not limit himself to an attack on Constant's "prodigious sophism,"[7] however. Indeed, this was merely the polemical opportunity that led him to develop a complex interpretation of the French Revolution, theological in inspiration and apocalyptic in tone, in which the Terror figures as a fatal and necessary consequence of the revolutionary process, partaking of both its satanic nature and its providential function.

Organized by what Maistre called "the infernal committee," the Terror was surely the "most terrible period of the revolution."[8] If one thinks about it, however, "it becomes clear that once the

---

[4] Benjamin Constant, *De la force du gouvernment actuel et de la nécessité de s'y rallier* (1796), in *OCBC/Œuvres*, I. All citations are from this edition.
[5] *De la force*, 338.
[6] Joseph de Maistre, *Considérations sur la France*, ed. P. Manent (Paris: Editions Complexe, 1988), 166.
[7] Maistre, 131.
[8] Ibid., 30.

revolutionary movement was under way, France and the monarchy could be saved only by Jacobinism."[9] It would be foolish to deceive oneself about the intentions of the other European powers: even if they had mobilized to defeat the republic and restore the monarchy, in case of victory they would have attacked France's territorial integrity. How could France have resisted such a potent military force? And how could it have foiled the European conspiracy? De Maistre gave this answer:

Only Robespierre's infernal genius could work this miracle. The revolutionary government hardened the French soul, by tempering it in blood. It roused the spirits of the soldiers and doubled their strength with fierce despair and contempt for life, which stemmed from rage. Horror of the scaffold, which drove the citizen to the border, strengthened the outward force by annihilating the last vestige of resistance within. All life, all wealth, and all power was in the hands of the revolutionary government. And this monstrous power, intoxicated by blood and victory – a terrifying phenomenon never before seen – was at once a terrible chastisement for France and the only way to save the country.[10]

Clearly, for Maistre, the Terror was providential in two respects: first, as an appropriate punishment of the French people, who were obliged to "taste" the bitter consequences of the Revolution, which would calm their atheistic and fanatical spirit; second, the Terror was the only way of saving France in exceptionally grave circumstances and of restoring its legitimate sovereignty with its territory and military glory intact. To be sure, the Terror had produced disastrous moral effects. It had created a situation in which the French considered "bearable and almost desirable any state of affairs in which people are not constantly cutting each other's throats"[11] and had made them narrowly and cruelly selfish, but now for the purpose of self-preservation. If we look beneath the surface of events, Maistre wrote, we can contemplate the wondrous power of Providence, which, making "sport of human will," creates order out of disorder. The Revolution and the Terror (and even Thermidor) were merely different phases of the same process, which in turn was the product of a providential design: to punish France for having

<hr />

[9] Ibid., 31.
[10] Ibid., 31–32.
[11] Ibid., 136.

abandoned her mission as a Christian nation. All that distinguished one phase of the Revolution from another was the intensity of the violence, but this depended solely on circumstances. The fundamental principles remained the same.

THE REVOLUTIONARY JUSTIFICATION OF THE TERROR: ADRIEN LEZAY-MARNÉSIA

In the same year that Maistre published his *Considérations sur la France*, in which he condemned (and indeed reviled) the Revolution as a whole, Adrien Lezay-Marnésia, a brilliant young admirer of the Revolution,[12] published *Des causes de la Révolution et de ses résultats*, whose purpose was to reconcile the French to all phases of their Revolution.[13] To that end he proposed to show that the Terror, despite its brutality, had fulfilled a necessary and providential function. Thus by a singular coincidence, two works appeared in the same year that could not have been more remote from each other in political inspiration but that contained interpretations of the Terror that were in many respects similar.

For example, Lezay invoked exceptional circumstances to explain the Terror. The financial and economic ruin caused by the *assignat* and the burden of fighting a war both inside and outside the country's borders had left France with a serious dilemma: either dissolve the state or apply harsh force. When the Committee of Public Safety chose to make terror the order of the day, Lezay argued, it had no choice. The effects of its decision were "prodigious": the government, at last liberated from the pressures of the street and the prejudices of deputies, found the strength it needed. Discipline

---

[12] Of noble origin (his father was a marquis who was elected to the Estates General, where he sat with the *monarchiens*, ultimately ending up among the *émigrés*), Adrien Lezay-Marnésia (1770–1814) spent the years of the Legislative Assembly and Convention abroad. Returning to France after Thermidor, he became a publicist, and his views gradually evolved from a pro-monarchy position to a moderate republican one. He became a spokesmen for the "right" under the Directory, that is, for the position that the Directory had no choice but to align itself with public opinion (which favored constitutional monarchy), and found himself opposing Constant on a number of occasions.

[13] Lezay-Marnésia's text (*Des causes de la Révolution et de ses résultats*) was published in April 1797 in the *Journal d'économie publique*. Citations are from the Italian version (Adrien Lezay-Marnésia and Benjamin Constant, *Ordine e libertà* [Turin: La Rosa, 1995]).

was restored in the army. Enemy armies and foreign sovereigns were gripped with fear. Thus the Terror had saved France.

Lezay developed what would come to be called the "theory of circumstances." For a long time this remained the most common explanation or justification of the Terror. (It was adopted by liberal historians of the Restoration from Mignet to Thiers, as well as by Jacobin and Marxist historians.) In this view, the Terror was a product of adversity. To be sure, it was a period of terrible violence with a high cost in human lives, yet absolutely necessary because in the circumstances it was the only way to save France. So, regardless of whether France was saved from dismemberment and delivered whole into the hands of either the monarchy or the republic, and regardless of whether this outcome was the fruit of divine Providence or of rationality at work in history, it remained true for both writers – the reactionary Maistre and the republican Lezay – that the Terror was fully justified and an integral part of the revolutionary process.

Lezay's analysis did not end there, however. He proceeded to develop his reflections on circumstances into a general theory. If Maistre was convinced that the Terror would remain a singular historical event, Lezay argued that it was destined to repeat itself in every popular revolution. In fact, all popular revolutions proceed through three phases. In the first phase they count on the ardor of the people and in the final phase on the general desire for peace. But in the middle phase, when the popular impetus has waned but before weariness has set in, the revolutionaries succumb to exhaustion if no reinforcements arrive. And "those reinforcements are the Terror."[14]

Lezay illustrated his concept by developing an acute analysis of the dynamics of popular revolution. In the initial phases, he wrote, the people are governed by their love of liberty, because this is essential for changing the status quo. Hence those who wish to lead the revolutionary movement must declare themselves to be in favor of liberty. Later, however, the people's love of liberty begins to decline and, with it, declines the influence of the early leaders of the revolution. Ultimately,

[14] Lezay-Marnésia, 18.

they are supplanted by those who hold out to the people the possibility of a kind of actual equality: a mirage which, combined with the natural hatred of the have-nots for the well-to-do, drives the people into a terrible war against the rich. And since this equality is also more popular than liberty because it promises wealth, whereas liberty promises only rights, its proponents inevitably prevail, and their preponderance is all the greater because the class they court is bolder, while the class they rail against is more timorous.[15]

The Terror is therefore a necessary phase in any popular revolution. When the revolution reaches this intermediate stage in its development, it is at risk, because the demand for liberty is no longer sufficient to motivate the active participation of the people. Then the revolutionaries, in order to save the revolution, are obliged to hold out the mirage of equality of property to the masses. The revolution thereby infuses itself with extraordinary new energy, but this needs to be channeled and controlled, and only the Terror can manage this successfully. The Terror then serves to guide the most tumultuous phase of the revolution. At the same time, it restores the habit of obedience in the population, and without this, no political order can be established.

We come now to Lezay's third argument in justification of the Terror: that it was a painful but necessary first step toward reestablishing liberty in both its political and moral aspects. According to the author of *Des causes*, the impetuous "unleashing of the people" is essential for the initial success of any revolution but becomes the most important obstacle to its ultimate success. Indeed, the "unleashing of the people" allows them to shake off the yoke of oppression but leaves them incapable of accepting another. Yet the people must always wear some yoke, whether of the monarchy or of law: free or slave, the people must be obedient. In Lezay's words,

the less the people are able to obey, the less suited they are for liberty, because the less they are able to control themselves and the more force it takes to control them. When anarchy has made them forget obedience, despotism is therefore needed to teach it to them again. It was fortunate that they found a despotism sufficiently violent to obtain the desired effect and then to destroy itself.[16]

[15] Ibid., 19.
[16] Ibid., 25.

Furthermore, this despotism greatly accelerated the changes in mores that inevitably accompany the birth of any new political order: "Eighteen months of Terror were enough to do away with age-old customs and establish others that might have taken centuries to put in place."[17] Thus, "violence" made a "new people"[18] of the French, paving the way for liberty. Without violence, liberty would never have taken hold. The relevance of this argument scarcely needs emphasizing: it contributed to the idea that terror is a necessary ingredient of revolution and that merciless dictatorship is a necessary stage on the road to freedom.

Lezay's justification of terror could not have been more complete: for him, terror is justified in part because it is *necessary*, in part because it is *consubstantial* with revolution as a popular uprising, and in part because it is the *indispensable political and ethical precondition* for the establishment of liberty. Once the French understood the deep historical necessity of the Terror, Lezay argued, they were able to let go of their hatred and resentment and prepare to live amid the splendors that the Revolution had made possible, albeit at the price "of innumerable crimes and misdemeanors."[19]

CONDEMNING THE TERROR IN THE NAME OF 1789: THE YOUNG CONSTANT

Constant took no notice of Maistre's views on the Terror but felt he had to reply publicly to Lezay's views. The reason is easy to guess: it was in a way obvious that a declared enemy of 1789 (such as the anonymous author of *Considérations sur la France*) would argue that the Terror had been necessary and was inextricably intertwined with the Revolution itself. For proponents of the Revolution, however, this argument was disastrous: to associate 1789 with 1793 after Thermidor was to link the Revolution to a development that the French had rejected almost unanimously. Looking to the future, moreover, it linked revolutionary principles to violence and dictatorship. And it was not so obvious – and quite dangerous – that

---

[17] Ibid., 26. Lezay says "eighteen months" because he dates the beginning of the Terror from the first emergency measures taken in March of 1793 by the Convention; see earlier (p. 1).

[18] Lezay-Marnésia, 26.

[19] Ibid., 5.

a pro-revolutionary, pro-republican writer such as the author of *Des causes de la Révolution* (who was also anonymous, but whom Constant knew to be Lezay-Marnésia) should make the same argument. When a second edition of Constant's *Des réactions politiques* appeared in 1797, he therefore added a brief preface entitled *De la Terreur* (On the Terror),[20] which is nothing less than a point-by-point refutation of Lezay's argument. To begin with, Constant rejected Lezay's thesis in principle: by invoking circumstances as a justification for the Terror, Lezay had raised circumstances to the level of principle, thereby opening the way to a complete divorce between the means and the ends of political action. To pardon individuals led astray by revolutionary excesses is one thing: this was necessary, Constant argued, if for no other reason than the wish to "pacify the Republic." But to "maintain that such excesses were *in themselves* salutary and indeed indispensable" is something else. To take this line was not to pardon individuals but to justify the principle itself. And to do this was to cross a line that Constant insisted must not be crossed. The principle at stake was the limitation of power:

There is a degree of arbitrariness that suffices to turn heads, corrupt hearts, and twist all emotions. Men and bodies invested with unlimited power become drunk with that power. *In no circumstances is unlimited power acceptable, and in reality it is never necessary.*[21]

Constant thus stated the cardinal principle of modern liberalism in its purest form: absolute power of any kind must be rejected. The reason for this is the universality of individual rights. Either this principle is shared, or it is not, like all ultimate values. Of course it is open to the kinds of objection that any political "realist" would make (and both Burke and Marx would object to its "abstractness" from their opposite ends of the political spectrum). In Constant's view, however, the very identity of the Revolution – which was at once a political and a philosophical event – hinged on this principle. The deepest significance of 1789 in fact lay in the birth of a political order based on the universality of individual rights and the rule of law. Since the Terror denied both, Constant rejected any attempt

---

[20] Constant's text appeared at the end of May 1797, about two months after Lezay's. *Des effets de la Terreur* can now be found in Benjamin Constant, *OCBC/Œuvres*, I. Subsequent citations refer to this volume.

[21] *Des effets de la Terreur*, 519 emphasis added.

to justify it and any attempt to depict it as an outgrowth of the principles of 1789.

Thus Lezay's thesis was unacceptable in principle, but more than that, Constant argued, it was also "dangerous in its consequences." "Terror, reduced to a system and justified as such, is much more horrible than the ferocious and brutal violence of terrorists, because wherever this system exists, the same crimes will be repeated again and again; whereas terrorists may well exist without reviving the Terror. Once terror is consecrated in principle, it remains enshrined forever."[22] Constant realized that arguments like Lezay's (which justified not spontaneous, accidental violence but violence erected into a "system of government") were like a virus infecting the ideals of 1789 and offered any government abundant pretexts to resort to force. In Thermidorian France, moreover, the first government to do so might well be a restored monarchical government, which could turn to Lezay for excellent arguments in favor of unleashing a "White Terror." To be sure, this was not Lezay's "subjective intent," but it was surely the "objective consequence" of his theoretical assumptions. By depriving political action of all normative guides, Lezay's thesis led to the sacrifice of principle and the justification of crime. It was no accident, moreover, that this outcome was welcomed both by those who had always detested the Republic (the monarchists) and those who had dishonored it (the Jacobins).

Finally, besides being wrong in principle and dangerous in its consequences, Lezay's doctrine was historically misleading. Not only was the Terror not necessary (the Republic was saved "despite the Terror"); not only was it counterproductive and useless as a means to an end; but its negative effects were not yet over, and its aftermath left the Republic under the Directory still "besieged with dangers on all sides."[23] The contrast between Lezay and Constant could not be clearer: whereas the former ended up justifying the Terror in all its aspects, the latter condemned it in a way that left no room for mitigating factors. Yet Constant's reasoning was not devoid of subtlety. His uncompromising rejection of the Terror did not apply to all the actions of the dictatorship, only to the "atrocities" (Constant borrowed the word from Lezay); lawful actions were acceptable.

[22] Ibid., 518.
[23] Ibid., 519.

To explain this distinction, it is useful to invoke Constant's concept of state power, which is already expressed in sufficiently clear if still fragmentary and disorganized terms in his youthful writings. In *De la Terreur*, Constant argued that any government, despotic or liberal, has a "legal, repressive, and coercive part" that forms the "basis" of its existence.[24] Without a legal monopoly on the use of force, no government can oblige its citizens to respect its decisions, in which case its very existence as a common power is called into question. For Constant, however, such power is of a contractual and instrumental nature. It is the means that society chooses to guarantee the full exercise of individual rights, which thus define the limits and at the same time the ends of state power. Coercion is still necessary. Indeed, it is clear that even a liberal state must have the power to enforce its judgments when necessary, for otherwise its decisions would remain purely hypothetical. Thus what distinguishes a liberal state from a despotic one is not the absence of coercion but the fact that state power in general (including the use of force) is limited in both manner and extent by a series of checks and balances (including both individual rights and constitutional procedures). It is a derivative and instrumental power. In such a conception of state power, "means" and "ends" are not distinct but mutually related, and it is this relationship that justifies the existence of power: the choice of means is a question of principle, which cannot be neglected. Form *is* substance. The absence of limits to the exercise of power not only upsets this relationship, reinstating the arbitrariness typical of a despotic state and corrupting the very nature of man, but also disrupts the delicate balance between limited power and sovereign society so that order and liberty can no longer coexist without succumbing to one of two opposing evils, anarchy or despotism.

To return to the government of the Terror, Constant argues that it, like all governments, had a legal and coercive aspect but that it also developed an "atrocious" or terrorist aspect. The men in power remained the same, but the exercise of power took on a dual nature. To justify Terror in the name of practical efficiency is to confound these two different ways of exercising power, attributing the effects

---

[24] Here, the term "government" is synonymous with state, state power, and sovereign power.

of lawful coercion to terror. In reality, when the government operated in its terrorist mode, its achievements were by no means prodigious but pointless if not downright harmful – harmful, because they fostered resentment that degenerated into rebellion. Any number of episodes demonstrated the truth of this assertion: if terror was so admirable, why crush the revolt in Lyons, the departmental insurrection, and the Vendée? But without the Terror, Constant argued, those rebellions would not have taken place – pointless, because what was obtained with the most brutal violence could have been obtained with legal coercion. If nothing else, Constant maintained, the government was obliged to act prudently, in accordance with the gravity of the situation. It had the power to banish citizens, to inflict the harshest of punishments on deserters, to punish conspirators and agitators, to restrict emigration, and to impose special taxes. But the Terror proceeded quite differently: it sent representatives to the armies and invested them with unlimited powers, which they used to commit unspeakable horrors; it created tribunals from which there was no appeal and sentenced countless individuals without due process; it left good citizens at the whim of greedy officials; and it sought to destroy the clergy. By committing atrocities in the name of justice, the Terror ruined the good name of the latter and achieved nothing beyond awakening universal compassion for its victims, regardless of their true responsibility.

Finally, Constant forcefully rejected Lezay's most shocking argument, namely, the "moral" justification of the Terror. The claim that the Terror had forged a "new people" endowed with republican mores was absolutely "false. The Terror associated the Republic with horrendous memories while restoring an appearance of morality to the most puerile practices and the most pointless forms of the monarchy. The Terror is to blame, moreover, for the decay of public spirit, the fanaticism that is contrary to every principle of liberty, and the infamy that attaches to all republicans."[25]

As for the argument that the Terror was an indispensable prelude to liberty, "once again," Constant observed, "nothing could be farther from the truth. The Terror prepared the people to accept any yoke imaginable, but it left them indifferent and perhaps unsuited to liberty. It made them bow their heads but degraded their souls and

[25] *Des effets de la Terreur*, 524.

shriveled their hearts."[26] As long as Terror was the order of the day, it served the Jacobins, but now that it was dead, it served the monarchists: in hammering repeatedly on this point, Constant sought to show not only who would benefit from the justification of the Terror but also what the real antecedents of "judgment pushed to the extremes" were.

Having refuted all of Lezay's arguments, Constant was ready to draw his own conclusions:

> Terror was not a necessary consequence of liberty or a necessary *reinforcement* of revolution. It was a consequence of the perfidy of internal enemies, of the coalition of foreign enemies, of the ambition of a few scoundrels, and of the aberrations of many senseless individuals. It devoured the enemies whose imprudence brought it into being, the instruments whose frenzy served it, and the leaders who pretended to control it.[27]

Of course it is no accident that the memory of the Terror was used above all by enemies of the Republic: they used the "memory of Robespierre to insult the shade of Condorcet and assassinate Sieyès. It was the frenzy of 1794 that caused weak and embittered men to abjure the enlightenment of 1789."[28] Against the idea that the Revolution formed a "bloc" (an idea shared by Maistre and Lezay), Constant insisted on the need to distinguish sharply between 1789 and 1793, between the Revolution and the Terror.

THE STRENGTHS AND WEAKNESSES OF THE YOUNG CONSTANT'S ANALYSIS

Constant's conclusions reveal the strengths and weaknesses of his analysis. The strengths stem from his criticism of any monolithic image of the Revolution – an image that had been characteristic of counterrevolutionary historiography from the beginning but that was just beginning, with Lezay, to affect proponents of the Revolution and would later come into its own in Jacobin–Marxist historiography. This image was certainly effective in inflaming the most radical political passions (since it lent itself to condemnation

---

[26] Ibid., 524.
[27] Ibid., 525.
[28] Ibid., 524. Sieyès is mentioned because an attempt had been made on his life on April 11, 1797.

or praise of the Revolution in toto), but as an interpretive device it was reductive: an exceptionally complex phenomenon like the French Revolution was narrowed to a single meaning, yet it shaped the political universe of continental Europe, with its multiplicity of philosophical currents and institutional models.

Another strength of Constant's analysis of the Terror stems from his having resisted the temptation to engage in historical apology and his recognition that to accept dictatorship and violence as a necessary phase in the struggle for freedom was to inoculate progressive ideas with a devastating "virus," offering endless pretexts for organized minorities to follow the example of the Jacobins by proclaiming themselves to be the sole interpreters of the will of the people, of historical progress, or of some supposed truth.

By contrast, the weakness of Constant's interpretation stems from his exaggeration of the contrast between 1789 and 1793, to the point of denying any link between the Revolution and Jacobinism. His interpretation of the Terror as a revival of absolutist rule prevented Constant (and all other proponents of the theory of circumstances) from recognizing the *novelty* of Jacobinism as both a historical phenomenon and an unprecedented form of despotism. Indeed, that novelty depended on the links between the Terror and a certain part of the revolutionary galaxy, namely, those revolutionaries who saw the event as a new beginning and who believed in the regeneration of man through politics. The young Constant failed to see how, given a specific set of circumstances, 1789 could lead to 1793. But this does not mean, as some have argued, that he "eliminated" the problem of violence by treating the Terror as an episode of gratuitous and senseless horror, whereas Lezay is supposed far more consciously to have "rationalized" the Terror by demonstrating its circumstantial necessity. In reality, Constant was fully *conscious* of the role that violence played in the revolutionary process. He returns to the subject at several points in his youthful writing and is neither complacent nor moralistic. At times he even seems to offer a full precautionary justification of revolutionary violence.[29]

---

[29] In *De la force*, 375, note a, Constant wrote that "it is almost always by way of some great evil that revolutions tend toward the good of mankind, and the more pernicious is the thing to be destroyed, the crueler the evil of the Revolution."

According to Constant, the many episodes of violence that mark the Revolution have nothing to do with the Terror:

> Sporadic disorders, terrible but temporary and illegal calamities, do not add up to terror. Terror exists only when crime becomes the system of government, not when it is the enemy of the government; when government orders crime, not when it combats it; when it organizes the scoundrels' frenzy, not when it calls on the support of decent men.[30]

Thus Constant did not repress the problem of violence. On the contrary, it was on the basis of a rigorous distinction between "spontaneous" revolutionary violence and the "institutionalized" violence of the Committee of Public Safety that he *consciously* rejected the Terror. This rejection was in no sense the product of historical-philosophical dread born of an inability to confront reality. In other words, to resort to a much-abused and unfortunate expression, Constant was well aware that you can't make an omelet without breaking eggs. Nor can his attitude be reduced to a mere strategic choice dictated by the circumstances of the moment, namely, the unpopularity of Jacobinism. It was, rather, based on two distinct considerations. The first was a typically liberal principle, namely, the inviolability of the human person and conscience, which was intended to take politics out of the realm of violence and to establish a close relationship between the means of political action and the ends. The second was a historical judgment: at a time when the system of privileges was being dismantled, individual rights were being ratified, a representative system of government was taking shape, and the possibility of controlling and influencing power was being established, there could be no further justification for the recourse to violence.

To sum up, Constant's reflections on the Terror can be criticized not so much for repressing the problem of violence as for his inability to recognize the antilibertarian implications of certain revolutionary principles. In other words, he can be criticized for having neglected, in his ardor to defend the liberal spirit of the Revolution, the "revolutionary roots" of the Terror. But the reason for this was that his political thought in the Directory period was still immature and

---

[30] *Des effets de la Terreur*, 526.

because his theoretical reflections on a "system of principles" – the need for which was already apparent in 1797 – would not begin until the political battle to establish a liberal republic seemed lost.[31]

CONSTANT'S MATURE INTERPRETATION OF THE TERROR

At the time Constant wrote *De la Terreur*, his philosophical and historical thinking had already yielded mature fruits of great interest, but he had yet to elaborate an independent and detailed political theory.[32] He saw himself in a general way as the heir of the French enlightened liberal tradition, which he absorbed without fully appreciating its internal tensions, contradictions, and weaknesses. His theoretical sources comprise a pantheon of thinkers from Montesquieu to Rousseau, Voltaire, and Condorcet.

His attitude toward this tradition had changed considerably by the time he completed the long intellectual journey that ended with the publication in 1806 of his magnum opus, *Les Principes de politique*. In this work, the first attempt after the revolutionary upheaval to provide a *liberal* political theory appropriate to a *modern* society, Constant brings together two key ideas: the distinction between the

---

[31] In *Des réactions politiques*, Constant wrote, "In days to come, if no cleverer writer precedes me in the endeavor, I shall perhaps attempt to set forth what I regard as the elementary principles of liberty." *OCBC/Œuvres*, I, 489.

[32] This thesis is shared, with various minor differences, by Etienne Hofmann (to whom we owe the first critical edition of the *Principes de politique* of 1806, preceded by a monograph offering an accurate and well-documented account of the long gestation of this treatise: *Le Principes de politique de Benjamin Constant*, Droz, Genève 1980); Marcel Gauchet, "Constant," in *Dictionnaire critique de la Révolution française*, ed. Furet and Ozouf; Éphraim Harpaz, in his Introduction to Constant, *De l'esprit de conquête* (Paris: Flammarion, 1986); and the late George Armstrong Kelly, "Constant and His Interpreters: A Second Visit," *ABC*, 6 (1986). By contrast, Stephen Holmes is rather dismissive of the youthful writings, which he regards as brilliant but immature; see his *Benjamin Constant and the Making of Modern Liberalism* (New Haven: Yale University Press, 1984). Mauro Barberis takes the opposite position, arguing that "to distinguish between the youthful and mature works" is to search for "a laborious evolution toward maturity, which in fact did not take place." See *Benjamin Constant. Rivoluzione, costituzione, progresso* (Bologna: Il Mulino, 1988), 250. For a complete reconstructions of the period 1795–1806, taking account of the continuities as well as the clear discontinuities between the Constant of the Directory period and the imperial counselor, I permit myself to refer the reader to my *Alle origini del liberalismo contemporaneo. Il pensiero di Benjamin Constant tra il Termidoro e l'Impero* (Cosenza: Marco Editore, 2003).

liberty of the ancients and the liberty of the moderns, which he and Madame de Staël[33] developed in the wake of Hume, Delolme, and Ferguson, and a critique of Rousseau's concept of sovereignty that owed a great deal to Sismondi's "British" influence.[34]

Constant and Madame de Staël took up one of the major themes of pre- and post-revolutionary debate – the contrast between the ancients and the moderns – and developed it with unusual historical and conceptual clarity. Modern societies, they concluded, were profoundly different from ancient ones with respect to geopolitical characteristics (the size and population of states), socioeconomic conditions (commerce instead of war), and moral traits (abolition of slavery, civilization of mores, and aspiration to well-being through labor), and these differences gave rise to different needs and attitudes. Taken together, the conditions of modern life fostered a strong sense of individual independence, and people sought to realize that independence without interference or oversight by the state in the realms of thought and religion as well as in the economic and cultural spheres. In ancient societies, by contrast, the material and moral conditions of life made it necessary for society as a whole to assert its clear dominance over its individual members, so that individuals saw participation in the state as the best way to satisfy their needs and realize their aspirations.

Hence there is a profound difference – not sufficiently appreciated until now, according to Constant – between the ancient conception

---

[33] I am referring to *Des circonstances actuelles*, which Madame de Staël wrote around 1798 and which remained unpublished at the time. (The critical edition by Lucia Omacini was published by Droz in Geneva in 1979.)

[34] "British" influence because the young Sismondi who wrote *Recherches sur les constitutions des peuples libres* (1796) drew on the Anglo-American constitutional tradition in conscious opposition to the French. He challenged the latter tradition's devaluation of experience and in his polemic against a universalist-rational vision of liberty argued in favor of a historical-evolutionary, empirical, and pragmatic conception. Two relevant consequences followed from this basic position: on the constitutional level, a preference for mixed government (with a tricameral legislature), and, on the political level, a closely argued critique of Rousseau's ideas, which Sismondi attacked first in terms of the ancient/modern distinction (following Hume, Ferguson, Millar, and Delolme in maintaining that only the moderns had experienced liberty) and second in terms of the relationship between the concept of sovereignty and that of liberty (objecting to the surrender of all individual rights to the sovereign). While Constant remained impervious to Sismondi's constitutional ideas, he was profoundly influenced by his political theory.

of liberty and the modern. Whereas the ancients identified liberty with direct collective participation in government, the moderns see it largely as independence from government. If ancient liberty was *exclusively public* and went hand in hand with subjugation of the individual, modern liberty was *predominantly private*, as reflected in a broad sphere of civil liberties coupled with and supported by political liberty (but exercised indirectly, through the representative system).

Now, modern thinkers who had not noticed this fundamental difference (Rousseau and Mably) and revolutionaries who had been influenced by their ideas (the Jacobins)[35] had made a significant error: they had tried to construct modern liberty in the image of ancient liberty, calling on contemporaries to subjugate themselves to society to a degree intolerable for a modern people.[36] The principal source of this error can be found, Constant tells us, in Rousseau: against the scourge of despotism (and later in thinking about liberty), the Genevan writer did not revise the concept of sovereignty by elaborating a *theory of the limitations of power* but limited himself to transferring the locus of sovereignty from king to people and then elaborating an *egalitarian theory of the distribution of power*. Looking to the ancient *pólis*, and especially Sparta, as an idealized model, he identified liberty with the social power and the general will: the only liberty available to the individual in his theory is that of obedience to the general will or conformity with it. Individual self-determination is totally subordinate to collective self-determination.

This solution, besides being despotic in itself (by virtue of its anachronism), posed as a serious threat for the future as Constant saw it: since power in a modern democracy based on the principle

---

[35] For an acute analysis of Jacobinism, seen in relation and contrast to liberalism, see Lucien Jaume, *Echec au libéralisme. Les Jacobins et l'Etat* (Paris: Editions Kimé, 1990). Jaume completed this analysis with a massive study of the French liberal tradition, *L'Individu effacé ou le paradoxe du libéralisme française* (Paris: Fayard, 1997).

[36] Constant's "big idea," argued Marcel Gauchet in the book that launched the French "rediscovery" of Constant's political writing, "is that modernity is strangely unconscious of itself, of its novelty, its fundamental originality with respect to earlier societies. The collective consciousness remained mysteriously old-fashioned when it came to the transformations that laid the basic foundation of political liberty." See "Benjamin Constant: L'Illusion lucide du libéralisme," preface to Benjamin Constant, *De la liberté chez les Modernes. Ecrits politiques* (Paris: Livres de Poche, 1980), 40, reproduced in abbreviated and translated form in this *Companion*.

of popular sovereignty always remains in the hands of a few, who exercise it in the name of all, Rousseau's doctrine lent itself to instrumentalization by an organized minority claiming to interpret the people's will and disposing of the coercive and persuasive means to act as though that will coincided with their desires. Hence Rousseau's idea was likely to lead not to the absolute domination of all (the people) over the individual but to the absolute domination of a few (the governing elite) over society and its members. Thus liberty would be expropriated twice over.

This close critical analysis found historical confirmation in the tragic events of the Revolution. As Constant wrote in the *Principes de politique* of 1806, the consequences of Rousseau's system developed

their most frightening scope... during our Revolution, when revered principles were made into wounds, perhaps incurably. The more popular the government it was intended to give France, the worse were these wounds... *It would be easy to show, by means of countless examples, that the grossest sophisms of the most ardent apostles of the Terror, in the most revolting circumstances, were only perfectly consistent consequences of Rousseau's principles.* The omnipotent nation is as dangerous as a tyrant, indeed more dangerous. Tyranny is not constituted by there being few governors. Nor does a large number of governors guarantee freedom. The degree of political power alone, in whatever hands it is placed, makes a constitution free or a government oppressive; and once tyranny subsists, it is all the more frightful if the tyrannical group is large.[37]

To be sure, the immediate causes of "our Revolution, and those horrors for which liberty for all was at once the pretext and the victim,"[38] lay in the particular interests of the Jacobins and at times in exceptional circumstances. But Rousseau's theory served as the veil that covered those interests and exploited those circumstances. It was the theoretical system that justified these things and that might allow such things to be justified again in the future.

Clearly, this analysis was rather more sophisticated than what Constant had written under the Directory. The ethical and political condemnation of the Terror remained now that Constant possessed, in the form of his theory of political modernity, a more effective

---

[37] *PoP* (1806), 19–20 emphasis added.
[38] Ibid., 13.

tool for interpreting the way it unfolded. The Terror could not be attributed to the reemergence of Old Regime–style despotism or to an outbreak of criminal behavior due to personal corruption; nor could it be blamed solely on circumstances (though these were not without influence). The Terror was the fruit of a revolutionary mentality steeped in archaic political myths and deprived of historical understanding, totally incapable of understanding the nature and requirements of modern society.

When events conspired to bestow revolutionary leadership on men governed by this same mentality, men who had nourished themselves on the ideas of Rousseau and Mably, they believed they could wield power as it had been wielded in the free states of antiquity. They believed that everyone would be obliged to yield to collective authority, that private morality would be obliged to fall silent in conflict with the public interest, and that any attack on civil liberty would be compensated by the enjoyment of the most extensive political liberty possible. But they succeeded only in undermining individual independence without destroying the need for it. Ultimately, Constant wrote, Jacobinism was a miserable parody of the noble example of the ancients. It undermined individual liberty without consolidating political liberty. Its only achievement was a bloodbath. And all this happened because the Jacobins sought to substitute political liberty for civil liberty in a modern state, leaving them no choice but to swim against the tide of history.

6 Constant's Thought on Slavery and Empire

Both Constant's broadly theoretical works and his immediate political interventions indicate his perception that empire and slavery were urgent political problems of the post-revolutionary world. He published his eloquent denunciation of conquest, *De l'esprit de conquête et de l'usurpation* (*Spirit of Conquest and Usurpation*), during the dramatic months of Napoleon's fall in early 1814, as his first published political statement since his falling out with the Emperor over a decade earlier.[1] It is significant that the essay dwelt on foreign conquest – its injustices abroad and its debasement of political life at home – as the distinctive abomination of Napoleonic politics. Constant had little occasion in the remaining seventeen years of his life to discuss conquest and empire, for during the crisis-ridden Bourbon Restoration, France was not in a position to regain the territories lost over the years to the British, or to expand into new ones.[2] The first major effort at colonial expansion, the conquest

[1] See Cecil Courtney, *A Bibliography of Editions of the Writings of Benjamin Constant to 1833* (London: The Modern Humanities Research Association, 1981). Between 1801, when a series of his Tribunate speeches were published, and the appearance of *De l'esprit de conquête*, Constant published only the play *Wallstein* (1809) and several articles in the *Biographie Universelle* (1811–13), although he wrote much of the political material that would later appear in the *Principes de politique* and other works. Courtney notes that on the day (January 30) that *De l'esprit de conquête* was published, Constant wrote in his journal, "La bombe est lâchée" (p. 28).

[2] The French lost their colonies in India and Canada to the British in 1763 after the Seven Years' War and a number of their Caribbean colonies in subsequent decades, including most significantly Saint-Domingue, which became independent Haiti in 1804, though it was recognized by France only in 1825. France ultimately regained Martinique, Guadeloupe, and Guiana from the British in 1814, 1816, and 1817 respectively.

of Algiers in 1830, took place just a few months before Constant's death. But the *Spirit of Conquest* identified with subtlety and prescience the social dynamics of a politics of conquest in a modern nation, and Constant's critique identified in advance many of the political and rhetorical strategies the advocates of the Algerian conquest would use to sell that conquest to the French nation.[3] During Constant's years as a legislator, he regarded slavery and the slave trade as the most pressing problems presented by the French Empire. He was considered one of the Chamber of Deputies' staunchest and most eloquent abolitionists, though, as I discuss later, his antislavery activities were at once radical and cautious, characteristic of his posture as a leading figure of the liberal opposition under the increasingly reactionary Bourbons.

Constant intertwined moral and historical arguments against what he identified as the "spirit of conquest," which had reached its apogee in Napoleon's empire but could be seen more broadly as a danger distinctive of post-revolutionary, indeed modern, politics. His moral claims are framed in historical terms: conquest is wrong *for us, now,* rather than in any universal sense. But his historical narrative is also given a moral cast as a tale of progress. This style of moral-cum-historical argument lends Constant's thought some of its most distinctive strengths as well as its oddities. By historicizing moral arguments as he does, Constant resists both complacent self-satisfaction and relativism, for he urges his readers to regard their own society as only one possible instantiation of human values while also conceiving of certain very broad moral commitments – above all, to human equality – as sanctified by the movement of history and to imagine their (our) own actions as contributing to a larger collective project of human emancipation. And yet Constant flattens his historical arguments by rendering them in moral terms, producing sometimes puzzling glosses and lacunae and studiously ignoring historical phenomena that might seem to disrupt his narrative of progress, including both commercial aggression and colonial slavery, as I discuss later in this essay.

[3] I discuss Constant's anticipation of the sorts of argument that Alexis de Tocqueville would use in favor of the Algeria conquest, as well as Constant's own brief and ambivalent commentary on the conquest, in Jennifer Pitts, *A Turn to Empire: The Rise of Imperial Liberalism in Britain and France* (Princeton: Princeton University Press, 2005), chap. 6.

It might be said that Constant's political approach to slavery, like his political thought more generally, was distinctly post-revolutionary: committed to progress, political and civil liberty, and human equality, but also pragmatic, moderate, and sometimes even traditionalist in its mode of expression.[4] He considered slavery an indefensible violation of the most basic human rights and the presence of slavery in a society a mark of its vice and barbarity. But he devoted little effort to developing the moral arguments against slavery and the slave trade, as earlier abolitionists such as Condorcet had done, for he believed that as a theoretical matter the idea that slavery is wrong no longer needed to be argued. What was required was to persuade an indifferent public of the daily atrocity of slavery, in order to move the French government and political classes to the actions necessary to abolish the trade and ultimately slavery. In attempting to do so, Constant sought to work effectively within the severe constraints, and the reactionary climate, of Restoration politics. He was cautious and gradualist, in recognition of the failings of radical reform during the Revolution. By devoting his efforts to attacking the slave trade, already illegal though widely tolerated in France, and defending the civil rights of free people of color in the colonies, Constant was able to pursue an abolitionist agenda based on what was ostensibly an existing consensus. But although he restricted himself to attacking the slave trade rather than slavery itself, his persistence on this subject placed him among the radicals in the French debates of his day, which were markedly cautious compared with contemporary British, or revolutionary French, opinion.

Slavery is also a recurrent theme in Constant's more theoretical works, although there is a peculiar disjuncture on the subject of slavery between these and his political writings and speeches. Except when he was directly addressing the slave trade, Constant consistently wrote as though slavery had been abolished in modern society. He was deeply invested in the contrast between ancient and modern societies, and the prominence of slavery in ancient societies and economies constituted an important part of this opposition. In light of this contrast, Constant might have handled the continuing,

---

[4] For one account of the "post-revolutionary" nature of Constant's thought, see Biancamaria Fontana, *Benjamin Constant and the Post-Revolutionary Mind* (New Haven: Yale University Press, 1991).

indeed increasing, presence of colonial race slavery in the modern world in one of several ways. He might, for instance, have argued, as he did about conquest, that slavery was anachronistic, antithetical to the spirit of modern societies: that it was bound either to destroy what was valuable in them or to succumb to the movement of history. He might even, as some recent scholarship has done, have identified colonial slavery as a distinctively and disturbingly modern phenomenon, one instrumental to the emergence of the global economy whose early growth he was witnessing.[5] But instead, when contrasting ancient with modern societies, Constant tended to write as though slavery simply did not exist in the modern world: that the movement of history had already destroyed it. As I argue further on, this was a puzzling argumentative route for a thinker who for a decade was one of the French parliament's most persistent opponents of the slave trade.[6]

CONSTANT'S THOUGHT ON CONQUEST AND EMPIRE

De l'esprit de conquête et de l'usurpation is at once a brilliant polemic against Napoleon and a much broader brief against imperial expansion in the modern age. It offers a subtle analysis of the anxious mentality of the "usurper" and a powerful social psychology of the nation that succumbed to his despotism and to the spirit of conquest, against its own interests and inclinations. Constant drafted the essay in late 1813, after the decisive defeat of Napoleon at Leipzig, though by his own admission, he had written portions of

---

[5] See, e.g., Sidney Mintz, Sweetness and Power: The Place of Sugar in Modern History (New York: Penguin, 1986).

[6] To be sure, slavery had been abolished within Europe proper, but the slavery thriving in European colonies had become central to European economies: it has been estimated, for instance, that by 1789, the colony of Saint-Domingue, with its half a million slaves and abundant sugar and coffee, accounted for 40 percent of the value of all French foreign trade. See Laurent Dubois, Avengers of the New World: The Story of the Haitian Revolution (Cambridge, MA: Harvard University Press, 2004), 21. As noted, Saint-Domingue became independent Haiti in 1804, and the other major French slave colonies, Martinique and Guadeloupe, were more marginal to the French economy. By the time Constant took up the battle against slavery, metropolitan French could regard slavery as less essential than it was to either their pre-revolutionary or the contemporary British economy. Constant addresses none of this directly, so one can only speculate about the reasons behind his curious disregard of modern slavery in his theoretical works.

the work many years earlier, "when the world still lay beneath the yoke of a tyrant."[7] The essay is relentlessly hostile to Napoleon – unlike Constant himself, who famously and perplexingly agreed to help the emperor draft a constitution during the Hundred Days, Napoleon's audacious and short-lived effort to recapture the throne after his escape from Elba.[8] But the essay's argument is otherwise complex, and its numerous and often competing strands of argument may owe something to its composition at several quite different moments of Napoleon's reign, as well as to Constant's persistent ambivalence about not only the modern French public, Napoleon's victims, but also his abettors.

It was shrewd of Constant to perceive how alluring the project of conquest could be for post-Revolutionary France. Enthusiasm for Napoleonic militarism was, to be sure, at a low ebb when the work was published, after the catastrophe of the Russian campaign and Napoleon's defeat at the hands of a united Europe. The loss of many of France's colonies after 1815 and the preoccupation among French legislators and political thinkers with domestic politics under the Bourbon Restoration meant that in the years immediately following the pamphlet's publication, imperial adventures were foresworn by political figures from across the political spectrum.[9] Members of

---

[7] From the preface to the first edition, in *PW*, 46. The essay's first two editions were published abroad, in Hanover and London, in January and March of 1814; two further editions were published in Paris shortly after Napoleon's abdication in April.

[8] Constant's decision has been attributed to his lack of alternatives and to Napoleon's charisma; see Dennis Wood, *Benjamin Constant: A Biography* (London and New York: Routledge, 1993), 214, and Paul Bastid, *Benjamin Constant et sa doctrine*, vol. 1 (Paris: A. Colin, 1966), 282–92. The constitutional *Acte additionnel* was known colloquially as the Benjamine in honor of its drafter. It is worth noting that Napoleon (partly in a failed effort to gain British support) decreed a ban on the slave trade early in the Hundred Days; for the text of Napoleon's decree, see Pierre Branda and Thierry Lentz, *Napoléon, l'esclavage, et les colonies* (Paris: Fayard, 2006), 345.

[9] Guizot, for instance, who was later to support aggressive policies of expansion in Algeria, in 1828 deplored what he described as fanciful and pointless military adventures; see Pitts, *A Turn to Empire*, 166–67. On liberal political thought under the Bourbon Restoration, see Cheryl Welch, *Liberty and Utility: The French Ideologues and the Transformation of Liberalism* (New York: Columbia University Press, 1984), chap. 6; Pierre Rosanvallon, *Le moment Guizot* (Paris: Gallimard, 1985); *Histoire du libéralisme politique: de la crise de l'absolutisme à la constitution de 1875* (Paris: Hachette, 1985); and Laurence Jacobs, "'Le Moment Libéral': The Distinctive Character of Restoration Liberalism," *Historical Journal*, 31 (2) (June 1988), 479–91.

the liberal opposition were especially vocal critics of conquest and militarism. But it would not be long before the Emperor's exploits, especially in Egypt, were remembered with nostalgia by a population weary of the polarizations of left–right politics. Conquests in "barbarous" lands seemed to many to offer an escape from those endless battles. When the liberals came to power in the 1830 July Revolution, just weeks after the assault on the city of Algiers that laid the foundations of France's North African Empire, many quickly concluded that France should assume its rightful status among the great powers and that this status would require colonial possessions. The July Monarchy's decision to erect the colossal Luxor obelisk at the center of the Place de la Concorde, thereby placing a unifying marker of French glory and superiority vis-à-vis the Orient at the former epicenter of revolutionary violence, represents a striking example of this phenomenon.[10] Constant, although he himself was sometimes tempted by the language of civilization and barbarism, consistently and eloquently opposed the national temptation to conquest and empire.

Against the spirit of conquest, Constant's pamphlet proposed a liberal counternarrative of post-Revolutionary France, a redemptive story according to which the nation might purge itself of its Napoleonic heritage and declare itself for peaceful, restrained, commercial relations with its neighbors and the globe. The essay offers what at times seems a naïve portrait of commerce as antithetical to war: commerce "rests upon the good understanding of nations with each other, it can be sustained only by justice; it is founded upon equality; it thrives in peace."[11] In making the case that commerce might make possible a new sort of mutuality among states, this essay, like so much of Constant's work, shows the mark of his Scottish enlightenment education. But eighteenth-century Scots like Hume and Smith had been clear-eyed about the dangers of the misalliance of commerce and war that Hume termed "jealousy of trade."[12]

---

[10] See Todd Porterfield's superb account of this episode in *The Allure of Empire: Art in the Service of French Imperialism, 1798–1836* (Princeton: Princeton University Press, 1998), 13–41.

[11] *SCU*, 65.

[12] See David Hume, "Of the Jealousy of Trade" (ca. 1759), in *Essays Moral, Political and Literary* (Indianapolis: Liberty Fund, 1985), 327–31; Adam Smith, *An Inquiry into the Nature and Causes of the Wealth of Nations* (Indianapolis: Liberty Fund,

They fully recognized the complicity of commercial motives in recent wars such as the Seven Years' War. They sought, rather, to show that commerce *need* not provoke wars of expansion and rivalry and that commercial nations could benefit by adopting a politics of mutual encouragement rather than militarized competition.

Constant, with his penchant for making moral arguments in historical terms, often put the case more deterministically, suggesting simply that commerce would "necessarily" replace war and that international commercial ties would make patriotism irrelevant and violence obsolete, unless men hungry for power disrupted this natural course of events.[13] The essay thus seems to ignore the role of commerce in sparking modern wars and imperial violence. But it also tells a more complicated story, for in insisting that the peaceful commercial spirit was a fragile achievement and in detailing the ways that modern governments co-opted their citizens for violent projects of expansion, Constant showed precisely that the spirit of conquest was far from obsolete. The essay suggests that modern self-interest may be seen to have moral value and moral purpose, but also that this purpose is threatened by other tendencies of the age and, indeed, of darker possibilities latent in self-interest itself. Much of the power of the essay comes from its persistent intimations that a moral direction to history can be perceived but that modern citizens must be prepared to struggle on its behalf.

Stephen Holmes has wonderfully illuminated the paradoxical argument that lies at the heart of *De l'esprit de conquête et de l'usurpation*. The work at once declares Napoleon to be utterly anachronistic, hostile to the spirit of the modern, commercial age and also reveals him to be "perversely in step with the disorienting, rootless, and contingency-conscious character of modern times."[14] Holmes shows the ways in which the essay complicates

---

1976), IV.vii.c.85; and Istvan Hont, *Jealousy of Trade* (Cambridge, MA: Harvard University Press, 2005), esp. 72–76.

[13] "The condition of modern nations thus prevents them from being bellicose by nature"; *SCU*, 54.

[14] Stephen Holmes, "Liberal Uses of Bourbon Legitimism," *Journal of the History of Ideas*, 43 (2) (April–June 1982), 229–48, at 235. Holmes's article brilliantly makes sense of the puzzling legitimist language of much of the section on usurpation, arguing that Constant uses legitimist claims in much the same way that he elsewhere uses ancient society: as devices of criticism against malign political projects

and ultimately undermines what sometimes appears to be its "simpleminded providentialism": the view that anachronistic political forms are simply impossible. If Constant was tempted by the thought that expansionist wars were inappropriate to an age of commerce, when peaceful trade afforded modern societies a more efficient way of "possessing what is desired," he also perceived the congruence between Napoleon's political strategies and the yearnings of post-revolutionary, commercial France.[15] By placing the discussion of conquest at the beginning of the pamphlet, Constant foregrounds imperial expansion as one of modern government's primary techniques for simultaneously mobilizing and dominating the public. Whereas part II of *De l'esprit de conquête et de l'usurpation*, on usurpation, addresses France's singular revolutionary and post-revolutionary history, the section on conquest is written in much more general terms, predicting dire consequences for *any* government that pursues an agenda of conquest in the modern age.

Conquest can stimulate public enthusiasm, but because modern peoples prefer peace and privacy to glory and can see that militarism is not in their interest, modern governments must peddle "sophistries" to sell their projects of conquest. So rulers will "talk of national independence, of national honour, of the rounding off of frontiers, of commercial interests, of precautions dictated by foresight, and what next? The vocabulary of hypocrisy and injustice is inexhaustible."[16] Public discourse and judgment are corrupted by this proliferation of cant and deception, as the government works to "banish logic" and "suffocate [the people's] humanity." Constant perceptively adds that the public realm and ultimately private morals are debased whether or not the people are actually deceived by the government's rhetoric, for when they see lies rewarded with success, they learn contempt for the truth.[17] And the military culture

[whether Bonapartist or Jacobin], but without any nostalgia or aspiration to resurrect these outmoded regimes.

[15] *SCU*, 53.

[16] Ibid., 64–65. Constant notes the novelty of the French Revolutionary pretext of "freeing peoples from the yoke of their governments" and cites Machiavelli for the thought that "the worst of all conquests is the hypocritical one."

[17] Holmes remarks on the proximity of hypocrisy and self-delusion: a sincere rejection of the tyrant in private alongside a cynical acceptance of the regime in public is, he argues, following Constant, both politically useless and ultimately unstable; Holmes, "Liberal Uses of Bourbon Legitimism," 245–46.

spawned by the conquests – a culture of obedience, uniformity, and impatience with difference – oppresses and further abases the people.

The dynamic is most spectacularly bad, as Constant argues in the usurpation section, when the ruler is a new man who aspires to despotic power but has no basis of legitimacy in either tradition or genuine public consent. The pamphlet portrays a vicious circle, in which the aspiring despot undertakes spectacular feats of conquest in order to command the attention of the public and then feels compelled to continue the performance because his insecure position means that he needs acclamation by the public in order to entrench his rule. The usurper, with no mandate independent of popular acclaim, requires the simulacrum of a public spirit. He needs visible popular support without the independence of mind that results from the free flow of ideas in a genuine public opinion. Constant explains Napoleon's Egyptian expedition as the result of his recognition that it was only by staging a military spectacle at the fringes of the modern world that he could rise to preeminence in a modern nation, even one as unstable as Revolutionary France. It is striking that Constant lapses into the language of barbarism as he tries to explain how Napoleon could have triumphed in France. Making rather uncritical use of a conventional dichotomy between civilized Europe and the "barbarism and ignorance" beyond, Constant argues that Napoleon saw that he would have to "leave the paths of civilization" to "lay the foundations of his preeminence." He then "worked to make Europe go backward." Arguing that domination by one man is nearly impossible in enlightened societies, Constant charges imperial expansion – which he portrays as diluting civilization with barbarian influences – with the destruction of moderate and relatively egalitarian politics in the metropole: referring to the Roman precedent, he writes, "it was almost always barbarian legions that created emperors."[18]

Constant betrays, throughout the work, an unresolved ambivalence about the French public and its relation to its former emperor. Were the French simply the victims of a tyrant, or were they complicit in his rule? The preface to the first edition, published before Napoleon's abdication, excuses the apparent "unanimity that so astonishes and offends the rest of Europe" as in fact "simply the

---

[18] *SCU*, 99–100.

effect of the terror experienced by the French people." But by the third edition, published just after Napoleon's fall, Constant admits "a degree of impatience against the nation that bore his yoke" and that acted "not only against her own interest," but against her natural sense of honor and propriety.[19] This simultaneous sense of alienation from the nation and desire to speak on behalf of its true self produces instabilities in the work, though it also contributes powerfully to the essay's tone of critical urgency. As he would do in the 1820s in the case of slavery, Constant offers in this essay an idealized portrait of the modern public, an image that he recognizes is in perpetual danger of betrayal by that public's actual opinion. Constant both argues that conquest is alien to the spirit of modern nations and demonstrates how prone such nations are to succumb to the lies and blandishments of expansionist despots.[20] Similarly, he would later maintain that modern societies have decisively and irrevocably rejected slavery while also insisting that the slave trade was able to continue only because the French public condoned it. In both cases, Constant set out to show that the movement of history is on the side of justice and equality; but also that these are fragile achievements, perpetually threatened by the machinations of the powerful and the venality of so many ordinary people.

Constant's final remarks on French imperial ambitions came in June 1830, a few months before his death. Although he was critical of the Bourbon regime's effort to prop itself up by a spectacular conquest of Algiers, he also claimed, perhaps in his own bid to appeal to public opinion, to "applaud the ruin of a nest of pirates, if we have the courage to carry it off, rather than respecting the character of sovereignty in a barbarian."[21] It is difficult to judge whether Constant might have maintained his resolute opposition to foreign conquest as expressed in 1814, had he remained alive to witness the feverish expansion of French power in Algeria over the next

---

[19] Ibid., 45, 47.
[20] Indeed, he notes, "[b]y a curious paradox, the more pacific the popular spirit, the easier would be the initial success of a state that sets itself to struggle against it"; *SCU*, 70.
[21] "Alger et les élections," in Constant, *Positions de combat à la veille de juillet 1830: articles publiés dans le Temps, 1829–1830*, ed. Ephraïm Harpaz (Paris: Champion, 1989), 191–92. See Pitts, *A Turn to Empire*, for further discussion of this episode. Unless otherwise indicated, all translations from the French are my own.

two decades. His liberal heirs were split on the question, with the majority, including Tocqueville most prominently, enthusiastically backing the conquest. But rare voices of opposition, such as the left-ist deputy Amédée Desjobert, faithfully reiterated Constant's key arguments, for instance about the ways colonial ambition corrupted public discourse with specious appeals to national honor.[22] And the first major Algerian contribution to French debates over the con-quest, Hamdan Khodja's searingly critical *Miroir*, published in Paris in 1833, paid tribute to Constant in an epigraph on the title page.[23] If such gestures were sadly futile in the France of the July Monarchy, when liberals, finally in power, lived up to few of the hopes they inspired while in opposition, Constant's analysis remained among the most powerful indictments available of the peculiarly dangerous interplay between populist politics and imperial adventurism.

COLONIAL SLAVERY IN CONSTANT'S THOUGHT

Constant's interventions in the Chamber of Deputies over the course of the 1820s convey what we might call the post-revolutionary cast of his anti-slavery politics. He was cautious and gradualist, seemingly concerned to avoid the counterproductive polarizations and rever-sals that had beset revolutionary politics. Abolitionist opinion in late eighteenth-century France lagged well behind that in Britain and relied heavily on the importation and translation of British tracts.[24] A few pre-revolutionary radicals such as the Marquis de Condorcet,

---

[22] See, e.g., Amédée Desjobert, *La Question d'Alger: politique, colonisation, com-merce* (Paris: Crapelet, 1837), 6–8; and *L'Algérie en 1846* (Paris: Guillaumin, 1846).

[23] Hamdan Khodja, *Aperçu historique et statistique sur la Régence d'Alger, inti-tulé en Arabe le Miroir* (Paris: Impr. De Goetschy fils, 1833); a modern edition is *Le Miroir*, ed. Abdelkader Djeghloul (Paris: Sindbad/Actes Sud, 1985). The pas-sage, from Constant's *De la religion considérée dans sa source, ses formes et ses développements* (vol. 1 [Paris: A Leroux et C. Chantpie, 1826], xxxvi) reads, "When it is egoism that overturns tyranny, it can only share the tyrants' plunder." The suggestion was that French pretensions to liberate Algeria from Ottoman despo-tism were empty; that in Algeria French liberalism had taken the form of egoism rather than a commitment to human equality and liberty.

[24] One influential import was Thomas Clarkson's *Essai sur les désavantages poli-tiques de la traite des nègres*... (Neufchâtel: [s.n.], 1789). See Serge Daget, "A Model of the French Abolitionist Movement and Its Variations," in *Anti-Slavery, Religion, and Reform: Essays in Memory of Roger Anstey*, ed. Christine Bolt and Seymour Drescher (Folkstone, Kent: Dawson, 1980).

Denis Diderot, and the Abbé Raynal offered (often anonymously) denunciations of slavery as a violation of natural right, but their proposed reforms were often deferential to the planter elite and contemptuous toward the slaves they wanted freed.[25] And as British abolitionism was becoming a mass movement beginning in the 1790s, French anti-slavery activity remained restricted to a small elite.[26] In 1794, the revolutionary Convention declared the emancipation of slaves in all French colonies, but it did so not so much as a natural extension of its egalitarian logic, but rather only when its hand was forced by the slave rebellion in Saint-Domingue, France's most important West Indian colony.[27]

When Napoleon restored slavery and the slave trade in 1802 (the same year Constant was expelled from the Tribunate and retired to the political wilderness), his government aggressively suppressed abolitionist publications and French anti-slavery opinion retreated into near invisibility.[28] Abolitionism's association in the public mind with the British contributed to the unpopularity of the cause

---

[25] See, e.g., Raynal's *Histoire philosophique et politique des établissements et du commerce des Européens dans les deux Indes* (Neufchâtel et Genève: Libraires associés, 1783–84); one of Diderot's anonymous contributions on slavery is included in Diderot, *Political Writings*, ed. John Hope Mason and Robert Wokler (Cambridge: Cambridge University Press, 1992), 185–88. Condorcet's anonymous *Réflexions sur l'esclavage, par M. Schwartz* (Neufchâtel: Société Typographique, 1781), declaring the "stupidity" of "les Nègres" (though blaming this on the masters), argued that freed slaves, "accustomed to obey nothing but force and caprice," could not be trusted to abide by the same laws as whites but instead would "have to be subjected to a severe discipline, regulated by law" (pp. 33, 36).

[26] See Edward Derbyshire Seeber, *Anti-Slavery Opinion in France during the Second Half of the Eighteenth Century* (Baltimore: Johns Hopkins Press, 1937); Lawrence C. Jennings, *French Anti-Slavery: The Movement for the Abolition of Slavery in France, 1802–1848* (Cambridge: Cambridge University Press, 2000); and Nelly Schmidt, *Abolitionnistes de l'esclavage et réformateurs des colonies, 1820–1851* (Paris: Éditions Karthala, 2000); Serge Daget, "L'Abolition de la Traite des Noirs en France de 1814 à 1831," *Cahiers d'études africaines*, 41 (1971), 14–58; David Geggus, "Haiti and the Abolitionists: Opinion, Propaganda, and International Politics in Britain and France, 1804–1816," in *Abolition and Its Aftermath*, ed. David Richardson (London: Frank Cass, 1985); Seymour Drescher, "Two Variants of Anti-Slavery: Religious Organization and Social Mobilization in Britain and France, 1780–1870," in *Anti-Slavery, Religion and Reform*.

[27] See Laurent Dubois, *A Colony of Citizens: Revolution and Slave Emancipation in the French Caribbean, 1787–1804* (Chapel Hill: University of North Carolina Press, 2004).

[28] See *1802: Rétablissement de l'esclavage dans les colonies françaises*, ed. Yves Bénot and Marcel Dorigny (Paris: Maisonneuve et Larose, 2003). The indefatigable

during this time of war and heightened anti-British sentiment. Even after Napoleon's fall, the restored Bourbons, despite having agreed to the ban on the slave trade imposed by the Treaty of Versailles, discouraged abolitionist opinion and surreptitiously supported the trade.[29] In this climate, so hostile to the formation of an abolitionist movement, Protestants – Swiss Protestants in particular – were among the most active conduits of anti-slavery arguments into France. Huguenot international networks, especially in finance and publishing, had long facilitated the movement of radical and abolitionist ideas and tracts, as the Neufchâtel imprint of many abolitionist publications suggests.[30]

Germaine de Staël, and the Coppet group in particular, long stood at the center of French and Swiss anti-slavery activity: indeed, in that context Constant might be seen as something of a latecomer to active abolitionism. De Staël's father, Jacques Necker, had begun to criticize slavery and the racism on which it was based in 1784; in 1789, he argued before the newly convened Estates General that they should not only abolish the hated corvée but consider the "unhappy people who are calmly made an object of traffic."[31] De Staël herself had first denounced slavery and the slave trade in several pieces of sentimentalist fiction written in her late teens, around 1786.[32]

revolutionary Abbé Grégoire was one of the few who continued to press the abolitionist cause (and did so through the 1820s); he evaded the censors by inserting his abolitionist arguments into a work apparently of literary scholarship; see Grégoire, *De la littérature des nègres ou Recherches sur leurs facultés intellectuelles, leurs qualités morales* (Paris: Maradan, 1808), and Geggus, "Haiti and the Abolitionists," 117; also see Ruth Necheles, *The Abbé Grégoire, 1787–1831: The Odyssey of an Egalitarian* (Westport: Greenwood, 1971).

[29] See David Brion Davis, *The Problem of Slavery in the Age of Revolution, 1770–1823* (Ithaca: Cornell University Press, 1975), 68, who notes that the precedent of Napoleon's 1815 decree abolishing the French slave trade forced the Bourbon government to accede to English demands to abolish the trade, but that the Bourbons "neglected to publish the new law, which provided for no enforcement and which failed to make slave trading a crime" (p. 68).

[30] See the excellent article by Thomas David, "Le rôle de la Suisse dans le movement abolitionniste français (vers 1760–1840)," in *Abolir l'esclavage. Un réformisme à l'épreuve (France, Suisse, Portugal, XVIII-XIXe siècle)*, ed. Olivier Pétré-Grenouilleau (Rennes: Presses Universitaires de Rennes, 2008).

[31] See Alfred Berchtold, "Sismondi et le Groupe de Coppet face à l'esclavage et au colonialisme," in *Sismondi Européen: Actes du Colloque international tenu à Genève les 14 et 15 septembre 1973* (Geneva: Slatkine, 1976), 169–98, at 171.

[32] These were published in a volume titled *Zulma, et trois nouvelles* (London: Colburn, 1813); they are available in Germaine de Staël, *Œuvres de jeunesse,*

Her short story *Mirza*, narrated by a European man visiting Senegal, includes poetic denunciations of slavery by the passionate and virtuous Wolof woman Mirza and describes experiments in plantation agriculture in Africa as a means of supplanting the trade.[33] De Staël's early letters make repeated reference to slavery and to the events of Saint-Domingue,[34] and her story *Histoire de Pauline* was set in Saint-Domingue, amid the avidity and depravity of the planter class. She was by no means an anti-imperialist; on the contrary, she was keen to keep the colonies in the possession of the French. She tried to intercede with Napoleon on behalf of an *homme de couleur*, Magloire Pélage, who had been instrumental in defending Guadeloupe against the British.[35] De Staël was also quick to press the abolitionist cause on Napoleon's defeat, publishing several essays in 1814 in an effort to persuade the negotiators of the Treaty of Paris to ban the trade as a condition of the peace. The political economist Sismondi, another Swiss Protestant and a close friend of de Staël

ed. Simone Balayé and John Isbell (Paris: Desjonquères, 1997). De Staël visited London in 1813, when she wrote the Wilberforce preface mentioned later. A translation of *Mirza* appears in *Translating Slavery: Gender and Race in French Women's Writings, 1783–1823*, ed. Doris Y. Kadish and Françoise Massardier-Kenney (Kent: Kent State University Press, 1994), 146–59.

[33] The story tells of the African Ximeo's love for and then abandonment of Mirza, a member of the rival "Jolof" tribe; his capture in battle by the Jolofs and his sale to a European slave trader; the faithful Mirza's offer to be enslaved in his place; and the release of both of them by the European governor, moved by her loving self-sacrifice. De Staël's descendant, the Comtesse Jean de Pange, speculated that Mirza – not beautiful but striking, with "enchanting eyes" and an "animated countenance" (p. 150) – was a stand-in for de Staël herself. See "Madame de Staël et les nègres," *Revue de France*, 5 (1934), 425–43. De Staël chose names recalling other antislavery texts, such as Saint-Lambert's *Ziméo* of 1769 and Olympe de Gouges's *L'esclavage des noirs ou l'heureux naufrage* of 1789 (in which a central character is Mirza).

[34] In a letter of 1786, she wrote, "What glory for a century the abolition of slavery would be!" She went on, "but it's horrible to admit: the negroes [nègres] are lazy when they are free, and that is the Europeans' great excuse," but then noted the "filial piety" that led young Africans to put themselves in the place of captured parents, so that the "barbarous European merchants" gained two healthy young men in place of an infirm elderly one, "profiting from the virtues of these same negroes whom they believe, with reason, to be of another nature than their own"; *Lettres de Jeunesse*, in *Correspondance Generale*, ed. B. W. Jasinski, t.1 (Paris: Pauvert, 1962), 141.

[35] See de Staël's letter to her father, quoted by Pange (p. 437). Pélage was deported in 1802 along with many other mixed-race officers and tried as an "enemy of the republic" but eventually freed after a long trial; see Dubois, *Colony of Citizens*.

and Constant, also wrote an antitrade essay at this moment, one that went into multiple editions over a few months.[36] Both de Staël and Sismondi were in contact during this period with leading British abolitionists such as William Wilberforce and Zachary Macaulay. The appearance of de Staël's and Sismondi's pamphlets as soon as Napoleon's censorship regime lost its power, and their insistence on this issue as central to the postwar treaty negotiations, suggests the importance of the issue to them. Constant, in contrast, seems not to have published on the trade until 1819.

De Staël died in 1817, but her son Auguste became the linchpin of the abolition committee of the Société de la Morale Chrétienne, the most active French abolitionist group of the early 1820s, and one with a strong Protestant presence. Constant, though a member of the society, and involved in its activities on behalf of the Greek independence movement, did not serve on its slave trade committee.[37] This group's focus on the slave trade, and its gradualist approach toward emancipation itself – its belief in the need to educate slaves before they could be liberated – typified the cautiousness of French abolitionism under the Restoration. The Duc de Broglie, the husband of de Staël's (and probably Constant's) daughter Albertine, was the foremost abolitionist of the Chamber of Peers. Also active during the 1810s and 1820s were the liberal political economists and journalists Charles Comte and Charles Dunoyer, who regarded Constant as an important influence on their thought, but who added arguments from political economy, such as the greater efficiency of free labor, to the case against slavery.[38]

---

[36] De Staël published two short essays. The first was an influential preface to a work by William Wilberforce (*Lettre à Son Excellence Monseigneur le prince de Talleyrand Périgord... au sujet de la traite des nègres* [London: Imprimerie de Schulze & Dean; Paris: Le Normand, 1814]). De Staël's second piece was a letter to the European sovereigns convening to conclude the Treaty of Paris, calling on them to include the abolition of the trade in the treaty. The Wilberforce preface was published in de Staël, *Œuvres complètes*, vol. 17, ed. Auguste de Staël (Paris: Treuttel et Würtz, 1820–21). Both appear in translation in *Translating Slavery*, 157–62. Sismondi's longer essay, *De l'Intérêt de la France à l'égard de la traite des nègres*, went through three editions in Geneva and Paris in 1814.

[37] See Jennings, *French Anti-Slavery*, 13–14, for a list of the committee's members; he notes that after Auguste de Staël's death in 1827, the society sharply reduced its abolitionist activities.

[38] On Comte and Dunoyer's abolitionism, see David M. Hart, *The Radical Liberalism of Charles Comte and Charles Dunoyer* (2003). This revised version

If Constant lagged behind his abolitionist friends in the first years of the Bourbon Restoration, he quickly became a leading spokesman for the movement in the Chamber of Deputies, though, in keeping with the movement's tenor in the 1820s, he remained nearly silent about the abolition of slavery itself. Constant instead focused his attention on two causes: the abolition of the slave trade, and the legal rights of free people of color [gens de couleur] in the colonies.[39] These were policies on which the country was in principle in agreement, and Constant was careful to appeal to longstanding French law and royal policy in making his case for each. As he noted, the French government had agreed to the abolition of the slave trade in the Treaty of Paris negotiations of 1815, though the trade continued with the knowledge and even encouragement of the French state.[40] And he repeatedly asserted that the legal equality of gens de couleur in the colonies had been recognized by the colonial laws promulgated by Louis XIII and Louis XIV.[41] Yet in the context of Restoration

of an unpublished Cambridge University Ph.D. dissertation is available at http://homepage.mac.com/dmhart/ComteDunoyer/index.html. On the ambivalent implications of early nineteenth-century political economy for abolitionism, see Seymour Drescher, The Mighty Experiment (Oxford: Oxford University Press, 2002), especially the treatment of Jean-Baptiste Say in chapter 4.

[39] Laurent Dubois notes that the English expression "people [or persons] of colour" was in use by some members of that group in the eighteenth century and that the expression was the favored term for nonwhites during the revolutionary period of emancipation; planters tended to favor racial classifications such as mulâtre and câpresse. See Dubois, Avengers of the New World, 6; and A Colony of Citizens, 252–66.

[40] The restored Bourbon government, in the Second Treaty of Paris of November 1815, had committed to the eventual abolition (in Constant's words) of a "traffic as odious in itself as contrary to the laws of religion and nature"; in Constant, "De la traite des nègres au Sénégal," La Minerve Française (August, 21, 1819), VII.113–24; in Recueil d'articles: le Mercure, lLa Minerve et la Renommée, vol. 2, ed. Éphraïm Harpaz (Geneva: Droz, 1972), 915–26, at 919. But Talleyrand, France's negotiator, did manage to obtain a five-year reprieve during which to build up the slave populations in French colonies. See Paul Michael Kielstra, The Politics of Slave Trade Suppression in Britain and France, 1814–48: Diplomacy, Morality, and Economics (London: St. Martin's Press, 2000), 22–25. It has been estimated that more than seventy-seven thousand slaves were secretly shipped to the French Caribbean between 1814 and 1831; see David Eltis, Economic Growth and the Ending of the Transatlantic Slave Trade (New York: Oxford University Press, 1987), 246.

[41] Louis XIV's Code noir of 1685 declared that masters who had reached their majority were free to emancipate their slaves at will and that freed slaves were to be considered native subjects of the kingdom, enjoying "the same rights, privileges

politics, as the government grew increasingly reactionary and the public remained supportive of or indifferent to the trade, even these causes were the preserve of radicals. Constant's speeches on the trade were regularly subjected to ridicule and heckling by the right wing of the Chamber.[42] His efforts to frame his arguments as appeals to longstanding tradition and a broad moral consensus seem calculated to rise above such partisanship.

One of Constant's first public statements on the slave trade came in August 1819, in an article in his weekly newspaper, *La Minerve française*, in which he summarized the findings of a leading British abolitionist group, the African Institution.[43] The article conveyed some of the main concerns of the British abolitionist movement at that moment: to promote the development of agriculture and "civilizational advancement" in Africa, and to encourage free and mutually beneficial commerce between Africa and Europe. Constant reported that both the French possessions in Senegal and the independent state of Sierra Leone had developed quickly during the brief time that the slave trade was effectively suppressed. Sierra Leone, moreover, proved the capacity of postemancipation societies to govern themselves effectively. Sierra Leone's short history proves how "easy and rapid" the process of civilization could be in the absence of the devastations of the trade. The colony's population, Constant writes, "presents all levels of moral faculty; from the almost brutish state of the recently freed captive to the perfected state of the businessman, farmer, and artist." Freed slaves were eagerly educating

and immunities as persons born free" (art. 55–59); see *L'esclavage à la française: le Code Noir (1685 et 1724)*, ed. Robert Chesnais (Paris: Nautilus, 2005). As Louis Sala-Molins notes, this formal legal equality of black, mixed-race, and white subjects was never recognized by colonial planters and was quickly compromised by discriminatory legislation; Sala-Molins, *Le Code noir ou le calvaire de Canaan* (Paris: Presses Universitaires de France, 1987), 196–201. Also see Laurent Dubois, *A Colony of Citizens*, 73–74.

[42] See, e.g., his speech of July 31, 1822, *Discours*, II, 179–80.

[43] The article summarized the "Thirteenth Report of the Directors of the African Institution, read 24th March 1819" (London, 1819); see Constant, "De la traite des nègres au Sénégal," *La Minerve Française* (August, 21, 1819), VII, 113–24; in *Recueil d'articles: le Mercure, la Minerve et la Renommée*, vol. 2, ed. Éphraïm Harpaz (Geneva: Droz, 1972), 915–26. The African Institution was founded in London in 1807 by antislavery leaders including Thomas Clarkson, William Wilberforce, and Granville Sharp; see the *Report of the Committee of the African Institution* (London: William Phillips, 1807), 10.

themselves, and men "snatched from the chains of the slave markets have been given judicial functions... which they fulfill with intelligence and integrity."[44] These claims anticipate Constant's later encouraging remarks about the successes of independent Haiti. Given the widespread hostility to emancipation that followed the violence of the Haitian rebellion, and the resurgence of French racism in response to that rebellion, the symbolic and ideological significance of these arguments should not be underestimated.

Constant's subsequent speeches in the Chamber of Deputies on the "atrocious crime" of the slave trade tied a critique of the trade to a broader attack on the Restoration regime's contempt for the rule of law.[45] He argued that the evils of the trade had recently increased, aggravated by the seemingly deliberate ineffectiveness of French legislation against it. The government had declared the slave trade "infamous," but its laws remained "scandalously indulgent": in contrast to harsh British and Dutch penalties, the French merely confiscated the slaves they captured, which did nothing to deter a business in which profits were so outlandishly great.[46] Traders now simply crammed their human cargo into even smaller ships, built to evade patrols, and more readily threw their victims overboard, now to evade discovery as well as rid themselves of the sick. And the government could not even regulate the trade and try to improve the lot of its victims, now that it was ostensibly committed to abolition.[47] Constant's parliamentary speeches also used the issue of the trade to criticize Restoration politics more generally, especially the government's hypocrisy and its surreptitious violation of its own laws out of a desire for profit. He also linked the issue to one of his most cherished causes of the time, freedom of the press, protesting that the government's allies were stifling abolitionist opinion.[48]

---

[44] "De la traite des nègres au Sénégal," *Recueil d'articles*, 919.
[45] Constant's major speeches on the trade occurred on June 27, 1821 (*Discours*, I, 548–60); April 5, 1822 (II, 137–44); July 31, 1822 (II, 179–81); and March 13, 1827 (II, 569–73); phrase quoted at I, 549. He also called the trade "the most abominable traffic that has ever dishonored the human race" (II, 290).
[46] *Discours*, I, 550–51. Constant accused the regime of quietly giving the slaves they captured to colonial governments, rather than freeing them, as the treaties and royal decrees demanded (*Discours*, I, 560).
[47] See, e.g., speech of April 5, 1822, *Discours*, II, 139–41.
[48] *Discours*, I, 471.

Constant's only major theoretical work to address modern slavery, the *Commentaire sur l'ouvrage de Filangieri*, extended his parliamentary case in several important ways.[49] By placing a chapter on the slave trade so prominently in a major restatement of his political theory and by linking the current fight against the trade to the campaign of an Enlightenment reformer of an earlier generation, Constant made clear that slavery was a matter of central concern to post-revolutionary politics. And he explicitly argued here, as he did in none of his other major statements on slavery, that it was racism that made possible such an egregious violation of modern morality. He maintained that although the ancients had possessed all the necessary rudiments for an adequate moral system, by allowing slavery to become entrenched in their society, they had become habituated to tolerating the worst violations of moral principle. Modern consciences rebelled at practices to which the ancients had become inured, and this fact marked a decisive advance. As I argue later, this contrast was one Constant drew frequently. But the *Commentaire* is remarkable, nearly unique, among Constant's writings in noting that the moderns' moral advance was severely marred by the racism that led modern Europeans to tolerate the enslavement of "*les nègres*," whom "some people unfortunately consider... not part of the human race." Such people would never deign to steal, but through racist "sophisms" they permitted themselves to rob other human beings of their labor and their very persons.[50]

Constant, always adept at diagnosing and anatomatizing self-delusion, perceived that the abolitionists' political strategy must respond to the peculiar nature of the evil. To set out to prove, as Filangieri and other early opponents of the trade had done, that

---

[49] This book was a substantial work of political theory for which the eighteenth-century Neapolitan of the title served more as provocation than as the real object of Constant's attention. Part I of the *Commentaire* was published in 1822; the chapter on the slave trade is placed prominently at the beginning of the work's second part, published separately in 1824: *Commentaire sur l'ouvrage de Filangieri* (Paris: P. Dufart, 1822–24).

[50] *Commentaire*, 1822–24, part II, 12. It is worth noting Constant's use of the term "nègre" at a time when, according to Serge Daget, abolitionists had almost universally forsworn that term in favor of "noir." See Daget, "Les mots esclave, nègre, noir, et les jugements de valeur sur la traite négrière dans la littérature abolitionniste française de 1770 à 1845," *Revue française d'histoire d'outre-mer*, 60 (1973), 511–48. Constant seems to use the terms interchangeably during the 1820s.

slavery is a violation of rights was at once no longer necessary and yet not sufficient. Contemporary reformers must instead move public opinion, must "produce [a] moral conviction" in the evil of slavery by dwelling on its grim facts and "incredible atrocities." This argument accounts for Constant's decision to detail the horrors of the trade in his parliamentary speeches, as in his account of the slaves on the ship *Rôdeur* in 1819 who, after being blinded by a contagion that rampaged through their fetid quarters, were thrown overboard to drown.[51] Constant rejected the common strategy of justifying or excusing the evils of the trade with reference to the violence committed by the rebel slaves of "Saint-Domingue" (by this time independent Haiti). "Yes, the Negroes who burst their chains were ferocious; they punished horrific cruelties with horrific cruelties. But who was to blame? Did they go to coasts inhabited by Europeans to bring flames and massacre?"[52] Constant's sympathetic reading of the actions of the Saint-Domingue rebels places him, again, in the radical wing of opinion in France, where many used the violence of that rebellion to justify the harshest reprisals, blanket denials of blacks as responsible political agents, and indeed the perpetuation of slavery.

The second colonial cause Constant took up in the Chamber was that of the civil rights of the colonial *gens de couleur*. As he had with the slave trade, Constant used the legislature's power of the purse to introduce political debate over conditions in the colonies, by refusing to approve allocations of funds for the colonies until the government had responded to criticism.[53] He countered the government's threat that public debate over the colonies would compromise peace and stability. On the contrary, "during ten years that our voice has been stifled, and they have persisted in the path of severity and arbitrary rule, the colonies have not made, it seems to me, any progress toward

---

[51] Speech of June 27, 1821, in *Discours*, I, 557–58. Always alert to the problem of censorship, Constant noted that the medical journal in which the story had first appeared had apparently published a second, "mutilated," edition, perhaps "to efface the traces of an atrocious crime?"

[52] *Commentaire*, 1822–24, Part II, 15–16.

[53] In December 1820, for instance, when the French Cabinet prevented a petition against the trade from being debated in the Chamber, Constant and General Foy used a discussion of the marine budget to attack the trade; see Kielstra, *Politics of Slave Trade Suppression*, 104.

tranquility."[54] As with the trade, in taking up this issue, Constant positioned himself as a moderate and a defender of French law, even as he occupied a radical place in the skewed spectrum of Restoration political opinion. Constant could thus advance the abolitionist cause – the cause of liberty and political and civil rights for blacks in the French colonies – without directly addressing what he considered the politically futile project of emancipation.

As he detailed in several speeches from 1824–26, a group of *hommes de couleur* from Martinique had been arrested, deported, and ultimately exiled to Senegal for circulating a French political pamphlet considered inflammatory by the island's paranoid and reactionary planter class. Constant pointed out that the pamphlet, which reprinted a speech by a member of the Chamber of Deputies, was perfectly legal in France. As Constant noted with outrage, the men had been denied any legal defense, any opportunity to confront their accusers, and any process of appeal. Illegally deported to France, where they should have been set free according to French law, they were held by the captain and sent on to Senegal, where many of them soon died.[55] Constant presented the case as evidence of a flagrant breach of French legal protections and constitutional principles, suggesting that such violations in the colonies presented merely a more extreme example of the authoritarianism of the Restoration regime. He called on the Chamber to pay reparations to those who had been so abused, and to follow Britain in granting equal civil and political rights to black freemen on grounds of both justice and prudence, "to reunite under the same laws the free population of these colonies, by interesting them all, without distinction of color or origin, in the maintenance of an equitable and impartial legislation."[56]

Constant's rhetorical position here, as on the slave trade, was self-consciously moderate, even conservative. As in the *Spirit of Conquest*, in his speeches on the *gens de couleur* Constant made use of almost floridly reactionary rhetoric – "rebellious subjects," "the threat of opposition to the royal will," "resist[ance] to the exercise of the royal prerogative" – for liberal ends.[57] Rather than calling

---

[54] *Discours*, II, 496.
[55] Three speeches on the "déportés de Martinique" are included in the *Discours*: June 16, 1824; January 8, 1825; and June 3, 1826.
[56] *Discours*, II, 495.
[57] Ibid., 292–93; also see *Discours*, II, 302–3.

for a full extension of metropolitan laws and rights to the colonies, as had been briefly the case during the Revolution, Constant more modestly proposed that the spirit of French law be respected in the colonies.[58] He recalled with praise efforts by Louis XIII and Louis XIV to begin to establish an "equitable system in the colonies."[59] Reversing the standard metropolitan trope of nonwhite colonial subjects as a constant threat of insurgency and violence, Constant portrayed the white *colons* as the true rebels. It was they, he said, who had declared that they would obey no new laws in the colonies and who were thus openly defying royal authority.[60] He accused the ministry, which had acceded to the *colons'* demands, of abandoning the most basic constitutional principles: first in flouting French law in the colonies and then in resisting parliamentary inquiry into colonial abuses. Constant respectfully but pointedly articulated the choice facing the king: whether to follow the course of wisdom and humanity and "return to the decrees of his predecessors [and] improve the fate of the *gens de couleur*," or to allow his government to continue abetting the lawlessness and insubordination of the *colons.* He thus suggested, indirectly but not subtly, that the colonies were evidence – perhaps advance warning – of the regime's authoritarian and anticonstitutional character.

Constant's speeches on Martinique, which call for full civil rights for the *gens de couleur* and political rights equal to whites' (i.e., with a property restriction), indicate his commitment to racial equality.[61] His hostility to racism is still more fully articulated in his critique of a fellow liberal, the political economist Charles Dunoyer, also an abolitionist. Dunoyer had lamented the misfortune of "inferior"

---

[58] "The article of the charter that provides a special regime for the colonies does not suggest that they will be protected by no legal regime at all"; "Sur l'administration des colonies," June 3, 1826, in *Discours,* II, 490; also see 497: "the colonies [must] finally be put under a regime conformable if not to the literal dispositions of the Charter, at least to its grounds [*bases*], that is to say to the rules of justice and the sentiments of humanity."

[59] *Discours,* II, 291.

[60] Ibid., II, 302. The king, he said, "knows that there exist in the colonies enemies of the blacks and of the men of color who have made every effort to destroy the ancient ordinances of our kings and put in place the most appalling system of inequity and cruelty."

[61] "In the English colonies, political rights are conferred on all those who, by their industry, their property, present sufficient guarantees; and under our ministers, the free people of color are deprived even of civil rights"; *Discours,* II, 495–96.

races and claimed that this inferiority did not license European subjugation of them, but he accepted racial difference as a scientific
fact, and a politically relevant one. Constant, without altogether
ruling out the possibility that science might some day learn something from the study of race, argued that great care must be taken
to keep the racial systems of "ingenious writers," in his derisive
phrase, entirely out of politics. He argued that colonialism had
thwarted the moral and intellectual progress of subjugated peoples of
all races, including African slaves, inhabitants of the Spanish New
World colonies, and Greeks under Ottoman domination. He saw
great promise in the short history of independent Haiti:

The blacks [noirs] of Haiti have become very reasonable legislators, quite
disciplined warriors, and statesmen as able and as polished as our diplo-
mats. They have placed themselves at the level of the most perfect races,
in terms not only of the necessary arts, but of social institutions. Their
constitution is better than most constitutions of Europe. Let us leave the
physiologists, then, to attend to the primitive differences that will be sur-
mounted sooner or later by the perfectibility with which the whole race
is gifted, and let us beware of arming politics with this new pretext for
inequality and oppression.[62]

Constant's attention to racism in this essay suggests that he very
specifically intended to include racial equality in his plea for equality
in the book's preface: "the most absolute equality of rights among
all individuals agglomerated into a national body must be, and soon
will be, in all civilized countries, the first condition of the existence
of all government."[63]

If the abolition of slavery itself was, in Constant's view, a quixotic
agenda in the immediate term, the abolition of the trade and the
entrenchment of civil rights and the rule of law in the colonies were
causes allied to abolition that could be framed as mainstream, even
if they were, at the moment, pressed only by a radical wing. Unlike
reformers of the eighteenth century, such as Diderot or Condorcet,
who called for the abolition of slavery with little hope of achieving

---

[62] "De M. Dunoyer et quelques-uns de ses ouvrages," in *Mélanges de littérature et de politique* (Paris: Pichon et Didier, 1829), 149–50. Constant's optimistic reading of the Haitian struggle for independence was unusual even among enemies of slavery; see Geggus, "Haiti and the Abolitionists," in *Abolition and Its Aftermath*, 130.
[63] "Préface," *Mélanges*, xiii–ix.

it and who, arguably, were making a broadly moral, as much as an immediately political, argument, Constant was engaged in a political process in which incomplete advances might be achieved, and he chose to press these.[64] This strategy might be seen as part of his post-revolutionary politics, in which the dramatic oppositions and purer moral positions of an earlier era gave way to pragmatism and caution. The result is that Constant's very few remarks on colonial slavery itself are strikingly timid; in the *Commentaire*, he concluded by saying that while slavery, like the trade, corrupted both master and slave, "the friends of humanity are resigned to see slavery continue"; and he allowed himself to hope that the abolition of the trade might at least "soften the slavery that we dare not abolish."[65] While he left no doubt, then, that he opposed slavery, he also said little against it. Paradoxically, it seems this was both because he believed the moral case had been won and because he found the political project of abolition, for the moment, unrealistic.

ANCIENT SLAVERY AND MODERN FREEDOM

We have seen that whatever his hesitations about agitating directly for abolition, Constant was deeply preoccupied with the evils of colonial slavery and the slave trade, and that by virtue of his connections with abolitionist circles, he was unusually well placed to understand slavery's presence and power in the life of the French Empire. Slavery is also a persistent theme in Constant's more theoretical political writings, as the antithesis of the liberal freedom he was concerned to elaborate and defend. Constant often used the term *slavery* to describe the most egregious forms of political subjection.[66] His comparisons between the ancient and modern worlds repeatedly invoke slavery as one of antiquity's most distinctive, and vicious, institutions. The triumph of equality and the gradual amelioration and ultimately eradication of slavery are the organizing principles of Constant's philosophy of history. Several decades before Tocqueville

---

[64] See Fontana's description of Constant as a "tractable political opponent" under the empire and restoration (*Post-Revolutionary Mind*, xii).

[65] *Commentaire*, 1822–24, part II, 19.

[66] On connections between antislavery and antidespotism arguments in the eighteenth century, see Sue Peabody, *"There Are No Slaves in France": The Political Culture of Race and Slavery in the Ancien Régime* (Oxford: Oxford University Press, 1996), chap. 6.

famously proposed that the progress of equality was the central phenomenon of European history over the last millennium, Constant declared the passion for equality the motive force of human history. Tocqueville was to describe the love of equality as a peculiarly modern sentiment and to hold it in some suspicion as a passion that can overpower, with disastrous consequences, people's love of liberty. Constant, in contrast, regarded it as a permanent feature of the human constitution, something "innate and indestructible."[67] He argued that equality is at once human beings' most fundamental desire – our most natural sentiment, our *"loi primitive"* – and the telos of humanity's historical development.[68] He sought to show that the laws of all societies, even the most despotic, implicitly recognize human equality and that even the most complete subjection cannot destroy our love of equality.[69]

This was a narrative that Constant tinkered with over the course of thirty years; his first sketch of a theory of progress was probably written in 1799, and his last published volume, the *Mélanges littéraires et politiques* of 1829, included several essays that continued to explore the idea that human progress is the gradual realization of equality.[70] In these essays, Constant's account of progress involves four "steps" toward equality: from theological slavery to civil slavery; then to feudalism; to hereditary nobility; and finally, after the French Revolution, to equality before the law.[71] He describes each stage as a successive triumph for the idea of equality. Whereas

---

[67] *Du moment actuel et de la destiné de l'espèce humaine, ou histoire abregée de l'égalité,* in *OCBC/Œuvres,* III, 1, 372. Although, like Tocqueville, Constant granted that people embrace equality more readily than they do political liberty, where Tocqueville depicted such a preference as a political malady, Constant saw it as natural and salutary. For equality is a deeply rooted human passion, he argued, while attachment to political liberty must be learned, and it comes only with the progress of civilization.

[68] *Du moment actuel,* 370.

[69] Constant distinguishes civil laws, which are "close to nature" and the "expression of universal needs", from political laws, which are the instruments of power, distant from nature. Political laws are used to entrench power, while civil laws always "consecrate" equality; though they are often temporarily powerless in the face of political laws, they preserve the sentiment of equality even in the midst of oppression ("Du moment actuel," 370–71).

[70] For several statements of this theory, see *Du moment actuel* and "Trois textes relatifs à la perfectibilité de l'espèce humaine," in *OCBC/Œuvres,* III, 1, 456–75. Also see "De la perfectibilité de l'espèce humaine" in *Mélanges.*

[71] The influence of the four-stage approach of the Scottish Enlightenment is apparent, though Constant's conception of the stages is very different from the Scots's

primitive theological slavery rested on the idea of a difference in nature between a priestly ruling caste and a subordinated populace, Roman civil slavery regarded slavery as the result of mere fortune and so, Constant argued, recognized the natural equality of masters and slaves. Although "undoubtedly horrible," it was "less humiliating" than the earlier form.[72] The advent of Christianity then introduced the idea of the "moral equality" of masters and slaves. Feudalism and later its abolition recognized further rights on the part of the subjected, and the gradual erosion of noble privileges was completed by the sudden introduction of legal equality during the Revolution.

Given this prominence of slavery in Constant's theoretical and historical writings, and his participation in abolitionist circles in France, it is striking that his theoretical works say so little about modern race slavery. Constant's belief that slavery corrupted ancient morality would seem to contain an implicit critique of New World slavery. But his narrative of the progressive eradication of forms of slavery in European history proceeds as though the revival of slavery in the New World had not occurred, or as though Europe's history could be read in isolation from the colonial slavery that was so central to European economies, and on which so many Europeans' livelihoods depended. Constant repeatedly referred to slavery as "destroyed." He cited, as evidence of moral progress, "the abolition of slavery, which is for us a clear truth, and which was the opposite for Aristotle."[73] The claim is odd, given the power of the colonial pro-slavery lobby and the resurgence of racist and paternalist defenses of slavery in this period. Here, as elsewhere, Constant seems to be analyzing Europe in isolation from its colonies, offering a schematic philosophy of history that had room for only one type of society at any moment. Since the current moment was that of post-revolutionary legal equality, the scheme would seem to leave no space to consider the persistence of colonial race slavery. Certainly, the treatment of earlier periods similarly abstracted away from complicating details, such as the church's longstanding complicity in slavery, despite Constant's own understanding of his

emphasis on modes of subsistence; and Constant insisted as the Scots tended not to do on the motive force of ideas.

[72] See *OCBC/Œuvres*, III, 1, 451.

[73] See "De la perfectibilité," in *OCBC/Œuvres*, III 1 at, e.g., 467, 473; cited passage at p. 465.

philosophy of history as one that married reason and facts. That Constant followed a widespread tendency to ignore colonial slavery is suggested by a remark made decades earlier by Adam Smith, that Europeans are "apt to imagine that slavery is entirely abolished at this time, without considering that this is the case in only a small part of Europe" and that slavery was still in use in most of the rest of the world, including "the greatest part of America."[74] Nonetheless, such silence on modern slavery was in marked contrast to the insistence of radicals like Diderot that modern Europe was deeply enmeshed in the crimes of conquest and slavery and that New World slavery represented a horrific reversion to barbarism, just as equality and liberty were gradually triumphing in Europe.[75]

Two moments in his theoretical writings that explicitly acknowledge the existence of modern slavery in the course of a contrast with ancient society suggest that Constant saw slavery as thoroughly corrupting of colonial society, but also quite separable from the life of the metropole. In the *Principles of Politics*, he argued that the existence of slaves – "a class of men who enjoy none of the rights of humanity" – inevitably changes the character of an entire society and destroys people's capacity for compassion, so that the prevalence of slavery made the ancients "severe and cruel." He added in a footnote that "[e]veryone knows how little susceptible to pity are men who have lived for a long time in the colonies."[76] Even

---

[74] Smith made this remark in his lectures on jurisprudence at the University of Edinburgh (lecture of February 15, 1763). He concluded, with a pessimism in striking contrast to Constant's historical narrative, that "[i]t is indeed almost impossible that it should ever be totally or generally abolished"; in Adam Smith, *Lectures on Jurisprudence*, ed. R. L. Meek, D. D. Raphael, and P. G. Stein (Oxford: Oxford University Press, 1978; reprinted Indianapolis: Liberty Fund, 1982), 181.

[75] In a contribution to Raynal's *Histoire des Deux Indes*, Diderot likewise compared ancient slavery with modern freedom but cautioned that "hardly had domestic liberty been reborn in Europe than it was buried in America" (Diderot, *Political Writings*, 186 [This is cited earlier in note 26.]). Montesquieu's *Persian Letters* compared Roman slavery favorably to modern slavery, and it criticized modern states involved in the slave trade as reversing the progress brought about by earlier Christian rulers, who had abolished slavery in Europe in accordance with the "principle" of Christianity, "which declares [*rend*] all men equal." See *Lettres persanes*, letters 75 and 115, in *Œuvres complètes*, ed. Roger Caillois (Paris: Gallimard, 1949), 244–45 and 301–2.

[76] *PoP* (1806), 358 (translation slightly altered) and accompanying footnote at 374 note N. David Hume had similarly noted (with reference to the ancient world and the American colonies) the "little humanity, commonly observed in persons,

this aside, a rare moment in which Constant acknowledged modern slavery when addressing the vices of ancient slavery, suggests that he thought the evils produced by slavery might be sequestered in the New World, with modern Europeans left untainted by any complicity with the institution. A key strategy of earlier abolitionists in France and especially in Britain had, in contrast, been precisely to insist on the guilt of metropolitan consumers of slave-made goods and the moral corruption implied by any participation in the slave economy. The radical British abolitionist William Fox, for instance, wrote in a pamphlet of 1791 that the public should not console itself with the thought that "the crime rests alone with those who conduct the traffic, or the legislature by which it is protected." The metropolitan consumer was not merely complicit but in fact the "original cause, the first mover in the horrid process."[77] A second moment of recognition of modern slavery in contrast to the ancient form occurs, as mentioned earlier, in Constant's *Commentary on Filangieri*, where Constant explained the modern toleration for New World slavery, so offensive to modern morality, as a result of the racism that excluded blacks from Europeans' circle of moral concern. Yet even in the *Commentary*, outside the chapter on the slave trade, Constant wrote of slavery as though it had been abolished in the modern world.[78]

Such tensions in Constant's treatment of slavery – his active abolitionism, alongside his frequently articulated view that slavery no longer exists – might be read as related to his ambivalence about how to assess the climate of public opinion in his day on the subject. As I have begun to suggest, two apparently contradictory thoughts

accustomed, from their infancy, to...trample upon human nature"; "Populousness of Ancient Nations," *Essays Moral, Political, and Literary* (Indianapolis: Liberty Fund, 1985), 383–84.

[77] William Fox, *An Address to the People of Great Britain, on the Propriety of Abstaining from West India Sugar and Rum* (London, 1791). Reproduced in *Slavery, Abolition and Emancipation: Writings in the British Romantic Period*, vol. 2, ed. Peter J. Kitson (London: Pickering and Chatto, 1999), 153–65. On the British abolitionists' campaign of the sugar boycott, see Adam Hochschild, *Bury the Chains* (Boston: Houghton Mifflin, 2005).

[78] He argued, for instance, that condemning criminals to labor is an utterly illegitimate appropriation of a person's faculties, the treatment of a human being as a beast of burden; he added that those who support penal servitude are in danger of bringing back slavery, which has been "abolished by religion and the advance of knowledge"; *Commentaire*, part III, 225.

recur in his work. One was that the moral battle against slavery had been won and indeed that this fact was one of the most decisive marks of difference between the ancient and modern (especially post-revolutionary) worlds. This was a claim he made not just in his philosophies of history, but also in some of the directly political writings, where such an argument allowed him to shame his opponents, to frame them as rebels against a social consensus, or worse, as hypocrites defying their own stated position. In his 1819 *Minerve* article, for instance, he noted that the French state had already committed to the abolition of the trade and that while government ministers bridled with "virtuous indignation" at any suggestion that they might be betraying that commitment, the trade was flourishing under the eyes of, and indeed with the apparent connivance of, French officials.[79]

The other thought, seemingly in tension with the first, was that public opinion in France had not yet turned definitively against slavery or even the slave trade and that popular indifference to or support for the trade had enabled the government to flout its own stated determination to stop it. There was, Constant argued, widespread public complacency about slavery and hostility toward abolitionists: "The names of atheist, Jacobin and bonapartist are pure flatteries if one compares them with that of philanthropist, which is given to those who condemn the trade in negroes."[80] In making both claims, sometimes within the same work, Constant was, in part, pointedly exposing the inconsistencies and hypocrisies of French public discourse on the slave trade. He was also suggesting that people's commitment to abstract moral principles was insecure unless it was underpinned by a more visceral sense of what a violation of those principles meant in lived experience. He was, finally, creating conceptual space for his own distinctive approach to reform, one that was at once progressive and moderate.

[79] "De la traite des nègres au Sénégal," in *Recueil d'articles*, 915. In a speech of 1822, he asked, "Why does the trade, this traffic declared infamous by our government and proscribed by all the governments of Europe, continue with such audacity?" His answer was that it was convenient and profitable for the government and its allies to allow the trade to continue: colonial judges themselves, he charged, "buy blacks from those very men that their duty and their oaths require them to condemn." Speech of April 5, 1822, in *Discours de M. Benjamin Constant à la Chambre de Députés*, vol. II (Paris: J. Pinard, 1828), 139–40.

[80] "De la traite des nègres au Sénégal," in *Recueil des articles*, 925.

Constant's optimistic and ameliorative philosophy of history permitted a reluctance toward forceful reform, a gradualism even on issues of the utmost moral urgency. If history can be shown to be moving steadily toward the realization of justice and equality, then radical reform can be regarded as unnecessary, even dangerous.[81] Constant was solicitous of public opinion, arguing that reformers should not too aggressively outpace – *"exagérer"* – the evolution of the public's ideas.[82] Constant criticized the radicals of a previous generation, such as Condorcet and Godwin, who undermined their often laudable projects by allowing themselves to engage in "bizarre conjectures" and overly precise and therefore "ridiculous" predictions of future developments. Reformers should instead embed their more radical arguments in commonplaces, so as to accustom reluctant publics to the "strange truths" they had to preach. This cautious approach to reform was surely one reason why Constant restricted his abolitionist arguments to an assault on the slave trade and largely avoided mentioning the abolition of slavery itself in his speeches in the Chamber. Indeed, he argued in the *Commentary on Filangieri* that even the movement for abolition of the trade had outdistanced public opinion and preceded "the moral conviction that makes reforms effective."[83] The ban on the trade was seen as imposed by authority rather than society, and worse, as a capitulation to the English. Convicted slave traders were seen as victims rather than as odious criminals. Reformers, then, in Constant's view, had to alter public opinion before they could hope to entrench change through legislation or decree.

And yet one of Constant's persistent arguments for patience in reform was that people should be allowed to suffer evils until they are ready to fight them. Slavery, in which the appeal for reform is being made to the oppressors, to those who are not suffering the consequences of an immoral policy, would seem to be a special case,

---

[81] On this "Burkean" aspect of Constant's thought, see Fontana 1991, 39–40, and Holmes 1984, chap. 3. Holmes argues that Constant portrayed "moral improvement as an irreversible process beyond moral approval or disapproval" partly in an effort to demonstrate to the reactionary ultras the futility of their political stance (p. 196).

[82] If we understand the march of progress, he argued, we will know what it means in our own age to accede to it, rather than resist it or "exaggerate"; "we will know what to fight and what to suffer with patience" (*OCBC/Œuvres*, III, 1, 446).

[83] *Commentaire*, 1822–24, part II, 8.

and one to which Constant himself was sensitive. In the *Spirit of Conquest*, in the course of defending the preservation of traditional institutions, even if they are unjust, he had named slavery as one of those injustices that can never be sanctioned or softened by lapse of time, because "in what is intrinsically unjust there is always an injured party, who cannot adjust to its sufferings."[84]

The issue of slavery reveals some of the broader tensions in Constant's thought, above all his combination of an acutely critical, even disillusioned, analysis of modern politics alongside a tendency to idealize modern history as a story of moral progress. From this followed his odd combination of recurrent disappointment in public opinion and continuing faith that the public would eventually come around to the right view. Constant's persistence in the abolitionist cause in the inauspicious climate of his day exemplifies, as well as any aspect of his career, his post-revolutionary liberalism, that is, his simultaneous commitment to the fundamental principles of the Revolution and deep hostility to the polarities of revolutionary politics. In the end France would abolish colonial slavery only in the course of yet another revolution. Given the difficulties of post-revolutionary political action, then, it is perhaps to be expected that Constant fell back at key moments on a faith in the movement of history to accomplish ends that seemed at once indisputably desirable and yet utterly out of reach.

ACKNOWLEDGMENTS

I am grateful to Bryan Garsten and Helena Rosenblatt for their helpful comments on earlier drafts.

---

[84] He had wryly invoked the memorable image of the cook who excuses the violence she does to the eels she skins by saying, "They are used to it. . . . I have been doing it for thirty years"; *SCU*, 75.

7   Benjamin Constant as a Second Restoration Politician

Much as he would have wanted, Benjamin Constant has attracted more attention as a writer and thinker than as a practicing politician, although the importance of his political career has long been recognized and biographies do provide extensive information concerning his contributions as journalist, pamphleteer, and parliamentarian. The latter works, however, view Constant from the perspective of the individual, rather than as part of a group. Thus, in order to view him in a new light, this essay will place Constant within the context of the Second Restoration Liberal Opposition as a means to discuss his role as a practicing politician.[1]

Although frequently referred to as the *parti libéral* by contemporaries, the Opposition was not a political party in the modern sense. The Opposition had no party platform, deputies voted according to their individual inclinations, and there was no card-carrying membership among supporters. Nor were all Liberals necessarily liberal in political or economic philosophy; among the Opposition there were many former Bonapartists or Jacobins whose liberalism was more a product of circumstance than doctrinal conviction.[2] Liberals

---

[1] Of the many biographies, Paul Bastid, *Benjamin Constant et sa doctrine*, vol. I (Paris: A. Colin, 1966), and Elizabeth Schermerhorn, *Benjamin Constant, His Private Life and His Contribution to the Cause of Liberal Government in France, 1767–1830* (London: W. Heinemann Ltd., 1924), provide the most detail on Constant's political career. Dennis Wood's *Benjamin Constant: A Biography* (New York: Routledge, 1993) focuses more on Constant's literary work and personal life, but is a far more reliable guide than Harold Nicolson's *Benjamin Constant* (New York: Doubleday, 1949).

[2] To avoid confusion, I have capitalized "Liberal" when referring simply to members of the Opposition and reserved the lower case for individuals who were liberal in doctrine.

were, however, linked by belief that they were the heirs of the Revolution; they saw themselves as the spokesmen for the "new France" that had emerged from 1789 onward. There were differences among them as to what they thought constituted the "true" Revolution (especially concerning the Terror and the First Empire), but during the Restoration such differences were submerged under a common defense against attempts to return to the institutions and values of the *ancien régime* political and social order. Liberals often argued on the basis of abstract principles, but their discourse as a whole tended to be historicist, based on an often emotive and subjective reading of the past.

Liberals believed in national sovereignty and representative government, and they interpreted the constitutional Charter of 1814 as a contract between the monarchy and the nation. Like most royalists, they sought to avoid the question of where sovereignty ultimately resided in the event of a clash between monarch and nation, and it was only during periods of crisis generated by what they perceived as reactionary aggression that Liberals openly asserted the primacy of national sovereignty. All the same, Liberals uniformly opposed the royalist *thèse* that sovereignty ultimately rested with the king, and they were determined that the Chamber of Deputies should have significant legislative and budgetary powers independent of the throne. Because it was elective, unlike the Chamber of Peers, Liberals viewed the Chamber of Deputies as the sole body that could claim to represent the nation, despite the narrowness of the franchise.

Through most of the Restoration, Liberals proclaimed a need to defend the Charter from extreme (ultra)royalists. Yet the Charter Liberals claimed to defend was a product of their interpretation, and much of their propaganda was directed toward developing what they termed the "representative element" in a constitution that was vague in many regards. Such development could occur along various lines: enhancing the powers of parliament in relation to the central government; replacing state appointment of local officials with elections; liberalizing press laws so as to enable writers to better inform, and reflect, public opinion; and enlarging the electorate. Very few Liberals favored immediate institution of full manhood suffrage, let alone granting the vote to women, but many believed the level of the *cens* (which restricted the electorate to roughly ninety thousand property owners who paid a minimum of three hundred *francs* annually in taxes) should be reduced to make elections a more accurate reflection of national will. One way or another, Liberals were highly critical of governments that failed to make sufficient progress as they defined it, and they inclined to view steps that reduced the representative principle as a betrayal of the Charter.

Liberal opposition to royal despotism was closely linked to resistance to any proposed restoration of privilege for the nobility or Catholic Church. The stridency of Liberal criticism tended to vary in accordance with the proximity of ultraroyalists (closely associated with both despotism and privilege) to power, but Liberals were consistent in defending freedom of opinion and conscience and insisting on legal equality (among men). Outbursts of anticlericalism or antinoble sentiment should not, however, be exaggerated; Liberals opposed privilege rather than nobility or Catholicism per se.

Establishing the dimensions of Liberal Opposition is difficult. Most Liberal efforts were directed at the electorate, but as the Restoration wore on Liberals distinguished themselves by their willingness to mobilize demonstrations of public support that reached far beyond the bounds of the franchise. Given the repressive nature of the regime, there were limits as to how far Liberals could go in orchestrating such demonstrations, but it is worth underlining that ties between enfranchised Liberals and disenfranchised popular elements were manifest throughout the period. In terms of parliamentary politics, the Liberal Opposition was composed of two main blocks of deputies: the Center-Left (moderates) and the Left (radicals). More frequently than not, the two tendencies voted in common, but the two sides could divide over any issue. On the whole, moderate royalist governments willing to compromise (such as those led by Decazes and Martignac) were more likely to provoke division than were intransigent ultraroyalist ministries (such as those led by Villèle and Polignac), but maintaining unity was always a central concern for the Opposition. Unity did not, however, preclude tactical alliance with other groups, depending on circumstance. Pragmatism guided Liberal politics as much as doctrine.

Such characteristics were reflected at the grassroots level. In the early years of the Restoration, Liberals began to organize at the local and departmental level. The level of sophistication varied according to region, but organization usually began in private salons and reading rooms and then developed into committees designed to secure the election of candidates for the Chamber of Deputies. Initially this process frequently led to rival committees, often along moderate and radical lines. Such splintering could contribute to victories for royalists, and hence a committee of deputies and journalists was established at Paris in 1818 to encourage Liberals in the departments to combine over agreed slates of candidates. Gradually, such efforts bore fruit in the form of central electoral committees that organized subcommittees of activists throughout a given department. In theory, the committees should have dissolved after elections had taken place, but in practice they became increasingly permanent features of local politics.[3]

Despite such advances, division – or at least the potential for it – remained. Defining the differences between moderate and radical Liberals is not a straightforward proposition, partly because temperament and personal or group rivalry born of material interest could play as great a role as disagreement over doctrine or policy. Nevertheless it can in general be said that radicals were more eager to push for enhancement of the "representative principle" of the Charter, were more fiercely critical of government infringement of political or civil liberties, and were more confrontational with the state administration. Radicals were more prone to resort to conspiracy and insurrection during the early 1820s; moderates generally confined themselves to legal means of opposition.[4]

* * *

Having sketched the character of the Liberal Opposition, we now can turn to Constant's place within it. Given his reputation as an old roué whose gambling debts reduced him to caging for loans, his independence as a thinker, and his role in coauthoring Napoleon's *Acte additionnel* during the Hundred Days, one might expect Constant

---

[3] During the Restoration, leading state officials, particularly departmental prefects, were responsible both for organizing elections and for securing favorable returns for the government in place.

[4] The aforementioned summary is distilled from Robert Alexander, *Re-Writing the French Revolutionary Tradition: Liberal Opposition and the Fall of the Bourbon Monarchy* (Cambridge: Cambridge University Press, 2003). For an earlier work on the subject, see Paul Thureau-Dangin, *Le parti libéral sous la Restauration* (Paris: E. Plon Cie., 1876). For a recent study of liberal emphasis on capacity as the means to determine voting rights, see Alan S. Kahan, *Liberalism in Nineteenth-Century Europe: The Political Culture of Limited Suffrage* (New York: Palgrave Macmillan, 2003).

to have been isolated during the Second Restoration, but in fact he played a crucial role in giving the Opposition coherence.[5] There were three principal causes for his centrality: his role as a spokesman for Liberal values, interests, and strategies; his frequent efforts to maintain unity within Liberal ranks and to forge tactical alliances with other groups; and his recognition of the importance of organization.

Many leading nineteenth-century politicians also were journalists, but few were as prolific as Constant. Early in 1817 he relaunched his political career by cofounding a revised version of the *Mercure de France*, which later appeared as the *Minerve française* in 1818 to avoid censorship problems. In 1819 he shifted from the *Minerve* to the *Renommée*, which served as a vehicle for left-wing deputies to address their constituents and the broader public generally. The following excerpt from a letter from his chief electoral agent, written in the summer of 1819, reveals the extent to which Constant's journalism raised his profile as a politician:

You have written a lot in the *Minerve* for the last three weeks; continue, it is necessary. All the subscribers, upon initial reception, search for your articles and those of Monsieur Étienne. Your piece in the 78th edition has been read and re-read with the greatest interest in all the [reading] societies. Do not neglect the *Renommée*, between you and me, most [people] think that it needs you. Here [at Le Mans] there are meetings of twenty to thirty workers solely to listen to readings of the *Minerve* and other journals. It is the same among the wealthier class of patriots. These societies have subscriptions with the bookstores; a single copy suffices for 100 people.[6]

After the *Renommée* merged with the *Courrier français*, Constant continued to contribute frequently, publishing, for example, twenty-four articles from April to June 1829. Toward the end of the decade he also published in the *Constitutionnel* and the *Temps*. He thus was associated with the leading Parisian journals and his articles were also published in regional newspapers such as the *Courrier du*

---

[5] Nicolson is particularly insistent on Constant's isolation; see his *Benjamin*, 248. During Napoleon's "Flight of the Eagle" in March 1815, Constant had rallied to the restored Bourbon king, Louis XVIII, and written in the *Journal des débats* that he would rather die than support the returning tyrant. Thus his decision a couple of weeks later to aid Bonaparte in writing a new constitution for the empire and to join the council of state shocked contemporaries and gave him a lifelong reputation for unprincipled opportunism.

[6] See Ephraim Harpaz, ed., *Benjamin Constant et Goyet de la Sarthe: Correspondance 1818–1822* (Geneva: Droz, 1973), 132. All quotation translations are by me.

Bas-Rhin. In terms of volume and range of subject matter, Constant's productivity was indeed "scarcely believable."[7]

The latter remark could also be made about this work in parliament, where he sat as deputy for the department of the Sarthe from March 1819 to November 1822, for the Seine from February 1824 to November 1827, and for the Bas-Rhin from November 1827 until his death in December 1830. Although he occasionally lost the order of his scribbled notes, Constant's knowledge, powers of reason, and mordant wit made him a formidable adversary capable of driving opponents into frenzies of outrage. He spoke no fewer than 265 times between 1819 and 1821, and he gave 49 speeches between January and August 1828. Partly because Chamber speeches formed a large part of newspaper reports, they also raised a deputy's profile. In May 1819 Constant's electoral agent wrote, "All the liberals of the Sarthe triumph in your debut in the Chamber. Your speeches are read and re-read here; they desolate the ultras and give joy to all those who desired your election." Constant's speeches and writings touched on virtually every topic of national interest – financial and budgetary matters, constitutional and judicial issues, civil and political liberties, educational policies, religion, foreign relations, the army, and abolition of the slave trade.[8]

Even brief consideration demonstrates to what extent his was a key Liberal voice, both in tone and in content, in the crucial battles of the period. On return in the fall of 1816 from self-imposed exile, Constant initially took a relatively conciliatory line with the Richelieu government. He was well aware that although they had lost control of parliament, ultraroyalists remained eager to continue exacting revenge against those who had rallied to Napoleon in 1815. Constant thus pressed the government to end the laws of exception that had formed the legal basis for repression after Waterloo, but supported

---

[7] See Wood, 224, 245. More particularly on Constant's political journalism, see Anna Shumway, *A Study of the Minerve Française* (Philadelphia, 1934); Ephraïm Harpaz, *L'école libérale sous la Restauration, le Mercure et la Minerve, 1817–1820* (Geneva: Droz, 1968); and the same author's "Benjamin Constant, 1820–1830: grandeur et limites de sa pensée," in *Benjamin Constant, Madame de Staël et le Groupe de Coppet, Actes du Deuxième Congrès de Lausanne et du Troisième Colloque de Coppet,* ed. Etienne Hofmann (Oxford: The Voltaire Foundation and Lausanne/Institut Benjamin Constant, 1982), 89–97.

[8] See Wood, 229, 237, 242; Bastid, *Benjamin,* I, 324–26; Schermerhorn, 322; Alexander, 273–76; and for the quote, Harpaz, ed., *Benjamin Constant et Goyet,* 92.

the Lainé law of February 1817 because it established direct elections. While calling for national reconciliation, Constant however took a firm line over the pretensions of ultraroyalism. In their disillusionment with the moderate policies of Louis XVIII, ultraroyalists such as Chateaubriand became champions of the constitutional powers of parliament, provided they controlled the latter. Constant's riposte to Chateaubriand's *La monarchie selon la Charte* suggested that a better title would have been "The Charter According to the Aristocracy," and he counseled skepticism of ultraroyalist constitutionalism until the extreme Right learned to respect the liberties of others.

As Liberal representation rose in the Chamber due to partial elections from 1817 to 1820, Liberals grew impatient with the slow pace of liberalization of successive moderate royalist governments. Constant was far from unique in demanding that justice be meted out to the perpetrators of illegal White Terror and in alluding to a secret ultraroyalist organization that was bent on destroying the Charter. Reference to "dark powers" lurking behind the throne soon became a standard rhetorical ploy for attacking government policies without directly impugning the King, even when everyone knew such policies reflected royal wishes. Disillusionment became strident opposition in late 1819 when Decazes, then head of the cabinet, decided to align with ultraroyalists to change the Lainé law and thereby reverse Liberal gains. Constant argued that such a step would violate the Charter by reversing development of the representative principle.

Politics further polarized in the spring of 1820 when ultraroyalists exploited the assassination of the Duke of Berry to engineer the fall of Decazes in favor of a second Richelieu ministry. The latter then passed the law of the Double Vote (which enabled the wealthiest landowners to vote for two sets of deputies), reimposed preliminary censorship, and enabled state detention of any individual suspected of sedition for three months without charges being filed. France seemingly lurched toward civil war as riots occurred outside parliament, and debate within descended to pure invective. Constant was at the Liberal forefront in attacking infringements of liberty and denouncing the "aristocratic" character of the new electoral law. He also excelled in baiting opponents. To counter claims that Liberals were bent on overthrowing the monarchy, Constant returned to charges of ultraroyalist conspiracy: "That invisible power exists;

it protects the manoeuvres [assassinations during the White Terror] that emanate from its heart. Let Your Majesty deign to deliver us from that invisible force that is neither legal nor constitutional, and that undermines the throne and threatens liberty."[9]

The period that followed was marked by failed revolt and increased repression as Liberal electoral fortunes plummeted and power shifted steadily to ultraroyalism. Many Liberals concluded that the laws of 1820 had indeed violated the Charter and set about provoking revolution. Although he considered the Villèle government that came to power in December 1821 to be counterrevolutionary in character, Constant played no part in attempts to raise insurrection. Instead he confined himself to frustrating battles in the Chamber, speaking twelve times between January 25 and February 16, 1822, against a series of laws that again renewed preliminary censorship, removed trial by jury for press infractions, and authorized prosecution of newspapers for seditious "tendencies." All the same, Constant was subjected to police surveillance and harassment. It did not help that two of his principal supporters in the Sarthe became involved in revolt at Saumur or that he was cited by one of the rebels as part of a planned provisional government. Press allegations eventually induced Constant to fight a duel with an ultraroyalist, an action that alienated his supporters in the Sarthe. Nor did likening French intervention against Spanish liberals to medieval religious crusades enhance the standing of Constant or Liberals generally, and he and they suffered massive defeat in the partial elections of November 1822.[10]

Exploiting patriotic sentiments after the French army had successfully restored Ferdinand VII to his rule of Spain, Villèle called a general election in 1824. Constant was returned to the Chamber as a deputy for the Seine, but across France, Liberals were decimated amid an ultraroyalist landslide. Despite the irritant of a spurious challenge to his right to sit in parliament, Constant soon set the tone for Opposition for the remainder of the Restoration: "If formerly

---

[9] See Alexander, 81–134; Bastid, *Benjamin*, I, 305–45; Schermerhorn, 310–35; Wood, 217–31; Harpaz, *L'école*, 145–53; and Alan B. Spitzer, "Restoration Political Theory and the Debate over the Law of the Double Vote," *Journal of Modern History*, 55 (March 1983), 54–70. For the quote, see Bastid, *Benjamin*, I, 340.

[10] Alexander, 135–86, 168; Bastid, *Benjamin*, I, 346–84; Schermerhorn, 335–44; Wood, 231–33.

some dreamed of the republic, did others not think that the representative system was inappropriate for us? And, however, who does not sense today that in our stage of civilisation the representative system is the most desirable, and who does not also today sense that given the customs of the old Europe the republic would be a chimera or an affliction?" Far from advocating revolution, he recognized that the throne and liberty were intimately bound, each requiring the other. From 1824 onward, Liberals would adopt a defensive posture, claiming their sole desire was to preserve constitutional monarchy from ultraroyalists. Such claims were not new, but with ultraroyalism clearly in the ascendant, the rhetoric of saving the Charter steadily gained credence.

That opposition was no longer automatic could be seen in Constant's acceptance of the abolition of partial elections, although he did propose an amendment that a deputy's mandate should be for four rather than seven years. Thereafter opposition hardened, but this could be attributed to the extreme nature of proposed legislation – an indemnity for émigrés whose land had been confiscated during the Revolution, a law making sacrilege punishable by execution, revision of inheritance laws in the direction of the aristocratic principle of primogeniture, and a press law designed to restrict the publishing trade in general. All of these measures could easily be depicted as regressive, but in opposing them Constant and his fellow Liberals took care to avow their loyalty to the throne. Under such circumstances, another old tactic also regained currency: the king's government was in danger of falling under the control of an occult organization somehow tied to the Jesuits.[11]

Intransigence, hubris, and factionalism in ultraroyalist ranks brought a vast reversal of fortunes in the national elections of November 1827, restoring Liberals to parity with ultraroyalists in the Chamber and leaving the balance of power with a minority of moderate royalists. As the Villèle government gave way to a centrist ministry led by Martignac, Constant adopted a position similar to that which he had occupied prior to 1820. While pushing the government to distance itself from ultraroyalism in 1828 and the first half of 1829, he also modulated his criticisms with encouragement. Thus while voting against new press laws Constant did admit they were

[11] Alexander, 187–237; Bastid, *Benjamin*, I, 385–411; Schermerhorn, 345–60; Wood, 233–42. For the quote, see Bastid, *Benjamin*, I, 390.

an improvement over past legislation, and when the government introduced bills to make local government office elective, he praised the initiative, though he opposed the narrowness of the proposed franchise.

Like most Liberals and moderate royalists, Constant believed that nothing good could come of the ultraroyalist Polignac ministry appointed by Charles X in August 1829, and he joined in the chorus of warnings against an alleged *coup d'état* whereby the government would try to rule despite an opposition majority in the lower house and, perhaps, seek to set aside the Charter. Constant had long drawn analogies between the Bourbon and Stuart dynasties, but he remained within the Liberal mainstream in advocating legal resistance – refusal to grant the budget, refusal to pay taxes should the government violate the Charter, and solidarity with the address of the 221 deputies that called on the King to appoint a new ministry. Liberal restraint served to maintain alliance with centrist groups such as the *doctrinaires* and moderate royalists such as the Agier defection and yielded electoral triumph in June–July 1830. When Charles X confirmed warnings of *coup d'état* with the July Ordinances, Liberals were no more prepared for revolution than was the government.[12]

Thereafter, Constant's relations with the July Monarchy evolved along lines similar to those of radical Liberals who formed the political bloc known as the Party of Movement. Liberal deputies played a vital role in channeling insurrection at Paris into the creation of a new regime, and Liberal committees in the departments assured that transfer of power was relatively bloodless. At the capital, Constant contributed to the foundation of the July Monarchy by dismissing conciliatory decrees brought by the envoys of Charles X to parliament, by drawing up an address asking the Duke of Orleans to take the position of lieutenant-general of the kingdom, and by preparing a proclamation to the people justifying the dethroning of the former king. Liberal unity had always been based on common opposition, however, and with the Bourbons removed fragmentation soon set in. Moderate Liberals joined with the doctrinaires and moderate royalists in a conservative coalition that sought to minimize change, while radical Liberals such as Constant grew disenchanted with the

---

[12] Alexander, 238–85; Bastid, *Benjamin*, I, 412–54; Schermerhorn, 361–64; Wood, 243–47.

limited progress achieved in the revolutionary aftermath. In particular, Constant was disappointed by rejection of his proposals for revised press laws and troubled by what he considered an insufficient purge of former ultraroyalists in the administration, but in truth his health was rapidly failing and his participation in parliament was not what it once had been.[13]

* * *

Thus Constant had played a major role in setting the tone, content, and strategy of Liberal Opposition. It would be a mistake, however, to view him, or any other Liberal, as wholly representative of the Opposition. Liberals were a heterogeneous collection of Bonapartists, Jacobins, and Liberals. Given their diversity, the pursuit of unity, either through emphasizing common ground or by ignoring difference, was crucial to Liberal fortunes.

Although in many regards he was a quintessential liberal, on his return in 1816 Constant found himself rebuffed by his old associates, the *doctrinaires*, and fell in with the former Jacobins and Bonapartists who haunted the salon of Madame Davillier. Germaine de Staël had previously warned against liberals combining with Bonapartists, but her words were largely ignored as diverse groups found common ground in defending what they saw as the heritage of the Revolution. In his willingness to associate with non-*doctrinaire* elements, Constant entered a far more numerous and politically significant movement. The *doctrinaires* were liberal, but their desire to find an exact balance between royal and national sovereignty made them distinct from the Liberal Opposition, though the two often allied in the 1820s.[14]

As a member of the Opposition, Constant sat with the Left. He shared the view that the Charter was a contract and, despite his fears of popular tyranny, he spent most his time denouncing the agents of royal despotism. In the heat of the parliamentary battles that

---

[13] Alexander, 286–310; Bastid, *Benjamin*, I, 455–76; Schermerhorn, 364–67; Wood, 247–50.

[14] For a description of the heterogeneous character of the Davillier salon, see Jean-Jacques Coulmann, *Réminiscences* (Paris: Michel Lévy Frères, 1862), I, 172–210. See also E. Cappadocia, "The Liberals and Madame de Staël in 1818," in *Ideas in History*, 182–98; Alexander, *Re-Writing*, 271–72; Charles H. Pouthas, *Guizot pendant la Restauration: préparation de l'homme d'état (1814–1830)* (Paris: Typographie Plon-Nourrit, 1923), 472–77; and Pierre Rosanvallon, *Le moment Guizot* (Paris: Gallimard, 1985), 11–32.

marked the crises of 1820 and 1830, Constant's defense of the rights of the nation could take on an almost Jacobin hue. Amid debate over change in the electoral regime in May 1820, Constant hectored royalists for their failure to respect the tricolor "under which the French people have fought."[15] Given the context, his speech fell just short of an avowal of republicanism. In August 1830 he would assert that the legitimacy of a monarch emanated from the will of the nation. Leaving extreme moments aside, it is however more instructive to note that Constant consistently supported the more progressive Liberal proposals for development of the representative element in the Charter. In 1817 he rejected indirect elections as aristocratic; in 1829 he lobbied for a broader franchise for local elections than the government was willing to grant, and soon after the July Revolution he called for a lowering of the *cens* by at least a third. Constant may not have been a democrat, but his emphases on granting full political rights to small-scale property owners, and on assuring as broad a distribution of property as possible, placed him well in advance of most his contemporaries.

Similarly, Constant consistently pushed for extending the powers of parliament. He was an early advocate of ministerial responsibility, arguing that while it was the prerogative of the king to appoint ministers, the Chamber of Deputies had a right to render wayward government inoperable through refusal to grant the budget. Constant also championed the right of citizens to refuse tax payment should the government violate the Charter, and in general advocated means by which government could be confined within the rule of law. There was much that was not clearly elaborated in the Charter, leaving a lot of leeway for interpretation, but what is noteworthy is that Constant argued for positions that moderate Liberals often viewed as extreme. All the same, he stopped short of advocating revolution and was to the right of a small number of more democratic, generally republican, Liberals such as d'Argenson or Lafayette.[16]

Constant rejected what he termed "military" discipline when it came to voting, but he also recognized the value of avoiding needless

---

[15] The quote is from Bastid, *Benjamin*, I, 342.

[16] See Bastid, *Benjamin*, I, 310, 329, 360, 402, 438, 457; Alexander, 85, 265; Wood, 239–40; Schermerhorn, 322; and Ezio Cappadocia, "The Liberals and Madame de Staël in 1818," in *Ideas in History: Essays Presented to Louis Gottschalk*, ed. R. Herr and H. T. Parker (by his Former Students) (Durham, NC: Duke University Press, 1965), 182–98.

division, and his pragmatism made him aware of the need to forge alliances. Paul Bastid put the point nicely when he stated that Constant's political philosophy was "simultaneously firm in principle and conciliatory in application." Most important was the need to preserve solidarity on the Left. Despite his distaste for Napoleonic despotism, Constant took care not to alienate Bonapartist voters in the Sarthe and, on the recommendation of his supporters in the Bas-Rhin, postponed the publication of letters on the coup of 18 Brumaire prior to the elections of 1830.[17]

Cultivation of unity at times required compromise, and on occasion Constant had to support initiatives with which he agreed in principle, but judged ill timed. In 1819 he backed calls for an end to the exile of regicides, although he correctly surmised that pressing the issue might drive the government toward the Right. Similarly, he opposed parliamentary refusal to confirm the election of the abbé Grégoire, a regicide by intention, though not in deed. Constant cited the Charter's call for past political conduct to be forgotten and pointed out that Fouché, a regicide, had been appointed to the ministry in the summer of 1815. Nevertheless, he privately regretted that Grégoire had been nominated in the first place and approved of Liberal strategy aimed at not alienating centrists whose votes would prove crucial in attempts to foil revision of the electoral law. Rather ironically, Constant's initially favorable response to the press bill proposed by the Martignac ministry in 1828 landed him in hot water with much of the Liberal press. In this instance Constant was forced to abandon a moderate Liberal position in favor of radical solidarity, although his desire not to adopt "systemic" opposition to the government was obvious to all.

Unlike some of his more intransigent colleagues, Constant recognized that unity sometimes required toleration of differing positions, rather than insistence on conformity. Writing on such a wide array of subjects, Constant was bound to clash with other journalists, including fellow radicals. In such instances, it was important to keep disputes within reasonable bounds. Amid a battle with de Pradt, a Liberal editor of the *Courrier français*, over the latter's support of

---

[17] See Bastid, *Benjamin*, I, 311, 358, 429, 452–53; Harpaz, ed., *Benjamin Constant et Goyet*, 41–43; Alexander, 272; and Robert Alexander, *Napoleon* (London: Oxford University Press, 2001), 38–45.

Simon Bolivar, Constant sought to assure readers that neither Liberal considered dictatorship appropriate for a European state – despotism was the goal of the extreme Right. Hoping for a wedge issue, ultraroyalists claimed that Constant had broken with the *Courrier*, but Constant published a note denying the allegation and continued contributing to the journal. Because it did bring forward significant reforms, the Martignac ministry posed an especially acute threat to Liberal unity in 1828–29. While radicals pressed for retribution against the former Villèle government for past illegalities, most Liberals concluded that the issue might bring the fall of a government that was moving in a positive direction. Constant backed the call for legal measures, but he came to recognize that nothing would come of the issue and moved on. When d'Argenson and Chauvelin resigned their seats in protest of Liberal inaction, Constant defended his fellow radicals from attacks in the press, but also wrote that they had taken the wrong course of action in weakening the Opposition.[18]

Constant's willingness to overlook differences becomes clear if we consider his relations with the conspiratorial organization known as the *Carbonari*. In the Chamber, Constant was most closely aligned with Lafayette, who was up to his neck in plotting insurrection. There is no evidence that Constant was involved in conspiracy, but it beggars belief that he did not know that Lafayette and a host of his Liberal colleagues had passed beyond legal opposition. There was thus something disingenuous in Constant's frequent attribution of revolt solely to government provocation. More to the point, however, is that Constant's electoral demise in 1822 was directly attributable to the illegal activities of others with whom he was closely associated; his electoral address calling on voters to reject rumors that "I am implicated in the prosecution of supposed revolutionary plots" achieved little.[19] Thus it seems plausible that Constant's apparent desire to block the highly compromised Manuel from running for election in Paris in 1824 signaled his wish for the Opposition to distance itself from the failed path of conspiracy. All the same, Constant's refusal to denounce or criticize those who had conspired helped subsequently to restore Liberal unity. For their part, radicals

---

[18] Bastid, *Benjamin*, I, 328, 421, 428–29; Harpaz, ed., *Benjamin Constant et Goyet*, 204–6; Schermerhorn, 362–63; Alexander, 268–69; and Harpaz, "Benjamin," 92.
[19] See Harpaz, ed., *Benjamin Constant et Goyet*, 722.

returned in 1824 to the legal strategies from which moderates had not strayed.[20]

In 1818 Constant had been taught a lesson when the administration blocked his first bid for election (in the Seine) by reaching an accord with a moderate Liberal candidate. Constant believed that a prior agreement had been betrayed, but he refrained from publicly expressing his anger and while the *Mercure* attacked administrative interference, no criticism was made of the moderate Liberal. Subsequently in the Bas-Rhin from 1827 to 1830, Constant would have to combat the strategy of a prefect who sought to divide him from moderate Liberals. Initially backed by radicals, Constant needed time to win over the local newspaper and the department's moderate Liberal deputies. He did so by speaking up for Protestant interests, by refraining from antidynastic rhetoric, and by throwing himself into lobbying for departmental economic interests. Nor did it hurt relations with local moderates that Constant blocked proposals that other radicals, such as d'Argenson, be asked to run in the department against moderates. Initially isolated in the departmental deputation, by 1830 Constant was leading it.[21]

Liberal fortunes were closely tied to tactical alliances with other groups. As early as 1818, Constant had in the *Minerve* counseled Liberals to combine with centrists and even ultraroyalists over individual issues whenever it served the cause of liberty. At times such strategies necessitated setting aside personal differences. His relations with the *doctrinaires* were complicated; former friends such as Broglie were inclined to sneer at Constant's Liberal associates, and matters became increasingly tense as the *doctrinaires* aligned with the moderate royalist governments of 1817–20, while Liberals increasingly attacked them. Nevertheless in 1819 Constant steered clear of the bitter invective that broke out in debates between the *Renommé* and Francois Guizot's *Courrier* and was thus able to

---

[20] For a brief summary of the relation between Liberal Opposition and the *Carbonari*, see Alexander, *Re-Writing*, 140–44, 165–77; for more detailed accounts, see Alan B. Spitzer, *Old Hatreds and Young Hopes: The French Carbonari against the Bourbon Restoration* (Cambridge, MA: Harvard University Press, 1971), and Sylvia Neely, *Lafayette and the Liberal Ideal 1814–1824* (Carbondale, IL: Southern Illinois University Press, 1991), especially 142, 173, 216–27. See also Bastid, *Benjamin*, I, 343, 358, 371, 385–86.

[21] Bastid, *Benjamin*, I, 313–14, 321–22, 429; Harpaz, *L'école*, 74–75; and Alexander, *Re-Writing*, 85, 273–76.

pursue departmental interests with Royer-Collard and Guizot regarding state appointment of local officials. Such restraint thereafter facilitated improved relations in the 1820s when ultraroyalism drove Guizot and Royer-Collard steadily to the Left. Indeed Guizot owed his election in 1830 to Liberal influence.[22]

More important was the alliance that Liberals formed with the Agier defection after Chateaubriand's expulsion from the ministry in the summer of 1824. Although they were formerly part of the ultraroyalist camp, a combination of personal rivalry (with Villèle and his faction) and unease at the increasingly clerical nature of ultraroyalist rule drove the Agier defection toward the political center. When outside power, Chateaubriand was a natural defender of freedom of the press, and ties were further cultivated when Liberals such as Constant joined him in championing Greek independence. By associating themselves with Chateaubriand, Liberals began to erode doubts about their dynastic loyalty and, better yet, the Agier defection was influential in a judiciary that began to reverse the administration's corruption of voter lists. Although Liberal representation in the lower house grew dramatically from the elections of November 1827 onward, the alliance of Liberals, *doctrinaires*, and the Agier defection was crucial to forcing Polignac and Charles X to resort to the ordinances of July 1830. Constant helped by continuously maintaining that Liberals were seeking only to defend the Charter and by calling for resistance within constitutional bounds. When a committee of the Chamber of Deputies debated how to respond to the threatening Crown speech that opened parliament in March 1830, Constant predictably pushed for a firm line, insisting that "the duty of all Frenchmen is to resist all that which is contrary to the Charter." More ominous for the Crown, however, was that Liberal moderates such as Faure, *doctrinaires* such as Royer-Collard, and members of the defection such as the Marquis de Cordoue joined in the call for a change in government.[23]

* * *

Constant also made an important contribution in promoting organization. Perhaps reflecting the influence of Guizot, historians have

---

[22] Bastid, *Benjamin*, I, 333; Schermerhorn, 321; Alexander, *Re-Writing*, 271–72; and Harpaz, *Benjamin Constant et Goyet*, 152–53, 157, 162.

[23] Bastid, *Benjamin*, I, 319, 402, 449, and Alexander, *Re-Writing*, 196, 208–9, 218–19, 243–44, 270, 280–81.

been too inclined to emphasize association of political parties with factionalism and thus have largely overlooked the strides that Liberals made in party formation. Much of contemporary criticism of parties was rhetorical, a means by which politicians denounced the organization of others while themselves organizing. Party formation was perhaps retarded by the formation of secret societies; most of the public disliked conspiratorial organization and the discovery of groups such as the Carbonari encouraged acceptance of state repression of all associations, whether illegal or legal. All the same, Liberal organization grew over the course of the Restoration. For his part, Constant considered parties a natural product of representative government; destruction of party systems was always accompanied by the death of liberty. Hence it is no surprise to learn that Constant was at the center of initiatives closely linked to party formation.[24]

Organization occurred at both the national and local level and Constant played a major role in each. In parliament, what became the Liberal Opposition began when members of the salons of Ternaux and Laffitte combined to form an electoral committee of self-styled "Independents" in September 1817. For a deputy, "Independent" signified intention to judge proposed legislation on its own merits, rather than automatically follow government wishes. For the electorate, "Independent" indicated willingness to vote on the basis of a candidate's qualifications and beliefs, rather than follow the directions of the government through its chief electoral agents – the administration. Shortly thereafter, in November, a group of deputies and journalists, including Constant, formed the *Société des Amis de la Presse* to support journalists undergoing state prosecution. Initially the society included moderate royalists, *doctrinaires*, and Independents, but it evolved in a partisan direction, inclining royalists and *doctrinaires* to cease attending. Eventually, the radicalism of the society led Decazes to bring legal action against them, forcing the association to disband. Nevertheless two precedents had been established by late 1819: Opposition deputies (now styled Liberals due to their penchant to "defend" the liberties of the Revolution) would continue to meet *en bloc*, and a steering committee would continue to chart strategy. According to Constant, in late 1819 approximately

---

[24] Alexander, *Re-Writing*, 311, 338–44, and Bastid, *Benjamin*, I, 311.

sixty Liberal deputies met on a weekly basis during the parliamentary session.[25]

Roughly parallel to the aforementioned developments were initiatives that linked national and local organization. In 1818 a group of Liberal radicals, including Constant, published the *Correspondant électoral*, which recommended slates of candidates to departments undergoing renewal. By 1819 Liberal journalists and deputies had established a central committee that came to be known as the *comité directeur*, and the *Constitutionnel* had begun to publish an "official" list of Liberal candidates in the departments. Frequently linked by royalists to the propagation of revolution, the *comité directeur* was in fact simply an attempt to coordinate the efforts of local Liberal committees. While agents of the committee did travel into the provinces to dispense advice, they could not impose candidates on local committees; the *comité* could counsel activists to combine their efforts and it could publish the names of candidates backed by local committees, but it could do little more.

Constant's role in these coordination efforts was threefold. In late 1818 he was asked to run for election in the Sarthe by Charles Goyet. Goyet, in turn, headed a committee at Le Mans that had organized a network of subcommittees throughout the departmental cantons. In previously securing the election of Lafayette, Goyet and his committee had already demonstrated impressive ability to turn out the Liberal vote by providing travel, security, and accommodation arrangements. They duly delivered a victory to Constant in March 1819, but more importantly, Constant and the Parisian *comité* decided to disseminate information about Goyet's organization to committees throughout France. In 1818–19, the *Minerve*, *Censeur*, and *Renommé* published extensive reports on Goyet's strategies.[26]

It seems highly probable that Constant was a member of the *comité directeur* from very early on, and he would remain a central figure in national organization for the entirety of the Restoration. Whether the *comité directeur* had much by way of permanency,

[25] Alexander, *Re-Writing*, 85–86; Bastid, *Benjamin*, I, 314, 334; Schermerhorn, 319–20; and Harpaz, ed., *Benjamin Constant et Goyet*, 214–17.

[26] Alexander, *Re-Writing*, 108–9, 185–86; Harpaz, ed., *Benjamin Constant et Goyet*, 52–55, 130; and, especially, Sylvia Neely, "Rural Politics in the Early Restoration: Charles Goyet and the Liberals of the Sarthe," *European Historical Quarterly*, 16 (3) (1986), 313–42.

especially after the abolition of partial elections in 1824, is difficult
to say; it seems more likely that it was formed and reformed solely
at the time of elections. One way or another, in the fall of 1821
Constant was part of the *comité* that established a subcommittee
to gather information from departmental correspondents. Constant
would again be part of the committee formed at Paris in 1824. In the
summer of 1827 he helped found a revamped version of the *Amis
de la Presse*, which combined Liberals with members of the Agier
defection, but Constant does not appear to have been part of the complementary organization known as *Aide-toi le Ciel t'Aidera*. The
Aide-toi was more directly involved in the coordination of provincial electoral committees and has gained greater notoriety, but government officials were at the time more preoccupied by the ability
of members of the *Amis*, such as Chateaubriand to entice royalists
into the Opposition camp. Subsequently, officials would become
even more perturbed as Constant (and other Liberal notables) began
what became a series of departmental tours designed to coordinate
the efforts of local activists. In his tour during the fall of 1827, for
example, Constant acted as a Liberal agent in the Bas-Rhin, the
Haut-Rhin, the Saône-et-Loire, and the Côte-d'Or. His role in directing strategy would again be apparent after the elections, when he
was part of a Liberal delegation that visited Villèle to question the
government's role in the riots of November.[27]

Constant also supported many seemingly minor initiatives that
enhanced Opposition coherence and gave it a measure of discipline.
Early in the Second Restoration he made himself a champion of voter
independence by writing two pamphlets that became part of a Liberal
tradition of informing voters of their rights so as to combat administrative manipulation of voter lists. When the *doctrinaire* Camille
Jordan published an account of his conduct as a deputy to his departmental supporters, ultraroyalists attacked this practice as unconsti-
tutional. Constant, however, praised Jordan, arguing that publicity
abetted representative government. Subsequently, Constant would

---

[27] Alexander, *Re-Writing*, 172, 210–11, 216; Bastid, *Benjamin*, I, 385–86, 412–14,
438–41; Harpaz, ed., *Benjamin Constant et Goyet*, 599–602; Schermerhorn, 355;
Pouthas, 369–80; Sherman Kent, *The Election of 1827 in France* (Cambridge, MA:
Harvard University Press, 1975), 81–106; and Raymond Huard, *La naissance du
parti politique en France* (Paris: Presses de la Fondation nationale des sciences
politiques, 1996), 49–50.

make his own "patriotic oath" to the electors of the Sarthe. Such oaths became a means by which voters could hold their deputies accountable. Conservatives disliked the practice, believing that it impinged on the independence of a deputy, but Liberals adopted patriotic oaths, making them a standard part of campaigning, even for reluctant royalists, by the late 1820s.[28]

The question of a deputy's obligations to his constituents is an interesting one where Constant is concerned. Like most Liberals, Constant relied on local activists for securing election – hence, the tone of Constant's reply to Goyet's initial query about becoming a deputy for the Sarthe:

The idea of being named by the citizens of a department which, in the last elections, manifested such an honourable attachment to liberty and such courageous persistence, and of thus becoming the colleague of General Lafayette, and part of such a distinguished deputation, infinitely flatters me. If, as I have no doubt, success crowns your benevolent intentions, I will undertake to merit that honour by devoting myself even more than I have done to this point, if that is possible, to the cause that we all cherish, and in particular to the interests of the department that I would have a special mission to represent and defend.[29]

Constant did not have the wealth of some deputies – say, the Periers or Lafitte. Nor was he ever a likely conduit for state patronage; even in the aftermath of the July Revolution Constant had limited success in securing places for his followers. Where he excelled lay in exposure of real or alleged injustices. Whether fighting to overturn faulty judicial verdicts, pushing for enquiries into murder at Nîmes, recounting religious and state persecution in the Sarthe, or accusing the administration of prejudice against Protestants in the Bas-Rhin, Constant could be counted on to bring grievances to light. Goyet expressed his gratitude as follows: "We have read with the keenest interest your article on the Sarthe in the journal [the *Renommé*] edition of Wednesday 21 January [1820]. I will have it circulated throughout the department. I will no longer say anything of the sentiments of gratitude and love, and even of the respect that

---

[28] Bastid, *Benjamin*, I, 319; Alexander, *Re-Writing*, 107–8, 263–64, 283; Schermerhorn, 313–14, 321; and Prosper Duvergier de Hauranne, *Histoire du gouvernement parlementaire en France* (Paris: M. Lévy-frères, 1857–72), IX, 467–74.

[29] See Harpaz, *Benjamin Constant et Goyet*, 16.

you have inspired among all Sarthois; I would repeat myself in each letter."[30] Constant's willingness to combat the state also greatly enhanced his appeal in the Bas-Rhin.

Neither the Sarthe nor the Bas-Rhin was a "rotten borough" for Constant. In 1820 he would voyage to the principal centers of the Sarthe to meet Goyet's *équipe*. Banquets, speeches, public promenades, and private dinners were means by which a deputy could bask in support, but they also provided opportunity to learn of local interests and plot strategy. The extensive correspondence between Constant and Goyet reveals a relationship based on mutual benefit and respect. On the whole Constant was free to concentrate on issues of national consequence, but he did lobby for replacement of ultraroyalist officials by individuals recommended by Goyet, and he put far more effort into coordinating the efforts of the departmental deputation than Lafayette. Mindful of the potential impact on voters, Constant sought Goyet's advice over the position to take concerning Grégoire's election in 1819, and it would appear that Constant's parliamentary reference to Fouché originated in a letter written by Goyet's "team." Goyet felt no reluctance over advising Constant concerning political and personal conduct – it would be better if he dined at home with his wife more often. When Constant fought his duel in 1822, he put his pride above the interests of his constituents, and Goyet and other Sarthois roundly criticized him for his irresponsible behavior.[31]

Matters were somewhat different in the Bas-Rhin. Constant was invited to run at Strasbourg in 1827 by a group of radical Liberals who had grown disenchanted with their former darling – Georges Humann. In part, the reasons for the rift between Humann and the radicals were ideological; as a deputy, Humann had become associated with the *doctrinaire* Royer-Collard and drifted toward the Center-Right in the mid-1820s. Moreover, the radicals believed that Humann's vast wealth and international trade contacts put him out of touch with the economic plight of most Alsatians. Prone to assert his independence, Humann refused to make a patriotic oath, and

[30] Ibid., 232.
[31] Bastid, *Benjamin*, I, 325–28, 346–57; Alexander, *Re-Writing*, 108–9; Schermerhorn, *Benjamin*, 320–23; and Harpaz, ed., *Benjamin Constant et Goyet*, particularly 78, 85, 169–213, 385–406, 683–93.

when he refused to take part in a banquet for Constant, opining that the latter was too thirsty for public acclaim, the radicals decided to dislodge Humann. When the prefect sought to exploit this rift by claiming that Constant was supported only by the "inferior classes" – butchers, bakers, and hatters – Constant responded with a wry "Letter by a Sausage-Maker" that reminded the prefect that middle-class elements not only fed and clothed the upper classes, but sometimes even gave loans to "grand *seigneurs.*" The latter shot at the prefect's indebtedness hit the mark and gave a fine example of Constant's ability to take on the administration. Nevertheless, Constant's subsequent election was partly due to the radicals' disciplining of a former deputy.

Seldom has a politician been as fêted as was Constant in Alsace between 1827 and 1830. For his part, Constant proved to be an excellent constituency man, consulting frequently with his advisors during three tours of the department, or by means of correspondence while in Paris. After his election in 1827 Constant solicited information on Alsatian interests and was consequently deluged with petitions, brochures, and letters outlining projects for economic development; at least one commentator remarked that Constant emerged from meetings with his pockets stuffed with papers requesting aid or proposing public works. Over the course of his parliamentary career, Constant had made himself an expert on financial issues, and he took this part of his mandate very seriously, frequently asking his Alsatian correspondents for further information and explanation. In fact, very little by way of economic benefit came of Constant's efforts, but as noted previously, his labors in this domain drew moderate Liberals into his orbit, and he became immensely popular in Alsace generally.[32]

It seems fair to conclude that Constant's promotion of Alsatian interests was partly rooted in self-interest; Constant loved his moments at the tribune of the Chamber and was by no means averse to addressing adoring crowds. All the same, it is also true that he had a distinguished track record when it came to promoting political rights. Part of such advocacy lay in defending practices designed to

---

[32] Alexander, *Re-Writing*, 233–36, 273–75, 283, 342; Schermerhorn, *Benjamin*, 356; and *Autour des "Trois Glorieuses" 1830: Strasbourg, L'Alsace et la liberté: Actes du Colloque de Strasbourg, 16–18 Mai 1980* (Strasbourg: Palais universitaire, 1981).

block administrative control of elections. Hence Constant pushed for secrecy of the ballot. Similarly, Constant defended the right of electoral committees to monitor voting lists so as to prevent prefectoral councils from stacking them with unqualified royalists while deleting qualified Liberal voters. Equally significant was Constant's lifelong labor on behalf of freedom of the press. Newspapers, especially local ones, could play a vital role in party formation by providing sustained ideological polemic; by linking local to national and international concerns; by giving accounts of the conduct, speeches, and attendance of deputies; and by supplying basic information as to voter lists, meetings, and the like. At a time when Liberal committees were supposed to spring into action only during elections, newspapers could provide continuity in discussion of issues and remind readers that they were part of a national movement.

Liberal committees did, however, find ways to make their activities semipermanent. One such means lay in the gathering of signatures for petitions to the Chamber of Deputies. Perhaps the greatest petition campaign was that of 1820 when Liberals sought to block change in the electoral law by using petitions to demonstrate that the nation was opposed, but there were many other such occasions, particularly against prefects who had "cooked" the voting lists or threatened civil servants who did not comply with ministerial voting directions. In 1820 royalists sought to ban collective petitions and Constant attacked the initiative. He also cofounded and then defended subscription campaigns by which Liberals sought to raise funds to defend or compensate individuals or newspapers brought to trial for political reasons. Given his arguments, it was only natural that in 1829–30 Constant defended the Breton associations designed to organize mass refusal to pay taxes should the government "violate" the Charter.[33]

In terms of core values, it is probably impossible to assess to what extent Constant was influenced by the counsels of his local allies. One can, however, note that he attracted followers with very advanced views. Goyet had great faith in the political aptitude of what he termed the "intermediary classes" – small-scale property owners who, more often than not, did not possess the vote.

---

[33] Bastid, Benjamin, I, 336, 340–41, 369, 402, 449–50; Harpaz, ed., Benjamin Constant et Goyet, 291–312; and Alexander, Re-Writing, 92–94, 239, 264–67.

Several of Constant's leading backers in the Bas-Rhin were partisans of full manhood suffrage. It would push matters too far to assert that Constant was a democrat, but it does appear that late in his career Constant became increasingly democratic. Battle with Bourbon despotism perhaps explains his complaint that while workers were allowed to celebrate publicly when news arrived of victory in Algeria, they were prevented from doing so when Liberals won elections. More significant was Constant's criticism of Guizot's proposed measures against popular societies in the aftermath of the July Revolution:

These men, acting on an entirely natural impulse, without any bad intention whatsoever, have seen that they have been promised [new] institutions, and they have assembled to discuss established institutions and the promises made. In theory, they have the right; otherwise why have you consecrated freedom of the press? You have done it so that any citizen can communicate his opinions to an immense number of citizens, and [yet] you want to prevent a handful of citizens from verbally communicating their opinions to a few others.

In July the people of Paris could have committed vast disorders, but they had refrained from doing so; guided by altruism and virtue, they had acted solely in the interests of France. Why then should they be treated with mistrust?[34]

* * *

In sum then, Benjamin Constant played a crucial role in defining the Second Restoration Liberal Opposition. He was a gifted and industrious writer and speaker who addressed all of the leading issues of the period and provided the Opposition with much of their intellectual ammunition, whether in seeking to block reaction or in pushing for fulfillment of the "representative element" in the Charter. In parliament, Constant was a leading member of the Left, and the positions he took consistently placed him in the radical wing of the Opposition. Yet Constant also had a shrewd appreciation of what could be accomplished given current circumstance – hence, the care

[34] Quoted in Jean-Pierre Aguet, "Benjamin Constant, député de Strasbourg, parlementaire sous la Monarchie de Juillet (juillet-décembre 1830)," in *Autour des "Trois Glorieuses" 1830: Strasbourg, L'Alsace et la liberté*, 104. See also Harpaz, *Benjamin Constant et Goyet*, 132, 698–700; Alexander, *Re-Writing*, 224–25, 309–10; and Bastid, *Benjamin*, I, 460.

he took to cultivate relations with moderate Liberals and to keep disputes with other groups (save, at times, ultraroyalists) within reasonable bounds. While he could be sharply critical of the failure of moderate royalist governments to liberalize, he also recognized that utterly uncompromising opposition might well foster the return of ultraroyalists to power. Thus he sought a carrot-and-stick approach to the Richelieu, Decazes, and Martignac ministries. Even when confronted by ultraroyalist government, Constant fought by legal means; he was thus well placed to help define the strategies that ultimately won the constitutional struggle of 1829–30.

Beyond the return to "loyal" defense of the Charter, Liberal success after 1824 had much to do with rebuilding the network that had yielded dramatic rewards prior to 1820, but thereafter collapsed under the weight of insurrection and repression. In publicizing Goyet's methods, Constant had helped to expand Liberal grassroots organization, and in the care he took to consult with, and support the efforts of, local activists, Constant put his theories of representative government into practice. It was logical, and telling, that he should have advocated patriotic oaths, collective petitions, secrecy of the ballot, the right of voters to monitor administrative preparation of voting lists, the right of workers to form political clubs, the right of taxpayers to refuse payment when governments acted unconstitutionally, and ministerial responsibility to parliament. Moreover, throughout the Second Restoration, either at Paris as a member of the *comité directeur* or in touring the provinces as one of its agents, he was at the heart of every major initiative to give the Opposition national coordination. Similarly, for tactical purposes Constant was quite willing to work with groups such as the *doctrinaires* and the Agier defection. Principally due to his coauthorship of Napoleon's *Acte additionnel*, Constant always had a reputation for opportunism, but like government, successful opposition is the art of the possible. Justly famous for his elaboration of liberal doctrine, Constant was far from doctrinaire as a practicing politician and his pragmatism was a major asset to an Opposition that ultimately blocked a return to despotism in 1830.

II. The Psychologist and Critic

8 Constant and Women

Benjamin Constant's relations with women have been a topic of endless fascination and attention. Almost every scholar of Constant's novel *Adolphe* has given in to the temptation to identify the real-life woman who was the model for the novel's main female protagonist Ellénore. (The principal candidates are Charlotte von Hardenberg, Germaine de Staël, and Anna Lindsay.) And many have insisted that the fictional Adolphe is a more or less transparent representation of Constant himself. Although such identifications are informative, they are less illuminating than analyzing how the important women in Constant's life influenced his reflections on interpersonal relationships, human sentiments, and the importance of both for understanding society and politics.[1]

Constant had casual and serious relationships with many women, and married twice. In 1789, as a young *conseiller de Légation* at the court of Brunswick, he married Wilhemine Luise Johanne "Minna" von Cramm, a lady-in-waiting. Due to Constant's absences, Minna's infidelities, and general incompatibility, by 1791 the marriage was in serious trouble; their separation in 1793 was legally codified in 1795. In 1808, he married another German woman, Charlotte von Hardenberg, with whom he remained until his death in 1830. All the evidence suggests that this was the most emotionally stable relationship of his life. Equally important, however, were Constant's intimate connections with the famous Dutch/Swiss writer Isabelle

---

[1] While the characters in *Adolphe* obviously "reflected" Constant's experiences, they were self-conscious literary constructions. Indeed, they are penetrating portraits that the fictional figure Adolphe likely would not have been able to construct. Constant, of course, could and did, indicating a degree of reflectivity that Adolphe lacked.

de Charrière from 1787 until her death in 1805 and with the equally renowned Germaine de Staël between 1794 and 1811. With the latter, he fathered a child, Albertine de Staël, born in 1797. These two major writers of late eighteenth-century and early nineteenth-century French literature were central to Constant's emotional and intellectual life. In addition, however, there were his ties to Marie-Charlotte Johannot, Julie Talma, Anna Lindsay, and Juliette Récamier, to name only the most important. His relations with women were, to borrow the words of Joan Hinde Stewart, "spectacularly complicated."[2]

Many scholars have discussed Constant's relations in the context of a consideration of his "character." During the nineteenth century, Constant did not fare well. In spite of being a political celebrity at the time of his death in 1830, he was often viewed as slightly disreputable. This was in part due to his gambling (he often was unable to pay his gambling debts), his political past (especially his cooperation with Napoleon during the Hundred Days), his being of Swiss birth (and therefore, in the eyes of some, non-French), and his being a Protestant divorcée married, during his final years, to a German divorcée. This negative reputation was reinforced by critical characterizations of Constant disseminated by descendants of Germaine de Staël (especially the Broglie family) after she and Constant had separated. There was also the unflattering portrait penned by Sainte-Beuve.[3] With the publication of an abridged version of the "intimate journals" in 1887, more information was available, not least concerning Constant's perception of his emotional and intellectual needs, and the important place of women in relationship to these needs.[4] He reveals himself to be sexually promiscuous, continually

---

[2] Joan Hinde Stewart, "*Adolphe*, by Benjamin Constant," in *Encyclopedia of the Novel*, vol. 1, ed. P. Schellinger (Chicago: Fitzroy Dearborn, 1998), 45–46.

[3] Sainte-Beuve was especially censorious, referring to Constant as "un esprit supérieur et fin, uni à un caractère faible et à une sensibilité maladive." This quote is from "Un Dernier mot sur Benjamin Constant," originally published in 1845; reprinted in C. A. Sainte-Beuve, *Portraits contemporains*, t. 5 (Paris: Calmann Lévy, 1889), 279. This article shows Sainte-Beuve at his prudish and hypercritical worst.
   For an analysis of Sainte-Beuve's view of Constant, see the discussion by Pierre Deguise, *Benjamin Constant méconnu: le livre De la religion* (Genève: Droz, 1966), 3–37.

[4] Constant's *Journaux intimes* were published in an altered, extremely abridged form in 1887. The complete texts have been available only since 1952. The most accessible edition is in *Œuvres*, 221–823. For an account of their publication history,

in pursuit of women for physical satisfaction, emotional warmth, social respectability, and apparent security, and at the same time chronically anxious and indecisive. He searched alternately for the security that a relationship seemed to promise or, once in a relationship, for freedom from the constraints it entailed. Obviously, saddened by the fragility of relationships and the difficulty of maintaining them, he was also obsessed by the tragedy of their failure and the emotional suffering that this entailed. Much of this personal experience informed *Adolphe* – "that most quietly disruptive of all French novels," in the words of Alison Fairlie[5] – which is about the failure of a relationship and, more broadly, about the tragic incompatibility of certain character traits with the structure and mores of modern society.

Twentieth-century analyses have generally been less censorious, though, arguably, this has as much to do with changing mores as anything else. Again, the issue of "character" has been central. Modern scholars comment on Constant's chronic anxiety and tendency to melancholia, his fear of ending relationships, but his inability to sustain them. Gustave Rudler and Georges Poulet have noted his obsession with death, his uncertainty about the future, his detachment, his tendency to indecision, and his oscillation between one quality and its opposite.[6] Etienne Hofmann points to doubt and moderation as the essence of Constant's personality and notes how these cohere uneasily with his desire for stability and certitude, and with his fear of ennui.[7] Kurt Kloocke also stresses the importance of Constant's ennui, linking this predisposition to the destructive nihilism of the Romantic sensibility.[8] Other scholars, more critically, see

---

see Roulin's "notice," 1476–82. There is now, however, a wonderful new scholarly edition: *OCBC/Œuvres*, VI. References will be to this new edition.

[5] Alison Fairlie, "The Art of Constant's *Adolphe*: 1. The Stylization of Experience," in *Imagination and Language: Collected Essays on Constant, Baudelaire, Nerval and Flaubert* (Cambridge: Cambridge University Press, 1981), 3.

[6] Gustave Rudler, *La Jeunesse de Benjamin Consant: 1767–1794* (Paris: Colin, 1908); Georges Poulet, *Benjamin Constant par lui-même* (Paris: Seuil, 1968).

[7] Etienne Hofmann, *Les "Principes de politique" de Benjamin Constant: la genèse d'une œuvre et l'évolution de la pensée de leur auteur (1789–1806)*, t. I (Genève: Droz, 1980), 80, 89, 194, 200.

[8] Kurt Kloocke, *Benjamin Constant: une biographie intellectuelle* (Genève: Droz, 1984), 32.

Constant as a spoiled, self-centered misfit. C. P. Courtney, for example, describes the young Constant in 1787, when he met Isabelle de Charrière, as "a mixture of shyness and aggressiveness, intellectually brilliant but emotionally immature." He was "a conceited monster and cosmopolitan *déraciné* constantly at odds with his milieu and family (including his well-meaning father)."[9] Harold Nicolson, noting Constant's "variations between egoism and remorse," judges that Constant "remained temperamentally adolescent to the day of his death."[10]

What is impressive, of course, is how successful and productive Constant was in spite of his unfortunate early life history and in spite of the emotional turmoil left in its wake.[11] Yet the psychologically oriented analyses of Constant's character have frequently exaggerated the negative valences of his relationships with woman at the expense of seeing their positive sides. These accounts have also often overstated the degree to which Constant was a weak plaything of stronger forces. In fact, many of Constant's relationships were characterized by deep mutual emotional attachment, and the most famous were characterized, in addition, by the shared delight of finding an intellectual partner of such high caliber. Constant's *Journaux intimes* reveal, as Tzvetan Todorov has pointed out, his emotional weaknesses with "a pitiless lucidity,"[12] but they also disclose an unusually acute and critical mind. As one would expect from the private daily ruminations of someone as perceptive as Constant, the *journaux* read a bit like life as it might feel to live it – a mixture of confusion, surges of power, crosscurrents of frustration, moments of triumph, recognition that things are not as they previously had appeared, and belated realization that in fact things *are* as they

---

[9] C. P. Courtney, *Isabelle de Charrière (Belle de Zuylen): A Biography* (Oxford: Voltaire Foundation, 1993), 381, 388.

[10] Harold Nicolson, *Benjamin Constant* (Garden City, New York: Doubleday & Company, 1949), 60.

[11] As George Armstrong Kelly has perceptively noted, "his resiliency and fortitude are far more impressive than his malignancy. Deprived of the normal sources of courage, he managed to show great courage amid a life pointed toward tribulation and decomposition." (*The Humane Comedy: Constant, Tocqueville, and French Liberalism* [Cambridge: Cambridge University Press, 1992], 8.)

[12] Tzvetan Todorov, *A Passion for Democracy: The Life, the Women He Loved and the Thought of Benjamin Constant*, translated from French (New York: Algora Publishing, 1999), 8.

previously had appeared. Constant's strength – which accounts for the continuing appeal of the diaries – was his persistent endeavor to see his emotional weaknesses as clearly as possible, to analyze the ways in which various character traits played a role in his personal life and in the affairs of the wider world, and to chart a course that would promote improvement. Constant's vulnerabilities were expressive of his sensitivity to the many and varied forces and settings in constant flux around him. Even his novel *Adolphe* is evidence of this. While it obviously "reflected" his experiences (something arguably true of all novels), it was a self-conscious literary construction of immense introspective power. It grew out of Constant's coruscating attempt at self-understanding.

Constant's relationships with women were varied and complex. He experienced personal obsessive desire (with Harriet Trevor and Juliette Récamier), being the object of obsessive desire (with Anna Lindsay), having intimate and confidential friendships (with his cousin Rosalie de Constant, Isabelle de Charrière, and Julie Talma), and being the intellectual companion of two of those impressive women of his time (Isabelle de Charrière and Germaine de Staël). He felt paternal love (for his daughter Albertine de Staël), contemplated a marriage of convenience (with Amélie Fabri), and ended with an emotionally stable marriage (with Charlotte von Hardenberg). No simple model can summarize Constant's relationships with women.

To begin to understand this complex life, we must first look at Constant's relationships with the most prominent and important of these women. There follows a consideration of Constant's own reflections about intimate relationships (his own and others), and how these reflections were intertwined with his broader consideration of that most illusive subject – the "self" – and with his theories of culture, society, and politics.

IMPORTANT WOMEN IN CONSTANT'S LIFE

Constant's Family

In the beginning were the important women in Constant's family. His mother Henriette-Pauline de Chandieu (1742–67) was of a Swiss Protestant family that traced its roots back to the Dauphiné region of France. She gave birth to Benjamin when she was twenty-five; tragically, she died sixteen days later. Benjamin's father, Louis-Arnold-Juste de Constant (1726–1812), was crushed, indeed suffered a seizure, but he survived and returned to his professional post as the commander of a Swiss regiment in Holland. Young Benjamin, as a consequence, was sent to his relatives for care: first to his maternal grandmother, François de Chandieu, and then to his paternal grandmother, "la Générale" Rose-Susanne de Constant.

Dennis Wood, in the best recent biography of Constant, draws from the clinical work of John Bowlby and Ian Suttie to suggest that Constant's character was largely the result of these early traumas: the early death of his mother; a father who was aloof, vain, secretive, stern, and emotionally unavailable for his son; a string of caretakers – relatives and itinerate and sometimes abusive tutors – who left the young boy feeling unloved and abandoned. These factors, Wood convincingly argues, provide a key to understanding Constant's fear of rejection, his depressions, and his difficulty sustaining a long-term intimate relationship. Constant, on this reading, remained psychologically locked in an inner world that revolved around the tyranny of his early deprivations.[13] Whatever one's assessment of the strengths and weaknesses of the mature Constant, there is little doubt that the self-enclosed sensual cycles of his life and many of his inner demons resulted from his early history.[14]

At the age of four, Constant was moved to the care of Jeanne-Suzanne-Marie Magnin (1752–1820), a young woman of twenty years, who cared for the young child between 1772 and 1774. There is a curious history associated with this. At the age of nine, Marianne Magnin (as she was called) had been kidnapped from her peasant family by Constant's father Juste, who took charge of raising and educating her. After the death of Benjamin's mother, Marianne Magnin became Juste's mistress and, subsequently (probably in 1792), his

---

[13] Dennis Wood, *Benjamin Constant: A Biography* (London: Routledge, 1993). In the words of Dan Hofstadter, who agrees with Wood's analysis, Constant "had the orphan's tendency to melancholia, to cramped self-reliance and compulsive nomadism." (*The Love Affair as a Work of Art* [New York: Farrar, Straus and Giroux, 1996], 10.)

[14] For a more classically Freudian account, see Han Verhoeff, *"Adolphe" et Constant; une étude psychocritique* (Paris: Klincksieck, 1976).

wife. Marianne Magnin gave birth to a son Charles in 1784 and a daughter Louise in 1792. Until 1798, Constant was unaware of the marriage and therefore of the fact that he had half siblings.[15] When Constant's father died in 1812, there was a dispute over inheritance, but cordial relations between Constant and Marianne Magnin remained.[16]

The other two important female members of Constant's family were his maternal aunt, Anne-Marie-Pauline-Andrienne comtesse de Nassau (1744–1814), with whom Constant corresponded until her death, and his cousin Rosalie-Marguerite de Constant (1758–1834). Rosalie never married, and she remained the "dear cousin" who Constant could rely on for kindness and support. A testimony of her importance is the voluminous correspondence between them.[17]

Early Infatuations

As a boy and young man, Constant had a series of flirtations and engrossing infatuations about which we have an unusually large quantity of information, most of it from Constant's own hand. Although these affairs were less important than his later connections with Isabelle de Charrière, Germaine de Staël, and Charlotte von Hardenberg (to name only the most significant), they do reveal Constant's impulsiveness and lifelong insecurities.

In 1781, at the age of thirteen, he seems to have become enamored of the daughter of David Grenier while living with his father in the garrison town of Geertruidenberg. What was probably his first love affair took place in Brussels four years later. Sometime between August and November 1785, Constant fell in love with Marie-Charlotte Johannot, the wife of a Genevan cloth merchant who later became a member of the Convention. Marie-Charlotte swept the young Benjamin off his feet, but she was prudent enough to insist on some distance, apparently recognizing that the relationship could not succeed. Constant remained deeply attached, as indicated by

---

[15] See the discussion in Wood, *Benjamin Constant: A Biography*, 282, note 75.
[16] See Paul Delbouille, "Le dernier procès de Juste de Constant et l'esprit de famille chez Benjamin et chez Marianne Magnin," *ABC* 26 (2002), 89–101.
[17] The first letter we have is dated March 19, 1786. See *OCBC/CG*, I.

a poignant passage in his memoir, the so-called *Le Cahier rouge*,
written in 1811.

> In this coterie [of Genevans in Brussels] there was a woman of about twenty-
> six or twenty-eight, with a very seductive figure and very distinguished
> intelligence. I felt drawn towards her, without clearly admitting it to myself,
> when, by a few words that at first surprised me more than they delighted
> me, she allowed me to discover that she loved me.

> Madame Johannot – such was her name – is set apart in my memory from
> all the other women I have known: my liaison with her was very brief,
> and reduced to a few things. But she never made me pay for the sweetness
> she gave me with any mixture of agitation or grief; and at forty-four years
> old I remain grateful for the happiness that I enjoyed with her when I was
> eighteen.

> The poor woman came to a very sad end. I was myself in Paris [when she
> poisoned herself years later] . . . and I have never been able to pronounce her
> name without being moved to the bottom of my soul.[18]

Madame Johannot was clearly more important than the next focus
of Constant's attention, Harriet Trevor (1751–1829), the wife of the
English ambassador in Turin. Constant met Harriet in 1786 at her
house on the outskirts of Lausanne, where Constant went to gam-
ble. There is an extremely entertaining description of his obsessive
infatuation in *Le Cahier rouge*, one that would find a strong echo
in *Adolphe*. Constant remembers how he convinced himself that he
was deeply in love with her.

> I took it into my head to win her favor. I wrote her an eloquent letter in which
> I declared my love for her. I handed her this letter one evening, and returned
> the following day for her answer. Agitation due to uncertainty about the
> result of my overture had put me in a kind of fever, which resembled the
> passion that at first I had only wanted to feign. Madame Trevor replied to me
> in writing, as the circumstances demanded. She spoke of her obligations, and
> offered me a tender friendship. . . . I thought that the adroit thing to do was
> to show the most violent despair because she offered me only friendship in
> return for my love. The poor woman, who probably had had affairs previously
> with men of more experience, did not know how to act in this scene, which

---

[18] "Le cahier rouge," in *Œuvres*, 128. There are three letters from Johannot to Constant in *OCBC/CG* I, 67–70.

was the more embarrassing for her because I made no movement that might have put her in a position to terminate it in a manner agreeable to us both.

I kept myself ten steps away from her, and whenever she approached to calm or console me I retreated, repeating that, since she had for me only friendship, there was nothing left for me but to die. For four hours she could get nothing else out of me, and I departed leaving her, I suspect, very annoyed with a suitor who would dispute about a synonym.[19]

Constant recounts that he continued his pursuit for months, "becoming each day more and more in love, because each day I ran up against difficulties that I myself had created." She responded with patience and became more attentive, but she resisted becoming his lover. *Le Cahier rouge* provides a hilarious description of his foolish actions. Jealous of an Englishman, he threatened him to a duel, even though, as it turned out, "he took not the least interest in Mrs. Trevor."

With the hopes of appeasing me, he declared to me that, far from wishing to take the wind out of my sails, he did not even find Mrs. Trevor attractive. I then wanted to fight him because he did not sufficiently respect the woman I loved. Our pistols were already loaded when my Englishman, who had no desire for so ridiculous a duel, got out of it very cleverly. He demanded seconds, and informed me that he would tell them why I had picked a quarrel with him. When I told him that it was his duty to keep such a matter secret, he laughed at me, and I had to renounce my brilliant enterprise.[20]

The episode ended when Benjamin's father took him to Paris, where he quickly lost interest in Mrs. Trevor. He was unmoved, he tells us, when he saw her three months later.

In Paris, there was a somewhat similar episode, with another desperately unsuccessful resolution, though the object of Constant's affection was not a mature woman in her mid-thirties, but a young woman of seventeen years. In May 1787, Constant met Jeanne-Jacqueline-Henriette "Jenny" Pourrat, the daughter of Augustine-Magedeleine Pourrat (ca. 1740–1818), who ran a Parisian salon that Constant frequented. Constant declared his love and proposed marriage. When he was rebuffed and confronted by the lover of Madame Pourrat (Jenny's mother), he impulsively staged an attempted

[19] "Le cahier rouge," 130.
[20] Ibid., 131.

suicide. "I repeated without ceasing that I wanted to kill myself, and by saying it I almost came to believe it, although at bottom I had not the least desire to do so."[21] He made a clumsy attempt to do so, but failed, and was (not surprisingly) barred from the house. His father sent for him again; or, rather, he sent a Lieutenant Benay to bring Constant to his residence in 's-Hoertogenbosch. Constant evaded the lieutenant and escaped to Scotland.

On his return, Constant was sent by his father to take up a position he had arranged for him at the court of Duke Karl Wilhelm Ferdinand in Braunschweig (Brunswick). Benjamin arrived in Brunswick in December 1788, and during the following year, he was given the position of a *conseiller de Légation* at the court. At the court he met Wilhemine Luise Johanne (Minna) von Cramm, a lady-in-waiting to the duchess. Constant became enamored and, equally significant, saw her as a wife that would bring him financial stability and independence from his father. They were married on May 8, 1789. Constant took Minna to Switzerland in July of the same year to present her to his family. He seems to have been very happy in the first two years of the marriage. It is only at the end of 1791 that his correspondence with Isabelle de Charrière indicates that there were difficulties. In December 1791, they had struggles over the fact that Minna, while Constant was away, had taken as a lover a young Russian prince named Gallitzine.[22] This led, by 1793, to a public scandal in Brunswick that contributed to Constant's feelings of isolation. The other reason for this isolation was his support of the Revolution in France. It was about this time, probably in January 1793, that Constant first met Charlotte von Hardenberg (about whom more will be said later). Constant and Minna agreed to an eventual separation on March 20, 1793. The divorce became final on November 18, 1795.

Isabelle de Charrière

Even before the dramatic episode with Jenny Pourat and before Constant went to Brunswick and met Minna von Cramm, he encountered, in early March 1787 at the Paris salon of the Jean-Baptiste

---

[21] Ibid., 138–39.
[22] During this period when the marriage with Minna had no future (and after Minna had taken a lover), Constant had an affair with an actress named Caroline (November 1792).

Suard, Isabelle de Charrière. Isabelle de Charrière was an accomplished writer whose productions included novels, short stories, plays, essays, verse, and operatic libretti. Born into a prominent family in Holland in 1740, she had known many famous suitors, including James Boswell, and had carried on, as a young woman, a voluminous correspondence with Constant's uncle, Constant d'Hermenches.[23] Following her marriage to Charles-Emmanuel de Charrière in 1771, she moved to Le Pontet in Colombier, Switzerland. She was forty-six when she met the nineteen-year-old Constant in 1787 in Paris. Constant was enthralled by this older woman, twenty-seven years his senior. He recounted in *Le Cahier rouge* that "it was during this epoch that I made the acquaintance of the first woman of superior intelligence whom I have known, one who had the most intelligence of all those whom I have encountered.... We passed some days and nights together. She was very severe in her judgements on all those she saw. I was by nature given to mockery. We suited each other perfectly."[24]

Whether or not the relationship was physical remains a mystery.[25] What is not in doubt, however, is how deeply attracted they were to each other and how profoundly important this connection remained for Constant for the next eighteen years, until Isabelle de Charrière's death in 1805. No doubt, there were some obvious similarities of background and experience that brought them together: both were non-French by birth, but both wrote in French; both were highly

[23] There is now an English edition of this correspondence: *There Are No Letters Like Yours: The Correspondence of Isabelle de Charrière and Constant d'Hermenches*, trans. Janet Whatley and Malcolm Whatley (Lincoln, NE: University of Nebraska Press, 2000).

[24] "Le cahier rouge," 135. On Isabelle de Charrière, see especially C. P. Courtney's recent authoritative biography, *Isabelle de Charrière (Belle de Zuylen)* (Oxford: Voltaire Foundation, 1993). Also see the wonderful short book, originally published in 1925, by Geoffrey Scott, *The Portrait of Zélide* (New York: Helen Marx, 1997). In addition, see Philippe Godet, *Madame de Charrière, d'après de nombreux documents inédits (1740–1805)*, 2 vols. (Genève: Jullien, 1906); Joan Hinde Stewart, *Gynographs: French Novels by Women of the Late Eighteenth Century* (Lincoln, NE: University of Nebraska Press, 1993), 96–132; Mona Ozouf, *Women's Words: An Essay on French Singularity*, trans. Jane Marie Todd (Chicago: University of Chicago Press, 1997), 21–44; Raymond Trousson, *Isabelle de Charrière: un destin de femme au XVIIIe siècle* (Paris: Hachette, 1994).

[25] See Roland Mortier, "Belle and Benjamin: Political Gradations," *Eighteenth-Century Life*, 13 (1) (February 1989), 16–25.

intelligent and extraordinarily gifted; both felt (or *had* felt in the case of Isabelle) hemmed in by the constraints of their families. But the real commonality seems to have been their caustically skeptical view of the world, a deeply felt unhappiness with their environments, and a strong desire for friendship, connection, and intimacy. It is difficult to resist a clinical interpretation: at forty-six, Isabelle must have seen Benjamin as the intelligent articulate son she never had; Benjamin must have seen Isabelle as the warm nurturing mother he never had.

Gustave Rudler attributes to Isabelle de Charrière a large responsibility for the birth and growth of Constant's skepticism, pessimism, and rebelliousness.[26] Most modern scholars see her influence as benign or positive. Cecil Courtney suggests that Isabelle understood Constant's rebelliousness, but that she did not encourage his unbridled individualism and anarchic behavior.[27] Dennis Wood sees the influence of Isabelle de Charrière as "a tonic" for Constant, a practical sustaining influence during Constant's years as a young man. She was the first woman in Constant's adult life to give him the stable affection that permitted him to accept without guilt his own perceptions: for example, his sense that all things and people are complex and mutable. She played a critical role in Constant's development as a novelist. And, she helped him find the strength to rebel against his obtuse and difficult father.[28] The correspondence between the two is justly famous for its literary quality, for its intellectual power, and for its political perspicuity.[29]

What is beyond dispute is the important role Isabelle de Charrière played in Constant's life during the next few years. He referred to Colombier, where Isabelle lived in her house at Le Pontet, as the haven to which he could always return.[30] In person or via correspondence, Isabelle was principal confidant and advisor during this early period of his life, a difficult time for Constant. Between

---

[26] Gustave Rudler, *La Jeunesse de Benjamin Consant: 1767–1794.*
[27] Courtney, *Isabelle de Charrière,* 384–91.
[28] Wood, *Benjamin Constant: A Biography,* 92–93.
[29] This correspondence, which is being published in *OSBC/CG* [currently up to 1799], is available in its entirety in an edition edited by Jean-Daniel Candaux, *Isabelle de Charrière Benjamin Constant: Correspondance (1787–1805)* (Paris: Desjonquères, 1996).
[30] He visited many times: December 10, 1787 – February 16, 1788; December 1791; several times between June 1793 and September 1793; August 1794.

January 1790 and November 1792, for example, there were a number
of enmeshed events that together led to his frustration and depression. There was, first of all, his boredom with life in Brunswick. He
found the people at court tedious and stupid, and he was progressively isolated because of his sympathy for the French Revolution.
Secondly, there was the deterioration of his relationship with his
wife Minna. And, finally, there were the legal and financial difficulties of his father, a consequence of a mutiny of the officers in Juste de
Constant's battalion that had taken place on October 29, 1787. Juste
lost the initial legal battle before the military court in Amsterdam
on August 25, 1788, and Constant spent an impressive amount of
time during the next few years working to save his father's reputation and wealth. Juste was eventually rehabilitated in 1796, but, as
C. P. Courtney has noted, it was "a hollow victory, for by this time
Just was completely ruined."[31] The result for Benjamin was despon-
dency and melancholy, expressed with such force in his letters to
Isabelle.

With the onset of the Terror in France, Constant's relationship
with Charrière was tested by diverging assessments of the Revolution. Isabelle, who always disliked abstract systems and favored
moderate reform, became more and more critical of the Revolution
following the events of August 1792. By late 1793, she was expressing
sympathies for the counterrevolutionary views of Antoine Ferrand
(author of Rétablissement de la monarchie) and of Mallet Du Pan
(author of Considérations sur la nature de la Révolution de France).
Constant had some criticisms of the Terror, but he remained a sup-
porter of the Revolution. In a letter of September 9, 1794, he told
Isabelle that

you were wrong, if you believed that I doubted the possibility of a Republic
without a tyrant like Robespierre, and consequently with liberty. I believed
that compression, in that moment of crisis [during the Terror], to be absolutely necessary. I believe it still, but I think that a time will come, a time
that is not far off, when this compression will no longer be needed and when
the Republic will be only liberty. . . . I am like a man who, obliged to travel
on a very bad road, tired of hearing his fellow travelers complain about the
rocks, the mud, the potholes, the chaos, plugs his ears, and fixes his eyes on
the tower of the village that is his destination.[32]

---

[31] Courtney, Isabelle de Charrière, 489.
[32] Constant to Isabelle de Charrière, September 9, 1794, 364.

Isabelle found this "ends justifies the means" attitude offensive, and she could not resist making fun of his metaphor. "It is very good not to complain of a bad road, but it is equally bad, that is to say it is a shame, for an intelligent person to take for the tower of the village that is one's destination a stick illuminated by the moon."[33]

The relationship survived this strain, but when Constant fell under the spell of Germaine de Staël, Isabelle de Charrière distanced herself. Perhaps Isabelle was jealous of losing Constant to a younger rival or found the rival an affront to and rejection of the way of life and set of values (so different from those of Germaine de Staël) that she assumed she and Constant shared.[34] It probably had elements of both. Shortly after their break, she referred to Constant's political positions as driven by his "desire to make a sensation."[35] Constant, nonetheless, remained immensely attached, and he was devastated when she died in 1805.

Germaine de Staël

Constant's richest intellectual collaboration, but also the most troubled emotional connection, was with Germaine de Staël (1766–1817).[36] Germaine de Staël was the daughter of Jacques Necker, a wealthy Genevan banker who was a finance minister of Louis XVI during some of the last years of the Old Regime (1777–81 and 1788–90). Her mother, Suzanne Curchod, presided over a fashionable salon in Paris, and as a result Germaine as a child met and delighted many of the luminaries of the late French Enlightenment. By all accounts, she was articulate, precociously brilliant, and self-centered to the point of grandiosity. Because of her father's position in the government, Germaine observed many dramatic events during the early months of the Revolution, which she discussed with liberal commentary in her posthumously published Considérations sur la Révolution Française. In 1786, she married Eric Magnus de Staël

---

[33] Isabelle de Charrière to Constant, September 10, 1794; iv, 559–60.
[34] Courtney prefers the latter explanation. See his Isabelle de Charrière, 546–84.
[35] Isabelle de Charrière to Huber, July 11, 1795; cited in Courtney, 581.
[36] The Constant–de Staël relationship is discussed in many sources. For the early years, I have found especially useful: Béatrice W. Jasinski, L'Engagement de Benjamin Constant: amour et politique (1794–1796) (Paris: Minard, 1971). For the period after January 1804, the essential source is Constant's Journaux intimes.

Holstein, the Swedish ambassador to France. Germaine de Staël was best known for her publications, *Lettres sur les ouvrages et le caractère de J.J. Rousseau* (1788), *De l'influence des passions* (1796), *De la littérature* (1800), and *De l'Allemagne* (1810), and for her novels *Zulma* (1794), *Delphine* (1802), and *Corinne* (1807). She also exerted cultural and political influence, especially during the empire when her château of Coppet in the *pays de Vaud* became a center of liberal opposition to Napoleon.[37]

From their first meeting on September 18, 1794, Constant was dazzled with Germaine's mind, wit, and enthusiasm. He was immediately infatuated and soon very much in love. De Staël, who at the time was the lover of Adolf von Ribbing, was not swept off her feet, though she was attracted to Constant's energy, sensibility, and generosity, and found great pleasure in their intellectual exchange. Constant became part of de Staël's entourage, but not her lover, in February 1795 when he moved into a room in her house in Mézery. Distraught that they were not lovers, Constant replayed some of the dramatic scenes of his youthful infatuations, including a threatened/attempted suicide in late March 1795. De Staël was touched by his devotion, but found him physically unappealing and experienced at most what Béatrice Jasinksi has called "amused compassion."[38]

They returned to Paris together on May 25, 1795, and became embroiled in post-Thermidorian politics. They both supported the Constitution of 1795 and worried about the restoration of the Bourbons, whose leader Provence (the future Louis XVIII) made it clear in his Declaration of Verona (June 24, 1795) that a royalist restoration was synonymous with a return to the Old Regime and revenge against republicans associated with the Revolution. They also opposed the Jacobin Left, whose activities (such as the insurrection of 1 Prairial, May 20, 1795), they feared, would return France to the Terror. De Staël's salon at the Swedish embassy on the rue du Bac became a central meeting place of moderate republicans

[37] See, especially, the publications of the *colloques* consecrated to the "groupe de Coppet," *ABC* (1988, 1994, 2003); and *Coppet, creuset de l'esprit liberal: les idées politiques et constitutionnelles du groupe de Madame de Staël*, sous la direction de Lucien Jaume (Aix-en-Provence: Presses Universitaires d'Aix-Marseille, 2000).

[38] Jasinski, *L'Engagement de Benjamin Constant*, 19.

and constitutional monarchists working to find a "liberal" middle way.[39]

Constant and de Staël became lovers in late January 1796. In mid-April, they signed an "engagement" that declared their intention to remain "indissolubly joined together" and "to devote our lives to each other."[40] Because of her political activities and reputation, de Staël was frequently forced to live outside of France during the Directory. There was a decree for her expulsion from France dated October 15, 1795, for example, and she left Paris for her father's château Coppet on December 20. She was in and out of France during the next few years, and, as the political leaders permitted, in Paris.[41] Constant was torn between pursuing his ambition to play a role in French politics and being with Germaine. As a consequence, he was often on the move between Paris, his residence outside Paris at Hérivaux, where Germaine often stayed when she was allowed to reside in France, and the de Staël château in Switzerland. On June 8, 1797, Germaine, in Paris, gave birth to Albertine de Staël, Constant's only child.

The connection between Constant and de Staël was buttressed, from the beginning, by similar political and intellectual concerns. They read and corrected each other's works; some, like de Staël's unpublished manuscript *Des circonstances actuelles qui peuvent terminer la Révolution et des principes qui doivent fonder la République en France*, were in essence collaborative projects. Their politics were deeply influenced by the constitutional ideas of Germaine's father, Jacques Necker.[42] Both embraced a middling "liberal" politics that recommended the protection of "rights," called for a constitutional and representative system that would ensure the

---

[39] During 1795, de Staël was close to the republican opposition around Pierre-Louis Roederer's journal *Le Journal de Paris*, while Constant in July 1795 moved closer to the partisans of the government around Jean-Baptiste Louvet's journal *La Sentinelle*. For the political maneuverings of this period, see Henri Grange, *Benjamin Constant: amoureux et républicain 1795–1799* (Paris: Les Belles Lettres, 2004).

I have argued in a previous publication that Constant and de Staël were the first to use the term "liberal" to refer to their political stance between the Old Regime and Terror. See my "Benjamin Constant, the French Revolution, and the Origins of French Romantic Liberalism," *French Historical Studies*, 23 (4) (2000), 607–37.

[40] These quotes are from Wood, *Benjamin Constant: A Biography*, 142.

[41] She was, for example, in Paris from May 1797 to January 1798.

[42] See Henri Grange, *Les Idées de Necker* (Université de Lille III, 1973); and Grange, "De Necker à Benjamin Constant ou du libéralisme ploutocratique au libéralisme démocratique," *Le Groupe de Coppet et la Révolution Française* (Lausanne: Institut Benjamin Constant, 1988), 63–71.

separation and balance of power, and insisted that a culture of public involvement was necessary for republican survival.[43] Constant published his first political pamphlets during their time together, and he worked on a large manuscript, *Fragments d'un ouvrage abandonné sur la possibilité d'une constitution républicaine dans un grand pays*, unpublished until 1972, that contained many of the political ideas that would emerge in his later works.[44]

Constant was clearly attracted by de Staël's intellect, but he was equally driven by passion. Unfortunately, their tastes were quite different, and from the middle of 1798 there were severe strains in the relationship. In a revealing letter to his aunt dated May 15, 1798, Constant complained that he was "isolated without being independent, subjugated without being united with her. I see the last years of my youth passing by with neither the repose of solitude nor the gentle affections of a legitimate union. I have tried in vain to break it off."[45] He and Germaine were reconciled the following month, when she arrived at Hérivaux, but this was the beginning of growing tensions and irritations. Constant was appointed to the Tribunate on December 24, 1799, and for the next few years (he was eliminated from the institution by a decree dated January 17, 1802, but continued to serve until March 21) his energies were consumed with his duties and activities at the heart of French politics. Germaine spent most of this time at Coppet.

While there remained mutual intellectual respect and influence between Constant and de Staël, the first decade of the new century was filled with dramatic confrontations interspersed with temporary reconciliations. They did not definitively part ways until May 10, 1811, but the emotional closeness of the first few years became more intermittent, and they were more and more apart. The strain is revealed most starkly in Constant's *Journaux intimes*, where he

---

[43] Constant's early political writings are in *OCBC/Œuvres*, I. For an analysis of Constant early liberalism, see my "Benjamin Constant, the French Revolution, and the Origins of French Romantic Liberalism."

[44] Recently, both have been published. Madame de Staël, *Des circonstances actuelles qui peuvent terminer la Révolution et des principes qui doivent fonder la République en France*, ed. Lucia Omacini (Geneva: Droz, 1979); Benjamin Constant, *Fragments d'un ouvrage abandonné sur la possibilité d'une constitution républicaine dans un grand pays*, ed. Henri Grange (Paris: Aubier, 1991).

[45] Constant to Anne-Marie-Pauline-Adrienne de Nassau, May 15, 1798, *OCBC/CG*, III, 335.

vacillates between his desire to rupture with Germaine and his desire to "return to this tie because of memories or some momentary charm."[46] There are extended entries where Constant sees Germaine as "the only person who understands him" and imagines a future in which they will be married. More frequently, he expresses his need for a quiet scholarly life and imagines (or celebrates) his escape from the exhausting rigors of the continuous sociability that surrounds Germaine.[47] Most arrestingly, the private journals record the dramatic gyrations from one to the other, sometimes in the same day.[48] One emerges from reading Constant's private journals with the sense that Germaine was such an immense presence – intellectually, physically, and emotionally – that Constant was alternately dazzled, enthralled, exhausted, and disgusted. Sometimes, he seems to have experienced all of these simultaneously.[49] As he himself put it in May 1804, "It is certain that in our union, I will always be the second person, cherished sometimes, but always subordinated. It is not less than half of my time – time which is so precious and which passes so rapidly at my age [he is 36 years old] – that will be taken by her."[50]

---

[46] This is a direct translation of the *code chiffré du journal abrégé* – that is, of the numerical code that Constant himself devised to refer to his shifting emotional states for the abridged version of his *Journaux intimes*. 2 = "Désir de rompre mon éternel lien dont il est si souvent question." 3 = "Retours à ce lien par des souvenirs ou quelque charme momentané." [*Journaux intimes (1804–1807)*, 44.]

[47] For example, on July 1, 1804, Constant, in his journal, wrote the following: "fatale liaison! ma santé, mon bonheur, ma gloire, tout en est victime. Jamais on n'a vu de caractère aussi misérablement faible que celui de Biondetta [Germaine], jamais égoisme qui se fit moins scrupule de peser sur les autres, et de se les immoler, jamais prétentions plus multiformes, et plus ombrageuses. Tout cela accompagne de beaucoup d'esprit, de grâce, de naturel, et de bonté. C'est là le malheur. enfin le tems s'avance ou je prendrai mon parti, et certes j'irai plutot en Laponie que de me laisser retenir plus longtems dans cet esclavage." [*Journaux intimes (1804–1807)*, 157.]

[48] On April 9, 1804, for example, Constant recorded "2" in his *Journaux intimes* (referring to the number indicated in footnote 46). On April 10, he recorded 3; on April 12, 3; on April 23, 2; on April 24, 2; on April 25, 2; on April 26, 2; on April 27, 2; on April 28, 2; on April 30, 2; on May 1, 2.3.2; on May 2, 2; on May 3, 3; on May 4, 3; etc. [*Journaux intimes (1804–1807)*, 102–20.]

[49] This speaks to de Staël's need always to be the center of the attention. As Henri Grange cogently puts it, for de Staël, Constant was "toujours nécessaire et jamais suffisant." See Grange, *Benjamin Constant: amoureux et républicain 1795–1799*, 134.

[50] *Journaux intimes*, entry of May 1, 1804, 117–18.

Julie Talma and Anna Lindsay

Two women who were extremely important to Constant during the final turbulent years with Germaine were Julie Talma and Anna Lindsay. Julie Talma (1756–1805) was an ardent republican who ran a salon in Paris that Constant frequented during the late 1790s. Constant and Talma became close friends, but probably not lovers, and spent a great deal of time together when he was in Paris. In the words of Harold Nicolson, "With gentle sagacity she steered their affair into the calm lagoon of a devoted and outspoken friendship. She became the firmest as well as the most penetrating friend that Constant ever had."[51] When she died in 1805, Constant was devastated.

Constant's relationship with Anna Lindsay (1764–1806), with whom he had a passionate and stormy affair, was very different. Anna Lindsay (born O'Dwyer) was the daughter of an Irish Catholic innkeeper from Calais, but she had been supported and educated by the Duchess de Fitz-James, who was impressed with her abilities. She subsequently accepted a number of male "protectors" to avoid poverty. At the age of twenty, she married a British officer, Louis Drummond, with whom she had a son (in 1788), but in 1789 he abandoned Anna and returned to Scotland. She then began an eleven-year liaison with Auguste de Lamoignon, a married man with whom she had two children and spent time in London. Constant met Anna Lindsay in the salon of Julie Talma on November 20, 1800. At this moment, Anna was distanced from Lamoignon, who was patching things up with his wife, apparently for financial reasons. Anna and Constant fell deliriously in love and had an intense affair during the next six months. Constant's letters suggest that this was the most emotionally consuming and physically fulfilling relationship of his life.[52] On December 13, 1800, he wrote to her that

you are the unique goal of my existence, the entire occupation of my thought. To live with you, to take you from the absurd and unnatural circle in which you live, to consecrate to you all that I am, all that I value, is my only hope.... My love, we shall consecrate all our existence to all the pleasures and to all the joys. We shall fulfill each other with all species of

---

[51] Nicolson, *Benjamin Constant*, 175.
[52] La Baronne Constant de Rebecque, *L'Inconnue d'Adolphe: Correspondance de Benjamin Constant et d'Anna Lindsay* (Paris: Plon, 1933).

enjoyment and union. Our souls, our spirits are made for each other. I have never known love before knowing you.... My love, my angel, my hope, all that I value in life is in you, each drop of my blood flows only for you alone![53]

The following day, he wrote the following:

I love you with all the power of my soul, because I understand you, because I resemble you, because I *also* have made the voyage of life *alone*, relying on the strength of my character, in the midst of battles that I have fought and of wrongs that have been ascribed to me. My love, we have traversed deserts peopled with shadows that we have taken sometime for realities! At last, we find this longed-for reality: what does it matter that the shadows have misled us?... Our true future is deep in our hearts.... I love to hear you, to see you, to possess you because you are the object of my love, respect, and veneration.[54]

Constant's letters indicate that he expected his union with Anna to continue forever. But, when Germaine de Staël returned to Paris at the beginning of January, he found that he could not break off his relationship with her, at least at this time.[55] Anna, not surprisingly, became jealous, resentful, demanding, and possessive; as she had put it in a letter in February, she could not accept a "divided affection."[56] Constant responded with pleadings for her to be patient and with protestations that he needed to retain his independence. Anna, in frustration and despair, escaped to Amiens in May 1801, demanding, in her letters to Constant and to Julie Talma (who was drawn into the situation as an intermediary), that Constant choose either Germaine or her.[57] Constant, faced with losing the woman he clearly loved, nonetheless refused Anna's conditions, insisting again that he needed independence and pleading that they remain friends.[58] Unable to accept this, Anna separated herself from Constant during the summer of 1801, though they remained friends and sometimes lovers for several years (1802–5). In July 1804, Constant wrote in his

[53] Benjamin Constant to Anna Lindsay (December 13, 1800), ibid., 18.
[54] Benjamin Constant to Anna Lindsay (December 14, 1800), ibid., 22–23.
[55] See, for example, the letter from Benjamin Constant to Anna Lindsay (January 19, 1801), ibid., 52–54.
[56] Letter of Anna Lindsay to Benjamin Constant (February 22, 1801), ibid., 70.
[57] See especially the letter from Anna Lindsay to Julie Talma (May 28, 1801), ibid., 124–27.
[58] See the letter from Benjamin Constant to Anna Lindsay (May 31, 1801), ibid., 129–42.

Journaux intimes that Anna "is perhaps the woman who loved me the most, and is the one who made me the most unhappy; but I owe to her having known in a woman all the ecstasy of physical and emotional love."[59]

The parallel between Anna Lindsay and Ellénore in Constant's novel *Adolphe* is remarkable: both are non-French; both have two illegitimate children with a "protector" on whom they are financially dependent; both are beautiful and passionate; both expect their relationship (with Constant and Adolphe, respectively) to provide more constancy than the indecisive, independence-demanding male is willing to give; and both, finally, are devastated when their love is not reciprocated in the manner they reasonably expect.

Mention needs also be made of Amélie Fabri (1771–1809), a resident of Geneva, with whom Constant contemplated marriage in 1803. Constant was reeling again from the difficulties of living with Germaine and considered, as an alternative, married life with a less demanding companion. Constant envied the successful marriage of his friends Thérèse and Ludwig Ferdinand Huber, and hoped to find something comparable.[60] His journal discussion, *"Amélie et Germaine,"* indicates that he was looking for stability, peace of mind, financial security, and permanence. He wished, in his own words, "to regularize his life."[61] As the condescending journal descriptions of Amélie indicate, Constant was not in love. He was carefully weighing the advantages and disadvantages of a marriage of convenience, and imagined finding intellectual and sexual satisfaction elsewhere. When Germaine heard of the marriage proposal, she raised such a storm that the project was not pursued.

Charlotte von Hardenberg

The other woman of great importance in Constant life was Charlotte von Hardenberg (1769–1845), who belonged to a Hanoverian family, though she herself was born in London. Cosmopolitan like Constant, she read and spoke French, German, and English. In 1788, Charlotte

---

[59] *Journaux intimes* (July 28, 1804), 177.
[60] See Benjamin Constant, "Lettres à Louis-Ferdinand et à Thérèse Huber (1798–1806), ed. Etienne Hofmann," *Cahiers staëliens*, 29–30 (1981), 77–128.
[61] Benjamin Constant, "Amélie et Germaine," in *OCBC/Œuvres*, III, I, 49–80; this quote is from p. 51.

had married Baron von Marenholtz, a man sixteen years her senior;
in 1789, she gave birth to a son. Constant first met Charlotte in
Brunswick on January 11, 1793. Although they saw each other frequently for the next couple of months, there is no indication that it
was a sexual liaison at this time.[62] Constant, reeling from his difficulties with Minna, found Charlotte attractive, sensible, uncom-
plicated, but not brilliant. Charlotte was strongly attracted to Constant, which aroused the jealousy of her husband and prompted her
father to warn her to be wary of scandal from being seen in public
with a man whose marriage was in trouble. To avoid such embarrassing complications, Charlotte left Brunswick in March, but she
kept in touch with Constant. They met briefly in Kassel on May 11,
1793. Charlotte clearly had fallen in love with Constant and subsequently wrote of her hopes that they could be together at some
future time. Constant, meanwhile, was nurturing his freedom and
by the autumn was reporting to Isabelle de Charrière that he was
no longer in love with Charlotte.[63] They continued, nonetheless, to
correspond through the summer of 1794.[64]

Constant would occasionally get a letter from Charlotte,[65] but
they were infrequently in touch for most of the next decade. In
1798, Charlotte had divorced Baron von Marenholtz and married
the Vicomte Du Tertre, an impoverished French royalist. In 1802,
they moved to a Paris apartment on the rue de l'Université. In the
late summer of 1803, she and Constant again began to correspond.
This was a couple of years after Constant's stormy affair with Anna
Lindsay and a few months after his contemplation of marriage to
Amélie Fabrie. He was often separated from Germaine, with whom
he found it increasingly difficult to live, but with whom he was
unable to break off definitively. He frequently spent months at his
new residence outside of Paris, Les Herbages.

---

[62] In a letter to Isabelle de Charrière (April 28, 1794), Constant referred to his "chastes
amours" with Charlotte. OCBC/CG, II, 313.
[63] See letter from Benjamin Constant to Isabelle de Charrière (October 8, 1793),
OCBC/CG, II, 157–58.
[64] Constant's letters have not survived, but thirty-two of Charlotte's letters of 1793–
94 are in OCBC/CG.
[65] In Cécile, Constant mentions receiving in late December 1795 a letter from Charlotte dated June 1795. See OCBC/Œuvres, III, I, 259.

Following a fruitful trip with Germaine to Weimar in 1803–4, during which Constant met Goethe, Schiller, and other luminaries of German letters, Constant returned to Les Herbages in December 1804. On December 28, 1804, he recorded in his *Journaux intimes* that he wished to see Charlotte again: "the woman who changed my whole life and who I loved so passionately for a few days. I am very curious to meet her again after twelve years of separation."[66] In early May 1805, the meeting took place in Paris, and Constant's infatuation was renewed. His diary entry, characteristically analytical, is revealing:

With Charlotte, I [would be] able to live in France, honorably and peacefully. She [would] bring me her charming character, plenty of intelligence (more in fact than I had believed), a distinguished family, enough money that I would be no poorer married than I am at present, and an attachment that has survived ten years of separation and ten years of my own indifference, during which I did not respond in an animated or decisive manner.... It is an unexpected port that the heavens have presented to me. It is necessary to head for it.[67]

It was the beginning of a turn that would change Constant's life.

The following day, May 5, Constant learned of the death of his close friend Julie Talma. Another friend, Ludwig Ferdinand Huber, had died in January; Isabelle de Charrière would die in December. Constant was grief-stricken by these deaths, and he slipped into depression. Even his journal entries became abbreviated following the death of Julie Talma. The emotional crisis of this period led him to reassess again – indeed, over and over again – the advantages and disadvantages of his stormy relationship with Germaine de Staël. Charlotte's patience and understanding helped Constant break free.

It took years, however, for Constant to find his way to this "unexpected port." Constant traveled to Geneva in July 1805 to be with Germaine and thus reentered the whirlwind of her social world. Constant and Germaine moved to and from Switzerland and eastern France during the next year. (They could not return together to Paris because Napoleon would not allow Germaine to reside there.) Finally, in October 1806, Constant received a letter from Charlotte

[66] *Journaux intimes* (December 28, 1804), 285.
[67] *Journaux intimes* (May 4, 1805), 387.

insisting on a commitment. Constant traveled to Paris to see her; his diary records that on October 20, after "thirteen years of resistance," they became lovers.[68] He was soon very much in love. In contrast to Germaine's "impetuosity, egoism, and constant preoccupation with herself," Charlotte's "gentle, calm, humble, modest manner of being" was attractive and endearing. "I am tired of the man-woman whose iron hand has enchained me for ten years; a truly feminine woman is intoxicating and enchanting me."[69]

There followed another four years of extreme emotional turmoil, marked by confrontations, illnesses, and apparent suicide attempts by both Charlotte and Germaine. Constant spent time with both, though his relationship with Germaine had ceased to be intimate – she had since long taken on a succession of other lovers. Constant first told Germaine of Charlotte in early November 1806; she predictably exploded with anger, an anger that would not abate in subsequent years. During the spring of 1807, DuTertre agreed to a divorce from Charlotte; on April 11, 1808, the Catholic Church declared the marriage null and void; on June 5, 1808, Constant and Charlotte married in Basel. Constant was so worried about Germaine's reactions to the news of his marriage that it was hidden from her until May 1809, when there was a stormy scene between Charlotte and Germaine. The emotional hurricane continued for another year and a half, during which time Constant was characteristically unable to make a decisive move to distance himself from Germaine. They saw each other briefly in Lausanne in early May 1811. They believed that they would likely never meet again – Germaine was planning her trip east into exile; Benjamin and Charlotte were headed to Göttingen, where they lived for the next few years. Germaine and Benjamin did meet again in Paris after the defeat of Napoleon in 1814, but by this time the old affection had been replaced by a mutually critical regard.

Following the stormy period between 1806 and 1810, the subsequent years were relatively calm. Constant recognized the positive and stabilizing force that Charlotte played in his life, though his diary records periodic boredom and disaffection. But, he also respected and

---

[68] The mention of "thirteen years of resistance" is recorded on October 19, 1806; on October 20, he notes that they became lovers. *Journaux intimes*, 467.
[69] *Journaux intimes* (October 26, 1806), 468–69.

was comforted by her good sense, her tolerance, and her deep affection. From 1816 to 1830, when Constant rewrote his work on religion and became active politically, they lived in Paris.

Juliette Récamier

There was one other significant love interest in Constant's life: Juliette Récamier (1777–1849). Récamier was a member of Germaine de Staël's circle, was well known for her poise and beauty (as represented in the famous paintings of Jacques-Louis David and François Gérard), and had many admirers. Constant had been an acquaintance for years, so he was surprised by his unexpected passion for her in late August 1814. In spite of his rational understanding of the obsessive and destructive nature of his infatuation, and in spite of all the evidence that Juliette had no great passion for him, Constant experienced sleeplessness, frustration, and ultimately exhaustion.[70] It was finally brought to an end when he left Paris at the end of October 1815, on his way to exile in Brussels and then London following the Hundred Days. By the time he returned to Paris in September 1816, he had settled back into a relatively routine life with Charlotte, with whom he would remain until his death in 1830.[71]

CONSTANT'S ANALYSIS OF INTIMATE RELATIONS AND CHARACTER

Constant obsessively analyzed his own character and relations with women. This analysis informed his thinking about intimacy, character, and the self, and more broadly, his thoughts about society and politics. This does not mean that he *theorized* about intimacy in the way that he did about politics and religion. The infrequent references to personal relations in his published works point to their elusive

---

[70] The critical source is Constant's *Journaux intimes* (September 1814 – October 1815), *OCBC/Œuvres*, VII.

[71] Dennis Wood discusses a series of love letters addressed to Constant between August 1818 and February 1819, strongly suggesting that Constant had an affair during this period with a woman in Paris who used the pseudonym of "Eliane." See Wood, *Benjamin Constant: A Biography*, 221–26.

quality. "In the present state of society," he wrote in 1806, "personal relations are composed of fine nuances, undulating, impossible to grasp, which would be denatured in a thousand ways if one tried to give them greater precision. Opinion alone can reach them."[72] Nonetheless, in ways indicated later, his reflections about intimacy were not restricted to women but deeply informed his views of character, *moeurs*, and politics.[73]

Constant's Melancholy and Views of Intimate Relations

Constant's extensive *Journaux intimes* are filled with ruminations about how he should move ahead with the women in his life, and they contain often-pitiful justifications of his own self-interested actions. They provide evidence of his chronic indecision and reveal how his plans were frequently overwhelmed by events and by his own changing emotions. These journals show Constant to have been plagued by the meditative, contemplative, anxious frame of mind that medicine at the time referred to as "melancholy" – what we today would characterize as depression. To hold at bay the stultifying effects of this self-absorbed withdrawn state, Constant looked in a variety of directions. Impulsively, he toyed with the idea of death, manifested in his frequent recourse to dueling. He was also a compulsive gambler, which can be interpreted as a flirtation with fate, or alternately driven by hope for a miracle. When he reflected about the existential dilemma of human isolation, he recommended connection with transcendent values through art and through religion. He also looked, especially in his mature years, to a public life in politics, which he believed would contribute benefits to society and to emotional health. Constant referred to politics as his "vocation," his "calling."[74] But, if political action could provide a temporary safe harbor against the storms of his emotions, it was to the intensity of

---

[72] *PoP* (1806), 371. I have altered this translation slightly.
[73] I have examined this issue in more detail in "Benjamin Constant, the French Revolution, and the Problem of Modern Character," *History of European Ideas*, 30 (2004), 5–21.
[74] See, for example, the letter of Constant to Mme De Nassau, January 20, 1800; cited by Stephen Holmes, *Benjamin Constant and the Making of Modern Liberalism* (New Haven, CT: Yale University Press, 1984), 45–46.

personal relationships that Constant looked for personal emotional health.

Curiously, while his famous novel *Adolphe* concentrates on the difficult nature of love in modern society, friendship is nowhere discussed in any depth in his writings. He had close friendships with men: with John Wilde in Edinburgh; with Jakob Mauvillon in Brunswick; with Prosper de Barante between, roughly, 1805 and 1815. But it is above all with women – particularly Isabelle de Charrière, Julie Talma, and his cousin Rosalie – that he had sustaining friendships. Not surprisingly, the deaths of these women were horrible blows to Constant's equilibrium.

Even in the best of times, however, Constant's relationships with women were difficult to sustain. Constant's *Journaux intimes* contain passages where he contemplates the type(s) of women that he needed and desired. They reveal, as many have pointed out, different and conflicting inclinations. Some passages reveal the desire for a woman who would be entirely subordinate to him and to his own emotional and social needs.

I need a being that I can protect, that I can hold in my arms, whom it would be easy to make happy, whose inoffensive existence yields effortlessly to mine. I need a wife, in a word, who is almost imperceptible, if not for my domestic affections, and who is a soft, intimate and light part of my life. But where can I find this woman?[75]

In this vein, Constant wrote of needing a woman who he could form to his own desires, a woman, in short, with no will or autonomy of her own.[76] As Tzvetan Todorov has put it, the "other" in these passages is reduced to "a purely auxiliary function."[77]

At other times, Constant longed for complete fusion with another. His relationship with Anna Lindsay, brief though it was, provided him with his own experience of this. This form of total sentimental

---

[75] "Amelie et Germaine," January 6, 1803, 50. Constant wrote in his *Journaux intimes* (p. 144) a year and a half later that he needed to spend his life with "a mistress who does not at all trouble my life."

[76] On July 16, 1804, in his *Journaux intimes* (p. 168), Constant imagined how marrying a young woman of sixteen years "would give one the chance to influence her character," though he recognized that the chance of this working was unlikely.

[77] Todorov, *A Passion for Democracy*, 104.

merging is similar to the spontaneous, natural, nonreflexive interpersonal form of communication that Rousseau had termed "transparency."[78] Believing that any long-term relationship can be sustained on such a level was seductively attractive for Constant. Jean Starobinski has suggested that Germaine de Staël, who suffered from melancholy and was preoccupied with thoughts of suicide, struggled with such dark thoughts because she believed in the possibility of total "transparent" intimacy.[79] Constant's novel *Adolphe* can be read as an account of the failure of such love: Ellénore in the novel imagines "transparency" to be possible, but when it proves unavailable she loses the will to live.

The third and most common manner in which love is depicted in the writings of Constant might be called the self-defeating dialectic of desire.[80] In this form, love is identified as the desire to attain the love of another, to overcome obstacles, to eliminate difficulties, and to obtain the object of love. But the "dialectic" is such that if the love is reciprocated then the desire disappears. Love, therefore, either is unfulfilled or dies. If the love object is unattainable, then desire is enhanced. If the love object suggests that a relationship should end, then desire is enhanced. But, once the obstacles and the difficulties are overcome, then desire lessens and love disappears. This is the emotional tension that Constant recognizes in his relationship with Germaine de Staël.[81] And, this informs the sequence of events at the center of *Adolphe*. Adolphe writes Ellénore a love letter; her negative response stimulates an intense love that he had previously only feigned. He presses his suit, and after some hesitation she yields and the pair become lovers. This is quickly followed, however, by Adolphe's disillusionment and restlessness. He experiences increasing discomfort as Ellénore develops a tenacious passion for him and becomes, due to her own social position and temperament, more and

---

[78] The classic study of this theme is Jean Starobinski, *Jean-Jacques Rousseau: La transparence et l'obstacle* (Paris: Gallimard, 1971).

[79] Jean Starobinski, "Suicide et mélancholie chez Mme de Staël," in *Madame de Staël et l'Europe* (Paris: Klincksieck, 1970), 242–52.

[80] I draw here from Tzvetan Todorov's discussion of the "logic of desire," in *A Passion for Democracy*, 108–14.

[81] See, for example, the extensive entry in the *Journaux intimes* (August 19, 1804), 191–92.

more dependent. As Constant famously put it, "she was no longer a goal; she had become a tie."[82] Love, in his mode, inevitably ends in disaster, and *Adolphe* is a recounting of the grim tale of Adolphe's indecision and Ellénore's dependence, isolation, and death. Constant himself experienced this type of love at various times in his life: as a young man, when Harriet Trevor and Jenny Pourrat did not respond to his declarations of love; in later life, when Juliette Récamier also resisted his advances.

On the most obvious level, *Adolphe* is an analysis of the fatal workings of the self-defeating dialectic of desire and of the unintended consequences of statements and actions of love. As Constant put it in the preface to the second edition,

there is in the simple habit of borrowing the language of love, and of fostering in oneself, or of exciting in others, transient emotions of the heart, a danger which has not been sufficiently appreciated hitherto. One heads down a road whose end one is unable to foresee; one knows neither what one will inspire, nor what one may experience. One makes light of the blows of which one can calculate neither the force, nor the reaction on oneself; and the wound that seems only to graze the skin may be incurable.[83]

Constant's Analysis of Character in Modern Society

Examining Constant's continuing discussion of personal relationships bears heavily on his analysis of the importance of character for modern society. *Adolphe*, for example, is not just about the failure of love. More deeply, the novel is about the tragic incompatibility of certain character traits and the structure and mores of modern society. Constant intentionally constructed the novel in a way that once the relationship between Adolphe and Ellénore was established, their natures would inevitably lead, given current social arrangements, to tragedy. As he put it in the preface to the second edition, "[Adolphe's] position and that of Ellénore were without resources, and that is precisely what I wanted." The central dilemma of the

---

[82] Benjamin Constant, *Adolphe*, in *OCBC/Œuvres*, III, I, 132.
[83] Benjamin Constant, *Adolphe*, "Préface de la seconde édition, ou essai sur le caractère et le résultat moral de l'ouvrage," in *OCBC/Œuvres*, III, I, 100.

novel is that Ellénore's love and society's expectations give Adolphe little room for maneuver; there is no way for him to respond that would not culminate in disaster. "I have shown him [Adolphe] tormented, because he loved Ellénore only feebly; but he would not have been less tormented if he had loved her more. He suffered because of her, for want of sentiment; with sentiment more ardent he would have suffered for her. Society, disapproving and disdainful, would have poured all its venom on the affection that its authority had not sanctioned."[84]

Therefore, while *Adolphe* is obviously about the failure of an intimate relationship, it is also about how this failure is related to the character of the protagonists and the nature of post-revolutionary society. In a passage in the unpublished preface to the second edition of *Adolphe*, Constant made this clear:

I wanted to portray in Adolphe one of the principal moral maladies of our century, this fatigue, this uncertainly, this absence of force, this perpetual analysis, which places a mental reservation beside all sentiments, and because of that corrupts them from their birth.... And it is not only in the intimacies of the heart that this moral weakness extends, that this impotence of durable impressions is evident; all is tied together in nature. Fidelity in love is a force as in religion, as with liberty. But we no longer have any strength. We no longer know how to love, to believe, to want. Everyone doubts that which he says, smiles with vehemence on that which he affirms, and hastens the end of that which he tries.[85]

In this remarkable passage, Constant suggests that just as successful love requires strength and consistency of character – qualities unfortunately not predominant in the character of the fictional protagonist Adolphe – religion requires belief and liberty requires enthusiasm. What Constant laments, and what the novel *Adolphe* analyzes with such penetrating rigor, is the failure of modern man to measure up. Character is not equal to the requirements of the modern age; the all-important values of love, belief, and enthusiasm are being lost because men's emotions and energy are damaged, weak, and vacillating.

The complexity, the tensions, of Constant's thought is related to the fact that the private sphere and the public sphere, while directed

[84] Ibid., 102.
[85] Ibid., 196–97.

toward different goals and animated by different emotions, could not be isolated from each other. He famously argued in his political writings that modern society needed to be organized so that individuals could develop their capacities, and find their personal satisfactions, in everyday private activities.[86] This required that the private sphere be protected from intervention by a despotic ruler or a tyrannical majority. But, the health of the public sphere was also critical, and both spheres required that individuals strive to actualize the positive sentiments of self-respect, compassion, and enthusiasm. In both spheres, moreover, there was a danger of being overwhelmed by isolation or, at the other extreme, by what might be called the logic of domination.[87]

This is made clearer by contrasting Constant's thought with that of Rousseau. Rousseau famously idealized the "sentiments prior to reason" that characterized "natural man" and argued that the "civilized" world was structured by corrupting layers of science, technology, art, sociability, and language. As a consequence, the positive sentiments of self-respect (amour de soi-même) and compassion (pitié) were transmuted into vanity and selfishness. In Rousseau's conjectural history, the primitive "noble savage" is the only individual thoroughly free of artificiality and of the domination and subordination that defines modern personal relations. In modern society, the benign "natural" relationships that affect all humans equally are overwhelmed by the "unnatural" dependencies of one individual on another, dependencies that are harmful to freedom and morality.[88] Constant also believed in the primacy of sentiments, and he also feared the danger of unnatural dependencies, but he believed

[86] This is famously argued in "The Liberty of the Ancients Compared with That of the Moderns" [1819], in PW, 308–28.

[87] For a more extended analysis of Constant's views of "the self," see Jerrold Seigel, The Idea of the Self: Thought and Experience in Western Europe since the Seventeenth Century (Cambridge: Cambridge University Press, 2005), 248–91; and my article "Elite Culture in Early-Nineteenth Century France: Salons, Sociability, and the Self," Modern Intellectual History, 4 (2) (August 2007), 327–51.

[88] In Emile, Rousseau contrasts "dependence on things," which is natural and affects all humans equally (dependence on the law of gravity, for example), and "dependence on men," which is unnatural and harmful to freedom and morality. See Rousseau's Emile in Œuvres complètes de Jean-Jacques Rousseau, vol. 4, ed. Bernard Gagnebin and Marcel Raymond (Paris: Pléiade, 1970).

interdependence to be our normal condition. Constant's recurring desire for independence from *specific* relationships did not mean that he longed for independence *from* relationships. Total independence would not define a life worth living; indeed, it would not be a livable life. In contrast to Rousseau's depiction of modern society as a corrupt arena where vanity and *amour propre* reign,[89] Constant applauded modern man's desire to obtain the approval of others. Vanity, he argued, is part of our being; the quest for the approval of others encourages moral behavior and helps constitute our identity. In Rousseau's world, emotional health is to be found in quiet contemplation and isolation from others.[90] In Constant's world, emotional health is to be found in intense relationships, in social interaction, and in emotional interdependence.

Constant thus believed that it was impossible to speak meaningfully about the modern "self" without taking into account intersubjective relations, that is, without considering human sociability and the nature of modern social exchange. What troubled him so deeply was that *modern* man seemed unable to attain a robust integrity. In 1814, he wrote the following:

We have lost in imagination what we have gained in knowledge; as a result, we are even incapable of lasting emotion; the ancients were in the full youth of their moral life, we are in its maturity, perhaps in its old age; we are always dragging behind us some sort of afterthought, which is born from experience, and which defeats enthusiasm. The first condition for enthusiasm is not to observe oneself too acutely. Yet we are so afraid of being fools, and above all of looking like fools, that we are always watching ourselves even in our most violent thoughts. The ancients had complete conviction in all matters; we have only a weak and fluctuating conviction about almost everything, to the inadequacy of which we seek in vain to make ourselves blind.[91]

The sentiments and attachments of the public and private spheres overlapped; they converged in the analysis of character. And, auspiciously, the character of modern individuals seemed to be weakening. Constant was intensely concerned with what Lucien Jaume

---

[89] I'm thinking here of Rousseau's first two discourses.
[90] Virtue, for Rousseau, is an innate feeling that can be heard only in the silence of the passions, and which may succeed in guiding behavior only when, through an effort of will, one overcomes selfish bodily desires.
[91] *SCU*, 104–5.

has referred to as the "moral culture" of societies.[92] This had both a public and a private dimension. Constant believed that a stable successful society must esteem public honesty, respect, and virtue. Equally important, there must be love, intimacy, and devotion in private lives. In both, it was important to foster the sentiments of self-respect, compassion, and enthusiasm. He learned this from his attention to the political and social upheavals of his era, but it was also an outgrowth of the disappointments and comforts that resulted from his varied and spectacularly complicated relationships with women.

ACKNOWLEDGMENTS

The author thanks Kimberly Bowler, Tony LaVopa, Linda Orr, Helena Rosenblatt, Bernard Wishy, and the participants in the Triangle French Studies Seminar for their comments on previous versions of this essay.

[92] Lucien Jaume, "Coppet, creuset du libéralisme comme 'culture morale'," in *Coppet, Creuset de l'esprit libéral*, 225–39.

9   Individualism and Individuality in Constant

> It is not to happiness alone, it is to self-development that our destiny calls us; and political liberty is the most powerful, the most effective means of self-development that heaven has given us.
>
> "The Liberty of the Ancients Compared with That of the Moderns"

This almost epigrammatic formulation conveys, I will argue, the essence of Benjamin Constant's liberal philosophy. Even as a formula it is not simple. Although its basic terms – "happiness," "self-development," and "political liberty," – may have to the contemporary ear the ring of ordinary language, they were for Constant terms of art, with their own historical contexts, problematic interrelations, and, not least, polemical thrust.

Perhaps the first thing to note about Constant's claim is the relationship it proposes between a definition of the self and a theory of politics. Political liberty, for Constant, is not an end in itself but a means. He defends it here on the instrumental ground of its effectiveness in promoting the good of the self.[1] Although the ostensible concern of the famous address is to reconcile ancient liberty, the ideal of political participation on behalf of the common good, with modern liberty's celebration of individual freedom in the private sphere, Constant's highest value is the individual self. The question he has set for his audience is "which self?" – for the self, in Constant's presumption, has two primary goals, and his felt need to argue for the goal of

---

[1] Earlier, in the unpublished version of *The Principles of Politics*, he had put it this way: "If political freedom is not one of the individual possessions nature has given man, it is what guarantees them." *PoP* (1806), 387.

self-development attests to his belief that the other, "happiness," is broadly acknowledged and little contested. Constant, then, is asserting that political liberty should serve both goals and that while its utility for happiness may be more evident, a case needs to – and can – be made that it is also the best context for self-development. Why should that even be in question? What does Constant mean by differentiating "happiness" from "self-development"? And politically, what might be the tensions between the conditions that serve each?

Many reasons have been suggested for the recent revival of interest in Constant's thought both in France and in the United States. Most prominent, perhaps, is the end of the political appeal of Marxism in France with the collapse of European Communism after 1989 and the desire of French political intellectuals to refurbish an indigenous liberal tradition. American political theorists have been only too happy to join in the enterprise, pleased that the French have finally seen the Anglo-American political light, though French writing on Constant is often marked with pessimism about modernity and the workings of democracy largely alien to American celebrations of him. Helena Rosenblatt points out that such "presentist" purposes have led to serious distortions and misrepresentations of Constant's thought and calls for a more historically grounded approach that does not exploit him for contemporary political partisanship.[2] But in the face-off between happiness and self-development, the perspective provided by current political-cultural debates does no violence to Constant's own historical context. To the contrary, Constant was one of the originators of a continuing debate within liberalism about the benefits of modernity and the ultimate purposes of individual freedom.[3]

Nothing stamps Constant as a "modern" more than the fact that the self is the starting point of his reflection. Clearly, that self is not defined by a narrow egotism. What the claim does mean is that Constant reflexively saw and examined the world, including that which he thought was beyond the world, transcendence, from the point of view of the human subject. He insisted on this perspective even

[2] Helena Rosenblatt, "Why Constant? A Critical Overview of the Constant Revival," *Modern Intellectual History*, 1 (3) (November 2004), 453.
[3] See, for example, Nancy Rosenblum, *Another Liberalism: Romanticism and the Reconstruction of Liberal Thought* (Cambridge, MA: Harvard University Press, 1989).

when he sounded most traditionally religious, toward the end of his life: "In the old belief [polytheism] that philosophy had subjugated, man was reduced to the rank of an imperceptible atom in the vastness of the universe. The new form [Christianity] puts him back at the center of a world that was created only for him: he is at the same time God's creation and God's goal."[4] The apparent subordination of man to God in this formulation is inverted by its teleological claim: if man is God's goal, then God himself, and what he intended with his creation, can only be understood through and as what man wants for himself.

Appropriately enough, Constant's ethical and ideological commitments were rooted in his own biography. "For forty years," he wrote in one of his last publications, "I have defended the same principles: liberty in everything, in religion, in philosophy, in literature, in industry, in politics."[5] The rhetorical order of the fields he lists as his battlegrounds for freedom is not incidental; it traces the intellectual stages through which his thought – and activity – historically evolved. Politics did not come first (though one of Constant's biographers makes a plausible case for Constant's early sensitivity to political oppression in his native Switzerland as a French-speaking Vaudois under the tyranny of the ethnically German Bernese[6]). During his adolescence he was, he tells us, caught up in the Enlightenment struggle with religion, indeed at the atheist extreme of intellectual opposition: "Nourished by the principles of the philosophy of the eighteenth century and especially by the works of Helvetius, I had no other thought than doing my part to contribute to the destruction of what I called prejudice."[7] Perhaps his early hostility to religion was a displaced outlet for even more dangerous opposition to authority closer to home – whether that of the Bernese or of his difficult father, the domineering army colonel Juste Constant, who

---

[4] Tzvetan Todorov, *A Passion for Democracy. The Life, the Women He Loved and the Thought of Benjamin Constant*, trans. A. Seberry (New York: Algora Publishing, 1999), 217.

[5] Benjamin Constant, *Mélanges de littérature et de politique* (Paris: Pichon et Didier, 1829), V.

[6] Dennis Wood, *Benjamin Constant: A Biography* (London and New York: Routledge, 1993), 70.

[7] Kurt Kloocke, *Benjamin Constant: Une biographie intellectuelle* (Geneva: Droz), 21.

exercised tight, even if distant, control over his son until his own death. Since, however, religion underpinned all claims to authority in the Old Regime, paternal or political, to fight the authority of religion was to fight the legitimating principle of authority at its very source. At the age of nineteen, at any rate, Constant finally rebelled against the paternal authority to which he had previously passively submitted by fleeing to England to avoid facing his father over a disastrous love affair and near-ruinous gambling debts. And the citation in the preceding text, though referring to later political events in Constant's life, also suggests the wider scope of that original revolt against authority: "By liberty I understand the triumph of *individuality*, as much over the authority which would wish to govern by despotism as over the masses which claim the right to subject the minority to the majority. [Italics added.]" His use of the term "individuality" indicates that for Constant the desire for liberty was the expression of a desire to be free as a whole self, not just of a rebellion against coercion in a particular sphere.

Equally telling for his idea of freedom, however, was his ranking the fight for liberty in industry before that of liberty in politics in his list of battles. Whatever its emotional origins in his biography, his *intellectual* road to political freedom ran through contemporary ideas about the modern economy. Constant made the connection between economics and politics in his very first political publication, the pamphlet of 1796 *De la force du gouvernement actuel de la France et la necessité de s'y rallier* ["On the Strength of the Present Government of France and the Need to Rally to It"]. There, he defended the republican Directorate against a threatened restoration of the monarchy as the only form of government that could revive the two main sources of French prosperity, commerce and the navy, both badly damaged in the recent wars. "The form of government influences commerce according to the degree of liberty it allows it," he wrote; "its growth depends on untrammeled individual initiative." The authoritarian nature of monarchical government precluded its being able to do anything to revive an enterprise whose very nature was individual freedom, whereas "the enthusiasm for [political] freedom can accomplish miracles."[8] Here Constant

---

[8] *De la force du gouvernement actuel de la France et de la necessité de s'y rallier* ([Paris?: s.n.], 1796), 49. My translation.

appears to consider republican liberty as an independent instrument for promoting commercial prosperity through their joint commitment to individual freedom. In later works, however, he made the much stronger causal argument that commerce was the very *source* of the modern idea of liberty in general and of political liberty in particular.

Constant's indebtedness to the economic ideas of the Scottish Enlightenment, especially those of Adam Smith and David Hume, and to the ideology of *"doux commerce"* shared by other thinkers such as Montesquieu, has been extensively documented.[9] Eighteenth-century enthusiasts of the commercial revolution had reveled in the paradox that modern commerce, though fueled by self-interest, avarice, and vanity, both created material prosperity for society as a whole and encouraged sociability and the refinement of manners. Constant extended this line of thinking to make even more radical arguments for the benefits of modern commerce in light of the events of the French Revolution. He rehearsed the standard argument that with the rise of modern commerce, civilized calculation and mutual agreement had replaced the dangers and uncertainty of war as humanity's method for obtaining and increasing its means of subsistence. But he claimed more for commerce than that: it "inspires in men a vivid love of individual independence. It supplies their needs, satisfies their desires, without the intervention of the authorities."[10] Put directly, Constant was asserting that the free market *creates* a taste for liberty in general because it is so successful in satisfying material needs and desires.

The satisfaction of desires is what Constant meant by happiness; for him the two were synonymous. "The progress of civilization, the commercial tendency of the age, the communication among peoples," as he put it, "have infinitely multiplied and varied the means of individual happiness."[11] His concept of happiness was anchored theoretically in Helvetius's doctrine that humans are motivated by

---

[9] See Helena Rosenblatt, "Commerce et religion dans le libéralisme de Benjamin Constant," *Commentaire*, 26 (102) (Summer 2003), 419. Rosenblatt points to the index to Constant's *Principle of Politics* (1806) compiled by Étienne Hofmann, with its many references to Adam Smith as well as to French political economists relying on him.

[10] AML, 315.

[11] SCU, 104.

the pursuit of pleasure and the avoidance of pain. Constant's political conclusion followed with blunt inevitability: "The people most attached to liberty in modern times is also that most attached to its pleasures. *It holds to its liberty above all because it is enlightened enough to see in it the guarantee of its pleasures.*"[12] In the context of Helvetius's atheist materialism, pleasure was by definition physical and material. The doctrine thus meshed well with the motive of material self-interest at the heart of Scottish economics. For Adam Smith, however, the existence of a free market was fully compatible with the traditional British monarchy. Constant by contrast argued that the pleasure-satisfying free market not only led to the demand for free political institutions but was also their strongest buttress. After the fall of the Directorate he no longer equated free political institutions with strict republicanism, though it was always his preferred form, but political freedom did entail for him at a minimum the liberal essentials of popular sovereignty, representative government, the separation of powers, and ministerial responsibility. The close theoretical connection that Constant made between hedonism and liberalism, however, has not been sufficiently emphasized, no doubt in part because Constant was so highly critical of Bentham's utilitarian reduction of right and morality to a pleasure calculus.[13] But it was just that connection between pleasure and free political institutions that he himself made that raised a question about the possible relationship between liberalism and self-development.

The causal link between happiness and liberalism was further cemented, and the dilemma for self-development consequently heightened, by Constant's theory about the role and origin of ideas. "It was ... to ideas alone," he had written in his first pamphlet, "that the empire of the world was given."[14] Ideas drive history when they are transformed into the sentiments, passions, and enthusiasms that motivate individuals. But ideas do not appear out of nowhere, and they certainly do not originate ex nihilo in the brains of individuals. They are formed, Constant argued in a rough anticipation of Marx's later dictum that men do not make history in circumstances of their own choosing, from reactions to external events and

[12] Ibid., 105. Italics added.
[13] *PoP* (1806), 41.
[14] Constant, "De la force...," 78.

circumstances not subject to the individual will. It followed that "it is impossible to establish ideas which the force of circumstance has not produced, as it is impossible to push back those which it has, or sustain the value of those ideas whose time has passed."[15] The "circumstances" he had in mind were also much the same as those Marx would make preeminent, the changing technologies and social structures through which humans produced their means of subsistence. The modern idea of liberty could have arisen only out of the economic and social institutions of modern commerce – international trade, entrepreneurship, the emergence of the middling ranks of society, an increasingly complex division of labor, and the rise of public opinion – all of which had not only promoted wealth but helped subvert traditional beliefs and social bonds. These historical developments had also given rise intellectually to the idea of fundamental individual rights and to the urge to codify and protect them. "The citizen possesses individual rights independently of all social and political authority," Constant wrote in one of the classic articulations of rights-based liberalism; "any authority which violates these rights becomes illegitimate."[16] Despite the apparent echo of Locke, however – and the occasional slippage of his own language – these rights for Constant were not "natural" but historical, though none the less solid for that; indeed they were more securely established by the weight of history than they could ever be by the airy supports of metaphysics. Constant used essentially Burkean historicist premises to argue radically anti-Burkean conclusions. Yet his argument for rights, one could say, was ultimately derived from his theory of human nature. During the stretch of history when warfare was the most efficient instrument for securing material welfare, man's pleasure-seeking drives had sanctioned the values of honor and glory in combat; now, given the evolution of technologies of wealth making, they as firmly sanctioned the pacific norms of free market and liberal government.

But from the very beginning of his political career, Constant made clear his deep ambivalence toward the very motivations that he saw as the foundation of modern liberty. His first public expression of that ambivalence was less jarring – no doubt even to himself – than it

---

[15] Ibid.
[16] *PoP* (1815), 180.

might otherwise have seemed, because it was yoked to his condemnation of the monarchy. Life in a monarchy, he claimed, is much
more drab and uniform than that in a republic because by shack-
ling its subjects' actions monarchy condemns a great part of human
hopes and faculties to inactivity. Deprived of any goal, interest, or
hope other than the narrowly personal, everyone – subject, minister,
or the monarch himself – becomes purely self-centered and egoistic. Life is dominated by an "arid and corrosive sentiment which
consumes our existence, drains all objects of color, and which, like
the burning winds of Africa, dries out and withers everything it
touches.... [T]he soul is always constricted when it is driven back
to egoism.... There is always something drab and faded about someone who thinks only of himself.... He is unable to forget himself,
he can't give himself over to enthusiasm, he is not electrified by the
recognition of his equals...."[17] But Constant could not in all consistency continue to identify the "arid and corrosive" sentiment of
self-interest with monarchy alone; it was after all, as he knew and
eventually proclaimed, the very principle of the economic modernity
he lauded.

His initial condemnation of self-interest already contained some
of the elements of quite another view of the self that he would spend
a lifetime exploring and that culminated in the magnum opus of the
last part of his life, *On Religion*. In a word, it was a Romantic view,
Romantic in the sense that he saw the self as a quest for the infinite,
for transcendence, but Romantic also in the sense that the fulfillment of the self in transcendent otherness had simultaneously to be
compatible with individual autonomy.[18] It was this second requirement that complicated Constant's lifelong preoccupation with religion, which he originally rejected as opposed to freedom but which
he later came to embrace as expressing the self's deepest aspirations. It was this same requirement to reconcile transcendence with
individual freedom that ultimately made the identity of liberal intellectual and active politician the one way Constant believed a person
could fulfill the needs of the Romantic dimension of self in reality.

---

[17] Constant, *De la force*, 71–72.

[18] See my *Impossible Individuality: Romanticism, Revolution and the Origins of
Modern Selfhood* (Princeton, NJ: Princeton University Press, 1992), where I lay
this thesis out in detail.

This Romantic self is what Constant meant by "individuality." The equation marks a substantial difference with the humanist conception of individuality defined by Wilhelm von Humboldt, the contemporary today most generally identified with the idea.[19] Unlike Humboldt, Constant never spelled out explicitly or in one place everything he meant by the term; its elements have to be assembled from his disparate writings on politics, religion, and love and inferred from his various critiques of self-interest. They can also be inferred from his life, because the ideal of individuality informed his actions as well as his theory. And though it underwent development with time and reflection, the ideal remained consistent throughout his life. While his religious "conversion" seems, and felt to him, like a dramatic inner change, not only his remarks about human motivation in "On the Strength of the Present Government" in 1796 are fully compatible with everything he says about religion in 1824–27, but they often use very similar language.

The most important, and most ambiguous, aspect of individuality was what Constant called in his first pamphlet "enthusiasm," a term he apparently got either from his close association with Isabelle de Charrière in the years just before the Revolution or from his subsequent association with Germaine de Staël in the 1790s.[20] By enthusiasm he meant the subjective feeling of passion that can only be experienced in the exaltation of self-surrender to an objective "something" outside the self and greater than it. By definition, enthusiasm was incompatible with the self-serving pleasure seeking that motivated the modern economy. It was further undermined by the self-consciousness created by modernity's elevation of the self to central principle of concern. "The first condition for enthusiasm," Constant acknowledged, "is not to observe oneself too closely," and this was precisely what was impossible for the modern self, so on guard not to look like a fool in the eyes of others that it avoided conviction and decisiveness. "The ancients had conviction in all matters," Constant lamented, "we have only a weak and fluctuating

---

[19] Although Humboldt's *The Limits of State Action* was not published in its entirety in his own lifetime.

[20] See the two articles by K. Steven Vincent, "Benjamin Constant, the French Revolution, and the Origins of French Romantic Liberalism," *French Historical Studies*, 23 (4) (Fall 2000), 619, and "Benjamin Constant, the French Revolution, and the Problem of Modern Character," *History of European Ideas*, 30 (1) (March 2004), 7.

conviction about almost everything, to the inadequacy of which we seek in vain to make ourselves blind."[21]

Thus modernity weakened morality, for in Constant's anti-Kantian view enthusiasm was the only possible foundation of morals. One key way that the self-forgetfulness of enthusiasm manifested itself was in the affections of friendship and the selflessness of generosity toward others; these were thus essential to Constant's definition of individuality. Yet important as sociability and morality were for the wholeness of the self, neither could provide it with that ecstatic sense "of being subjugated, dominated, exalted"[22] that characterized the most intense expression of enthusiasm. Nor was either sufficient to fulfill the striving for what Constant called "perfection."[23] Such exalted feelings could only be excited in the finite human being by a sense of the infinite, by a striving for that which truly transcends all limitations.

Being guided by enthusiasm, however, threatened a danger that Constant never analyzed in the abstract, though he did so, brilliantly, in one of its specific manifestations: the danger of error and self-deception in passion. Making enthusiasm the very criterion of the higher self meant that one could recognize the authenticity of one's striving not by any precise sense of the reality of its object but by the subjective nature of the emotion that drove it. Constant ultimately identified three emotions that expressed the most intense degree of enthusiasm: love, religious sentiment, and "the passion for freedom."[24] Of these, however, love and religiosity suffered from deficiencies that could not be rectified; however indispensable for the individual life, they could, therefore, not in themselves sustain the praxis, the activity, that true fulfillment of selfhood required. In the end only the passion, and the concrete quest, for political freedom as Constant understood it could do so.

Constant himself, of course, made the case against the adequacy of love foremost, though not exclusively in his novel *Adolphe*. Tzvetan Todorov has brilliantly dissected the sinews of love in Constant's life

[21] *SCU*, 105.
[22] B. Constant, "Préface," *De la religion considerée dans sa source, ses formes et ses développements*, vol. I (Paris: Bossange, 1824–31), 18. Translations from this text are my own.
[23] Ibid., 26.
[24] Todorov, *Constant*, 217.

and work. Love for Constant is partly egoistic, bent on conquest to satisfy vanity. Love hopes for fusion with the other as one's equal and partner. But above all love is a lack, and as such is reduced to the self-defeating "logic of desire":[25] either the beloved responds to one's love, and desire dies, or she does not, and desire remains unfulfilled.[26]

It is the first and last of these faces of love that dominate *Adolphe*. The self-confessed vanity that is one of the two motives Adolphe offers for trying to make another man's mistress fall in love with him is in part a manifestation of the way in which modernity has corrupted all aspects of the private sphere, infecting even the most powerful of other-regarding emotions with self-interest. But Constant also suspected that love could never escape the taint of selfishness, because it was organically linked with (sexual) pleasure. "It has as its aim a specific enjoyment," he wrote in his *Principles of Politics* (a locus for a discussion of love, which says much about its intrinsic connection with politics for Constant), and "because that aim is close to us. . . . it results in egoism."[27] Egoism, however, is not even the most serious problem for Adolphe's love. As he says rather ruefully of himself, despite his impatience with any ties holding him down, "I was not as profoundly self-centered as such characteristics would seem to suggest: it is true that I was only interested in myself, but even that interest was not strong. Without being aware of it, I nursed in the depths of my being a longing for emotional experience."[28] Not self-aggrandizing vanity but the passive need to be loved drives Adolphe most powerfully, a need manifesting the "lack" that Todorov identifies as the ground of love's inevitable disappointment.

Adolphe wins Ellenore, but his victory is his downfall (and of course hers). Todorov offers two different reasons for the tragedy of desire in Constant, one psychobiographical, and the other less easily characterized but more consistent with the notion of a universal "logic" of desire. With regard to virtually all the women he met, Todorov shrewdly points out, Constant was torn between two

[25] Ibid., 110.
[26] Ibid., 115.
[27] *PoP* (1815), 278.
[28] Benjamin Constant, *Adolphe*, trans. L. Tancock (Hammondsworth, England, New York: Penguin, 1964), 39.

contrary attitudes: on the one hand, he needed them to fill the gaping hole left open by the untimely disappearance of his mother, who died in childbirth, but at the same time, he needed to punish them in retaliation by abandoning them in turn. Women had to love him so that he could leave them and show everyone, most importantly himself, that he had no need of them.[29] The pattern both fits the facts of Constant's erotic life and will be familiar to anyone who has seen the apparently irrational syndrome undermine time and again the desperate craving for love in those who have been deprived of it early in life. It explains the apparently contradictory emotions and behaviors that marked the twists and turns of Constant's real and fictional affairs, from the devaluation of the beloved and ensuing boredom once she has succumbed to the desperate need for independence as her loving fidelity becomes suffocating, to the tormenting guilt at one's emotional abandonment of her and the difficulty of leaving her physically. But this biographical explanation, however plausible in Constant's case, does not amount to a *logic* of desire as such; it describes only an individual psychological syndrome. The other explanation entails the more radical, ontological argument that the very fulfillment of love inevitably entails its death.

Love inevitably dies if it is a quest of the sacred object, for no human object of love can measure up to this essentially religious demand. And Adolphe could not be more explicit that this is what his love for Ellenore meant. "I looked upon her," he writes of his passion, "as a sacred being, and my love was closely allied to religion."[30] Love as religion, however, is idolatry, because it seeks the infinite in the finite, and as more than "merely" human affection, it is bound to be disappointed. Brought before the tribunal of a severe logic, Constant would write years later in *On Religion*, love loses its raison d'être because it is an exclusive preference for an object we have been able to do without for a long time and which in any case so many others resemble: "The religious sentiment is not, like love, a passing inclination" – or, one could add, an inclination for the passing.[31]

---

[29] Todorov, *Constant*, 129.
[30] Constant, *Adolphe*, 61.
[31] Constant, *De la religion*, I, 32–33.

This is the lesson that Adolphe learns too late, after the tragedy of Ellenore's death. It is implicit in the acknowledgment that what he sought in falling in love was, in his words, "emotional experience"; as the modern cliché has it, he was in love with love, with the ecstatic feeling it created rather than with its apparent object, who is in tragic fact incidental to the emotion. The disastrous outcome of the affair is all the more tragic because Adolphe's behavior was not just the result of his flaws but of what in fact was best in him. As his acquaintance writes to the putative publisher of the confessional manuscript Adolphe left at his death, "You will see him in many varied circumstances, but always the victim of the mingled selfishness and emotionalism which worked together in him for his own undoing and that of others. . . . punished for his qualities even more than for his defects because his qualities had their origin in his emotions and not in his principles."[32]

Perhaps there is indeed a causal connection between biographical events and metaphysical understanding; perhaps the psychological deprivation caused by the premature death of his mother and the physical and emotional absence of his father attuned Constant to the ontological problem of desire as ultimate lack. Author and character, however, are not wholly congruent. Constant, unlike Adolphe, was ultimately able to find happiness in the love of his second wife. But it was not by all accounts the tempestuous, ecstatic love of a sacred being, rather the comfortable domestic love he was able to settle for when he turned the focus of his quest for enthusiasm increasingly to the thing for which he came to realize that love was a substitute, religion itself.

If love is the most "mixed" of the passions that share an affinity with religious sentiment, religion for Constant was the "purest."[33] By this he meant that it was not intertwined, as love was, with physical pleasure, so that it did not, like love, "vanish together with youth." But it was pure in another sense as well. Although it could be and throughout history had been corrupted by clerical castes, which used their claims to special knowledge of religious truth to establish power over others, true religion was not about dogma. It had no concrete object as such. It was about what Constant called

---

[32] Ibid., 124.
[33] *PoP* (1815), 278.

"the conjectures of the imagination and the needs of the heart."[34] In *Principles of Politics, Adolphe,* and *On Religion,* there is more than a hint of defensiveness about the vagueness of the protagonist's or author's religious effusions. "If I were accused... of failing to offer a sufficiently precise definition of religious feeling," Constant says in the first, "I shall ask how we can define with precision that vague and profound part of our moral sense, which by its very nature defies all the efforts of language. How would you define the impression of a dark night, of an ancient forest, of the wind moaning through ruins or over graves, of the ocean stretching beyond our sight? How would you define the emotion caused by the songs of Ossian, the church of St. Peter, meditation upon death, the harmony of sounds or forms? How would you define reverie, that intimate quivering of the soul, in which all the powers of the senses and thought come together and lose themselves in a mysterious confusion? There is religion at the bottom of all things. All that is beautiful, all that is intimate, all that is noble, partakes of the nature of religion."[35]

This invocation of things that might evoke in his contemporaries what Constant's conservative Romantic counterpart Chateaubriand called "*le vague des passions,*" the passion for the indeterminate, may read to contemporaries like an overripe Romantic cliché. Repetition, time, and postmodern irony have largely stripped them of their power to evoke anything today, but historical analysis. That was hardly a problem for Constant, but in terms of what religion might mean for life, defining it in terms of the religious sentiment did pose another. Keeping religion "pure," free of identification with anything less than the infinite, meant depriving it of all concrete belief, institutional form, or ritual practice – in other words, of any specific implications for living a life. If religion was all (beautiful and noble) things, it was nothing in particular, at most awe in search of an object. Adolphe unwittingly pinpoints the dilemma in his defense of the mourners praying for Ellenore on her death bed. "What surprises me," he claims, "is not that man needs a religion, but rather that he should ever think himself strong enough or sufficiently secure from trouble to dare to reject any of them. I think he ought, in his weakness, to call upon all of them. In the dense night that surrounds

---

[34] Ibid., 279.
[35] Ibid. Virtually the same words reappear in *De la religion,* I, 35.

us is there any gleam of light we can afford to reject?"[36] This is not quite Constant, but it might as well be. In *On Religion*, he not only acknowledged but insisted that "the dogmas, the beliefs, the practices, the ceremonies are the forms which the religious sentiment takes and which it later breaks.... While the base [the religious sentiment] is always the same, the eternal, the form is variable and transitory."[37] The syncretism this approach entails (and implicitly recommends) is ultimately both empty and paralyzing. If it is not religious "truth" that is true and if only the religious *sentiment* that underlies all religions is universal, then the very element that is necessary to practice any particular religion – the belief that its specific answers to the human needs religious feelings express are the right answers – is missing.

Of the three emotions Constant named as epitomes of enthusiasm, the partial disqualification of both love and religion left the passion for freedom only as the motive force for a viable, and concrete, way to fulfill one's individuality. But that passion too was threatened by dangers intrinsic to it that could undermine it, indeed turn it into the opposite of individuality. On the one side, political passion, even the passion for freedom, could all too easily shade into fanaticism. This is precisely what had happened in the Terror.[38] For a very brief moment, in fact, Constant had supported the Terror as a necessary means of defending the Revolution in its direst crisis, when it appeared that it would succumb to enemies from within and without. Furthermore, the Terror at its peak had been justified by its masters in the name of republican virtue, devotion to the good of all; it demanded the sacrifice of self to the common good that for Constant was the very definition of a morality inspired by enthusiasm. On the other side, political freedom, as we have seen, was for Constant historically both the effect and the instrument of happiness, of that "self-interest properly understood" which Constant consistently excoriated as the soul-destroying opposite of enthusiasm.

There was a form of politics, however, that escaped both of these dangers: liberalism, the form of politics that put individual liberty

---

[36] Constant, *Adolphe*, 119.
[37] Constant, *De la religion*, I, 13, 26.
[38] See Constant's trenchant remarks on the unholy alliance of fanaticism and freedom in *PoP* (1806), 415ff.

rather than some abstract, reified notion of "the common good" at its center but that, by universalizing that goal, set it above the self-interest of any one individual, making it also a higher moral cause. Liberal politics had at least three distinct advantages from the point of view of fulfilling the needs of the whole self.

By making the abstract individual and his/her rights the supreme value, it sought to protect the private sphere in which both the goals of happiness – pleasure or self-interest – and the transcendental desires of the heart – love and religion – could be served. The individual needed above all to be free from external coercion, not least from the coercion of government, to pursue those basic needs. Liberalism included the basic rights of private property and the freedom of religion necessary to fulfill both sides of the self. The paradox of Constant's liberalism, as one may think of it, is that the public sphere of politics exists above all to promote the private sphere, yet as such it is also an end in itself. In defending this paradox Constant was applying the bitter lesson France had learned from making politics a matter of serving "an abstract being [the entire nation] who never has positive existence"[39] in the time of the Terror. "During the French Revolution," he wrote, "men thought they could make public power work as they saw it done in the free States of antiquity. They believed everything must still today yield to collective authority, that private morality must be silent before the public interest.... But collective authority did nothing but harm individual independence.... Private morality was silent; but since the public interest does not exert the same sway over us as over the ancients, it was to a hypocritical and ferocious egoism that private morality saw itself sacrificed."[40] Only by rejecting the concept of "the public interest" could the true public interest – the needs and rights of the individuals who composed it – be served. "Where the individual is nothing," he wrote aphoristically, "the people are nothing."[41]

Secondly, liberalism as Constant understood it put a very high premium on the concrete details of the constitutional and institutional structures necessary to avoid the Scylla and Charybdis of despotic tyranny on the one side and democratic tyranny on the other. Nor

[39] Constant, *PoP* (1806), 331.
[40] *PoP* (1806), 366.
[41] Ibid., 384.

was it sufficient just to work *out* those details theoretically; it was necessary to work *on* them as well, to translate them into political actuality. Liberalism demanded practical activity, commitment to the life of politics to fight for the realization of liberal institutions against the constant threats from both "Right" and "Left." Freedom of speech, press, and assembly were just the necessary preconditions for such political activity. Not the least of the reasons for Constant's continuing importance to liberalism is his intense interest in the minutiae of constitutionalism, not necessarily the particulars of his own recommendations – though many remain relevant despite the passage of time – but the spirit, the example, of such detail work itself. His specific proposals for constitutional structures followed from his recognition that there can be no freedom without attention to its institutional armature. Coming to grips with the "historical" Constant thus means among other things engaging with those proposals as politics: there is no exercise more appropriate to his spirit than trying to answer that supposedly superannuated old question of political philosophy, what is living and what is dead in Constant's constitutional theory. Enlisting Constant in the recent historical battle against totalitarianism may in a sense be anachronistic, but the spirit of his effort to devise institutional structures to protect liberty amid changing historical threats is not. The strictures against the tendency of "people or princes" to attempt to create uniformity in society[42] hardly sound irrelevant in a posttotalitarian world, let alone a totalitarian one. His insistence on the dangers of unlimited sovereignty, whether that of a majority or of the law itself, is as fresh a reminder of the threat that even a constitutional democracy can pose to individual liberties as it was in the aftermath of the Revolution. In any case, however, and unlike the implications of his notion of religion, the defense and extension of liberty, civil and political, provided Constant with a constant program for action.

And finally, the appeal of liberalism was that it satisfied in a concrete way the desire of enthusiasm to rise above purely individual concerns and strive for moral self-perfection through submission to a transcendent good. Fearful of tyranny of any kind, Constant would not make participation in politics an obligation enforced by coercion, but for him it was a necessary part of the ethos of a modern liberal

[42] *SCU*, 73.

state that protecting the liberty of all was the moral obligation of each.[43] Political service to the liberal state enabled the individual to circumvent the inevitable dissatisfactions of the purely private quest for transcendence, whether the tragedies of love or the frustrations of an objectless faith, to reach a level of moral and emotional fulfillment without the sacrifice of liberty. In effect, indeed almost literally, Constant's liberalism sacralized freedom. It became a quasi-religious value, to be worshipped and fought for. The peroration of his preface to *On Religion* more than hints that the very purpose of his defense of the religious sentiment is to serve a new modern religion of liberty: "Friends of liberty, proscribed in your turn by Marius and Sulla, be the first Christians of a new late Roman Empire. Liberty is nurtured by sacrifice. Deliver the power of sacrifice to the exhausted race which has lost it. Liberty always wants citizens, sometimes heroes. Do not extinguish the convictions which are the foundation of civic virtues, and which create heroes by giving them the power to be martyrs."[44]

If the tone of this appeal seems a little melodramatic, it is not simply attributable to the rhetorical style of the age. Constant wrote and acted when liberalism, as he conceived it, was new and embattled. The call to martyrdom on behalf of freedom was not an empty trope when exile, harassment by the secret police, potentially deadly duels with political opponents and even trials for treason, all of which Constant himself underwent during the regimes of Napoleon and the Restoration, could be the price of fighting for liberty. But when Constant spoke of raising altars to "that divinity of proud and noble souls" who gave their lives in defense of freedom,[45] he was speaking more than metaphorically. Constant's sacralization of liberty anticipates an argument that Emile Durkheim, a nonbeliever who nonetheless understood the power of religion, would make more than seventy years later in his essay on "Individualism and the Intellectuals," where he countered the attack of anti-Dreyfusards on the corrosive effect of modern individualism on communal belief

---

[43] Castigating the Terrorists for requiring attendance at the ceremonies and assemblies marking national holidays, Constant wrote, "A duty was made of what should be voluntary. Celebration of freedom was surrounded by constraint." *PoP* (1806), 369.

[44] Constant, *De la religion*, I, xliv.

[45] Ibid., xxix.

by referring to individualism as modern society's own sacred value. In an earlier age, Constant did not, as Durkheim did, replace God with the sacred value of the individual; rather he put divinity in the service of the value of individual liberty.

Constant's liberalism demanded the kind of political culture that both accommodated enlightened self-interest, self-interest "properly understood," and understood, preached, and practiced its limitations. Constant's writings, and just as much his political service, his entire career, were intended as a contribution to the creation of just such a culture. Todorov was absolutely on the mark in titling his book on Constant *A Passion for Democracy*, even if he erred in calling Constant a democrat rather than a liberal.[46] "Passion" here must be taken in a philosophical, perhaps even a theological, sense, not in the watered-down meaning of ordinary language. In the Weberian understanding of the term, liberalism for Constant was a vocation, a higher calling. Only thus, he believed, could liberalism serve the needs of "individuality" even as it protected the material pleasures and interests of individualism.

---

[46] Constant was unapologetic and adamant that the franchise be restricted to property owners. "Only property," he wrote, "can render men capable of exercising political rights. Only owners can be citizens." *PoP* (1806), 166. Although he wrote this in 1806, he did not change his mind as a liberal deputy in the late 1820s.

10 Literature and Politics in Constant

That Constant saw a close relationship between his literary and his political writing is evident from the title of his *Mélanges de littérature et de politique*, published in 1829, one year before his death.[1] It is also evident from the way Constant structured this collection, which became his intellectual testament. The key essay on "Literature in Its Relations to Liberty" is placed squarely in the center of the book. (It is the tenth of twenty essays.) But it does not divide the book into a literary and a political half. On either side of the central essay are pieces covering a variety of topics, and the final essay of the collection suggests that the ability to move easily between one domain and the other is itself a sign of political freedom. "There are periods in history when man seems to enjoy the fullness of his faculties. The arts, the professions, the talents are not such separate spheres as to prevent him from passing from one to the other.... It is especially or even exclusively in free states that are observed that speedy and varied application of every faculty to every need" (p. 469). Such a statement also shows that Constant's political vision is not the narrowly "liberal" one of people pursuing their private interests with little concern for citizenship. On the contrary, it is in the absence of freedom that a sharp division of labor arises, so that "the writer abstains from action, the warrior from thinking, and the statesman from writing" (p. 470). And what is true in practice should also apply to reflection on those practices: one domain should not be isolated from the others.

---

[1] Benjamin Constant, *Mélanges de littérature et de politique* (Paris: Pichon et Didier, 1829). Unless otherwise indicated, all references to essays in the *Mélanges* are to this edition.

Yet, the very intimacy of the connection between literature and politics makes it difficult to define the terms of the relationship. To begin with, it is not always easy to define what counts as "literature" for Constant. Works with clear generic markers, such as the novel *Adolphe*, represent only part of Constant's output. His many critical essays, in which we find some of Constant's most innovative thinking, are not easy to classify. What exactly distinguishes literary from political writing? In the *Mélanges*, essays announcing literary themes are suffused with political considerations. The essay devoted to Constant's translation and adaptation of Schiller's dramatic trilogy, *Wallenstein*, for example, develops some of Constant's most important aesthetic ideas, but fully a third of it consists of notes about German history and the politics of the Thirty Years' War. Conversely, the short essay contrasting the British politicians Fox and Pitt is as much a character portrait, a genre with a long literary pedigree, as it is an assessment of their policies.

Another difficulty is that Constant uses the word "literature" to mean at least three different things. First, and most conventionally, it designates works of artistic creation. Here, Constant defines his thinking about literature and politics in terms of a simple analogy. Thus, in the often-quoted words of the preface to the *Mélanges*, he declares, "For forty years I have defended the same principle, freedom in everything, in religion, in philosophy, in literature, in industry, in politics" (p. vi). Freedom, he goes on to say, is "the triumph of individuality" over the despotism of authority from above and the tyranny of the majority from below (p. vi), and literary freedom, like its political counterpart, begins with liberation from these two forms of oppression. (How it culminates in "individuality" is not defined here; we will return to this point.) Thus, Constant declares his "aversion for those jealous rules that for so long have hindered the progress of our literature" (p. vii). These rules are the conventions of style and decorum inherited from seventeenth-century classicism, which imposed strict limits on what art could represent and how. In this context, the despotism "from above" is exercised primarily by the critics (who may well, as under the Napoleonic regime, be instruments of political authority). But critics are not alone in forcing the author to follow the rules. There is also the unwillingness of the general French public to accept any artistic novelty. As Constant struggled with his adaptation of Schiller's *Wallenstein*, he was particularly mindful of the tyrannical majority of theatergoers who insisted that the conventions of French tragedy should still be respected. Those conventions are not merely matters of artistic decorum. Like the ban on showing noble characters perform household tasks on stage, they may have implications for the progress of political equality. Others, such as the one that prevents virtuous female characters from speaking openly of the power of love, may also indirectly affect the spirit of political freedom by restricting the artist's freedom to transcend the limits of social custom.

Not that Constant advocates unlimited literary license. On the contrary, he shares with his French contemporaries a concern for good taste and what he calls literary "perfection." Again, he is less interested in defining his positive ideal than in rebutting the argument of conservative critics who seek to restrict the scope of artistic expression. The essay "Literature in Its Relation to Liberty" was first drafted in 1805 in response to critics supporting the imperial regime.[2] They argued that art flourished best under the rule of absolute monarchs such as Louis XIV or Augustus.[3] When writers take sides in party quarrels or promote a political cause, they compromise their craft. With political questions settled once and for all, they are more likely to achieve that unsullied perfection of style and taste that defines great art. He revised the essay in 1817, after the restored Bourbon king Louis XVIII had granted a charter that made him a constitutional rather than an absolute monarch, but when some unnamed opponents resurrected the same authoritarian argument, giving it a new, almost Orwellian twist. They cannot condemn artists for being concerned with freedom, but they claim that the spirit of true liberty was nowhere better expressed than, once again, in the writers who flourished under Louis XIV. The *Mélanges* of 1829 reprints the essay in slightly revised form, at a moment when Charles X was trying to reinforce monarchical power.

Constant's reply illustrates both his commitment to artistic freedom and his acceptance of prevailing aesthetic standards. The latter move is in part a strategic one, as we can see by comparing the final

---

[2] "Fragments d'un essai sur la littérature dans ses rapports avec la liberté," *OCBC/ Œuvres*, III.1, 495–519.
[3] Constant's target includes La Harpe and Suard. See Delon's introduction, *OCBC/ Œuvres*, III.1, 491–93.

form of the essay with the manuscript version. He omits a passionate defense of the literary merits of controversial Enlightenment writers like Montesquieu and Rousseau[4] and confines his discussion to those Latin authors who enjoyed universal esteem.[5] The result is a less provocative, but perhaps all the more effective, rebuttal of his opponents' arguments. Constant makes two main points. The first is that "for a writer to have ideas of liberty, it is not essential that he should attach himself to specific forms of social organization, that one might consider to be more or less favorable to liberty" (pp. 226–27). Whether a writer is a monarchist or a republican does not matter in itself. Constant acknowledges that during the Revolution many writers who boasted of their republicanism were in fact enemies of liberty. What counts is the presence of an underlying impulse in the writing showing that whatever the writer's allegiance, the writer is no friend of despotism (p. 227). Horace or Virgil may praise Augustus, but by refusing to disavow his earlier struggles against tyranny, by alluding in positive, even if veiled, terms to republican heroes like Cato or Cicero, or by expressing hopes for greater freedom within the new regime, the poet is telling us that the ruler's favors "are more a necessity to which he bows than a fortune for which he strives" (p. 237).

Constant's second point is to deny any connection between the consolidation of Augustus's rule and the flourishing of literature. The Latin writers we value most either died before Augustus's ascendancy (Cicero, Lucretius, and Catullus) or came to maturity in the republican and civil war period (Horace and Virgil). Clearly, the tumult and partisan atmosphere of the preceding period did not corrupt the purity of their taste. On the other hand, writers who grew up under the imperial regime begin to show signs of "decadence," of a less flexible, more vulgar style. The obscurity and strain in Tacitus's writing is the unhappy effect of despotism (pp. 238–39). Unfortunately, Constant does not discuss how oppression affects Tacitus's

---

[4] He also omits the polemical remark that the work most identified with French absolutism, Bossuet's *Politics Drawn from Holy Scripture*, is just as much a partisan work as any written by the later *philosophes*, and therefore must be judged bad literature by his conservative opponents if they are to be consistent. "Fragments," 512.

[5] The version published in the *Mercure de France* announces a second instalment devoted to the age of Louis XIV, but it was never published.

style, just as we are not told how Horace's or Virgil's "ideas of liberty" contribute to their artistic excellence. The nature of that excellence is assumed as matter of general agreement. It is, Constant writes, "that flexibility in mind, that finesse in manners, that quickness in allusion, that propriety in words that make for the perfection of art" (pp. 231–32). The implication is that these qualities are not to be analyzed so much as instinctively recognized by others who can do so because they possess something of those same qualities. Indeed, it would seem that Constant wishes his own writing to be appreciated in the same manner.[6] This rather aristocratic view of art downplays the element of content and craft in favor of the general quality of mind above and beyond the particular work, a quality that begins to fill out what Constant means by individuality.

This brings us to a second, broader meaning of the word "literature." Constant's essay on Madame de Staël discusses her *Considerations of the French Revolution* as well as her novel *Corinne*, while that on William Godwin cites his novels *Caleb Williams* and *St. Leon* as well as his treatise on *Political Justice*. What matters here is the subject's distinctive outlook on life as it is reflected in the full range of his or her writing. The expression of individuality can take many forms; any or all of these can count as literature, or be the object of reflection that also counts as literary. Attention to the quality of individual character is even more marked in the essay on Julie Talma, a close friend of Constant who died in 1805. She was neither a public figure nor an author; her legacy consists of cherished memories in the hearts of her friends, not of books. One cannot appreciate Julie's character, however, without taking into account her passionate republicanism. Constant's eulogy may be one of the first of its kind to consider specific political convictions (as distinguished from general sentiments of liberty or loyalty) as integral to the personality of a private individual, and to make discussion of these convictions part of a literary memorial.

---

[6] As an example of Constant's quietly subversive style, one may take the sentence in which he says that the Augustus's favors were, for the true genius, "plutôt une nécessité qu'il subit qu'une prospérité qu'il ambitionne" (p. 237). The surprising juxtaposition of "necessity" and "prosperity" adds to the conventional contrast between sad fate and good fortune, a more acutely ironic one between well-being and neediness: the benefit turns the recipient into a beggar.

Another striking feature of the essay is the discussion of Julie's atheism, which again is not presented as an abstractly "philosophical" attitude, and still less as a matter for moral judgment. Rather, it is also a personal conviction to be discussed in relation to other aspects of her character and the particular historical circumstances in which she lived. The portrait of Julie thus connects with other essays in the *Mélanges* devoted to the historical development of religious ideas. While religion might seem to be something separate from literature or politics, it in fact belongs to both. This is because Constant's interest in religion focuses less on its content than on its imaginative forms and on the power structures it engenders or upholds. The dogmas of religion resemble political laws or poetic rules, depending on the context, and can be illuminated by comparison with either of these. For Constant, a genuine religious feeling belongs to human nature, but like other expressions of individuality it can emerge only through a struggle against forces from above and below, in this case from despotic priesthoods and from popular prejudice.

On another level, one could argue more broadly that any analysis based on suggestive analogies is a literary one, if we think of literature in terms of the humanist tradition of grammar and rhetoric. This tradition of *belles lettres* was reconceived in the Enlightenment as part of that reflection on the way ideas of any kind are combined and formulated, which constituted an essential part of *philosophie*, but in the post-Revolutionary period, *littérature* emerged as the more comprehensive term in Germaine de Staël's pathbreaking study *On Literature, Considered in Its Relationship with Social Institutions* (1800).[7] There, she defined literature as "everything that concerns the exercise of thought in writing, the physical sciences excepted."[8]

---

[7] One might wonder why this role is not assigned to philosophy. The explanation may lie partly in the cultural circumstances of the period. In the post-Revolutionary years, conservative writers identified "philosophy" with the confidently positivistic and militantly anticlerical attitudes of the Enlightenment *philosophes*. Even liberals such as Constant and de Staël were dissatisfied with what they saw as the intellectual narrowness of the *philosophes'* successors, the *idéologues*. On the other hand, they admired the sweeping comprehensiveness of German idealist thought, fully understanding it required technical skills they did not possess. It was also a style of thinking they thought was too foreign to French habits of mind.

[8] Madame de Staël, *De la littérature considérée dans ses rapports avec les institutions sociales*, ed. A. Blaeschke (Paris: Infomédia Communications [Classiques Garnier],

The distinctiveness of her claim can be seen by comparing it with the report Marie-Joseph Chénier presented in 1808 to Napoleon on behalf of the Institut de France, and published under the title *Tableau historique de l'état et des progrès de la littérature française depuis 1789*. A chapter on "moral thought, politics, and legislation" appears there between other chapters on grammar, rhetoric, history, and poetics. But Chénier was hardly staking a claim for the intellectual's right to pass independent judgment on political affairs or to transgress disciplinary boundaries. Rather, his report simply gives a more rationalized, indeed bureaucratic, version of traditional notions about literature as stylistically eloquent speech. The boundaries of genre and subject matter remain fixed, and eloquence itself, which endows ideas with communicative life, is subordinated to political needs. Chénier does not reduce literature to propaganda, but he agrees that the overall direction and pace of literary "progress" is to be directed by imperial policy. De Staël, by contrast, in exploring the relations between literature and social institutions, refuses to subordinate the former to the latter, even if she recognizes that circumstances shape what is said at any given place and time. The "perfectibility" of society, she declares, requires that literary intellectuals take a leading cultural role, not least in determining the meaning of perfectibility itself.

Constant certainly agreed with de Staël's expansive view of literature. Yet, it is important to notice a key difference between the forms taken by his own "literary" writing as compared with that of his longtime partner. Whereas de Staël's key works, *On Literature* and *On Germany* (not to mention her novels *Delphine* and *Corinne*) are ambitiously programmatic, Constant's essays, like his novel *Adolphe*, tend to be brief and suggestive. While they address topics such as freedom and perfectibility from a broad historical perspective and formulate principles Constant believes to be generally valid, they do so in response to specific circumstances. Often published in newspapers and journals, or if in book form as extended

---

1998), 16. It is not clear from this definition whether "physical" includes the biological sciences and should be translated as "natural," given that de Staël would certainly see such matters as the psychology of temperaments as susceptible of "literary" analysis. She probably has in mind any field of inquiry that requires specialized mathematical or other technical knowledge, in which case "hard sciences" would be the best translation.

pamphlets rather than formal treatises, and characterized by a deliberately low-key style (flights of speculative fancy are rare), they have a contingent quality at odds with claims for literature as a meta-discourse. Even when gathered for posterity in the *Mélanges*, Constant reasserts their contingent nature by revising them to offer first impressions of new developments such as the rise of Romantic drama or of utilitarian doctrine.

The somewhat ironic contrast between the circumscribed form of Constant's essays and the vast domain claimed for literature brings us to a third sense in which he uses the word "literature." In a journal entry dated November 6, 1804, Constant writes of his eagerness to publish his book on religion, so he can take his place "in literature."[9] Here, the word designates a symbolic space that transcends time and place. Room is made "in literature" for those who have published a work recognized as having the substance and enduring significance of a cultural monument. Implicit here is Constant's judgment that the essays and pamphlets he had published in the 1790s were too ephemeral to count as real literary achievements. Just as he aspired to play a role in government that would allow him to make his mark in the political world, Constant yearned for a place in the literary pantheon.

Although "literature" in this third sense of a symbolic space recalls the older notion of the "republic of letters," it carries different connotations. The republic of letters was built up as much out of correspondence, occasional essays, commentaries, and other informal modes of intellectual exchange as it was out of books. It represented a protest against the political division of Europe into states and religious confessions demanding the individual's absolute allegiance. Under Napoleon, the "Coppet circle" of which Constant was a member continued this tradition. On the other hand, like other early Romantic writers, including de Staël herself, Constant was equally driven by the desire to overcome what from the post-Revolutionary perspective was lamented as the fragmentation of knowledge and imagination of the early modern era and to offer a more integrated and comprehensive account of the human mind and its expressions in a work that would itself exemplify that ambition. Only such a work would qualify as "literature" in this third exalted sense.

---

[9] *Journaux intimes*, in *OCBC/Œuvres*, VI, 250.

In the event, the volumes of *De la religion* did not begin to appear until 1824, but the fact of its publication fortified Constant's belief in the value of his legacy, even though he could take satisfaction in his achievements as a champion of freedom in the Chamber of Deputies. Indeed, I believe Constant might not have published the *Mélanges* had the volumes on religion not already started to appear. The decision to collect his miscellaneous essays may have been part of a campaign to get Constant elected to the Académie Française. Yet, it was only when his *Religion* had already earned him a place "in literature" comparable to the one he enjoyed in politics as a long-term member of the Chamber of Deputies that those essays could finally be claimed *for* literature, and the dichotomy between literature as monument and literature as flexible occasional reflection overcome. As for literature in the first sense of creative work, it can be argued that Constant's political career under the Bourbon Restoration, more solid and successful than any of his efforts under earlier regimes, would not have been possible had he not completed his novel *Adolphe* and offered it to the public in 1816. Ironically, Constant himself regarded this book less as an artistic accomplishment than as a way to work through problems in his personal life, something to be forgotten once it was done, and it is primarily thanks to *Adolphe* that Constant enjoys a place "in literature" today. As we shall see, the novel is in fact the culmination of a reflection on the relationship between language, individuality, and society that runs through all three kinds of literature practiced by Constant, but which achieves its densest and most dramatic expression in this deceptively slight book.

* * *

Constant took from Condorcet and the intellectualist current of the Enlightenment his belief that human progress depended fundamentally on the generation of new combinations of ideas. In his essay "On the Perfectibility of the Human Species," he asserts that progress toward the ideal of equality depends on humanity's ability to articulate new ideas and discern the interrelationships between them.[10] Elsewhere, he adds that progress in such countries as China has been blocked simply because people there do not have the words

---

[10] "De la perfectibilité de l'espece humaine," in *EP*, 706.

they need to think their way into the future. Along with this confidence in the power of ideas is a conviction that "never has a true idea which has been put into circulation been removed from it" (p. 443). While the person who discovers a new principle – that is to say, a combination of ideas that captures something of the way things are – may be forgotten, "his thought will nevertheless remain imprinted on the indestructible whole" of human knowledge (p. 388). Constant's confidence on this score is remarkable, given the ideological as well as political upheavals he had witnessed.[11] Perhaps he had to insist on this point because it allowed him to downplay the role of collective human will exalted by Rousseau and then, to disastrous effect, by his Jacobin followers. Thus, the first duty of literary-political intellectuals is to make sure these thoughts remain freely available as resources for future exploration. (One thinks of the way Constant himself created a stock of manuscript reflections on which he could draw when the occasion was ripe.) Writers must resist attempts from above and from below, by society's rulers, but also sometimes by the people themselves, to hinder the progress of ideas, either by refusing to rethink old notions or by adopting fashionable notions whose potential is in fact more limited and limiting than the ideas they replace.

The words one chooses and the style of their combination are thus more than a matter of good taste. They contribute in a crucial way to human progress. This is because the verbal texture of their work has value independent of the immediate persuasiveness of the ideas to which they refer. In his first important pamphlet, "On the Force of the Present Government" (1796), Constant writes,

Words have such an influence on us that they bring back [ramènent] ideas. Separated from the latter by a foreign cause, they rejoin them, as soon as that cause exists no longer. The forms perpetuate the spirit, and while they can be horribly perverted, they resemble those trees that are easy to bend, but whose elasticity straightens them, when one ceases to compress them.[12]

---

[11] It should be emphasized that Constant first formulated this conviction, not in the years of his triumph, but in the midst of the Revolutionary upheavals and the manipulation of the language of freedom by its ideologues. One thinks of the equally idealistic slogan advanced in the Soviet 1930s by Mikhail Bulgakov in *The Master and Margarita*: "manuscripts don't burn."

[12] *De la force du gouvernement actuel et de la nécessité de s'y rallier*, OCBC/Œuvres, I, 369.

The passage is particularly remarkable for Constant's use of the word "form" in a positive sense. Generally speaking, Constant considers cultural forms (religious or literary) as an impediment to the free progress of the mind and spirit. Only in the realm of judicial practice does he praise respect for "the forms" (in the sense of procedural rules[13]) that provide some small defense against the immediate execution of arbitrary will. Here, a similar sense of defensive preservation is given a much more dynamic quality through the use of the tree image. Only young trees can bend and spring back in the way suggested by the image, which suggests that the words being preserved (and the ideas behind them) can demonstrate renewed vitality.

A good example of Constant's attention to particular words may be found in his essay on Charles Dunoyer, a French disciple of the English utilitarian Jeremy Bentham.[14] Constant criticized Dunoyer's reductively positivistic form of liberalism. Yet, he realized that he himself had not reflected enough on the ways unfettered freedom of trade might compromise the liberty and well-being of ordinary people. He does so now, but most notably by reacting to Dunoyer's terminology. We must, he writes, maintain the distinction between the idea of right and that of utility. "Right is a principle, utility is only a result; right is a cause, utility is only an effect" (p. 145).

He then moves from the conceptual distinction to the psychological dimension of the use of the two words.

The expressions that Bentham wishes to proscribe recall ideas much more clear and much more specific than those he would substitute for them. Tell a man: You have the right not to be executed or despoiled arbitrarily; you give him a very different feeling of security than if you say to him: It is not useful that you should be executed or despoiled arbitrarily ... in speaking of right, you present him with an idea independent of all calculation; in speaking of utility, you seem to invite a reconsideration of the thing in question, by submitting it to further verification (p. 146).

In another essay, Constant suggests that even appealing to "justice" may narrow the scope of legitimate human aspiration. "On the

---

[13] Following a common French sense of the word *forme*.
[14] Dunoyer's *L'Industrie et la morale dans leur rapport avec la liberté* (note the echo of Constant's essay on literature) was published in 1825.

Present Moment and the Destiny of the Human Species, or Short History of Equality" was probably written in 1799, at a time when, so it seemed to Constant, the ruling Directory was taking a disturbingly conservative turn. All of history, Constant wrote, can be thought of as a long struggle for equality against authoritarian structures.[15] Humanity's aspiration to equality may be obscured by the people's tendency to adapt to social circumstances and to accept as given many particular inequalities, some of which may well have been seen as just. Consequently, one should not equate the "sentiment of equality" with the "sentiment of justice." "Justice" is nothing other than "equality invested with the force of law," and thus always a more limited (and limiting) idea. Indeed, "there is this disadvantage in not giving equality its true name, that in then paying tribute to it under one designation, one believes oneself authorized to attack it under another." Constant is attacking those who seek to limit political equality in the name of justice and equity.[16]

These examples concern words from the past. What about the articulation of emerging realities? French classical critics had frowned on the invention of new words, and while Madame de Staël was willing to take a few risks,[17] Constant is wary of neologism. He prefers to focus on the generation of new intellectual associations from the vocabulary already available. We have seen how Constant's writing sometimes works through discreetly transgressive metaphors, but his critical reflections do not theorize the use of figurative speech as a literary critic might do. Rather, he speaks of the dynamics of language or, more precisely, of the articulation of ideas of which language is the vehicle, in terms reminiscent of Condorcet's vision of science. Thus in his essay on perfectibility, Constant writes that "even when our current ideas may be false, they carry in them

---

[15] How these first arose remains a mystery. Constant speculates that they were a response to some early calamity that disrupted the peaceful development of humanity from its original state.

[16] *Du moment actuel et de la destinée de l'espèce humaine, ou histoire abrégée de l'égalité*, in *OCBC/Œuvres*, III.1, 372.

[17] De Staël offended reviewers of *On Literature* by her use of the term *vulgarité* as a general term for lack of refinement in language and thought. This term would later come into common use, but at the time represented, in relation to the word *obscénité*, an attempt to reconceptualize the categories of inappropriate speech. See Jean-Claude Abramovici, *Obscénité et classicisme* (Paris: Presses Universitaires de France, 2003), 10.

the germ of perpetually new combinations, of rectifications more or less prompt but infallible, and of uninterrupted progression" (p. 393).

In order for this progression to occur, people must not be too wedded to any given combination of ideas. This principle may be easy enough to adopt in scientific experimentation, but in ordinary life people do not like having their comfortable mental habits disturbed. In his novel *Adolphe*, Constant shows his hero's irritation with the conventional wisdom expressed by the nobles of the little German principality that employed him. "Some obscure instinct warned me to distrust these general maxims which are so free of any qualification, so innocent of any subtlety. Fools make of their morality a compact, indivisible whole, in order that it may affect their actions as little as possible, and leave them free in all the details."[18] Instead of changing their ideas in light of their experience, they keep theory and practice separate from each other. In doing so, whether consciously or not, they not only block the way of progress, but also distort the reality of the world around them. Maxims of conventional wisdom may perhaps be suited to the unchanging order of primitive culture, but not to the complexity of modern society. "In the present state of society," Constant writes in the *Principles of Politics*, "individual relations are made up of fine nuances, changeable and elusive, which would be distorted in a thousand ways if one tried to give them clearer definition."[19]

Progress toward greater freedom and equality involves more than just intellectual flexibility, however. It requires sacrifice. For Constant, the willingness to give up immediate or instinctual gratification for the sake of a future or higher good is an important element in humanity's moral development, but just as important is what we might call intellectual sacrifice, by which we let go of primitive ideas, even about virtue, in order to allow the development of higher-order intellectual or moral concerns. Ideas based too closely on sensation, whose impulses are always the same, or to moral notions congealed into a solid mass, he condemns as "stationary," that is to say, as impediments to progress, while ideas based on higher-order,

---

[18] Constant, *Adolphe*, trans. Margaret Mauldon, ed. Patrick Coleman (Oxford: Oxford University Press, 2001), 10. All quotations from *Adolphe* are from this edition. See also the essay "On Madame de Staël and Her works," in the *Mélanges*, 178.
[19] *PoP* (1806), 371.

more flexible intellectual combinations are better because they are more adaptable to correction and improvement.

Constant calls the most important of these combinations "principles." These are not transcendent concepts or norms. Principles abstract from empirical data only to escape the "compact mass" of the given and to open up the possibility of mediating between primary values such as justice and equality and the diversity of human circumstances. Thus, to take his most prominent use of the term, Constant's "principles" of politics are applicable to all governments precisely because they do not depend on any particular constitutional form. As in his essay on literature and liberty, what matters is the presence of an underlying spirit of freedom. On the other hand, principles are more than mere regularities derived from the observation of human behavior. They have a moral dimension in that their purpose is to protect men's freedom to combine their ideas and channel their activities as they wish.

Principles, one might say, are for Constant combinations of ideas whose purpose is to safeguard the generation of further combinations of ideas, even ones that lead to modification of the principles themselves, should they start to impede the mind's freedom of combination. As Constant puts it in the chapter "Of Principles" in *On Political Reactions,*

A principle is the general result of a certain number of particular facts. Every time the whole of these facts undergoes some changes, the principle that resulted from it is modified; but then this modification itself becomes principle.[20]

Constant does not detail the process by which principles are generated, but a clue may be found in the way he uses the word "result" [*résultat*], which he derives from Condorcet's influential *Sketch for a Historical Picture of the Progress of the Human Mind.*[21] In reflecting on advances in human knowledge, Condorcet often uses "result" to mean something more specific than "outcome" but less rigid than

---

[20] *Des réactions politiques*, in *OCBC/Œuvres*, I, 490.

[21] A long-awaited critical edition of this work is now available: Condorcet, *Tableau historique des progrès de l'esprit humain: projets, esquisse, fragments et notes (1772–1794)*, ed. Jean-Pierre Schandeler and Pierre Crépel (Paris: Institut national d'études démographiques, 2004). The word *résultat* appears no less than four times in the preamble alone.

the end of a chain of causes and effects. A result is a conclusion reached by the kind of flexible blend of perception and reasoning needed to make one's way through the thicket of data and the multitude of rules that might be applied to the case. Writing in a situation of hardening ideological conflict, Constant wants to maintain Enlightenment optimism about humanity's ability to arrive at practical truth, but at the same time he wants to avoid the error of directly subordinating facts that belong to the "nuances" of life to any "compact mass" of rules, even "enlightened" ones, that, by its very compactness, distorts the search for genuine results by leaving no room for feedback and modification.

The word "result" also plays a key role in one of Constant's most important essays on literature, his tribute to Madame de Staël. Responding to criticisms of the heroine's unconventional behavior in de Staël's novel *Corinne*, Constant maintains that she is generous, sensitive, and true, and even when her actions are unconsidered. Indeed, *Corinne* is a truly moral work because its focus is not on specific actions or conventions, but on the whole of existence. Its morality, "resulting from natural emotions, influences the general tenor of life" (p. 177). Isolating particular moments in the actions of the heroine for moral judgment is a mistake. "The morality of a work of imagination consists in the impression the whole of it makes on the soul" (p. 176). The same emphasis on the whole appears in Constant's depiction of the reader's reactions: "If, when one puts down the book, one is more filled with sweet, noble, and generous sentiments than before one began it, the work is moral, and of a high morality" (p. 176). The language here sounds naively pious to the modern reader, but Constant's main point is that judgment cannot be rendered without introspection. This includes consideration of moral principles, but as part of a whole whose shape and direction cannot be anticipated or dictated by universal principle. As Constant goes on to say, in what will become his most often quoted statement about the relationship between literature and life, "a work of imagination should not have a moral goal [*but*], but a moral result. It should, in this respect, be like human life, which has no goal, but which always has a result in which morality necessarily finds a place" (p. 178).

Constant's concern for process is echoed in his attack on the aesthetic as well as the moral rules governing the French literature

of his day. These rules reflect the national preoccupation with producing "effects," in implicit contrast with results.[22] An effect, we
may infer, is a simple reaction, confirming or reinforcing ideas or
feelings already present and underpinning the generation of further
effects through the exercise of peremptory judgment on the world
beyond the work. A result is a more reflective complex of thought
and emotion, which enhances the reader's sense of self in relation
to the "general tenor of life." Simply disregarding literary conventions, however, will not bring about such results, since these are a
function of the work as a dynamic whole. To forget this is to confine
"literature" within the narrow bounds of poetic rules. In a broader
and truer sense, writing qualifies as literature when it helps us to
become more aware of the difference between effect and result. This
happens through reflection on the ways ideas are combined, sacrificed, and recombined, as Constant does in his critical essays. Or
it can happen by dramatizing what Constant calls "individuality"
in the life of a real or imaginary person, as Constant tries to do
in his portrait of Julie Talma and more expansively in *Wallstein*,
Cécile, and *Adolphe*. Just as political principles result from facts
and moral refinement results from art, we develop an understanding
of individuality by seeing how a variety of (sometimes apparently
contradictory) character traits combine within a particular personality to form a distinctive and dynamic whole. Appreciation of such
individuality in art enhances our own. On another level, as another
kind of dynamic whole, the successful literary work may also be said
to have its own kind of individuality (which Constant, in his essays,
identifies with that of the author's personality). In both cases, individuality can be recognized by the quality of the reaction it should
provoke in the reader: a desire to arrive at a principled judgment
combined with a willingness to subject that judgment to further
consideration.

* * *

Constant's adaptation of Schiller's *Wallenstein* is a fascinating
experiment, all the more instructive where Constant fails to follow
through on his most creative insights. Condensing this massive

---

[22] The French is *faire effet*. See the preface to *Wallstein*, in *OCBC/Œuvres*, III.2, 594.

dramatic trilogy into a single play would challenge the most talented dramatist, but Constant made things worse by his unwillingness to stray very far from the conventions of French classicism. The frozen vocabulary of French tragedy could not accommodate the semantic nuance and stylistic flexibility that gives Constant's other writing its literary quality.[23] Indeed, the twenty pages of historical notes appended to the play illustrate both the ambiguities and ironies of historical action more pointedly than Constant was able to do in the play itself.[24]

On the other hand, the conception of the hero's situation Constant developed in his lengthy preface to the play, while also departing from the German source, is much more original. For Schiller, the decision to set the play in the baroque atmosphere of early seventeenth century reflected both an interest in the German past and a more metaphysical fascination with "the incommensurability between agent and act and the indistinguishability of dreams and deeds."[25] Constant's Wallstein (he shortened the name for his public's convenience) illustrates more concretely the complexities of historical change. As the embodiment of a chivalrous *"esprit militaire"* increasingly out of place in a modern era of rational calculation and *Realpolitik*, Wallstein is an anachronism, not a metaphysical alien. Constant's play differs from Schiller's in underscoring how much the hero's character – bold but strangely passive, loyal but self-centered, contradictions for which Constant himself was often reproached – possesses an individuality that contrasts with the flattened uniformity of character that is the product of modern despotism. Constant was thinking of life under Napoleon, but he will later

---

[23] In a letter to his friend Prosper de Barante (September 18, 1808), Constant writes that in France's current state of decrepitude, literary creation is "galvinism and not life." Benjamin Constant, *Wallstein*, ed. Jean-René Derré (Paris: Société d'édition "Les Belles lettres," n.d. [1965]), 5.

[24] Constant could also rely on the readers of these notes, as he could not on the audience of his play, to enter into the play of allusion to the course of Napoleon's career.

[25] Julie A. Carlson, *In the Theatre of Romanticism: Coleridge, Nationalism, Women* (Cambridge: Cambridge University Press, 1994), 77. Constant's contemporary Coleridge also adapted Schiller's play, and while the result is also judged a failure, the two projects are worth comparing. In France, one would have to wait for Musset's *Lorenzaccio* for an original rethinking of Schiller's metaphysics in terms of a Romantic psychology of the self. Significantly, Musset's play is in prose, and was not intended for the stage.

return to the issue of anachronism and give it a new twist. In his *Spirit of Conquest* and other polemics against the emperor, he will accuse Napoleon, the erstwhile embodiment of post-Revolutionary modernity, of being, like war itself, an anachronism in the age of peaceful commerce. Instead of indulging in nostalgia for the past and its great individuals, Constant will likewise criticize ancient liberty as an outmoded political ideal that blinds us to the advantages of a modern, more flexible, and pluralistic form of individuality.

However, for Constant, *Wallenstein* was more than a history play. His fascination with Schiller's hero was matched by his feeling for Thekla, a young woman in love with Wallenstein's idealistic follower Max Piccolomini. Thekla's love, he claimed, was not that of a French heroine, a passion to be mastered or channeled by reason. It reflects a "German" idea of love as something sacred, "an emanation of the Divinity itself," linking two souls not only to each other but also to the world above.[26] Here, Constant underscores the metaphysical dimension he downplayed in his depiction of the hero. Thekla's purity of heart and confident trust in the transcendent power of love clashes dramatically with Wallenstein's vacillation and superstition. Regrettably, Constant's concern for French decorum leads him to make his Thecla (again, he changed the name) enter a convent after her lover's death instead of committing suicide over his grave. From a figure of transcendence, she turns into a pious cliché. The real problem, however, is that Thecla plays no role in the dramatization of Wallstein's individuality. In Schiller's trilogy, the connection between Thekla as a figure of transcendent love and Wallenstein's ambivalence about worldly action is grounded in a panoramic vision of the moral universe in which they live. *Wallenstein's Camp*, for example, shows us the common soldiers who followed the charismatic general in his rebellion against his Austrian masters in order to depict the cultural, religious, and political context for the action. Since Constant felt obliged to sacrifice Schiller's comprehensiveness to meet French expectations for a more concentrated plot, the connection between Wallstein and Thecla is too thin to spark any productive combination of ideas in the reader.

Cécile and *Adolphe* are more successful, precisely because the relationship between a vacillating hero and a loving woman lies at

[26] *OCBC/Œuvres*, III.2, 604.

the heart of the plot and because the author has found original ways to mediate between social and metaphysical or religious conceptions of life. *Cécile*, written in 1810 but not published until 1951, is an unfinished initiatory romance whose narrative is shaped by signs of an unexpectedly beneficent fate. Grounded in Constant's own experience, the story is that of a man seeking to extricate himself from a dead-end affair with the imperious Madame de Malbée. His chance reunion with the sweet Cécile, a woman from his past, allows him to imagine a new beginning. Although his guilty feeling of obligation to his former lover leads him to cause Cécile much anguish – the story breaks off in the middle of a particularly painful moment – a happy end is in sight.

Curiously, what enables the hero of *Cécile* to move forward is not any capacity for decisive action. On the contrary, he is sustained by abandoning himself to God's will. Why, then, does he not meet the same fate as the superstitious Wallstein? The difference seems to lie in the mode of his passivity. Whereas Wallstein wonders whether his choice of action corresponds to fate's immutable decrees, *Cécile*'s hero lives in a psychic world whose structure has already collapsed. His surrender to the divine will is thus a form of action, and it opens a space for something new to happen. Such an interpretation is supported by Constant's use of the term "era" (*époque*) for each successive episode of the story, the same word used by Condorcet for the stages of humanity's historical progress.[27]

Yet, the gesture of surrender in *Cécile* involves much more than the sacrifice of closely held ideas. It also involves the affections and the will, but in a particular way that links them closely with the more intellectual operations of the mind. In the disenchanted world of modernity people's attachment to particular idea combinations may reflect their reluctance to prefer freedom over short-term interest, but it may also include a determination to defend against a fear of psychic emptiness or chaos. We do not learn how the hero of *Cécile* moves from the initial moment of surrender to the resolution he announces at the beginning of the story. Perhaps Constant was too close to the experience, bound up as it was with his relationship to Charlotte, the model for Cécile, to give his story a finished, dramatic

---

[27] The word had already been popularized in cosmology by Buffon in his *Epoques de la nature* (1778).

form. Yet, the freshness and flexibility of its prose displays the successful result of a struggle through which good and bad order, good and bad openness, can be distinguished, even if it is unable fully to dramatize how the hero can work through the principles involved in that struggle.

Adolphe, too, began as a private exercise, but in 1816, when Constant's career was in shambles, he decided to publish it. When Napoleon returned to power in 1814 from his exile on Elba, he had invited his eloquent adversary to draft the constitution for a new, more "liberal" regime. To everyone's surprise, Constant accepted, only to have his hopes dashed by Waterloo. Distrusted now by both Right and Left, Constant beat a strategic retreat to London, where he first read his short narrative to groups in private homes and then published the novel. (A Paris edition and a London English translation appeared soon after.) He gave the need for money as the reason, but he had two other motives: to make sense of his past (including his relationships with the various women in his life) and to prepare the way for a return to public life. The tension between self-exploration and self-vindication, between the need to give form to explanatory principles and to dramatize their limitations, produced a masterpiece of literary art.

The story of *Adolphe* is a tragic one in that the relationship between Adolphe and Ellénore is doomed from the start. His birth and talents qualify him for a distinguished career in the public service of the German state where his father is a government minister, while Ellénore has for many years been the mistress of the noble Count de P. Marrying her would doom his career, but Adolphe makes things worse by his inability either to join his life to Ellénore's or to make a clean break, while she throws away what tranquility and social position she had achieved by publicly and masochistically clinging to an indecisive man. Neither character is idealized, and while there are intimations that through the characters' suffering can be glimpsed a higher dimension of meaning, there is no appeal to an arbitrary (because unexamined) transcendence as in the two works we have just discussed.

Aggravating the effect of the characters' flaws are rigid conventions of the society around them, which allow for immorality but not for scandal, and which condemn people to isolation but grant them no privacy. However, here again Constant avoids easy dichotomies.

In an essay published near the end of his life, Constant suggests that the tragedy of the future will focus on the tension between individual aspirations and outmoded social forms. In contrast to *Wallstein* (and to earlier French political tragedies, such as those of Corneille), society, not the hero, is the anachronism. Instead of flattening individuality, society prevents it from emerging.[28] There is something of this idea in *Adolphe*, which offers a scathing indictment of the world of petty pre-Napoleonic German principalities in which it is set.[29] Yet, the story does not suggest that historical progress is the answer to the issues it raises.

Instead, the narrative is framed by a set of texts that encourage readers to think for themselves about the relationship between character and circumstance. *Adolphe*'s first-person narrative is preceded by an "editor's foreword," which offers us an external (but still partial) view of Adolphe as he appeared some years after the end of his story. Freed from his ties to Ellénore, Adolphe has not entered a career but lives out a blasted life in melancholy wandering. At the end of the book, there is an exchange of letters (added by Constant not long before the novel's publication) between the editor of the "found manuscript" of the story and an anonymous man who knew Adolphe. The correspondent assures the editor that publishing the story would not now harm anyone's feelings and indeed would be useful in proving to women that "the most passionate feeling is not capable of fighting the established order."[30] The editor responds by agreeing to publish the story, but not of its usefulness to women, who will always delude themselves about their lovers, or because it illustrates the power of social convention. Rather, "it is to men that the lesson is directed," the lesson that "circumstances are of little import" and that "character is everything" (p. 79). He also advances a thesis that invites (and has generated) much debate about both

[28] Benjamin Constant, "Réflexions sur la tragédie," in *Œuvres*, 925. The play in question was a translation (apparently never published) of *Die Macht der Verhältnisse* by Ludwig Robert (1778–1832), a brother of Rahel Varnhagen. Behind the play's ostensible subject of class prejudice is a critique of anti-Semitism. Constant's essay, which appeared in the *Revue de Paris* in 1829, was written too late for inclusion in his *Mélanges*.

[29] It is unclear when exactly the story takes place, but the references to Poland suggest that it is before the final partition of that country. In any case, from a political point of view, to speak of "Poland" in 1816 also has an anachronistic quality.

[30] Constant, *Adolphe*, 77.

its application to Adolphe's life and its status as a moral principle. "The great question in life is the suffering we cause, and the most ingenious metaphysics do not justify the man who has broken the heart that loved him" (p. 79). Does the emotional authority of the second part of the sentence give the first part absolute validity? The decision is left to the reader.

The debate over the relative importance of character and circumstance also points to an exploration of individuality in the novel that differs from what we have seen in Constant's essay on Julie Talma and in *Wallstein*. In both these works (and in Constant's tributes to writers he admired, notably Madame de Staël), individuality of character is presented as an almost entirely positive quality. To be sure, individuality is composed of conflicting traits, including some, such as Julie's atheism and Wallstein's superstition, that Constant views as flawed. Yet, compared with the leveling of personality by oppressive regimes and reductive philosophies of self-interest, individuality is something to be prized. In *Adolphe*, the characters' individuality is not presented as an historical or political ideal, colored either by nostalgia for the past or by optimism about the future. It is, first and foremost, a reality of complex motives and contradictory expressions, to be recognized as such. In a preface he added after the book's first publication, Constant suggests how difficult it is for people to see this psychological reality, so caught up are they in their own desires and deconstructive schemes, just as the characters in the story fail to acknowledge the stubborn reality of the world around them. While the artificiality of that world's conventions, like the characters' illusions, calls for critique and proposals for reform, any real progress depends on recognizing reality before applying any principles to it. This is why he deliberately devised a story for which an alternative happy ending was not available (p. 83).

In the version found in the so-called second edition of *Adolphe*,[31] this preface bears the subtitle "Essay on the Character and Moral Result of the Work."[32] One might suggest that the difficult recognition of reality is a crucial part of what Constant meant when he

[31] In fact, it was added to some unsold copies of the first edition. A shorter version of this preface, without the subtitle, appeared in the third edition of 1824.
[32] Regrettably, in light of the lexical observations given earlier, the Oxford edition translates "*résultat*" as "effect" (p. 81).

said a work of art should not have a moral goal but a moral result. Another, related, clue may found in the author's own subsequent career. The appearance of *Adolphe* marked Constant's farewell to literary invention as much as it did to his inflated political ambitions (not to mention the self-delusion of his unrequited passion for Madame Récamier). In the remaining years of his life, Constant would continue to write about literature and, eventually, to publish his literary monument, his work on religion, but in a different context: that of his day-to-day work as a member of the liberal opposition working for independence of the press, for transparency in government, and for other principles of intellectual and political freedom.

11 The Theory of the Perfectibility of the Human Race

Translated by Arthur Goldhammer

De la perfectibilité de l'espèce humaine is the title of the seventeenth chapter of *Mélanges de littérature et de politique*, which Constant published in 1829. For this work he chose what he judged to be pieces most representative of his thinking. In order to afford readers an overview of his vast and relatively scattered writing, he scoured his papers and previously published articles for items he particularly valued. Another reason for bringing the volume out in 1829 was that the author was a candidate for the Académie Française and hoped that it would add luster to his reputation as a writer. *De la perfectibilité* was the revised version of a text written twenty-five years earlier, and in it Constant reverted to a subject that might have seemed rather out of date by the time it was published. To be sure, the nineteenth century celebrated the triumph of progress even more than the eighteenth had done, and soon Marx's historical materialism and Comte's positivism would provide the notion with theoretical underpinnings. Yet "perfectibility" had fallen out of favor. Both the word and the idea smacked too much of tiresome Enlightenment debates at a time when the younger generation was drawn to the new values of militant Romanticism. Still, Constant was by no means a writer of the past forgotten by the young. At his funeral in December 1830 students turned out to demonstrate their sincere devotion to Constant, the tireless defender of freedom. The students' esteem was no doubt reserved more for the politician than for the philosopher, however. In due course I will explain why the theory of perfectibility met with a relatively unfavorable reception, but let me turn first to its inception and to the way in which Constant became its champion.

THE GENESIS OF THE TEXT

On January 10, 1805, Constant received Charles de Villers, who had introduced Kant's philosophy in France. In his diary he wrote, "Visit of Villers. I found him full of enthusiasm for the Enlightenment. . . . He proposed that I participate in an anthology of German writing that the Institute hopes to put together. This suits me perfectly. Later, after mulling over what I might contribute, I came up with five pieces."[1] *De la perfectibilité de l'espèce humaine* figures in third place in the list that follows. The next day he wrote to Villers confirming his intention to contribute to the new journal and noted that *De la perfectibilité* could serve as an "introduction to the excerpt from Herder's *Ideas on the Philosophy of History*."[2] The proposed publication never saw the light of day, but we find among Constant's papers two manuscript versions of the essay, on which he later drew in preparing the text for the *Mélanges* of 1829, along with another text entitled *Fragments d'un essai sur la perfectibilité de l'espèce humaine*.[3] The precise date of these *Fragments* is unknown, as is the date of the text that Constant proposed to Villers in January 1805, which may have been written in 1803 or 1804. What is certain is that he had been pondering the idea for some time.

Rousseau seems to have been the first person to use the term "perfectibility," in his *Discours sur l'origine de l'inégalité*: he defined it as "the faculty of perfecting oneself" and claimed that it was what distinguished human beings from animals. He doubted, however, that this difference of essence was advantageous to man: "It would be sad for us if we were obliged to admit that this distinctive and virtually unlimited faculty was the source of all man's woes."[4] As is well known, Rousseau's argument in the first *Discourse* flew in the face of prevailing opinion, for he took the position that the development of science and the arts was inversely proportional to progress in morality and virtue. Constant rejected that pessimistic view, however, and

---

[1] *Journaux intimes*, OCBC/*Œuvres*, VI, 299.
[2] Benjamin Constant, Germaine de Staël, and Charles de Villers, *Correspondance*, ed. Kurt Kloocke et al. (Frankfurt am Main: Peter Lang, 1993), 94.
[3] Patrice Thompson has published all of these texts in OCBC/*Œuvres*, III, 431–75.
[4] See Jean Starobinski's edition of this text in Jean-Jacques Rousseau, *Œuvres complètes*, vol. 3 (Paris: Gallimard Pléiade, 1964), 142, 1317–18, for the detailed note on the term "perfectibility."

chose instead to follow Turgot, whose ideas on progress, dating from 1750, had been taken up by Condorcet in his *Tableau historique des progrès de l'esprit humain*, which Condorcet's widow published in 1794. After Constant came to Paris in 1795, he frequently encountered members of the group known as ideologues (Cabanis, Destutt de Tracy, Fauriel, de Gérando, and Volney) at the salons of Sophie de Condorcet and Madame Helvétius. In this circle there would have been numerous opportunities to discuss man's progressive faculty, which Condorcet described as "unlimited": "The result [of my work] will be to show, by reasoning and facts, that no limit has been set to the perfection of the human faculties; that the perfectibility of man really is unlimited; and that progress toward perfection, which no power can henceforth arrest, will end only when the globe upon which nature has placed us ceases to exist."[5] To be sure, Constant did not share all of Condorcet's ideas, but Condorcet's influence on him is beyond doubt. In 1798, moreover, Constant began work on a translation of William Godwin's *Enquiry Concerning Political Justice*, which again brought him into contact with a writer who affirmed a theory of progress. In Godwin's work Constant would also have detected something of the flavor of Scottish thought, with which he was already familiar from his stay in Edinburgh in the years 1783–85. The Scottish Historical School probably left a permanent imprint in his mind. Before Condorcet and along with Turgot in France, Smith, Hume, and Ferguson had conceived a progressive history of mankind, which proceeds by stages (hunting, husbandry, agriculture, and commerce) toward ever-greater freedom and equality. Godwin gave chapter 6 of his book 1 the title "Human Inventions Capable of Perpetual Improvement," and in it he wrote that "[t]here is no characteristic of man, which seems at present so eminently to distinguish him or to be of so much importance in every branch of moral science, as his perfectibility."[6]

The next phase, which would bring Constant into the heart of this debate, was the so-called perfectibility controversy, over which

---

[5] Condorcet, *Tableau historique des progrès de l'esprit humain. Projets, Esquisse, Fragments et Notes (1792–1794)*, ed. Jean-Pierre Schandeler and Pierre Crépel (Paris: Institut National d'Etudes Démographiques, 2004), 234–35.

[6] *De la justice politique (1798–1800)*, in *OCBC/Œuvres*, II, 1, 397, for the English version and p. 962 for Constant's translation, which remained unpublished until 1972.

much ink flowed in the years 1800–1802 following the publication of Madame de Staël's celebrated work *De la littérature*. Indeed, one can even hypothesize that the text that Constant did not publish until 1829 was written in the context of this controversy and that Constant had originally intended it as his personal contribution to the debate initiated by his friend's book. *De la littérature* can in fact be regarded as a second manifesto on perfectibility. Madame de Staël took the argument a step further than Condorcet by associating literature with progress in science and the arts. By "literature," of course, she meant all the means by which thought expresses itself; nowadays we would be more likely to say philosophy or the human sciences. Although she believed that one could not really speak of progress in poetic forms, she also contended that other kinds of literature adapt to the natural evolution of society. Every form of expression is a child of its time, and every period marks a stage surpassing those that have gone before. Like Condorcet, Madame de Staël held that progress is unlimited, but whereas he had primarily technical progress in mind, she insisted on intellectual and moral advances. That she took this position is not surprising: as an heir to the Enlightenment, it was natural for her to espouse a progressive philosophy of history. What is surprising is the violence of the polemic that her book aroused. The *Mercure de France*, the *Journal des débats*, and the *Année littéraire* all joined the chorus, with articles by Fontanes, Fiévée, Chateaubriand, Geoffroy, and Roederer, all of whom pounced on the theme of perfectibility and the author who dared to defend it. On December 11, 1800, for example, Geoffroy wrote in the *Année littéraire* of "this fatal chimera of perfectibility... this dangerous spirit of innovation and reform, which has turned the world upside down [and] become a serious threat to public tranquility."[7]

This statement strikes to the heart of the problem. Madame de Staël's work appeared just as the new consular regime was consolidating its power. The new regime quickly revealed its authoritarian nature and lack of tolerance for debate. Although the ideologues had supported Bonaparte in his quest for power, he had no intention of sharing it with philosophers or "metaphysicians," as he soon began

---

[7] Quoted by Axel Blaeschke in his edition of Madame de Staël, *De la littérature considérée dans ses rapports avec les institutions sociales* (Paris: Garnier, 1998), lxxxii.

calling them. By January 1800 the press was muzzled. Censors saw to it that no criticism of the regime saw the light of day, regardless of whether it came from the Jacobin left or the reactionary and royalist right. A majority of the public believed that the coup of the 18 Brumaire and the constitution of the Year VIII that followed had put an end to the period of revolutionary unrest. A consensus formed around the idea that after ten years of crises, political debate, and abortive innovations, the nation had grown tired of pointless and dangerous discussion and needed a rest. Bonaparte filled the role of providential hero to perfection: he was both a military and an administrative genius who could be entrusted with the reins of power.

Under the circumstances, the theory of perfectibility, especially when propounded by a woman who did not exactly enjoy the favor of the First Consul, could only be regarded as subversive. Unlike the regime's flatterers, she believed that existing institutions were less than perfect and would need to be adjusted to conform to evolving new ideas. Perfectibility also assumed freedom of expression, freedom of the press, and freedom of parliamentary assembly. Now, Constant, who was known to belong to Madame de Staël's coterie, had already begun to voice his opposition to the Tribunate in his first speech, in January 1800. In such a situation, the theory of perfectibility could hardly be regarded as innocent speculation. It seemed to be the work of a cabal and smacked of conspiracy. Hence it comes as no surprise to discover that the few newspapers still publishing seized on the theme, which served as a pretext for discussing political issues indirectly. To attack Madame de Staël and her perfectibilist thinking was to flatter the government in power and support the new regime. A more or less artificial split developed over this seemingly innocuous idea, which acquired a surprising political and polemical edge. After all, had not Condorcet himself been sought by the police when he was writing his *Esquisse*? Rather than give in to despair as the Revolution veered toward terror, he chose as his swan song a paean to progress, which he hoped would define the future of mankind. Wary politicians may have thought that to follow in Condorcet's footsteps in 1800 was to draw a parallel between the new regime and the Convention. Indeed, in the preface to the second edition of her book, Madame de Staël wrote, "No government other than a despotic one can set itself against the perfectibility of the human race." This was a clever way of saying that the more critical the Consulate was of her theory, the more it resembled other despotic governments. Ultimately, perfectibility became a touchstone for measuring the degree of liberty in any political regime. The controversy is reminiscent of another famous dispute, between the Ancients and the Moderns at the end of the seventeenth century, except for one important difference: in the 1680s the Moderns flattered Louis XIV by suggesting that his century might rival that of Augustus. The new Moderns of 1800 found themselves cast, not altogether willingly, among the opponents of the First Consul.

In translating Godwin in 1798, Constant had read Jean-Baptiste Salaville's *L'homme et la société ou nouvelle théorie de la nature humaine* and admired the chapters about the English writer.[8] In 1801, the same Salaville published *De la perfectibilité*, a short work of just seventy-one pages, of which he sent copies to Madame de Staël and Constant.[9] Constant refers to the work, moreover, in the version of his text that was published in 1829. Neither Constant nor Madame de Staël was influenced by Salaville. For one thing, their views were already mature by the time he wrote. For another, he differed with them on two key points. First, Salaville rejected the sensualist metaphysics of Locke and Condillac, to which Condorcet, Madame de Staël, and Constant remained more or less loyal. Second, he argued that perfectibility was not infinite and that men would cease to perfect themselves when, "knowing all that can be known, ... we will no longer be perfectible because we will already have been perfected. Our perfectibility will cease to exist, just as any cause ceases to exist when its effect has been achieved." Despite these differences, Madame de Staël and Constant no doubt looked favorably on Salaville as an ally amid the hostility stirred up by *De la littérature*. A statement like the following was perfectly compatible with their views, for example: "The enemies of perfectibility point to the profound demoralization that afflicts us at the present time. They conclude that, far from growing more perfect, we are becoming ever more degraded.... Even if we grant that the sum total of our present woes is greater than in the past, we shall see that this

---

[8] Salaville's book was published by Carteret in Year VII (1798–99). Constant's comments on it can be found in *OCBC/Œuvres*, I, 1418, 1426, 1434.

[9] Parts of letters thanking Salaville have been found: see Madame de Staël, *Correspondance générale*, ed. Béatrice Jasinski, vol. IV, no. 2 (Paris: J.-J. Pauvert, 1978), 400–401.

cannot count as an objection against the system of perfectibility." Salaville showed himself to be a true friend of liberty, clearly concerned about the authoritarian turn that the new regime was taking. He was acutely sensitive to the fact that the hostile reaction to a theory as anodyne as the theory of perfectibility was indicative of a climate unfavorable to freedom of thought and expression.

Indeed, this controversy marked the beginning of Madame de Staël's tribulations, as she faced increasingly zealous harassment by the consular administration. After being denied the right to reside within forty leagues of the capital, she was ultimately exiled in 1803. Constant accompanied her on her travels through Germany. Under the circumstances, belief in the idea of perfectibility afforded a certain consolation. In an unpublished work entitled *Histoire abrégée de l'égalité*, Constant wrote that "of all the scourges that afflict mankind, discouragement is the worst.... The remedy... is to escape one's circumstances for a time and to cast one's eyes over both the past and the future, without which it is impossible to judge the present, because in concentrating on the present alone one mistakes its true nature." By taking this lofty view of history, which he compares to a general's view of the battlefield, Constant is able to reach the conclusion that "taken as a whole, the human race has never regressed; whenever one people has forfeited its enlightenment or its freedom, a greater freedom and enlightenment have emerged somewhere else in the mass of mankind."[10] In *De la perfectibilité*, moreover, he asserts that only the theory of perfectibility is capable of "giving purpose to our efforts, motivation to our search, support in our uncertainty, and consolation in our discouragement."[11] Of course the period in which he was living was hardly a testimonial to the progress of enlightenment. In *De la littérature*, Madame de Staël did not hesitate to compare the Revolution to the Middle Ages, to a return to barbarism. Yet at the same time, following Turgot and contradicting Condorcet, she saw the Middle Ages, so reviled by the men of the Enlightenment, as a period when progress did not cease but simply went underground, ready to reemerge when the time was ripe. This, too, was a consoling thought for an "intellectual" condemned

---

[10] *Du moment actuel et de la destinée de l'espèce humaine ou histoire abrégée de l'égalité*, in *OCBC/Œuvres*, III.
[11] *Du moment actuel*, 456.

to exile. It was a thought that would define the mission of what was to become the Coppet group: namely, to be a harbinger of hope in a troubled time and to announce useful truths, regardless of the cost – truths that derived their power from the very difficulty involved in making them public.

In Germany, Constant again encountered the philosophy of Kant, to which he and others (including Villers, Henri Crabb Robinson, Humboldt, and before long Schlegel) introduced Madame de Staël. Kant clearly marked an important milestone for the philosophy of progress. In Weimar, however, Constant's major discovery was the work of Herder, especially his *Ideas on the Philosophy of History of Humanity*, which appeared in stages between 1784 and 1791. Thus the book was not particularly new when Madame de Staël and Constant discovered it, but Herder had died shortly before their arrival in Weimar, so it was natural for his work to have been a subject of discussion. We do not know whether Constant had previously read *Another Philosophy of History*, which was published in 1774. What we do know is that *Ideas* was his daily reading matter in January and February of 1804, as he indicated in his diary, from which we also learn that on April 24 he discussed perfectibility with August Wilhelm von Schlegel, who was soon to become the tutor of Madame de Staël's children and one of the leading lights of the Coppet group. Can we assume, therefore, that it was this reading and these conversations that led Constant to write *De la perfectibilité*? If so, that might explain why he proposed this text a year later to Villers "as an introduction to Herder's *Ideas on the Philosophy of History*." Chronologically, the hypothesis is tenable, but comparison of the text as it has come down to us with Herder's work raises a number of problems. In the first place, we do not know which excerpt or excerpts from Herder's work Villers proposed to publish in his new journal. Constant's text would not have served as an introduction for any arbitrary selection. Furthermore, Herder's name is not mentioned in either *De la perfectibilité* or *Fragments d'un essai sur la perfectibilité*, which is strange for a text intended to be an introduction to an anthology of Herder's writing. Finally, Constant's views on the subject are in many respects quite different from Herder's. These discrepancies suggest two possible hypotheses. Either the text entitled *De la perfectibilité* that Constant offered to Villers is not the surviving text that bears that title. Or, more likely, it is the same text, and Constant wrote it before he had read Herder carefully, in which case he would have revised it to serve as an introduction to the collection of Herder's writing in Villers's proposed *Revue germanique* only if the planned journal had actually come to fruition. Constant's Weimar reading influenced not the essay on perfectibility but rather Constant's ongoing work on religion.[12] In this respect, German writers helped Constant a great deal in his evolution beyond a narrowly French view. When it came to the philosophy of history, by contrast, Constant was surely much more indebted to the thought of the Enlightenment. Herder's conception of history was highly providentialist. For him, progress was the result of a divine plan, in which human reason played a relatively limited role.[13] Constant, despite some differences, retained the idea that Condorcet and the ideologues had favored: that mankind forges its own destiny. This idea can be described as a secularization of providentialism, or what Georges Gusdorf calls "mythistory."[14]

CONSTANT'S PERFECTIBILITY

Having examined the context in which Constant, at some point in the period 1802–4, wrote what appears to have been an article on perfectibility, we turn now to the definitive 1829 version of his theory.

The seventeenth chapter of *Mélanges* can be divided into three parts plus an introduction and a conclusion. The first part sets forth the natural law of perfection, the effects of which can be seen in the individual. The second part seeks to extend this law to the entire human species. Finally, the third part attempts to provide empirical and historical evidence for the existence of perfectibility. This structure is very much like what Condorcet had in mind when he distinguished "metaphysics" from "history": "If we limit ourselves

[12] As shown in a recent article by Kurt Kloocke, "Johann Gottfried Herder et Benjamin Constant," *ABC*, 29 (2005), 55–72.

[13] On this question, see Max Rouché, *La philosophie de l'histoire de Herder* (Paris: Les Belles Lettres, 1940), esp. 542–45, as well as the introduction to his bilingual edition of *Idées pour la philosophie de l'histoire de l'humanité*, selections trans. Edgar Quinet (Paris: Presse Pocket, 1991).

[14] See Karl Löwith, *Meaning in History: The Theological Implications of the Philosophy of History* (Chicago, IL: University of Chicago Press, 1950), and Georges Gusdorf, "La mythistoire de la raison," in *L'avènement des sciences humaines au siècle des Lumières* (Paris: Payot, 1973), 379–428.

to observing and gaining knowledge of the general facts and invariable laws that the development of these faculties demonstrates, the science in question would be called metaphysics. But if we consider this same development in the light of its results as they affect the mass of individuals who coexist at a given time in a given place, and if we follow it from generation to generation, what we seen then is a portrait of the progress of the human spirit.... This portrait is therefore historical, because, being subject to endless variations, it is based on the observation of human societies through many different periods of their history."[15] As we shall see, Constant followed his illustrious predecessor in another way as well, borrowing from him the sensualist theory of the origin of ideas but developing it in a new direction.

Let us turn first to the author's introduction of his argument. He describes perfectibility as both a "system"[16] and an "opinion." Although he uses the two terms as if they were synonymous, they are not in fact identical. A "system" carries conviction by the logical power of its construction. An "opinion" can be contested more readily, since everyone has the right to his or her own. A system imposes itself; an opinion can be combated. This ambiguity runs through the entire chapter, but it is especially striking at the beginning:

For anyone who does not share this *opinion*, the social, like everything else that depends, I would say, not solely on man but on the universe, is merely one of a thousand random possibilities, a thousand more or less fleeting forms destined to destroy and replace one another perpetually without leading to any lasting improvement. Only the *system* of perfectibility saves us from the inevitability of complete destruction, in which no memory of our

---

[15] Condorcet, *Tableau*, 234. Regarding this special sense of "metaphysical," André Lalande has observed that "in the eighteenth century and among the Ideologues, 'metaphysics' often denoted the science of the mind, of ideas and their origin." *Vocabulaire technique et critique de la philosophie* (Paris: Presses Universitaires de France, 1976), 617.

[16] In this connection it is worth recalling Fontenelle's definition of a "philosophical system": "The philosopher has before him a certain number of effects of nature and experience. He must try to uncover their probable causes, and from what he has seen and what he divines, he composes a seamless whole. That is his system. The historian also has a certain number of facts of which he imagines the causes and upon which he builds as best he can a system of history, which is something even more uncertain and subject to caution than a system of philosophy." See "Sur l'histoire" in Fontenelle, *Œuvres*, vol. 3 (Paris: Fayard, 1989), 174.

efforts or trace of our successes remains. . . . People speak in vain of enlightenment, freedom, and philosophy. Abysses yawn beneath our feet, savages lurk in our breasts, impostors may arise from within ourselves, and still more readily may our governments become tyrannical. If there is no permanence in ideas independent of human beings, we ought to close our books, abandon our speculations, forget our useless sacrifices, and devote all our efforts to those useful and agreeable arts that make our hopeless lives less insipid and temporarily embellish a present that has no future.[17]

Perfectibility here seems to be introduced as one belief among others: one is free to believe in it or not, and the only advantage of belief is that it holds out a better promise of rescuing us from despair at the absurdity of our condition. We remain free to reject this salutary idea, but if we do, we risk embracing a chaotic vision of the future of mankind. Later, the tone changes, and the author takes a more positive approach. Perfectibility is no longer one way of conceiving of mankind among others; rather, it can be shown to be an objective reality: "I therefore propose to investigate whether man has a tendency to perfect himself and, if so, what the nature and cause of that tendency might be. Are there limits to perfectibility, or is it boundless? Finally, what obstacles might impede it or stand in its way?" (p. 389). Still later, he adds, "I believe that I have given rational proof of the perfectibility of the human species and empirical evidence of its progress" (p. 414). Without notice we have shifted from an *opinion* to a *system*.

The system of perfectibility draws heavily on eighteenth-century speculation about the origin of ideas in the work of empirical philosophers from Locke to Condillac and the ideologues.[18] By borrowing from "sensualism," Constant hoped to place his "system" on a firm scientific footing, using what was presumably the most advanced thought of the time to armor his work against criticism. As stated earlier, however, by 1829 this choice may have seemed old fashioned, a throwback to the outlook of the Enlightenment. According

---

[17] Emphasis added. Benjamin Constant, *Mélanges* (Paris: Pichon and Didier, 1829), 387–88.

[18] Constant nevertheless insisted on the originality of his approach: "In all ages, writers of varying opinions have concerned themselves with these questions, but their investigations remain incomplete and their writings have only obscured their thinking. . . . To date, so far as I know, no one has attempted to develop this idea in a systematic way" (389–90).

to sensualist philosophy, the natural perfectibility of man is a consequence of the difference between sensations and ideas. Sensations are fleeting, but ideas have duration. Everything therefore depends on whether man is governed by sensations or ideas: "If sensations rule, the human species stands still; if ideas rule, it will progress" (p. 393). Constant promises, moreover, to "convince us that man governs himself wholly and exclusively through ideas" (p. 393) and therefore that perfectibility is an inherent faculty. To that end, he employs the notion of *sacrifice*, which played a crucial role in the thinking of the Coppet group. The principle was that man always sacrifices sensations to ideas: in other words, he would rather suffer "a real pain in the hope of a future pleasure.... From this it follows that there exists in human nature a disposition that invariably gives men the strength to immolate the present to the future and therefore sensations to ideas" (p. 394). Constant saw this tendency as universal and believed that it influenced men unconsciously, including those who appeared to be most in thrall to their selfish pleasures. It was in this capacity for transcendence that the force of reasoning and the seed of perfectibility lay: "Human nature is so prone to sacrifice that a present sensation is almost inevitably sacrificed when it stands in the way of some future sensation, which is to say, in the way of some idea" (p. 396). In other words, man is capable of dominating his passions without external intervention (moral or political authority), because reason, which is among his natural gifts, leads him to compare present and future sensations and thus to sacrifice the former to the latter. Constant also refers to this faculty as man's "free will" and "moral independence." These are intrinsic qualities, which men should always seek to cultivate, yet over the course of history some had contrived to hinder their development. The notion of "sacrifice" set Constant apart from his predecessors, especially Condorcet and the ideologues. In contrast to the latter, who defended a utilitarian ethics based on the concept of "self-interest properly understood" and who portrayed man as in thrall to his sensations, Constant claimed that human behavior is not selfish and that its aims are lofty rather than mundane: "The supremacy of ideas over sensations" (p. 396) tends to make "men their own masters and to preserve their moral independence, which is a source of dignity, tranquility, and happiness" (p. 397). It is important to note that the psychological mechanism of perfectibility is a source of "strength" and "energy" that makes human progress possible: "The indestructible seed of perfectibility lies exclusively in the faculty for sacrifice. The greater the use a man makes of this faculty, the more energy it acquires, and the broader his view becomes" (p. 398). This cumulative process brings him ever closer to the truth.

So much for what can be observed in the development of individuals, Constant now turns to the perfectibility of the species. How does he see this individual faculty for sacrifice leading to perfection of the community? His explanation is psychosociological: "Because certain truths, when repeated continually and universally, eventually inculcate the habit of seeing them as immediately self-evident" (p. 399). Perfectibility might almost be called contagious. To be sure, the argument is neither sound nor convincing, especially in view of the rather simplistic arithmetic example Constant gives: "We see immediately, without calculating, that two plus two equals four" (p. 399). One might have expected a rather different sort of example: heliocentrism, say, an idea that took a long time to be accepted but that eventually came to be taken for granted. Established truths accelerate the cumulative process of reasoning: each person "starts not at the point he would have reached on the basis of his individual experience alone but rather at the point he has reached through the experience of association" (p. 400). Constant's lapidary formulations are often better than his examples.

In the third part of the chapter on perfectibility, Constant sought to offer empirical and historical evidence of its existence. He began by distinguishing between two types of perfectibility, internal and external. Internal perfectibility is the same as morality: in Constant's highly optimistic reckoning, "the most absurd people of today cannot, despite themselves, regress to the point where the most enlightened people stood in centuries past. When time and reasoning have completely done away with a bad institution, not even stupidity or self-interest would dare call for its restoration" (pp. 400–401). Unfortunately, Constant took slavery as his example of a "bad institution" at a time when the slave trade, which he himself had contested, was still going strong. Did he perhaps wish to suggest that this abominable practice was an inconceivable anachronism? If so, contemporary facts contradicted his theory. As for external perfectibility, Constant seems to have had in mind nothing more than a series of discoveries (and perhaps inventions), which he briefly enumerates:

the discoveries "of Galileo, Copernicus, and Newton; the circulation of the blood, electricity, and a whole host of machines that every day make human beings more and more the masters of the material world; gunpowder, the compass, printing, steam, and other physical means of conquering the world" (p. 401). The very brevity of this account of the "progress" characteristic of modernity shows that for him the important point lay elsewhere. With a broader perspective, perfectibility becomes more obvious as one begins to contemplate the whole of human history, where overall progress is clear. "Those who do not want to recognize this progress assume that mankind is doomed to move forever in a circle, to proceed endlessly from ignorance to enlightenment and enlightenment to ignorance. . . . They believe this because they dwell on only a few parts of the globe, a few more or less circumscribed societies, a few remarkable individuals" (p. 403). Perfectibility is incompatible with myopic vision; to see it requires distance. With distance differences blur, and the law of large numbers eliminates accidents. Perfectibility has one thing in common with liberal economic thought: regulation is automatic; an "invisible hand" corrects momentary aberrations. "The progress of perfectibility can be suspended, and mankind may even seem to regress, but it tends to return to where it had been before. . . . Thus the upheavals of the French Revolution disrupted ideas and corrupted people, but once those upheavals ended, people reverted to the moral ideas they had held immediately before, so that we can say that the excesses of the Revolution perverted individuals but did not replace the existing moral system with a less perfect one. Yet such a regression is what one would need to show in order to prove that mankind had deteriorated" (pp. 401–2). Indeed, but Constant does not show that it has progressed either, for he claims only that after the "upheavals" people *reverted* to the moral system that had existed before. And if that system was a good one, why had the Revolution occurred? Constant has perhaps failed to find the proper example to substantiate his thesis. In other work, especially in political philosophy, he does a better job of integrating the Revolution into an evolutionist view, something he fails to do in the passage quoted previously in this chapter.

This point bears further elaboration, in order to show the degree to which perfectibility remained the basis of all his thinking. Why do revolutions take place? So that institutions can catch up with ideas. Ideas evolve, but institutions tend to remain frozen and to impede regular individual growth. We see the same phenomenon in the history of religion, where *religious forms* inhibit the perfectibility of *religious feeling*. Thus every revolution is a natural rebalancing, which allows the normal pace of historical progress to resume. "The more pernicious the thing destroyed, the crueler the revolution" (p. 411). Constant and Madame de Staël insisted that the excesses of the *ancien régime* were responsible for those of the Terror. Unlike others nostalgic for absolutism, they did not believe that the "upheavals" were a logical consequence of the Revolution itself. The ideas of equality and liberty did not necessarily lead to violence. Rather, violence was a consequence of the opposition, on the part of the privileged under the *ancien régime*, to the reforms desired by prevailing opinion. Despite what the preceding quotation might suggest, therefore, Constant was convinced that the Revolution not only failed to indicate regression but must actually be counted as a decisive step forward for humankind. Like the rest of the Coppet group, he held in Kantian fashion that 1789 signified the emancipation of the human race, which had finally achieved maturity by freeing itself from the authority of both the church and the absolute monarchy.

Any philosophy that bestows meaning on man's fate, especially any philosophy that describes that fate as progress, must identify a series of stages that illustrate this supposed progress. During the Enlightenment it was common to divide human history into four ages: the Age of Pericles (or sometimes Alexander), the Age of Augustus, the Age of the Medicis (or sometimes Pope Leo X), and finally the Age of Louis XIV.[19] Constant did not escape the influence of this tradition, but his periodization was more interesting, relatively original, and largely derived from his work on religion. His schema of four distinct phases dates back to his early work under the Directory. In 1796, in *De la force du gouvernement actuel*, he proposed an outline, which he then developed in his *Histoire abrégée de l'égalité*,

[19] See the article entitled "Siècle" by Jochen Schlobach in Michel Delon, ed., *Dictionnaire européen des Lumières* (Paris: Presses Universitaires de France, 1997), 994–97. Schlobach shows that this division did not necessarily imply belief in progress; it pointed, rather, to a succession of civilizations, which one after another rose, fell, and disappeared.

Fragments d'un essai sur la perfectibilité, and ultimately *De la perfectibilité.* Thus it was in the decade 1795–1805 that he definitively settled on this periodization, according to which human history was marked by four "revolutions" or "destructions." "Theocracy" was the first regime to go, followed by "slavery," "feudalism," and "nobility" (p. 404). With each new stage an abuse was destroyed, thus alleviating the human condition. The abuses themselves were not all of the same severity. The oldest were the worst: "If we sought to make nobility more oppressive, we would turn it into feudalism. If we sought to make feudalism more odious, we would turn it into slavery. If we sought to make slavery more execrable, we would transform it into theocracy. And moving in the opposite direction, to mitigate the regime of castes, which theocracy proscribes" (p. 405). This gradation of abuses accounts for the acceleration of history: "The destruction of abuses has something in common with the acceleration of falling bodies: the closer they come to the earth, the faster they move. This is because the cruder and more comprehensive the abuse, the easier it is to maintain, for it debases its victims all the more. Slavery was easier to maintain than feudalism, and feudalism was easier to maintain than nobility" (pp. 405–6). In an earlier passage he put the same point somewhat differently: "Privileged nobility is closer to us than feudalism, feudalism is closer than slavery, and slavery is closer than theocracy" (pp. 404–5). In other words, the interval between revolutions tends to diminish with the passage of time. Constant's chronological estimates are approximate but not uninteresting: "We do not know how long theocracy lasted, but it is likely that this detestable institution endured for a longer time than slavery. Slavery is known to have existed for more than 3000 years and feudalism for 1200, whereas the privileges of nobility without feudalism date back scarcely more than two centuries" (p. 405). Thus the rate of change accelerates as we pass through each of the four stages.

But what causes this movement? Constant rejects the notion of direct causes, which people all too often tend to ascribe to great events: "History[20] proposes the establishment of the Christian religion and the invasions of barbarians from the north as causes of the destruction of slavery; the Crusades as the cause of the destruction

[20] Here Constant means "historians" and not "events."

of feudalism; and the French Revolution as the cause of the destruction of noble privileges. But these destructions *were not accidental effects of particular circumstances*. The barbarian invasions, the establishment of Christianity, the Crusades, and the French Revolution were *the occasion, but not the cause"* (p. 406, emphasis added). Constant's subtlety here is worth noting. He rejects an overly mechanical idea of causation, in part because this attributes too much influence to circumstances and the people who manipulate them and agitators who always have a tendency to become despotic. He ascribes greater importance to what he vaguely calls "the eternal force of things" (p. 406). Once again, he encourages his readers to neglect the details of history in order to discover hidden causes, relationships that are less obvious but ultimately more essential. On the surface perfectibility seems to manifest itself in "occasions," "revolutions," and "circumstances," but in reality it is inherent in the human condition. Another reason why Constant plays down the importance of direct causes is his dislike of violent revolution: "One cannot help noticing that revolutions, which tend to the good of humanity, almost always do great harm along the way."[21] His whole discussion of perfectibility comes down to saying that it is pointless to oppose what he sees as mankind's inherent tendency to perfect itself. Any attempt by religious or political authorities to impede that tendency risks degenerating into revolution, with its usual train of misery and misfortune. If, however, a broad consensus were to develop in favor of the theory of progress, man could dispense with the need for revolution. Gradual adaptation would limit the violence of social conflict, and man would proceed without upheaval from one stage to the next. "It is to be hoped that those who govern might come to this realization.... It would spare them much bloody conflict and fruitless effort" (p. 414).

What is the main reason for this progress of the human spirit? For Constant, it is "the tendency toward equality" (p. 407). He linked the idea of perfectibility to his outline of a history of equality. Yet

---

[21] *De la force du gouvernement actuel,* in *OCBC/Œuvres,* I, 375, note a, which also includes the comment that "the more pernicious the thing to be destroyed, the crueler the Revolution," a remark that appears again, as we have seen, in *De la perfectibilité* (p. 411).

this yoking together of two of Constant's fundamental ideas was not without problems. When he states that "these four revolutions ... count as steps toward the *restoration* of natural equality" (p. 407, emphasis added), the idea of perfection realized over the course of time is rejected in favor of a return to the origins. Constant thus wavered to some degree between two paradigms: that of cyclical history and that of never-ending linear progress. Markus Winkler makes this point clearly in showing the role and importance of mythology in the work of Schlegel, Madame de Staël, and Constant.[22] Analyzing *Réflexions sur la tragédie*, Winkler lays stress on Constant's pessimistic view of the individual as overwhelmed by the constraints of society. This observation leads him to the conclusion that "the crushing of the individual" owing to "the action of society on man ... is the only source of modern tragedy that can compete with fate as a source of tragedy for the Ancients." Thus Constant, "in depicting the action of society as a source of tragedy, substitutes the immobile for the progressive, the closed circular horizon of myth for the open linear horizon of history."[23] Indeed, passages such as the following offer a marvelous illustration of the way in which the individual is confined within a social straitjacket:

When man, weak, blind, and lacking both the intelligence to guide him and the arms with which to defend himself, is hurled unwittingly and unwillingly into the labyrinth we call the world, that world envelops him in a set of circumstances, laws, institutions, and relationships both public and private. Without his being aware of it, and without his consent, a yoke is thus placed around his neck, and it weighs on him with a weight that existed before he arrived; when he learns to recognize it and sense its burden, he can nevertheless fight against it only from a position of distinct inferiority, and the struggle is fraught with danger. It is obvious that nothing in the life of man is more important than this action of society on the individual. It is the beginning and end of everything, and man must submit to society's unwanted and unknown requirements or risk destruction.[24]

---

[22] Markus Winkler, "De la fatalité des Anciens aux préjugés sociaux des Modernes. La présence du mythe chez August Wilhelm Schlegel, Madame de Staël et Benjamin Constant," in *Le Groupe de Coppet et l'Europe, 1789–1830* (Lausanne-Paris: Institut Benjamin Constant–J. Touzot, 1994); *ABC*, 15–16 (1994), 199–216.

[23] Winkler, 213–14.

[24] *Réflexions sur la tragédie*, in *Œuvres*, 910.

Reading these words, which the author wrote shortly after publishing the *Mélanges*, one would hardly guess that they came from the same pen that wrote *De la perfectibilité*. Is there any indication here of man's inherent energy and strength, the driving force of progress? The image of the conqueror has given way, it seems, to that of the slave. Does this mean, as Winkler suggests, that "radical doubt has been cast on the doctrine of perfectibility?"[25] Perhaps not. Earlier, in the same *Réflexions sur la tragédie*, Constant wrote, "In pointing out what I regard as one of civilization's inevitable consequences, I do not wish to appear to speak ill of the progress that civilization also brings, and which pleases me."[26] This affirmation is to be taken seriously. The difference in the subjects of the two essays should also be taken into account: in *Réflexions sur la tragédie*, the goal was to explore the sources from which tragedy might spring in the modern era, when audiences were no longer moved by either passions or characters as in the past, whereas in *De la perfectibilité*, the goal was to reflect in a much more general way on the future of mankind. What is more, the contradiction between the two texts is more apparent than real. The highly pessimistic view that the modern individual is weighed down by the yoke of society must rather be seen, I believe, in light of a view of history that, as we saw earlier, abstracts away from individual variations in order to focus exclusively on broad general tendencies. This is quite evident in another text that Constant wrote at about the same time as *De la perfectibilité* (ca. 1805): the *Esquisse d'un essai sur la littérature du XVIIIe siècle*. In this unfinished draft, Constant wondered about how best to paint the portrait of a century and rightly rejected the method of simply listing major authors. He rejected the "pantheon" approach precisely in order to avoid placing too much stress on individuals, who in his view should receive less attention than the "general spirit," the "tendency of the times," the "atmosphere," or "the dominant idea of the century."

Each author was influenced by that tendency.... Even those who were spurred on by their nature, their opinions, or their interests to fight against it unwittingly submitted to its yoke and carried its colors.... Each author is marked by the dominant idea of his century. Those who march at the head

---

[25] Winkler, 215.
[26] *Réflexions sur la tragédie*, 904.

of victorious doctrines have in fact merely obeyed the dictates of that idea. Those who seem to struggle against it capitulate."[27]

Later he develops this idea further:

It is not a fancy that causes men in a given period to be religious or irreligious, enthusiastic or calculating, energetic or pusillanimous. It is the effect of an impetus they received, which they could not help receiving, which was altered in them and, so altered, passed on to subsequent generations to be altered yet again in turn, thereby becoming different from what it was and gradually crating a new spirit. . . . Each person is free individually. . . . But as soon as the individual joins a group, he ceases to be free, because he is caught up in the movement of the group and not only subjugated but also altered by it. A century's superior writers do not impart their opinions to the century, as is often believed; they are rather influential because they express the century's views strongly and clearly. They seem to carry the century with them because they serve it; they seem to be its guides because they are its interpreters; they seem to persuade it because they reveal its own secret. No doubt the influence of such writers is great, yet it does not direct the general movement so much as accelerate it. What they borrow from their century they return with interest. The spirit of a century is a necessary fact, a physical fact.[28]

Both passages suggest that individuals play only a limited role in history. They are portrayed as the playthings of a transcendent social reality. Constant's interpretation might be described as holistic: the whole is greater than the sum of its parts. Such a view is quite compatible with the idea that perfectibility is a faculty of the species as much as of the individual. The preceding excerpt beautifully combines the dissolution of the individual into the mass with the power of an irresistible collective evolution. An irresistible force impels the entire collectivity and, like it or not, each individual within it toward a less harsh, more moral condition: this is a weightier argument than any that can be offered by the opponents of perfectibility,

---

[27] "Esquisse d'un essai sur la littérature du XVIIIe siècle," in *OCBC/Œuvres*, III, 527.
[28] "Esquisse d'un essai," 528. Agreeing with Constant, Prosper Barante has this to say about great men: "A man, no matter how great he is, bows to the general view of the times. All men are merely blind instruments of universal events that are independent of individuals." Letter to Madame de Staël, February 9, 1809. She had criticized Barante for failing to mention Necker in his *Tableau*. Cf. Simone Balayé, "Un article inconnu de Mme de Staël: *Tableau de la littérature française au XVIIIe siècle, par M. de Barante*," *Cahiers staëliens*, 20 (June 1976), 23.

who, Constant maintains, dwell too much on the particular and fail to take note of the overall tendency. In order to show the degree to which the ideas of "perfectibility," "equality," and "effacement of the individual" were compatible in Constant's mind, one could also cite another manuscript fragment: "It is obvious to any attentive observer that the means to glory and personal power have diminished and are continuing to diminish with each passing day; that individuals are losing their prominence as generations perfect themselves; and that equality is becoming greater as mankind lifts itself up, and because it does."[29] Clearly, one should be careful not to exaggerate the "individualist" aspect of Constant's thought as presented in his political works. Yet it is also clear that the gradual effacement of the individual as a consequence of perfectibility preoccupied him more than anything else. He was a "perfectibilist" as well as an anxious liberal.[30] The anxiety that plagues him is the same anxiety he feels in discovering that the liberty of the ancients tends to give way to the liberty of the moderns, so that selfishness, calculation, self-interest, and utilitarian thinking will likely take the place of generosity, self-denial, sacrifice, and civic virtue.[31] Here we detect a faint Rousseauian note: progress, yes, but at what price? The contradictions that sometimes appear in successive texts result not from uncertainty as to his convictions but rather from the polemical nature of the writing.[32] When attacking his reactionary enemies, he tends to emphasize the liberty of the moderns, accentuate his intransigent individualism, and champion perfectibility. But in addressing well-meaning liberal friends such as the ideologues, Benthamite utilitarians, economists, and Saint-Simonians, he tends to blow the trumpets of the Last Judgment rather than those of renown. It is as if he were saying to the one group, "There's no use

[29] [Le règne des hommes est passé], title ascribed to a fragment published in OCBC/Œuvres, III, 454.

[30] To borrow a phrase from the title of Thierry Chopin's Benjamin Constant: le libéralisme inquiet (Paris: Michalon, 2002).

[31] See the analysis of Giovanni Paoletti, soon to appear in Benjamin Constant et les Anciens (Paris: Honoré Champion, forthcoming) in the series Travaux et Recherches de l'Institut B. Constant.

[32] On the apparent contradictions in Constant's reasoning, see Emeric Travers, Benjamin Constant, les principes et l'histoire, preface by Philippe Raynaud (Paris: Honoré Champion, 2005), Travaux et Recherches de l'Institut B. Constant, 7.

retreating, an irresistible force is driving us forward," and to the other, already convinced of the reality of progress, "Have you fully appreciated everything that will have to be given up for the sake of progress?" As Florence Lotterie has noted, there is a good deal of "uneasiness" in Constant's notion of perfectibility.

Constant did not believe that history had ended with the French Revolution, unlike Hegel, who saw his own era as the "end of history," a culmination that could not be surpassed. For Constant, the period inaugurated by the Revolution was one of "legal conventions." He showed that this was a transitional era, a compromise: "The human spirit is too enlightened to go on being governed by force or deception but not yet enlightened enough to be governed by reason alone" (p. 412). He viewed the "legal conventions" in question as temporary, "artificial things, susceptible to change, created to replace truths not yet well known in order to meet temporary needs and consequently in need of amendment, improvement, and above all limitations as those truths are discovered and those needs change" (p. 413). Yet he never ventures to predict what the future holds and is severe toward those who, like Condorcet writing on the "tenth period," claim that the discovery of what determined the past means that there is no reason not to calculate what the future will bring. Although more of a philosopher of history than a historian in the narrow sense, Constant was wary of speculation that strayed too far from heuristic research.

Georges Gusdorf has shown that while the effort to secularize fate could liberate man from any form of divine intention, it could also lead to fanaticism every bit as virulent as that combated by this-worldly progressives.[33] Constant seems to have avoided this error, as can be seen in his discussion of "abuses." Indeed, the perfectibilist often sallies forth to do battle against prejudice, but Constant adopts a less radical position and concedes that errors "may for a time be useful, necessary, and preferable to the alternative" (p. 410). He admits that opinions "that we regard as indispensable, and which are indeed indispensable for us, may in centuries to come be rejected

---

[33] "Intolerance in the name of reason is as dangerous as Christian intolerance and unreason. Voltairian historiography bears signs of the fearsome fanaticism of anti-fanaticism." Gusdorf, 394.

as abuses" (p. 410). This relativism put him at odds with the writers of the French Enlightenment, who tended to judge everything exclusively from their own point of view. Here we may perhaps detect something of Herder's influence, for Herder insisted on the intrinsic autonomy and value not only of each nation but also of each epoch.

The question raised at the beginning of this essay remains. Published in 1805, *De la perfectibilité* would have found a natural place in the controversy I have described. It might even have extended that controversy. In 1829, however, the public seemed to have lost interest in the question, at least as it was formulated by Constant. How are we to explain this delay, such as it was?[34] The explanation most likely lies in the apparent similarity of the two political contexts: by 1805 imperial despotism had already reared its head; in 1829 the accession of the Polignac ministry in August marked the arrival in power of the *ultra* faction after the moderate intermezzo of the Martignac ministry. With the benefit of hindsight we now know that Polignac's assumption of power actually marked the beginning of the end of the Restoration, but in 1829 there was good reason to fear an attack on the Charter and the modest guarantees of liberty that it offered. Constant frequently dredged up arguments that he had used in the imperial years for reuse in his political battles during the Restoration. For instance, in preparing political texts after 1814 he drew regularly on his *Principes de politique*, which he had written in 1806 but left unpublished. Thus it is not surprising that he should have revived the theory of perfectibility at a time when liberal spirits had fallen prey to a certain discouragement following the brief but timid respite afforded by the Martignac government. In articles and speeches Constant liked to remind his audience of the principles he espoused, principles on which all of his political activity was based. Perfectibility and the associated idea of equality figured as part of his credo, which he was keen to reaffirm.

ACKNOWLEDGMENTS

Any work on this subject owes a considerable debt to the works of Florence Lotterie, especially her thesis, *L'idée de perfectibilité entre*

---

[34] Axel Blaeschke, in his previously cited introduction to *De la littérature*, lxxxviii, mentions two other authors who discussed perfectibility during the Restoration: Pierre-Simon Ballanche and Pierre Leroux.

Lumières et Romantisme (1750–1822) (Paris: X-Nanterre, 1997), and "Le progrès désenchanté: la perfectiblité selon Constant ou le malaise libéral," in *Le Groupe de Coppet et le monde moderne. Conceptions-Images-Débats*, ed. Françoise Tilkin (Geneva: Droz, 1998), 283–88. See also Bertrand Binoche, ed., *L'homme perfectible* (Seysssel: Champ Vallon, 2004), which includes Ghislain Waterlot, "Perfectibilité et vérité de la religion chez Benjamin Constant," and Jean Starobinski, "Benjamin Constant: la pensée du progrès et l'analyse des réactions," *ABC*, 23–24 (2000), 39–62.

III. The Analyst and Historian of Religion

12 Religion According to Constant*

Translated by Arthur Goldhammer

Benjamin Constant, the great theorist of liberal democracy and peerless connoisseur of human psychology, had a third ambition, which was more important to him than the vocation of politician or writer: he hoped to analyze one of the most notable aspects of human existence, namely, *religion*. He conceived this project in 1785, when he was eighteen, soon after finishing his studies. And he was still correcting his manuscript in October 1830, a month before his death. Between those two dates, the idea and the text were always with him, and despite repeated interruptions he worked on them constantly. The first volumes of *De la religion* (*On Religion*) appeared in 1824; the last, volumes four and five, were published shortly after his death, in 1831.

The book was the work of a lifetime, yet it stirred little debate when it appeared and was quickly forgotten. Only erudite historians and devotees of Constant are even aware of its existence. No other edition of the complete work ever appeared until 1999. What accounts for this reception? It must be said that the book's timing was not propitious. In nineteenth-century France, the devout and the anticlerical were locked in fierce battle for or against religion. Impossible to place in relation to this conflict, Constant was of no use to either side. By the twentieth century, when the history and anthropology of religion gradually emerged as fields of study, the work seemed anachronistic: its erudition was musty, and the overweening ambition to discuss all the religions of the world in all times

* This essay first appeared under the title "Un Chef-d'œuvre oublié," in Benjamin Constant, *De la religion considérée dans sa source, ses formes et ses développements*, ed. Tzvetan Todorov and Etienne Hofmann (Arles, France: Actes Sud, 1999).

and places seemed excessive. In truth, Constant's project was rather more limited than his title suggests: he studied only polytheistic religions, touching on monotheism only indirectly, and he stopped before reaching what he regarded as the decadent phase of polytheism, namely, the religion of the Romans. Still, the range of the work was vast and general, whereas the new sciences favored specialization. Only philosophers still dare to discuss religion in general; specialists speak only of particular religions, preferably during a limited period of time.

This neglect of Constant's work is profoundly unjust, not only because Constant in many respects played a pioneering role that deserves to be recognized but also because his reflections on religion and its historical destiny are among the most enlightening that exist. Indeed, he may have more to say to twenty-first-century readers than he did to their forebears two hundred years ago. Contrary to what people believed then, religion was not on the wane. Benjamin Constant can help us to understand why.

Constant's thinking about religion was novel in three respects: in his method, in his analysis and assessment of ancient religious forms, and, finally, in his ideas about the place of religion in the modern world.

A REVOLUTIONARY METHOD

In order to understand what was new about Constant's study, we must first understand the context in which he worked. Constant reached adulthood on the eve of the Revolution, at a time when religion had been under steady assault by the so-called *philosophes*, who saw it as the principal enemy of the Enlightenment. After 1789, the conflict moved out of books and into the streets. Churches were profaned, and Christianity was vilified. Under the Empire, the priests returned; under the Restoration, they triumphed. The *ultras* elaborated theological projects; others called for renewal of the faith, transformed to suit contemporary taste.

In the midst of these tumultuous conflicts came Constant, who proposed not to be for or against religion, but simply to study it. To us this might seem an obvious thing to do, but at the time it was shocking and was immediately interpreted in relation to the ongoing conflict and condemned: anticlericals saw Constant as tepid, while religious zealots saw him as too much of an atheist. Yet his goal was not to attack or defend religion but to understand it.

To begin his study, he needed to define its subject: Constant called it "religious sentiment." He started with an empirical observation: as far back as we look in history, we find no society without some kind of religious practice. No other animal species exhibits such behavior. Hence religious sentiment is a distinguishing trait of the human species. Paradoxically, both zealots and atheists failed to see that religious sentiment was an intrinsic human trait and tried to explain it as the effect of an external cause: divine intervention (revelation) for the former, and fear, need, and circumstances for the latter. By contrast, Constant proposed to study existing religions in order to shed light on "the human heart and human nature" (617; all page references are to the 1999 edition of *De la religion* published by Actes Sud). Thus he became one of the founders of religious anthropology.

Curiously, however, although Constant saw religious sentiment as timeless and inherent in the very definition of man, he chose to study it not as a philosopher but as a historian. He made no room in his work for fictions of the sort that appealed to the philosophers of his day: the state of nature, the social contract, and prereligious man. He was interested only in facts. From the first, therefore, he laid down a distinction that enabled him to relate what was permanent to what was not: if religious sentiment was immutable, religious "forms" evolved constantly. These forms were the result of the interaction between religious sentiment and changing circumstances: climates, institutions, and sequences of historical events. Change was inevitable: once a form emerged, it tended to solidify and become an impediment to what it was supposed to express. In time, it would therefore inevitably be rejected. History is no less intrinsic to man than is religion, and history consists in the substitution of one form for another. This conclusion was quite difficult for believers to accept.

Of course Constant was not the first historian of religion. He differed from his predecessors, however, and not only because he introduced an anthropological perspective into his reasoning. What distinguishes him from other well-known eighteenth-century writers on the subject such as Warburton, de Brosses, and Court de Gébelin is immediately apparent: whereas they still tended to confuse fiction with history, Constant worked with facts alone. On the other hand, no one would confuse his work with that of the great German scholars who began publishing in this same period. Think, for instance, of the monumental treatise by Friedrich Creuzer, *Symbolik und Mythologie der alten Völker* (Symbolism and Mythology of Ancient Peoples, 1810), which was soon translated into French. Not unlike psychoanalysts today, Creuzer set out to unify religions, decipher symbols, and uncover the true meaning of all the rites and myths of the past. By contrast, Constant followed the example of Montesquieu. (*L'Esprit des lois* was in many respects the model for *De la religion*.) His approach was above all contextual and structural: the first prerequisite was to relate each religious form to its historical and social context, for without the context the form had no meaning.

Following Montesquieu took Constant down a different path from the historians, but in the end he was also obliged to part company with Montesquieu, who was far too systematic for his taste. Constant searched for a middle way, still nameless, between history and system: a discipline interested in abstract principles yet solidly based on fact. Nearly a century later Max Weber would name the object of Constant's quest: the "ideal type," which Weber regarded as the quintessential object of the social sciences. Constant worked with a similar concept, which he called "combination," and he invoked it constantly. A "combination" consisted of a stable core of fundamental features, yet this stable core was compatible with any number of differences in detail. Thus he was able to argue that both Egyptian religion and Hinduism were examples of the same "combination." The concept of combination also led him to analyze the "trinity" in various religions, anticipating the work of Georges Dumézil.

All of these features of Constant's scientific approach were adopted by his successors (many of whom were unaware of his work and even his name). In much the same way as his ideas about democracy, his methodological innovations are today part of our common intellectual baggage, and we feel no need to attribute them to anyone in particular, but this was not true at the time of their inception. The seed dies in bearing fruit. Today's consensus departs from Constant, however, in renouncing the universalist framework he adopted. We hesitate to describe a society as "primitive" or to claim that one practice is more "advanced" than another; we are content merely to say that they are "different." Constant had no such scruples. He assumed the unity of the human species from the outset: "Whether man is savage or civilized (policé), he has the same nature, the same primitive faculties, the same tendency to use them" (p. 139). He therefore maintains the same criteria of judgment: the terms "savage," "barbarian," and "civilized" have for him an absolute rather than a relative content. In the spirit of Lessing and Condorcet, moreover, he also believed in historical progress, though reversals and overlapping cycles sometimes made this progress difficult to perceive.

Constant's erudition is obviously out of date as well. Yet it was vast for his time, for he drew on literature in Greek, Latin, German, English, and French and kept abreast of the latest developments. For detailed information about the beliefs of native Americans or Scandinavians we would no longer turn to Constant. But is that not the fate of all scholarship? As he said himself, "profundity lies not in erudition that compiles but in perspicacity that appreciates" (p. 478). What Constant can still teach us is how to think: given a particular set of facts, these are the questions that need to be asked and these are the answers that can be given. This lesson remains valid to this day. How can one fail, moreover, to admire the art with which Constant was able to distill the essence of the thought of his contemporaries – Lamennais, Chateaubriand and de Maistre – and subject it to critical analysis? Or his ability to paint brilliant comparative portraits, of Aeschylus and Sophocles, for example, or of the Ramayana and the *Iliad*, or, more surprisingly, of Euripides and Voltaire?

POLITICAL ANTHROPOLOGY OF THE RELIGIOUS

The first postulate, then, is that religious sentiment will not disappear. This is true not only because no people in history has been without religion but also because religion is the expression of an irreducible trait of the human species, a trait so general that Constant is unsure about what to call it and speaks now of a "sentiment," now of an "enthusiasm" or "perfection." In other words, the human being is never entirely at one with itself; man incorporates not only sensations and experiences but also self-consciousness, which enables him to imagine himself as other than what he is, hence to imagine something "better" outside of himself, which he can either aspire to achieve or else reject. Because men are self-conscious and therefore divided, they know freedom and act in accordance with something other than their original identity or immediate self-interest. In a fundamental sense, religion and history exist for the same reason, namely, man's capacity to transcend himself, to imagine an otherness that impels him to change.

Religious sentiment and the human ability to change are not the only instances of this capacity and need for self-transcendence. Other members of the same family include love (although Constant reminds us that love is sometimes a disguise for egoism), tenderness, sympathy, devotion, pity, and contemplation of nature. All of these activities might be said to reveal an aptitude for sacrifice, since all imply that we may prefer something beyond ourselves to our own selfish interests, to the assertion of our will to power, or to values associated purely with self-preservation. This "something beyond ourselves" may be above us, as in religion; or alongside us, as in human relations; or apart from us, as in nature.

Constant's primary adversaries in this book are therefore those who deny not just the need for the religious sentiment but also the need to transcend and in some cases to sacrifice ourselves. Among them were the Utilitarians of his day, followers of Bentham, who believed that "self-interest properly understood" should suffice as an ideal for humanity, as well as thinkers ranging from Democritus and Epicurus in ancient times to the materialist Encyclopedists, Hume, and Helvétius (whom the younger Constant had admired). The first step should not be to argue that religion is useless, that it is nothing but the opium of the people or an illusion of the past (as would later be claimed). Rather, it should be to observe that religion *exists* wherever human beings exist. It was commonplace, Constant noted, for his contemporaries to denigrate themselves and to describe themselves as animals or machines entirely determined by their nature and by the pursuit of self-interest. In reality, they could not live without positing something beyond themselves. In this respect, men differed from animals in nature, not just in degree.

These were not his only adversaries, however. Against the atheist materialists it was necessary to invoke the irreducible existence of the religious sentiment. That said, it remained to choose among different religious forms. Constant now shifted his fire from Voltaire and d'Holbach to Bossuet and Maistre. Rather than attack them head on, however, he shifted the ground of the debate to polytheism. Despite the infinite variety of historically attested forms of polytheism, it was possible to identify two main types: *sacerdotal* religions, that is, religions dominated by a priestly caste, and *free* or independent religions in which no priestly mediation was necessary. The religions of the Egyptians, Hindus, and Persians typified the former; that of the Greeks, the latter. What Constant hinted at here without really developing the theme was that within monotheism Catholics stood in similar opposition to Protestants, who thus remained faithful to the initial inspiration of Christianity: "We are all priests," Tertullian said. Not content to study these two varieties of religion, Constant also judged them: free religions were undeniably superior. If there was anything wrong with religion, it could only come from the priesthood and church.

The structure of the book was linked to this fundamental opposition. Book I served as a general introduction to the subject and Book II as the historical introduction, devoted to primitive religions. These were followed by studies of sacerdotal religions (in books III, IV, VI, X, and XI) alternating with studies of nonsacerdotal and therefore free religions (in books V, VII, XII, and XIII), with Book IX devoted to a comparison of the two. Book XV contained the conclusion of the work. Only two books did not fit into this plan: Book VIII, which contained a digression on Homer, and Book XIV, which summarized information about Scandinavian religions. The central argument dealt with the opposition between sacerdotal and nonsacerdotal religions and the superiority of the latter.

Constant justified this judgment in two ways. First, a priestly caste inevitably imposes a fixed order and common rituals and opposes any transformation of these because they become the caste's distinctive sign. In other words, sacerdotal religions tend to be static because of their very structure. But mankind is necessarily a part of history. It is condemned to change, because the conditions of life evolve and yesterday's answers no longer meet today's needs. In this respect, free religions are truer (in relation to human nature), because they admit of improvement, of the search for something better, whereas sacerdotal religions are stationary and constantly threatened by dogmatism. This also explains why the description of free religion among the Greeks became a chapter in another history, of the conquest of independence and the right to participate in the elaboration of the common law rather than submit passively to a law imposed from without.

The second reason why free religions are preferable to sacerdotal religions is that priests have a tendency to become part of the state political apparatus. The theological and the political aspire to become a single category, and not just in theocracies. Unlike other men, priests are not content merely to seek to know the gods; they also covet the means to govern other men. Both the theological and the political suffer from this confusion of the two. Religious sentiment ends up turning into its opposite: interest takes the place of disinterest, the selfishness of caste supplants the spirit of sacrifice, and the temporal drives out the spiritual. Better to leave religion out of such compromises and not hold God responsible for the imperfections of this fallen world. By contrast, men have an interest in governing themselves, in feeling responsible for their behavior on earth rather than relying on a law emanating from somewhereelse.

Constant thus takes his place in the great tradition of modernity, which begins in the Middle Ages with Marsilio of Padua and William of Ockham, who called for separation of the spiritual power from the temporal power, and ends with the legal separation of church and state. The religion of the future, Constant suggests, should stay out of politics, which in turn should keep its hands off religion. Both politics and religion are well advised to limit themselves and not aspire to undisputed dominion. In this respect, *De la religion* was not just a study of the past but a weapon in an ongoing battle.

THE FUTURE OF RELIGION

The sentiment that impels man to look beyond his immediate interests and not settle for the status quo is fundamental, but it is not necessarily religious. The same need can be satisfied by devotion to another human being. Constant has thus far identified the genus to which religion belongs but not its specific difference. What is it? Is there not a possibility today that religion may be replaced by other forms of the same sentiment?

The past is not of much help to us here, because religion was at times able to absorb foreign bodies that later split off from it. Ancient religions stood in for science, explaining the origins of the world and the nature of things. Physics and biology later assumed these roles. Religion once recounted the past, a responsibility that now falls to history. Religion, in the form of magic, sought to influence natural processes and human practices; technology and medicine subsequently took over these functions. Religion sometimes became mixed up with politics, but according to Constant little good came of this and it was better for the two to remain separate. So what is left of religion?

In the modern era some people have believed that religion was the same as morality or at any rate its foundation. Constant was not averse to this view. He was afraid that if religion disappeared, men would be guided solely by the calculation of their interests; that the absence of a belief in life after death would cause us to judge everything in terms of worldly needs; that the lack of an ultimate supernatural sanction would make human laws far too fragile. Yet, at the same time, he offers counterarguments against each of these threats. Immortality of the soul and the afterlife were unnecessary if people thought about the others among whom they lived and without whom they were nothing. Concern for all of mankind could serve as the basis for each country's law. Morality had no need of a religious foundation. Conversely, we often have occasion to judge the religions of the past, and we do so with the aid of moral criteria. Such standards allow us to say that this religion was mild and that one harsh, or that this one was generous, while that one was good only for those who practiced it. Morality even allows us to choose among the various teachings of a given religion and to prefer, for example, the precept "Love thy neighbor as thyself" to "Outside the church no salvation" or "Whoever is not with me is against me." In this respect, as Constant says, "morality becomes a kind of touchstone, a test to which one subjects religious ideas" (p. 469).

Another point needs to be made: Constant was not part of the effort by German philosophers writing at about the same time to substitute morality, or indeed philosophy, for religion and thus to turn philosophy into a secular faith. He rather said that religion was not competent to distinguish good from evil or to define duty any more than it was competent to describe the structure of the atom or the origin of life or make crops grow faster or guide affairs of state. Nevertheless, it neither could nor should disappear.

Even if man managed to satisfy all his immediate desires, protect his interests and bring all his relations into conformity with the rules of morality, and even if he experienced tenderness, devotion, and love, he would still lack something. What might that be? In a general sense, one might say that there would still be times when he would feel that his life lacked meaning. But what meaning? Man is torn between his finite being and the infinite horizons to which consciousness grants him access. The meaning of a life is the possibility of inscribing the finite in the infinite. We know that we are mere grains of sand in a vast universe, that our lives are but an instant in the eternity of time. We feel the need to situate ourselves in relation to the absolute, the infinite, the unlimited. We want to feel included in a network of relationships. But the universe denies us the key to this riddle. We must fabricate it ourselves. As we approach this goal, we gain a sense of inner accomplishment, and our life takes on a meaning.

Broadly interpreted, this is what "religious sentiment" is for Benjamin Constant: the aspiration to make contact with the infinite, to live in harmony with nature, and to define our place in the temporal flux. Neither science nor morality gets us there, because neither can help us to situate ourselves in the cosmos, to find our place in life's unfolding. Science yields specialized knowledge; it exists only because it explicitly refuses to answer questions about ultimate foundations. Morality governs human relations by rising above the narrowness of particular interests. But no matter how much knowledge science achieves, no matter how willingly human beings submit to the dictates of duty, the need for meaning remains. Other practices are more likely to get us where we want to go – for instance, religious experience in the narrow sense of contact with the invisible forces that animate the world (which is why religions recount the story of creation and describe the structure of the cosmos), or contemplation of nature, or the ecstatic experience of a beautiful work of art. All of these things bring us into contact with the infinite. "The contemplation of beauty of all kinds detaches us from ourselves, inspires us to forget our narrow interests, and transports into a sphere of greater purity and unimagined perfection" (p. 340). That is why religious sentiment will retain its place as long as men exist, be they savages frightened by the rumble of thunder or modern individualists who place their faith in science.

We are most likely to make contact with the infinite when our senses perceive it as something incarnate existing apart from us: a painting, a statue, or nature itself, "in the silence of the night, on the ocean shore, in the solitude of the countryside" (p. 48) – at night, when objects lose their well-defined contours; in solitude, when we forget the constraints imposed by others; when we contemplate the starry heavens above. In other words, religious sentiment is something that each of us feels in isolation, in confrontation with the universe and eternity. On this view, religion no longer functions as a bond among men – a function that some claim to find in the very etymology of the word. Of course collective religions take us toward that goal. But the role of social cement, which often strikes us as being essential to religion, is no more necessary to it than the role of grounding moral norms. The isolated individual can achieve harmony with creation by following a course of his own choosing.

Thus religious sentiment has become synonymous with an aspiration to spirituality. The plurality of religions that we see in modern society is a consequence of this purging of the religious sentiment. Plurality is not disappearance, however. Constant would say that modernity is destined to be pluralist, not atheist. He sees no problem in this. On the contrary, because no one religion can identify itself with the temporal power and therefore be corrupted by it, it is impossible for religion to become the basis of a fanatical identity politics or proselytizing intolerance. Furthermore, individuals will be more likely to find their way to a form of the infinite that suits them. "Plunged as we are in deep darkness, can we afford to reject the slightest glimmer of light?" Adolphe asked (in chapter 10 of his eponymous novel). Constant would add that to leave the religious quest to the individual is to allow him to perfect himself without limit: "Divide the torrent, or, rather, allow it to divide itself into a thousand rivulets. They will fertilize the earth that the torrent would have devastated." These are the final words of *De la religion* (p. 577).

Is this a choice that can be freely made? There is reason to doubt it. A free man can act as he will, but he cannot will as he wishes. To be other than one is, it is not enough to will it. "No one believes because he wants to believe," Constant wrote. Yet we can know that achieving what he calls "religious sentiment" is the way to fulfillment for man. Hence we can also allow that sentiment, that need, to invade us rather than resist it. We can tell ourselves that the greatest self-mastery consists in letting go of our selves. Here the future of religion fuses with the future of man.

13 Constant on the Religious Spirit of Liberalism

Benjamin Constant's writings have not generally been considered an interesting resource for political theorists concerned with the relation between religion and liberalism. Today Constant is best known for his 1819 lecture comparing ancient and modern liberty.[1] In that lecture, he defended the freedom of the moderns against the nostalgic rhetoric of republicanism that he thought had been used to justify dangerous political programs during and after the Revolution. Against those writers who suggested that freedom required Spartan self-sacrifice and public spiritedness, Constant argued that commercial society attaches us to a distinctively modern sort of liberty, a freedom concerned not primarily with involvement in politics but instead with the protection of private "enjoyments" and the opportunities for personal self-development. The memories of Robespierre, of Napoleon, and of other efforts to hijack the language of ancient republicanism had left Constant deeply opposed to any government program that sought to impose on citizens a particular understanding of moral or political virtue.

With this familiar view of Constant in mind, it would be natural to assume that his position on religion would simply aim to ensure that the state did not impose any form of worship on its citizens. And since liberal theorists today already agree that the state should be neutral with regard to religions and religious sects, it might seem that Constant's thought does not offer them anything that they do not already know. But while Constant did insist on "utter freedom of worship for all sects," he did so for different reasons than the ones

[1] Benjamin Constant, "The Liberty of the Ancients Compared with That of the Moderns [AML]," in *PW*.

often advanced by many liberal theorists today.[2] He rested his case not on the moral importance of recognizing or respecting all systems of belief, nor on a pragmatic sense that doing otherwise would lead to violence. In fact, his adamant stance in favor of *government* neutrality among religious sects did not arise from a sense that *liberalism* itself should be neutral or indifferent with regard to what sorts of religious beliefs and sentiments citizens entertained. Far from being neutral, his liberalism grew out of and was most comfortable with a particular sort of religiosity. Constant thought that a liberal politics of representative government was congruent with, and even deeply dependent on, a *liberal* sort of religiosity – a privatized, sentimental, antidoctrinal, and anticlerical religion close to the Protestantism of Swiss contemporaries such as Germaine de Staël. This essay aims to bring out the distinctiveness of his position about the religious spirit of liberalism, to explore the underlying logic linking one particular form of religiosity to representative government, and to show that Constant's liberal endorsement of government neutrality rested on a theory about how religions tended to develop over the course of history.[3]

The point about history is important because it resolves what otherwise seems to be an impossible difficulty at the heart of Constant's

---

[2] *PoP* (1815), 275–76.
[3] There is a growing body of work that has begun to integrate Constant's religious thought into his politics, though none takes precisely the tack of this essay. See Helena Rosenblatt, "Re-Evaluating Benjamin Constant's Liberalism: Industrialism, Saint-Simonianism and the Restoration Years," *History of European Ideas*, 30 (2004), 23–37; Rosenblatt, "Commerce et religion dans le libéralisme de Benjamin Constant," *Commentaire*, 26 (102) (Summer, 2003), 415–26; Tzvetan Todorov, *A Passion for Democracy: Benjamin Constant* (New York: Algora, 1999); Todorov, "Un Chef-d'œuvre oublié," in Benjamin Constant, *De la religion considérée dans sa source, ses formes et ses développements*, ed. Tzvetan Todorov and Etienne Hofmann (Arles, France: Actes Sud, 1999); Alan Pitt, "The Religion of the Moderns: Freedom and Authenticity in Constant's *De La Religion*," *History of Political Thought*, 21 (2000), 61–87; K. Steven Vincent, "Benjamin Constant, the French Revolution, and the Origins of French Romantic Liberalism," *French Historical Studies*, 23 (2000), 607–37; Biancamaria Fontana, *Benjamin Constant and the Post-Revolutionary Mind* (New Haven: Yale University Press, 1991). Major studies of Constant that skirt the religious issue include Stephen Holmes, *Benjamin Constant and the Making of Modern Liberalism* (New Haven: Yale University Press, 1984), and Andreas Kalyvas and Ira Katznelson, "'We Are Modern Men': Benjamin Constant and the Discovery of an Immanent Liberalism," *Constellations*, 6 (4) (1999), 513–39.

thought. Constant believed that political life under representative government required citizens to have certain habits of mind and thought, and yet he opposed all government efforts at fostering such virtues. How, then, was the success of representative government to be assured? The forces of history accomplished the task that Constant thought was too dangerous to leave to political actors or governments, and his endorsement of a laissez-faire government stance toward religion cannot be understood without emphasizing his faith in history. Today, most liberals find it difficult to maintain a similar faith in progress, and yet many also find it difficult to deny Constant's point about the interdependence between a liberalized religion and liberal politics. Liberals therefore often find themselves in a deep puzzle about how to treat religion in liberal democracies; they are habitually torn between the wish to respect existing religions and the desire to reform them. Although Constant's thought does not in the end offer an escape from this dilemma, it does offer a useful reminder that the difficulty cannot be evaded.

BEYOND COMMERCIAL SELF-INTEREST

Ever since Karl Marx dismissed Constant as nothing more than a spokesman for the bourgeoisie, scholars have misread his writings, portraying him as a theorist who wholeheartedly defended and even glorified the coming of the modern commercial world and its politics of material interests and property rights.[4] This view not only ignores Constant's admission, at the end of his 1819 lecture, that modern citizenship required an attachment to ancient as well as modern liberty. Depicting Constant as an unapologetic apologist for commercial interests also neglects the richest and most interesting part of his thought, his passionate concerns about the new moral and psychological challenges that modern individuals confronted in the rising commercial society. Free to choose for themselves rather than defer to the authority of their communities or spiritual advisors, modern individuals faced a novel set of insecurities. The nostalgia for ancient politics that Constant decried in his lecture arose from these modern insecurities; people turned to various forms of nostalgic politics

---

[4] Karl Marx, "The Eighteenth Brumaire of Louis Bonaparte," in *The Marx-Engels Reader*, ed. Robert C. Tucker (New York: Norton, 1978), 595.

because those forms of politics promised to eliminate the instability that modernity brought. To minimize the attraction of faux-Rousseauian solutions, Constant thought it was necessary to find for modern citizens a source of moral and spiritual depth. At the end of the lecture on ancient and modern liberty he said that the goal of combining the two forms of freedom was to help citizens pursue "self-development" (*perfectionnement*), a higher end than mere "happiness" (*bonheur*). He said that he bore witness not to a self-satisfied politics of commercial self-interest but instead to "the better part of our nature, that noble disquiet which pursues and torments us."[5] This was not an isolated rhetorical flourish, for a reading of Constant's work as a whole shows that such concerns were central to all of his writings.

In particular, it was with such thoughts about the insufficiency of understanding the human good solely in terms of self-interest that Constant introduced and explained the need for the work that he considered his magnum opus, an enormous history of ancient polytheistic religions, *De la religion, considérée dans sa source, ses formes et ses développements*.[6] Constant wrote that both commercial society and Enlightenment tended to encourage the calculating spirit through which men sought to understand their world in terms of self-interest. He was adamant that no doctrine of "self-interest well-understood" could be adequate for the needs of an individual psyche – not even for modern individuals, and perhaps especially not for them. "Nature has not placed our guide in our interest well understood, but in our intimate sentiment," he insisted. The reign of interest well understood during the past twenty years had led to a degradation of intellect and spirit, he wrote, and the dominance of the calculating spirit in the wake of the Enlightenment had left each individual his own center, isolated. "Friends of liberty," he wrote, "these are not the materials with which a people obtains, founds or conserves liberty." All systems of thought, he asserted, reduced themselves to two, one taking interest as a guide to one's own well-being and the other proposing sentiment as a guide to one's self-development.

---

[5] AML, 327.

[6] Benjamin Constant, *De la religion, considérée dans sa source, ses formes et ses développements*, ed. Tzvetan Todorov and Etienne Hofmann (Arles, France: Actes Sud, 1999) [*DLR*].

While the former could domesticate men and serve them well enough in peaceful times, it could never inspire the sacrifice necessary to defend liberty in other times. Constant's peroration at the end of the preface to this work was filled with talk of citizens, heroes, and self-sacrifice. "Friends of liberty," he declared,

liberty nourishes itself on sacrifices. Return the power of sacrifice to the enervated race which has lost it. Liberty always wants citizens, and often heroes. Do not let fade the convictions that ground the virtues of citizens, and that create heroes, giving them the strength to be martyrs.[7]

Such words do not seem to come from the pen of someone wholly pleased with the modern politics of commercial self-interest.

These writings against self-interest and in favor of religion cannot be dismissed as incidental to Constant's intellectual projects. The history of polytheism was the project on which Constant worked longest and hardest. He conceived of the idea for this project at the early age of eighteen, soon after having attended a set of lectures on "universal history, ancient and modern" in Scotland by Alexander Fraser Tytler, who focused a great deal on ancient Egyptian and Greek religions, polytheism, and the priesthood.[8] He continued to work on the project, modifying its purpose and outlook, throughout his life, publishing most of it as *De la religion* in the last years of his life and leaving in manuscript two final volumes on the Romans, which his wife published shortly after he died. Although *De la religion* is concerned almost entirely with ancient polytheistic religion, tracing developments from Homeric systems of beliefs about the gods to later Athenian thought and eventually to Roman paganism, Constant regarded his project as an effort to tell the grand story of the development of man's consciousness (*"la marche de l'esprit humain"*). In this way his history of religion may almost seem to parallel Hegel's *Phenomenology* in its ambition and scope, if not in its achievement. At various times in his correspondence and journals, Constant referred to the project on polytheism as his one project of real worth, as when he wrote in 1804 that his research on the history of religion was "the sole interest, the only consolation in my life."[9]

---

[7] *DLR*, 34, translation my own.
[8] Dennis Wood, *Benjamin Constant: A Biography* (London; New York: Routledge, 1993), 61–62.
[9] Wood, 269, note 20, citing Benjamin Constant, *Œuvres*, 289.

A complete examination of Constant's thought would therefore require study of *De la religion* as a whole, as other authors in this volume have undertaken. But to gain a quick sense of the thrust of the work on religion we can also consult a set of lectures on the topic that Constant gave to the Athénée Royale in 1818, just a year before his famous lecture on liberty.[10] In these three lectures he offered a synopsis of what he regarded as the primary findings of his long research up to that point, and perhaps most interestingly, he mentioned the broad lessons that he thought his research yielded for the politics of his own time. Indeed he insisted at the beginning of the first lecture that while the substance of his talks would concern details separated from him and his audience by centuries, his topic was nevertheless directly relevant to the defense of liberty in his day. His research into the early origins and development of religion was, he explained, a way of "seeking within our most intimate sentiments new supports for our most sacred rights."[11] He declared that he intended his work not as an attack on religion, but as an effort to ensure that no external authority exercised undue influence over it. "It is not the cause of philosophy, only, but also that of religion that I want to plead," he insisted.[12] If he seemed prematurely defensive on this point, which is perhaps because he knew that the fierce attack

[10] These lectures have not been published, but they are among the manuscripts in the archives of the Bibliothèque cantonale et universitaire in Lausanne, Switzerland: Benjamin Constant, "[fragment de la copie des lectures à l'Athénée Royal sur la religion]," Lausanne, 1818, CO 3279, referred to hereafter as "Lectures on Religion." The first two lectures are incomplete, with large sections crossed out, but the third lecture seems to be complete. For a description of the manuscript, see Etienne Hofmann, *Catalogue raisonné de l'œuvre manuscrite de Benjamin Constant* (Genève: Slatkine, 1992), 96. See also Patrice Thompson, Pierre Deguise, and Boris Anelli, *Les Écrits de Benjamin Constant sur la religion: Essai de liste chronologique* (Paris: H. Champion, 1998), 108–9. For a few biographical details about the lectures, see Wood, 225. Finally, some of the same points can be found in Constant's essay "Du développement progressif des idées religieuses," in *EP*, 629–53.

[11] "Nous occuper des institutions religieuses des différents peoples, ce n'est donc point sortie de la sphère de la politique... C'est au contraire faire entrer dans cette sphère une partie importante de l'existence humain, et l'on verra peut être, par le résultat, que c'est chercher dans nos sentiments les plus intimes, de nouveaux appuis pour nos droits les plus sacrés." Constant, "Lectures on Religion," 3. Translations of this text are my own. Page numbers refer to the folio page of the manuscript, of which there are ninety-eight in total.

[12] "Lectures on Religion," 4.

on clericalism he was about to deliver could easily be misunderstood to be an attack on religion itself, it was a misunderstanding he was eager to avoid. Constant was not merely tolerant of religion. Following Germaine de Staël, who in her *D'Allemagne* had associated the term "toleration" with an "indifferent" attitude toward religion, Constant insisted that he treated religion with the "respect" owed to all sincere sentiments of the heart. To uncover the sentiment worthy of respect, though, Constant thought it necessary to disentangle pure religion from its various deformations, all of which were the result of political authorities having tried in one way or another to convert religion into privilege. Sometimes authority pressed religion into serving as a pretext for many crimes; at other times authority institutionalized religion and thus turned it into a "mechanical and frivolous habit."[13] The assumption of his analysis throughout was that beneath the various perversions that authorities imposed on religion lay such a thing as true or pure religious sentiment. The source of religion was, he said at the beginning of the third lecture, to be found "not in reasoning, fear or hope, but rather in a need of the soul inherent to the nature of man, indestructible, which seeks always to satisfy itself according to the state of enlightenment and the stage of civilization."[14]

The major analytical distinction running through the lectures was that between priestly religions and independent ones. The importance of this distinction was that it made authority out to be something separable from religion. In the first two lectures he argued that the root of religion lay in a natural human need and that the first manifestation of this need could be found in primitive man's attachment to and worship of certain inanimate objects, which Constant called "fetishism." In the third lecture he said that these arguments all led to the question of how priestly power ever came into being, and why it arose in some communities but not in others. The question supposed that priestly authority was not naturally a concomitant of religion, but was something external to it, foisted on it, something to be explained. In the lecture Constant considered various possible explanations, including climate and the accident of natural disasters. In the end he concluded that the origin of priestly power lay ultimately in the dependence of some nomadic peoples

[13] Ibid., 2.
[14] Ibid., 44.

on observation of the stars and the elements for navigation and survival.[15] Those tribes that had depended strongly on such study had required a class of individuals who could devote themselves to it and who had been designated the authoritative interpreters of the celestial signs. This class had come to be regarded as the holders of science and knowledge more generally, and they eventually interpreted not only the stars but also their importance for human events; they had moved from astronomy to astrology. Constant thus announced with some fanfare his "first principle": that "all the cults founded on astrology gave to the priests an immense empire, while all those that took their origin from fetishism gave to them only a small amount of power."[16] As examples he cited first and foremost the Egyptians on one side and the Greeks on the other. Alongside the Egyptians as examples of astrological and priestly powers he named the Carthaginians and the ancestors of the French, the Gauls, who had been tyrannized over by their Druids. The final part of his story, he indicated, would be to show how the Greeks, who had avoided priestly power early on, confronted efforts to import elements of sacerdotal authority into their ranks, and how the Romans, whose colonization had imported both priestly and independent religions, negotiated the conflict between them. The independent religions were clearly the heroes of Constant's story. The history he summarized in the lectures was one that sought a form of religiosity free from the perversions caused by priestly influence.

The broadest question that the lectures raise is exactly how Constant sought to enlist religion, that vestige of the ancient regime, to meet the challenges of modernity without thereby falling into the nostalgia for premodern politics that he so famously decried. The lectures on ancient religion may be read to raise this question, but they do not even try to answer it. For an answer, one must turn to Constant's more political writings, where we find a solution so familiar to us now that its distinctiveness is difficult to see: Constant supported unfettered religious freedom for all. But while he unambiguously supported freedom for each individual to choose how and what to worship, he just as firmly seemed to favor a particular sort of religiosity, the sort that he thought such freedom would be likely to encourage. The pure religious sentiment that Constant

[15] See also Constant, "Du développement progressif des idées religieuses," 644.
[16] Constant, "Lectures on Religion," 59.

found through his historical research into ancient polytheism was closely akin to the pure Christian sentiment that would emerge in modern times; both declined to exercise political authority. Constant thus thought that government neutrality with regard to religion would foster the sort of religion that representative government required – a religion of private sentiment, stripped of doctrinal and rational content and thus made useless to those who might try to wield it as an authority over others. To see how he arrived at this position it is necessary to look more closely at his treatment of ancient polytheism.

A REEVALUATION OF ANCIENT POLYTHEISM

Constant was certainly not the first modern writer to study ancient polytheism when trying to find a sort of religion compatible with liberal toleration. Enlightenment authors had often noticed that there had been no pagan Inquisitions, and they had concluded that ancient polytheism had therefore been superior to Christianity in its attitude toward pluralism. David Hume attributed the relative tolerance of polytheism directly to the fact that it included multiple sources of divinity. In chapter 9 of his *Natural History of Religion*, titled "Comparison of These Religions [Polytheism and Monotheism], with Regard to Persecution and Toleration," he wrote,

Idolatry [polytheism] is attended with this evident advantage, that, by limiting the powers and functions of its deities, it naturally admits the gods of other sects and nations to a share of divinity, and renders all the various deities, as well as rites, ceremonies, or traditions, compatible with each other.[17]

Hume went on to give historical evidence for "the tolerating spirit of idolators" and for the inverse, "the intolerance of almost all religions which have maintained the unity of God." Christianity had been an exception, he argued, only when civil authorities had forced toleration upon it. "The intolerance of almost all religions which have maintained the unity of God is as remarkable as the contrary principle of polytheists," he argued.[18]

---

[17] David Hume, *The Natural History of Religion* (London: Bonner, 1889), sec. 9, 39.
[18] Ibid., 40.

A figure even closer to Constant than Hume was the historian Edward Gibbon, who was an occasional member of Germaine de Staël's circle and whose monumental *Decline and Fall of the Roman Empire* Constant had considered translating into French as a young man. Gibbon's assessment of ancient polytheism was similar to Hume's, and in his history he made no secret of his preference for polytheism over Christianity precisely on the grounds of its superior tendency to foster toleration. He described the beliefs of polytheists as uncertain and imprecise, easily taken up and abandoned, and thus unlikely to inspire deep devotion, much less fanaticism. "As long as their adoration was successively prostituted to a thousand deities," he wrote of the pagans, "it was scarcely possible that their hearts could be susceptible of a very sincere or lively passion for any of them."[19] Gibbon thus praised "the universal toleration of Polytheism."[20]

Monotheists, in contrast, Gibbon described as "a sect of people [that] separate[d] itself from the communion of mankind," that "claim[ed] the exclusive possession of divine knowledge," and that "disdain[ed] every form of worship except its own as impious and idolatrous."[21] Like Hume, Gibbon saw the root of intolerance and fanaticism in the very heart of monotheism, in the claim that there was only one source of value. Christianity was therefore inherently prone to intolerance, and the Inquisition was not a deviation from but a realization of its essential nature. Gibbon concluded his chapter on the topic with the "melancholy truth" that "the Christians, in the course of their intestine dissensions, have inflicted far greater severities on each other than they had experienced from the zeal of infidels."[22] But of course, to praise ancient polytheism in this way does not supply moderns with a solution. Obviously, neither Hume nor Gibbon was suggesting a return to polytheism. Their arguments on behalf of the pagan mentality mainly served to illustrate by contrast the failings of Christianity and, thus, to bolster their case against religion as such.

---

[19] Edward Gibbon, *The Decline and Fall of the Roman Empire*, ed. Hans-Friedrich Mueller (New York: Modern Library, 2003), chap. 15.
[20] Gibbon, chap. 16
[21] Ibid.
[22] Ibid.

Constant seems to have initially approached his project on polytheism with a similar point of view in mind. He wrote in his journal that he had begun the project inspired by the eighteenth-century materialist Helvétius and that he had wanted to expose religious beliefs as nothing more than "prejudices." But he found over time that his sympathy for these merely critical views of Christianity faded. In fact, he later wrote of his changing thoughts on religion that they provided "singular proof" of what Francis Bacon had written in his essay on atheism: "It is true that a little philosophy inclineth man's mind to atheism, but depth in philosophy bringeth man's mind about to religion."[23] If Bacon was right, then it seemed that many of Constant's peers in France had only a little philosophy. The common view on the Left, as de Staël summarized it, was that "to love liberty it is necessary to be an atheist."[24]

What Constant eventually found in his studies of ancient polytheism was something quite different from a new reason to endorse atheism. He acknowledged that the pagans had a certain tolerance for one another, but he regarded their attitude toward religion as a shallow and callous one of "indifference" rather than any sort of mutual respect or appreciation. If the ancient pagans seemed more tolerant than Christians, he argued, that was because they were ultimately indifferent to religious feeling in general. The truer and deeper toleration had come only later in the development of religious sentiment. The indifference of the polytheists was quite different from the *enthusiasm* that Constant thought followers of the true, pure religion would feel. And in Constant's enthusiasm *for* enthusiasm – evident in his (and de Staël's) effort to recuperate the word itself – we can see a key difference between his thought and Hume's.[25] Mutual respect came neither from a cool and detached assessment of religion's social function nor from a newly scientific worldview,

---

[23] Constant, letter to Claude Hochet, October 11, 1811, in *Lettres à un ami [par] Benjamin Constant et Madame de Staël*, ed. Jean Mistler (Neuchatel: Baconnière, 1949), 194, translation my own.

[24] Germaine de Staël, *Considerations on the Principal Events of the French Revolution* (London: Baldwin, Cradock and Joy, 1818), 2.335.

[25] See Vincent, "Benjamin Constant, the French Revolution, and the Origins of French Romantic Liberalism," 628–32; Michael Heyd, *"Be Sober and Reasonable": The Critique of Enthusiasm in the Seventeenth and Early Eighteenth Centuries* (Leiden: E. J. Brill, 1995); David Denby, *Sentimental Narrative and the Social Order in France, 1760–1820* (Cambridge: Cambridge University Press, 1994).

but instead from a passionate enthusiasm for the true sentiment in which all religions have their roots.

Furthermore, Constant noticed that while the indifference of ancient religions toward one another might have provided a simulacrum of tolerance, it had not solved the other major problem that he thought plagued religion – the support that religion provided for the rule of priests. Much of Constant's research into ancient polytheism was devoted to explaining the simple observation that some ancient sects, such as the ancient Egyptians, had developed strong priestly castes, while others, such as the Greeks, had not. In the end, as we have seen, he concluded that the origin of priestly power in societies such as Egypt lay ultimately in the dependence of their nomadic predecessors on observation of the stars and the heavens for navigation and survival. In attributing the rise of a priestly cast to a cause so clearly external to the nature of religion itself, Constant was arguing that priestly authority was foreign to religion.

Thus while Hume and Gibbon found in the contrast between Christianity and ancient polytheism evidence that Christianity was inherently intolerant, Constant drew a more nuanced view from his research. He found in the divergent paths of ancient polytheism evidence that one did not have to reject religion itself in order to reject the political scourges of priestly authority and intolerance. One only had to insist on the distinction between the natural sentiment that was the pure heart of religion and the social forms that the sentiment was forced to adapt by various authorities seeking to use it for their own purposes. Constant eventually revised the work *On Religion* to structure the whole narrative around the distinction between religious sentiment and religious form, and he made this distinction even more central to his enterprise than the distinction between priestly and independent religions. From a philosophical vantage point one can say that he was right to do so, for the idea of a pure religious sentiment was crucial to his defense of religion against its many detractors. It allowed him to attack both Old Regime religion and Enlightenment atheism. Influenced by incipient German Romantic philosophy, Constant came to think that the solution to fanaticism lay not in the rationalizing spirit of the high Enlightenment but instead in purifying the emotions surrounding religion. What liberalism needed, he seems to have thought, was a religion of pure sentiment.

WHY A RELIGION OF SENTIMENT SUITS
LIBERAL POLITICS

Constant was notoriously vague about exactly what he meant by religious sentiment. In his *Principles of Politics*, published just a few years before the lectures on religion, he addressed this complaint directly:

> If I were accused at this point of failing to offer a sufficiently precise definition of religious feeling I shall ask how we can define with precision that vague and profound part of our moral sense, which by its very nature defies all the efforts of language. How would you define the impression of a dark night, of an ancient forest, of the wind moaning through ruins or over graves, of the ocean stretching beyond our sight? How would you define the emotion caused by the songs of Ossian, the church of St. Peter, meditation upon death, the harmony of sounds or forms? How would you define reverie, that intimate quivering of the soul, in which all the powers of the senses and thought come together and lose themselves in a mysterious confusion? There is religion at the bottom of all things. All that is beautiful, all that is intimate, all that is noble, partakes of the nature of religion.[26]

Any reader could be forgiven for thinking that this passage only makes his meaning less clear. But the passage does offer insight into the feature of pure religious sentiment that Constant seemed to think most important – the fact that it is *undefinable*. The "very nature" of the religious sentiment is to "defy all the efforts of language," to resist definition. If the passage seems unlimited in its notion of the divine, if it seems promiscuous in the objects of its adoration – "there is religion at the bottom of all things" – that seems to be precisely Constant's point. Religious sentiment is meant to starkly contrast with the neatly defined parameters of one's economic interests. It is also meant to defy authority, including the authority of anyone who would seek to define it. Constant's tone in this passage suggests that he chafed at the insinuation that the religious sentiment should be defined; whoever would define it would control it; its very nature was to be independent of such control.

With these reflections we can begin to see why such a view of religion might have attracted Constant the man, at least as the biographies portray him – a man of unsettled habits and tastes, inconstant

---

[26] Constant, *PoP* (1815), 279.

in love and morals. We might also see why it suits modern individuals as Constant described them, ill suited to believing in any doctrine on faith or maintaining any firm and settled conviction. But leaving these psychological speculations aside, it is also possible to think through the way in which the idea of religion as sentiment seems particularly well suited to address the most fundamental *political* problems with religion that concerned Constant as a liberal.[27]

One problem that we saw him take up in his lectures was the problem of priestly dominance. Recall that he located the origin of this dominance in the need that some primitive societies had for experts in celestial navigation. What that tale highlights is the fact that priestly authority relies on a claim to special expertise or insight. To eliminate the justification for priestly rule it would, therefore, be necessary to eliminate any possibility of expertise in religion. Religion would have to be the sort of thing about which no one could have special knowledge. The Reformation did not fully achieve this, since giving everyone the chance to interpret the Bible left open the question of whether some were more skilled interpreters of that book than others. Diversity of interpretation does not remove but only displaces the question of authority, as the subsequent history of Protestantism adequately demonstrates. Perhaps Locke's notion that each is orthodox to himself came close to addressing the issue, but even the exercise of conscience requires the use of reason, which people seem to have and exercise to different extents. Religion understood purely as private sentiment is different in that it removes the possibility that some people have privileged access to religious truth. The final determinant of that truth is one's own sentiment, which is something that no one else can feel directly. Whereas a piece of reasoning or interpretation can be demonstrated to be wrong or at least debated, a moment of intense and deep feeling is undeniably intense and deep to the one who claims that it is. As long as that intensity is the determinant of religious truth, no one else can have special knowledge or insight about one's own religious claims. Religion understood as sentiment would therefore seem to remove the

---

[27] Here I follow closely the strategy of Arthur Melzer, who adopted a similar approach when examining Rousseau's "Profession of the Savoyard Vicar" in Rousseau's *Emile* (without calling Rousseau a "liberal"). Arthur Melzer, "The Origin of the Counter-Enlightenment: Rousseau and the New Religion of Sincerity," *American Political Science Review* 90 (June 1996) 344–60.

justification for priestly authority and to make individuals spiritually self-sufficient in a much more profound way than other forms
of Protestantism do.

A related problem in earlier Christianity was intolerance. Recall
that Hume, Gibbon, and others thought intolerance was endemic
to Christianity as a monotheistic religion. The reason, in Gibbon's
words, was that Christians "claim[ed] the exclusive possession of
divine knowledge." This meant that those of other faiths who
claimed to know something different about God implicitly challenged their claim; any claim of divine knowledge was implicitly
intolerant of those who disagreed. But we have just seen that when
religion is understood as sentiment, such claims of knowledge virtually disappear. Different people may be inspired by different objects
to feel a strong sentiment that puts them in touch with the infinite,
and so long as the feeling is accepted as the criterion of religiosity, the differences in the objects of our worship should not lead
to argument. "Pure" sentiment is "pure" in that it needs no confirmation from outside itself. Opinion is different; opinion wants
to be recognized as true and so seeks to be recognized as true by
others; religion understood as opinion therefore naturally tries to
persuade or convince others; it has a will to rule. Compare this
desire to convince with the important lines from the Savoyard Vicar
in Rousseau's *Emile*, who articulates something approaching Constant's style of religion as sentiment: The Vicar tells Emile, "I do
not want to argue with you or even attempt to convince you. It is
enough for me to reveal to you what I think in the simplicity of my
heart . . . [And, later:] Always remember that I am not teaching my
sentiment; I am revealing it."[28] While the Vicar may hope that Emile
feels something similar, he cannot utilize anything like the force of
argument against him. Religion as sentiment naturally gives up the
aspiration to convince or to convert; it is naturally tolerant.

For this reason religion understood as sentiment would seem to
yield a kind of diversity that is similar to polytheism. Hume's explanation of why polytheistic religion tends to be tolerant – that it
"admits the gods of other sects and nations to a share of divinity" –
finds a surprising echo in a passage from Constant's novel *Adolphe*:

---

[28] Jean-Jacques Rousseau, *Emile*, trans. Allan Bloom (New York: BasicBooks, 1979),
book 4.

What surprises me is not that man needs a religion, but rather that he should ever think himself strong enough or sufficiently secure from trouble to dare reject any one of them. I think he ought, in his weakness, to call upon them all. In the dense night that surrounds us is there any gleam of light we can afford to reject? In the torrent bearing us all away is there a single branch we dare refuse to cling to?[29]

What is striking about this passage is the combination of sincere religious passion with indifference to the distinction between religions. Such indifference is possible because a religion of sentiment makes no claims to authority over its adherents. In *De la religion*, Constant asserted that religious sentiment in itself contained "no principle, no element of slavery."[30] A principle is an element of slavery because in asserting the correctness of a principle we implicitly claim that it merits attention from everyone. Principles are assertions of authority. Religion understood as sentiment was religion stripped of ruling principle and thereby stripped of claims to authority.

A final problem with traditional Christianity that liberals might be concerned with is the one that Rousseau emphasized in his chapter on civil religion in the *Social Contract* – the problem that Christianity seems to make its followers concerned with the other world rather than this world and thus detaches them from caring deeply about politics. Christianity seems to demonstrate that one can detach people from their private interests only by detaching them from politics. The otherworldliness of Christianity turns believers into poor soldiers and bad citizens; if Christianity inspires sacrifices, it is not for the sake of the state. Does Constant's view of religion as sentiment address this problem? As we have just seen, his religious sentiment does not itself seem to be politicized; it does not tie its adherents to any particular political entity or authority; in fact, it does just the reverse. But religion as sentiment does seem to combat the problem of otherworldliness in a different way. It divinizes this world, looking for sources of sublime feeling in nature, in the very earthy experience of love (as in *Adolphe*) and, more generally, in the quest for self-development. This means that understanding

---

[29] Benjamin Constant, *Adolphe*, trans. Leonard Tancock (New York: Penguin, 1964), 118–19.
[30] *DLR*, 86, translation my own.

religion as sentiment gives one a worldly interest – an interest in protecting the opportunity to pursue such earthly experiences. That opportunity is precisely what Constant thought a liberal society of secure rights should protect, and the interest in pursuing those opportunities is what Constant thought might motivate us to make sacrifices for the sake of liberty. The experiences of sublime sentiment and self-development are "private enjoyments," but they are private enjoyments of a very different kind from the material ones presumed in most readings of Constant and in most readings of his liberalism. Religion as sentiment offers a source of agency and motivation that is deeper and more powerful than ordinary self-interest, and yet which does not tie one to an authority outside oneself.

In these ways a religion of sentiment tries to solve three of the political problems that Constant as a liberal was most concerned about: the rule of priests, the persistence of intolerance, and the insufficiency of material self-interest as a source of political agency strong enough to motivate citizens to defend their liberties. The problems are addressed by features of the peculiar sort of Protestantism that Constant admired, features that arose as radicalizations of Protestantism's tendency to value private judgment.[31]

In emphasizing the importance of authentic religious sentiment in Constant's work, we need not conclude that the traditional reading of Constant as primarily a defender of freedom is incorrect or that "freedom is subordinate to authenticity in Constant's work," as one author insists.[32] In fact, the arguments just rehearsed suggest that the Romantic element of Constant's thought was deeply connected to his understanding of freedom, that viewing religion as pure sentiment was a part of Constant's effort to make liberal representative government possible. As George Kateb has written, "the very notion of ruling and being ruled is alien to the spirit of representative democracy."[33] The question that Constant confronted was how religion, which seems so closely allied to the notion of being ruled by a higher authority, could fit into this spirit.

---

[31] Helena Rosenblatt, "Madame de Staël, the Protestant Reformation, and the History of 'Private Judgement," *ABC*, 31–32 (2007), 143–54.

[32] Pitt, "The Religion of the Moderns," 76.

[33] Kateb, "The Moral Distinctiveness of Representative Democracy," *Ethics*, 91 (April, 1981), 357–74 at 358.

These arguments suggest that there is a deeper connection between the Romantic aspect of Constant's thought and his political liberalism than has been recognized. Both Nancy Rosenblum and Stephen Holmes have emphasized the fact that Romanticism gave Constant a special reason to prize liberal rights, since those rights protected the realm of privacy in which a warmer, more expressive, and richer sort of life could be safely lived. The argument that we have seen so far accepts this, but goes further and in some ways reverses the logic. It suggests that a certain sort of Romantic sentimentalism was not just one possible mode of enjoying private liberty and one motive to protect that liberty, but that it was necessary to make religion compatible with liberty. Rosenblum sums up Constant's position as the view that "the only hope for Romantic souls is the peace and privacy of liberal society."[34] But an even more powerful, and more controversial, argument can be drawn from Constant, an argument that can be stated as the converse of Rosenblum's argument: the only hope for liberal society is the Romantic soul. Or, more precisely, a certain Romanticization of our religiosity – an individualization, subjectification, and sentimentalization of it – was necessary to tame religion's impulse to rule and thus make liberal political society possible.

CONSTANT'S INVISIBLE HAND

If political authority is intrinsically corrupting to the religious spirit, then that spirit cannot be inculcated by authorities. This is why Constant opposed all suggestions for anything resembling a civil religion, eventually arguing in the 1820s against not only the ultramonarchists on the right such as de Bonald and Maistre, but also Comte and the Saint-Simonians on the left, who were concerned enough about "moral anarchy" to consider various sorts of new state-sanctioned religion.[35] In his *Principles of Politics*,

---

[34] Nancy L. Rosenblum, *Another Liberalism: Romanticism and the Reconstruction of Liberal Thought* (Cambridge, MA: Harvard University Press, 1987), 26. See also Holmes, *Benjamin Constant and the Making of Modern Liberalism*, 174: "This paradox lies at the heart of Constant's liberalism: as the legal framework of social life becomes increasingly cold and impersonal, the chances for personal intimacy, emotion and expressivism are markedly increased."

[35] Rosenblatt, "Re-Evaluating Benjamin Constant's Liberalism," 31–33.

Constant had attacked this sort of argument at its source, arguing against Rousseau's case for civil religion in the *Social Contract*. Rousseau had insisted that the sort of civil religion he had in mind could not be used to support intolerance, since the only "negative dogma" allowed was that intolerance itself would not be allowed. But Rousseau had also licensed the sovereign to fix articles of sociability and banish anyone who did not accept them.[36] Constant quoted this passage at length and argued that it had had the effect of justifying a civil intolerance that was even more dangerous than religious intolerance, because it was born of calculation rather than a sincere feeling of duty.[37] Constant detected examples of such civil intolerance "disguising itself" in various places: when the newly emancipated Jews insisted that tolerated sects not be permitted to subdivide; when others insisted that only certain sects be tolerated, or that all existing sects be tolerated but not new ones, or that sects wanting to change their doctrines had to first seek approval from the authorities; when any of these policies were recommended, Constant thought they were in fact threatening forms of civil intolerance. He recognized in this impulse an echo of the antireligious fanaticism that he detected in the writings of materialists like Holbach and which he thought lay behind much of the violence of the Terror. In fact, anything less than "complete and utter freedom of all forms of worship" seemed intolerant and therefore intolerable to him.[38] Even if the efforts of authorities were designed to ensure tolerance, he thought those efforts led to forms of interference that were in the end intolerant. "Who would believe it!" he wrote. "Political authority causes harm even when it wishes to bring within its jurisdiction the principles of tolerance: this is because it imposes upon tolerance positive and fixed forms which are opposed to the latter's own nature. Tolerance is nothing but the freedom of all present and future forms of worship."[39] Thus attempts to liberalize religion by wielding authority could not succeed.

And yet a liberal temper of mind was necessary for representative government to succeed, and so a transformation of religion would

---

[36] Jean-Jacques Rousseau, *On the Social Contract*, trans. Judith R. Masters, ed. Roger D. Masters (New York: St. Martin's Press, 1978), 130–31.

[37] *PoP* (1815), 275.

[38] Ibid., 275–276.

[39] Ibid., 284.

be required. Constant's preference for a laissez-faire policy toward religion was not born out of the idea that all sects deserved equal respect, but instead out of a faith that open competition between them would tend to have a generally liberalizing effect on many of them. He thought that the complete religious liberty he was arguing for would lead to the proliferation of religious sects and that this would eventually encourage the purification of religious sentiment and enthusiasm while discouraging fanaticism and superstition.

Constant may have found the roots of this argument in Adam Smith's *Wealth of Nations*, and a look at Smith's treatment helps to bring out Constant's approach to the problem.[40] Smith had begun his consideration of the topic by noticing that an officially sanctioned and well-established church tends to lose the support of the common people as it matures and becomes more "learned" and "elegant," and that this opens the door for "a set of popular and bold, though perhaps stupid and ignorant enthusiasts" to stir up the people. While the established church might be superior in many respects, Smith had noticed, "the arts of popularity, all the arts of gaining proselytes, are constantly on the side of its adversaries."[41] The established church, defenseless against such rhetoric, tends to find itself calling in political authorities to support it, and from there, religious and political conflicts intertwine and escalate. Smith had argued that this cycle would never have developed had government left religion alone and thus not given the smaller sects cause for complaint. With this argument he was replying to Hume, who had argued in his *History of England* that the state should provide financial support to organized religion in order to weaken its vitality. Hume had suggested that since anyone on the public payroll tended to become indolent, the best way to influence priests into inactivity

---

[40] Constant visited Edinburgh during the early 1780s and read Smith closely. See Etienne Hofmann's note in Benjamin Constant, *Principes de politique applicables à tous les gouvernements*, vol. 2, ed. Etienne Hofmann (Geneva: Droz, 1980), 165, note 15. Adam Smith, *An Inquiry into the Nature and Causes of the Wealth of Nations*, ed. R. H. Campbell and A. S. Skinner (Indianapolis: Liberty Fund, 1981), V.I.iii.3, 792–94. For a good account of Smith's treatment of the topic, see Charles L. Griswold, *Adam Smith and the Virtues of Enlightenment* (Cambridge: Cambridge University Press, 1999), 266–92.

[41] Smith, 789.

was to "bribe their indolence" by subsidizing them.[42] Smith's line of reasoning was intended to show how such efforts to undermine religion had the unintended consequence of promoting religious fanaticism.

Smith proposed that it was under conditions of competition that the leaders of sects would find themselves "obliged to learn that candor and moderation" that was rarely found among priests who were officially sanctioned by the government. While he admitted that religious freedom might not produce "good temper and moderation" in all or even most religious sects, he thought that competition would dilute zeal to a manageable level and that it would encourage mutual toleration. It would not eliminate enthusiasm but it would render it "innocent" or free from the impulse to claim political authority. The effect of competition would be to produce a "pure and rational religion" that philosophers could endorse:

The teachers of each little sect, finding themselves almost alone, would be obliged to respect those of almost every other sect, and the concessions which they would mutually find it both convenient and agreeable to make to one another, might in time probably reduce the doctrine of the greater part of them to that pure and rational religion, free from every mixture of absurdity, imposture, or fanaticism, such as wise men have in all ages of the world wished to see established.[43]

Smith did see that unleashing a competition among sects would fire the enthusiasm of sectarian leaders in some ways, but he thought it would also remove one great cause of resentment – the official backing that some sects had from the state. That resentment, he thought, was what fueled the worst sorts of fanaticism.

The crux of the matter, as Smith saw it, was that political rulers could not challenge the authority of religion directly, but instead had to learn to manage religion indirectly. Smith recognized that "the great interest" of the clergy was "to maintain their authority with the people" and that their authority rested ultimately on the validity

[42] Smith quotes Hume's argument on pp. 790–91. Cf. Hume, *History of England*, iii, 30–31.
[43] Also, "The teachers of each sect, seeing themselves surrounded on all sides with more adversaries than friends, would be obliged to learn that candour and moderation which is so seldom to be found among the teachers of those great sects, whose tenets being supported by the civil magistrate, are held in veneration by almost all the inhabitants." Smith, 793.

of the doctrine they taught. That doctrine concerned matters of eternal punishment, and Smith pointed out the consequences directly: "The authority of religion is superior to every other authority." Why? "The fears which it suggests conquer all other fears." Thus political sovereigns could wield their own authority only by learning how to manage and persuade the clergy into adopting a set of doctrines consistent with it; the alternative of trying to wield force against clergy would always lead to unintended negative consequences.[44] The strategy of allowing for and even promoting a multitude of sects, and competition among them, was part of this effort to manage religion and influence it indirectly.

Constant was more careful than Smith to distinguish between religious sentiment and what he thought of as its dogmatic and superstitious perversions. He praised pure religious feeling, which was linked to "all the noble, delicate, and deep passions," and argued that it was not those emotions but rather the fanatical ones that posed a threat to society. But having made this distinction, Constant closely followed Smith in thinking that the dangers of dogmatism were best addressed by allowing a multitude of small religious associations to compete for adherents: "This multitude of sects, of which some are so frightened, is precisely what is most healthy for religion. Its effect is that religion remains a feeling and does not become a mere formality, an almost mechanical habit, which unites itself with every vice and sometimes even with every sort of crime."[45] Constant suggested that when the possibility of creating a new sect was open, people tended to be more reflective about their religion, more likely to let it influence their morals rather than inflame their passions.

In answer to those who pointed out that the appearance of new sects had always been marked by conflict, Constant provided the now classic liberal response to those who ask why religion has so often been a source of violence: "It is because authority has meddled with it. Through its [authority's] voice, by its indiscreet action, the most trivial of differences, until then innocent and even useful, have

---

44 Smith, 797–99.
45 *PoP* (1815), 285. Etienne Hofmann suggests in his notes to the early version of this work that Constant may have adopted this argument from Adam Smith's similar point in *The Wealth of Nations*. See Smith, 792–94.

become seeds of discord."[46] Constant went on to argue that sovereigns would better achieve their own political goals with regard
to religion by adopting the indirect strategy that Smith had recommended than by attempting to directly influence religion:

> In opposing the multiplication of sects, governments misunderstand their
> own interests. When sects are very numerous in a country, they exercise
> mutual control and free the sovereign from the need to come to terms with
> any of them. When there is only a single dominant sect, power is forced to
> use a thousand stratagems in order to have nothing to fear from it. When
> there are only two or three of them, each sufficiently formidable to threaten
> the others, uninterrupted surveillance and repression become necessary.
> Strange expedient! You say that you want to maintain peace, and in order to
> secure this you prevent opinions from diverging in such a way as to divide
> men up into small, weak and virtually imperceptible groups.[47]

In this talk of dividing men and weakening the groups to which
they belong Constant revealed that his support for religious freedom
did not emerge from a respect for all religions or for all sorts of religion. In fact he preferred those sorts that relied less on group dynamics and that allowed more room for individual judgment. Like Smith,
he thought that government neutrality between various religious
sects was the best way to indirectly manage religion. The multiplication of sects that both authors encouraged represented a relatively
thin form of pluralism, as it aimed to create beneath the veneer of
diversity a shared style or spirit of religion. While Smith emphasized
the "pure" and even "rational" quality of the desired sort of belief,
Constant longed for a different sort of purity, that of sentiment.

The competition between sects does not fully account for the progressive path that Constant thought religion would take, however.
The multiplication of sects was just one mechanism that Constant
mentioned by way of trying to explain the larger phenomenon of
religious progress. In his lectures on religion he actually put the
emphasis not on this mechanism but on his understanding of history
itself. This understanding was drawn in part from liberal German
Protestant theologians' notion of "progressive revelation," a doctrine of historical progress that he called "the doctrine of religious

---

[46] *PoP* (1815), 286.
[47] Ibid., 286–87.

perfectibility."[48] And yet while the Germans would have located the ultimate source for progress in a divine cause, Constant's interpretation more often than not accented the very human "need of the soul," a nervous emptiness that would not rest content without finding some religious form in which to acknowledge something larger than oneself. Whatever the ultimate source of energy, the main point for Constant was that a general direction of progress could be discerned in the long history of religion, that this progress went more smoothly when the natural religious sentiments were left unfettered by authority, and that the implicit goal was a pure religion of personal sentiment.

REPRESENTATIVE GOVERNMENT, HISTORY, AND POLITICAL AGENCY

If it is true that Constant followed Adam Smith in thinking that the most effective way to exert a positive formative influence on the character of religious beliefs was to subject them to the sort of competition that religious freedom would introduce, then the apparent neutrality of representative government with regard to religion might in fact be seen as a strategy meant to shape religion indirectly. The reason that the strategy had to be indirect is that the campaign to shape citizens directly was precisely what representative government was designed to avoid. Representative government was first and foremost a program to limit government; in this way it differed fundamentally from both government by divine right and government justified by popular sovereignty. Representative government was limited because in claiming merely to *represent* society it refrained from claiming the right to *reform* society. The very idea of "representative" government suggests an activity of reflecting rather than one of reforming or ruling.

Representative government understood in this way can survive only if the forces in society – such as religion – allow themselves to be represented rather than seek to exercise rule for themselves. *Society* in the sense that it emerged with the birth of liberalism can

---

[48] See Constant, "Du développement progressif des idées religieuses." See also Helena Rosenblatt, *Liberal Values: Benjamin Constant and the Politics of Religion* (Cambridge: Cambridge University Press, 2008), chap. 5.

be understood as the set of practices and institutions that do not insist on exercising direct political rule for themselves. But how can religion be made a part of *society* understood in this sense? How can religion be made to relinquish its claim to direct political authority? Some strains of some religions seem to be in need of reform if they are to give up their claim to rule. The question that arises is who will do the work of reforming them. A representative government, defined as "representative" precisely by its unwillingness to engage in reform, cannot be the answer.

Constant evaded this dilemma as many early liberals did, by letting history do the work of reform through the competition among sects and also through the more diffuse process of spiritual development. The notion of historical progress promised that the emergence of a representative system of government could itself be understood as something representative rather than something imposed. No founder or Rousseauian lawgiver was necessary to give a people its institutions or to render it sociable. People were naturally sociable, and they would gradually come to express their sociability in institutions without the need for a reformer. The notion of historical progress is deeply affiliated with the notion of representative government; both are different ways of expressing an aspiration to escape the need for formative politics, the need for ruling and reforming, being ruled and being reformed.[49]

Still, the philosophical affinity between the idea of representative government and the impulse to grant agency to history does not adequately explain Constant's position, for he was more than a fan of representative government cheering from the sidelines of history. He regarded himself as a partisan of that form of government, an agitator anxious to be involved in politics and to institute and defend new liberal institutions and practices. As he boasted himself in the course of the lectures on religion, he wanted to defend the rights that he thought must come along with representative government, such as the right to a free press. He was also eager to be involved in the work of writing constitutions – even when doing so required him to

---

[49] *SCU*, 75: "The past has made itself without our assistance; nobody can claim the glory for it." And see also Benjamin Constant, *PoP* (1806), 369: "Institutions have to be created by the spontaneous motion of sentiments. For them to be powerful but not tyrannical, their origin must be lost in the night of time... They are useful as a heritage; they are merely oppressive when drafted as laws."

work with Napoleon, whom he had condemned. He actively rejected the influence of Catholic ultramonarchists instead of trusting their demise to the progress of history. His liberal project of rejecting the asserted authority of others was therefore as much a political program as the programs it rejected; his liberalism was not without its own partisan and reforming impulse. But his liberal platform was a particular sort of program, one designed to create a system resistant to the programs of others. Constant found it necessary to clear the path for history. He sought to eliminate the institutions and interests that diverted religion from its natural progress toward pure sentiment. Thus his stance was habitually oppositional rather than constructive; he often seemed to be suspicious of all authority.[50] In this style of political activity and commitment we can catch a glimpse of just how complex the liberal political stance of "neutrality" actually is in practice. The main theme of this sort of liberalism is neither an apathetic indifference to religion nor an indiscriminate respect for all forms of religiosity, but instead a deep commitment to creating the conditions under which religion can reform itself.

In presuming the need for "reform" Constant's thought was recognizably Protestant. The movement of thought and feeling brought about by the Reformation, in general, and by German Pietism, in particular, had already been headed in the direction of viewing religion as a private sentiment. Constant, together with de Staël, saw the advantages of such a movement for the new liberal politics of representative government. From the perspective of politics, what is important about religion understood as sentiment is that it is religious feeling disentangled from opinion and authority, unable to justify imposition on others. Once understood as private sentiment, religion was well on its way toward becoming a chosen facet of an individual's identity rather than an external source of authority – well on its way, that is, toward becoming a part of liberal society and therefore compatible with modern liberty.

The implication of Constant's approach is not that liberalism is only for Protestants, but rather that certain styles of religiosity may

---

[50] Pierre Manent characterizes Constant's position as a "liberalism of opposition." Pierre Manent, *An Intellectual History of Liberalism*, trans. Rebecca Balinski (Princeton: Princeton University Press, 1994), 84–92 (quoting the title of the chapter).

resonate especially well with the presuppositions of liberal politics. The habit of conceiving the source of transcendence as internal and sentimental rather than external and doctrinal, the value put on private judgment, the preference for moral over theological commitments, the aesthetic sensibility that emphasizes the importance of imagination and representation, the focus on self-development – all of these features of the religion that Constant admired were central to the spirit of liberal democracy as he understood it. Of course many of these features exist also in non-Protestant religions. The Catholic Jansenists, for example, were important supporters of liberalism in post-Revolutionary France, in part due to the emphasis they placed on private judgment.[51] Research into other religions and sects would find parallel movements that might be similarly well suited for liberal society.

On reflection we might wonder whether Constant left out certain traits of character that liberal citizens require. For example, can the religion of sublime sentiment that he endorses offer sufficient resources of self-discipline? But once we begin to ask such questions, we have already conceded to Constant the main point, which is that liberals should attend carefully to the varieties of religious experience, distinguishing among different sorts, with an eye not only to what provides social or moral stability, but also to which are most supportive of the habits of mind that citizens of liberal democracies need. Constant, one of the first writers to name and describe a theory of political "liberalism," was not content to remain veiled in ignorance about religion. He spent a lifetime of research attending closely to the content of various sorts of religion, and he rendered judgments about what sort of religion was best suited for liberals. He did not regard doing so as a departure from the sort of neutrality that liberalism requires. In fact, his support for government neutrality among religions was based squarely on his view about what sort of religion was most consonant with the spirit of liberalism and about the conditions under which that sort of religion would be most likely to emerge.

---

[51] Cheryl Welch, "Jansenism and Liberalism: The Making of Citizens in Post-Revolutionary France," *History of Political Thought*, 7 (Spring 1986): 151–65.

14 Constant and Religion: "Theism Descends from Heaven to Earth"

The aim of this essay is to complicate the standard picture of Constant as a "modern liberal" and as a proponent of what Isaiah Berlin famously called "negative liberty" by showing that from the beginning to the end of his life Constant's "liberalism" was always informed by religious values – mainly liberal Protestant ones but also ones which, since the late seventeenth century, have been associated with what was then called "philosophic theism."[1] Theism, as we shall later discuss, is a religious tradition that was just beginning to be discovered and understood as a tradition in the seventeenth and eighteenth centuries. Indeed, entries on theism in dictionaries and encyclopedias of the period are infrequent – which is why A. E. Taylor was right to remind twentieth-century readers of two things: that theism is a "purely modern" word, and that it was just beginning to be used as a neologism in French, German, and English religious discourse in the late seventeenth and eighteenth centuries.[2]

As we shall also see, the word came into vogue through the philosophical writings of Cudworth, Shaftesbury, Diderot, Voltaire, Rousseau, Hume, and above all, Kant. In their writings, it turns out that theism is linked to a conception of God in which providential considerations in a transcendental sense and ethical considerations in an immanent sense are conjoined – thought together in Kant's

---

[1] Ralph Cudworth, *The True Intellectual System of the Universe* (London: Richard Royston, 1678).
[2] A. E. Taylor, "Theism," in *Encyclopedia of Religion and Ethics*, ed. J. Hastings (New York: R. A. Kessinger Publishing Co., 1921), 261.

terms – to form a theological anthropology that makes moral perfection the purpose of human life.[3]

At an early age – between 1794 and 1804 – Constant can be seen writing about the relationship between religion and morality in theistic terms.[4] What is more, he does so while associating himself with the religious values of what he called the "new theism."[5] As he well knew, however, this new theism involved recovering values of a religious tradition that began with Plato and persisted in much pre-Christian and Christian religious thinking down to the time when the seventeenth-century Cambridge Platonists (e.g., Cudworth) began to use the word "theism" to designate the tradition they were trying to rehabilitate and modernize in the early days of what is now called the "Christian Enlightenment." In keeping with what the aforementioned thinkers wrote about theism, Constant called the tradition "philosophical theism" and allowed it, so I shall argue, to guide him on religious and moral matters his entire life.[6]

Complications regarding the interpretation of Constant as a liberal begin here, for it is well known that Constant did not live a religious life either in public or in private. Similarly, and like many liberal Protestants of his day, he never hesitated to criticize organized religions – Protestant as well as Catholic – for their many failings, including their dogmatism (e.g., on original sin), their intolerance of religious and philosophical dissent, and their inclination to align themselves with illiberal (i.e., throne and altar) political regimes throughout Europe.

---

[3] Immanuel Kant, *Religion and Rational Theology*, trans. Allen Wood and Goerge Di Giovanni (New York: Cambridge University Press, 1996).

[4] Frank Bowman, "Benjamin Constant, Germany, and *De La Religion*," *Romanische Forschungen*, 74 (1962), 77, notes Constant's early interest in the relationship between religion and morality. Helen Hogue, *Of Changes in Benjamin Constant's Books on Religion* (Geneva: Droz, 1964), chap. II, is helpful on the relationship between the two and on how the interplay between the two relates to the emergence of theism in Constant's early thinking.

[5] The phrase can be in a manuscript of 1794 that scholars often identify as "New System of Theism" (NST). The manuscript has been printed as an appendix in Patrice Thompson, *La Religion de Benjamin Constant: Les pouvoirs de l'image* (Pisa: Pacini editore, 1978), 543–51. It can also be found in Bowman, "Constant," 77–81. My citations to NST are to the former.

[6] See Constant, quoted in Hogue, 38–39.

And yet, by his own admission "religion" meant a lot to Constant,[7] which is why he devoted much of his life to studying the histories of Western religions in their fetishistic, polytheistic, and theistic stages. As we shall see, two themes were of special importance to him in this regard: the history of the transition in Greek religious thinking from polytheism to theism, and the circumstances surrounding the emergence of a "new system of theism" among liberal Protestants in Germany during the late eighteenth century. By that measure, Constant certainly was religious, but he expressed what religion meant to him in the form of historical arguments that we now know fit into an emerging tradition of liberal Protestant scholarship that not only studied pre-Christian and Christian religions historically and contextually,[8] but also regarded Greek religion in the philosophical key of theism as the moment when Western thinkers began to realize the importance of the connection between a "fitting" (i.e., moral and purified) conception of God and the moral perfection of humanity.[9] To paraphrase G. Simmel, liberal Protestants were religious people who proposed to save pure religion (i.e., inner religiosity) from institutionalized religion (i.e., positive religion) by defining piety in moral/ethical terms rather than in doctrinal/dogmatic ones.[10] In this, enlightened, tolerant, and

---

[7] For Constant's statements, see Dennis Wood, *Benjamin Constant: A Biography* (London: Routledge, 1993), 62, 112–13, 131.

[8] See Anthony Grafton, "Historical Thought in F. A. Wolf," in *Aufklärung und Geschichte: Studien zur deutschen Geschichtswissenschaft im 18. Jahrhundert*, ed. Hans Erich Bödeker et al. (Göttingen: Vandenhoeck & Ruprecht, 1986), and idem, "Prolegomena to F. A. Wolf," in *Defenders of the Text: The Traditions of Scholarship in an Age of Science, 1450–1800* (Cambridge: Harvard University Press, 1991), chap. 9, on the so-called mythological school of German historical interpretation.

[9] Students of Greek religion have identified the Greek idea of *theoprepes* – what is fitting/appropriate/seemly discourse for human discussion of God – as crucial to the progressive nature of Greek religious thinking between Xenophanes and Plato. See, e.g., Werner Jaeger, *The Theology of the Early Greek Philosophers*, trans. Edward Robinson (Oxford: Clarendon Press 1947), chap. III, and Walter Burkert, *Greek Religion: Archaic and Classical*, trans. John Raffan (Oxford: Basil Blackwell 1985), chap. VII. Seneca, *Moral Letters*, #95, offers a precise formulation: man "will never make sufficient [moral] progress until he has conceived a right [i.e., morally fitting] idea of God."

[10] Georg Simmel, *Essays on Religion*, ed. and trans. Horst Helle (New Haven: Yale University Press, 1997), 9, 11, 162. Liberal Protestants, in other words, are not content with pure inwardness – the religious fruit of the "first Reformation" –

anticlerical liberal Protestants, while certainly critical of what Kant called "ecclesiastical faith"[11] saw themselves less as antireligious thinkers than as heirs of the teachings of earlier Christians – certain Renaissance humanists, Platonizing and Stoicizing Protestants, and Erasmians (e.g., Bucer and Grotius)[12] – who minimized the dogmatic claims of the visible church and emphasized instead the practice of piety in a community of ethicoreligious fellowship (i.e., in what Kant called an "invisible church").[13]

The main contention of this essay is that when Constant's life is viewed against the backdrop of his lifelong study of religion, especially the parts that probed the relationship between religion and morality during various theistic moments in Western religious

for they insist that inner religiosity is a sentiment/disposition that demands ethical objectification in the world (the aim of the "Second Reformation"). Ernst Troeltsch, *Religion in History*, trans. James Adams and Walter Bense (Minneapolis: Fortress Press 1989), famously calls this the "dispositional ethic" of modern Protantism. As he says elsewhere (*Protestantism and Progress: A Historical Study of the Relation of Protestantism to the Modern World*, trans. W. Montgomery [London: Williams & Norgate, 1912], 206), this ethical disposition is the basis of a "religion of freedom" that makes human beings responsible for their religious and ethical lives. Strikingly (p. 183), he sees this ethic as arising from "a theism that has taken up into itself the idea of immanence." As I shall argue, Constant's notion of "improved Protestantism" (in George Ripley, *Philosophical Miscellanies*, [Boston: Hilliard, Gray, and Company, 1838], 311) anticipates key aspects of Troeltsch's – very liberal Protestant – later argument.

[11]   Kant, *Rational Theology*, 136ff, 262f. Ernst Cassirer, *Kant's Life and Thought*, trans. James Haden (New Haven: Yale University Press, 1981), 377–78, shows that Kant had developed opposition to positive religion as early as 1775. Ernst Cassirer, *The Question of Jean-Jacques Rousseau*, trans. Peter Gay (Bloomington, IN: University of Indiana Press, 1963), 71–73, links Kant to Rousseau on this. The latter, *On the Social Contract, with Geneva Manuscript and Political Economy*, ed. Roger Masters, trans. Judith Masters (New York: St. Martin's Press, 1978), 127–28, rejects the "empty ceremonial" of organized religion for what he calls the internality of "true theism."

[12]   There is a vast literature on this. For starters, see Peter Miller, *Peiresc's Europe: Learning and Virtue in the Seventeenth Century* (New Haven: Yale University Press, 2000), chap. 4; Hugh Trevor-Roper, "Hugo Grotius and England," in *From Counter-Reformation to Glorious Revolution* (Chicago: University of Chicago Press, 1992); and Margo Todd, *Christian Humanism and the Puritan Social Order* (New York: Cambridge University Press, 1987). All discuss the minimalist tradition with an eye to the Erasmian inspiration behind it. Troeltsch, *Progress*, 201, follows J. Semler in calling the theology of eighteenth-century German liberal Protestantism Erasmian. Karl Aner, *Die Theologie der Lessingzeit* (Halle: M. Niemeyer, 1929), esp. 50–51, follows Troeltsch in this. Both depend on Wilhelm Dilthey, *Selected Works*, vol. 4, ed. Rudolf Makkreel and Frithjof Rodi (Princeton, NJ: Princeton University Press, 1996), 49–50.

[13]   Kant, *Rational Theology*, 135, discusses the invisible church.

history, his liberalism can be shown to have deep roots in theism and late eighteenth-century Protestant (mainly, though not exclusively German) religious thinking.[14] As it so happens, Constant scholarship has been trying for years to incorporate the religious dimension of Constant's thinking into discussions of his liberalism. For example, J. Starobinski, G. Kelly, and J. Isbell have argued that Constant's commitment to Protestantism began early (in the 1790s), grew in breadth and sophistication as his knowledge of German religious scholarship expanded, and intensified in the 1820s as his fears about the demoralization of his world deepened.[15] Even more recently, J. Lee and H. Rosenblatt have demonstrated, respectively, how Constant's Protestantism shaped his doux-commerce liberalism as well as his political engagements with French Catholics over the course of a lifetime.[16] To this end, Lee and Rosenblatt join with the others in portraying Constant as a liberal Protestant who wished to open religion to the world and, by so doing, create what Constant called an "improved Protestantism" that would reform the world in a moral sense without abandoning the Platonic notion that God is the measure of moral things in a religious sense.

This, I shall argue, is what Constant thought "philosophical theism" helped him do – accommodate religion to the world without secularizing it (or, in his words, helped him bring theism "from heaven to earth").[17] For all that, Constant's theism has seldom figured in conventional discussions of his liberalism, for modern scholarship has consistently interpreted Constant as a secular thinker

---

[14] The Genevan Church of the eighteenth century produced many liberal-minded theologians. See, e.g., David Sorkin, "Geneva's 'Enlightened Orthodoxy'," in *Church History*, vol. 74 (2005); and M. Klauber and G. Sunshine, "Jean-Alphonse Turretini on Biblical Accommodation," in *Calvin Theological Journal*, vol. 25 (1990).

[15] Jean Starobinski, *Blessings in Disguise, or, the Morality of Evil*, trans. Arthur Goldhammer (Cambridge, MA: Harvard University Press, 1993); George Kelly, *The Humane Comedy: Constant, Tocqueville and French Liberalism* (New York: Cambridge University Press, 1992); and John Isbell, *The Birth of European Romanticism: Truth and Propaganda in Staël's De l'Allemagne, 1810–1813* (Cambridge: Cambridge University Press, 1994).

[16] James Lee, "Benjamin Constant: The Moralization of Modern Liberty," Ph.D. thesis, History Department, University of Wisconsin, Madison (2003); and Helena Rosenblatt, *Liberal Values: Benjamin Constant and the Politics of Religion* (Cambridge: Cambridge University Press, 2008).

[17] Throughout this chapter the idea of "accommodationism" is a constant theme. For a helpful introduction to the idea, see H. R. Niebuhr, *Christ and Culture*, chap. III. The quote concerning theism can be found in Ripley, *Miscellanies*, 315.

whose conception of modern liberty promoted a form of "self-reliant humanism" that stressed the freedom and moral autonomy of the individual and defined liberty in terms of the ever-expanding opportunities for self-realization that civil society furnished individuals.[18] To support this interpretation of Constant, scholars emphasize his obvious economic and political liberalism. At the same time, some Constant scholars now suggest that on the level of cultural values Constant embraced a form of individualism that was "romantic" in inspiration.[19]

As familiar as this portrait of Constant is, it hardly squares with the arguments he actually makes in his writings about modern liberty and civil society in the modern world. Take, for example, what he says in his famous 1819 address/essay entitled "The Liberty of the Ancients Compared with That of the Moderns" (AML).[20] In the first part of the essay, he carefully sets the argument for modern liberty in an historical framework that is governed by what scholars today call liberal doux-commerce considerations.[21] However, from what Constant says about modern liberty in the closing pages of the essay it is obvious that he is worried about two things: the moral future of modern civil societies, and the wisdom of expecting the demoralized and depoliticized citizens of civil society to somehow become willing agents of the kind of "moral elevation" that Constant deemed necessary to save modern society from self-destruction. Moreover, the language Constant uses at the end of AML – which constitutes an indictment of *doux-commerce* liberalism for its false

---

[18] As Niebuhr, *Christ*, 113, and in "foreword," to Ludwig Feuerbach, *The Essence of Christianity*, trans. George Eliot (New York, Harper, 1957), ix, would put it, "self-reliant humanism" is "humanism without theism." The latter is an "all-too-human humanism" according to Troeltsch, *Progress*, 206.

[19] The argument that Constant is a Romantic hinges on the notion that he held a view of what Gerald Izenberg, *Impossible Individuality: Romanticism, Revolution, and the Origins of Modern Selfhood, 1787–1802* (Princeton, NJ: Princeton University Press, 1992), 23, calls the "infinity of the self." That self is unconditioned and is encouraged spiritually to express itself any way it chooses. That is not Constant's self.

[20] Page citations in the narrative refer to AML, in *PW*, 309–28.

[21] On *doux-commerce*, see Albert Hirschman, *Rival Views of Market Society and Other Essays* (New York: Viking, 1986), 106–9. I have discussed the concept and the historiography in Dickey, "Appendix IV," in Adam Smith, *The Wealth of Nations*, ed. Laurence Dickey (Indianapolis: Hackett, 1993), and in "*Doux-Commerce* and Humanitarian Values," in *Grotiana*, vol. 22–23 (2001–2).

moral promise about the future – introduces into the discussion of modern liberty religious and religiomoral considerations that had long been connected in Constant's mind with the religious outlook being articulated by liberal Protestants in Germany at the end of the eighteenth century. If this is the case – and it decidedly is – then it becomes difficult on the face of it to continue to interpret Constant as a modern secular liberal, for the liberal Protestant tradition with which he identified from at least 1794 on can be interpreted as secular only if the moral values of theists in general and of liberal Protestants in particular are defined beforehand as ideological masks that Protestants used to conceal their "bourgeois" secular identities.[22]

Of course, this kind of reductionism is on display in many modern studies of the intellectual history of Christianity during the Enlightenment. And, as I shall argue, it is a definite problem in the interpretation of Constant as a liberal, for when he appeals in AML to "heaven" (p. 327) to support his moral elevation/moral perfection argument, he knowingly inserts a religiomoral purposefulness into his discussion of modern liberty that is at once theological and teleological. The argument is theological because, as his religious writings reveal, the initiative for purposefulness comes from above – from a transcendental source that (like Rousseau, Lessing, Kant, Herder, and Hegel before him) he variously called God or Providence or the divinely ordained plan for the moral education of the human race. On that score, it is difficult to argue that moral purposefulness is "natural" to man in any secular sense. The argument is teleological because even though human beings pursue ends of their own choosing, the idea that moral purpose is an imperative for mankind – its "end" and "destiny" – calls into question the notion of man's moral autonomy and the unconditioned, open-ended, and criterionless quality of his efforts at self-realization. Indeed, in AML, man is

---

[22] Although Barth is not a reductionist in a Marxian sense, he treats liberal Protestantism of the eighteenth century as an expression of "bourgeois" interests. See Karl Barth, *Protestant Thought in the Nineteenth Century* (Valley Forge: Judson, 1973), chap. III. Before Marx and Engels had done so, Saint-Simon, "New Christianity," in *Social Organization, the Science of Man and Other Essays*, ed. and trans. Felix Markham (New York: Harper & Row, 1964), 108, had talked about "improved Protestantism" in reductionist terms. He uses the phrase in 1825, linking it to the "famous philosophers" of liberal Protestantism in northern Germany (p. 107). Constant's usage of the phrase in 1826 may be a response to Saint-Simon.

called to a destiny of moral perfection by means of an argument that involves fulfilling a specific telos that is part of a providential plan for man's religious salvation.[23] For this reason, we need to ask what kind of liberal is Constant if he insists on locating the initiative for moral purpose in an ethical Providence exercised by God over man and on grounding his call for moral elevation in a purposefulness that has a transcendent teleology infigured in it?[24] In addition, we need to ask, does the idea of ethical Providence register Constant's confusion over the matter of whether God or man has the initiative in the divine–human relationship? Is he just expressing the general confusion of a period of historical transition in which liberal Protestant thinkers – in the mode of the so-called compromise theology of accommodationists[25] – oscillate between religious (i.e., world-denying) and secular (i.e., world-affirming) ways of explaining moral purpose in the world? Is he recoiling from his own liberalism or enlarging liberalism by respiritualizing it in the face of a deteriorating moral situation in

---

[23] Mona Ozouf, "Liberty," in *Dictionary of the French Revolution*, ed. François Furet and Mona Ozouf, trans. Arthur Goldhammer (Cambridge: Harvard University Press, 1989), and Quentin Skinner, "The Idea of Negative Liberty," in *Philosophy in History: Essays on the Historiography of Philosophy*, ed. Richard Rorty, Jerome Schneewind, and Quentin Skinner (Cambridge: Cambridge University Press, 1984), explain why teleology in an ethical sense and liberalism are often at loggerheads with each other. Alasdair MacIntyre, *After Virtue: A Study of Moral Theory* (Notre Dame, IN: University of Notre Dame Press, 1981), chap. 5, presets teleology as an alternative to the "modern" thinking of the Enlightenment. Of special importance for us here is that he (pp. 50–53) links teleology to "theistic" theology. That will be our strategy too.

[24] Infiguration involves eliminating something outwardly but preserving it inwardly. For examples of the argument, see Meyer Abrams, *Natural Supernaturalism: Tradition and Revolution in Romantic Literature* (New York: Norton, 1971), esp. 201, and Louis Green, *Chronicle into History: An Essay on the Interpretation of History in Florentine Fourteenth-Century Chronicles* (Cambridge: Cambridge University Press, 1972), 122, 130, 143. In Christopher Dawson's words (*Progress and Religion* [New York] 1934, 190), "Over-ruling Providence . . . [is] desupernaturalized and fitted into [a] rational scheme of contemporary philosophy . . . that could not divest itself of the Christian teleological conception of life."

[25] Ernst Troeltsch, *The Social Teaching of the Christian Churches*, vol. 2, trans. Olive Wyan (New York: The Macmillan Company, 1931), 999ff, claims that "compromise" becomes essential for early Christianity following the "delay" of the "Second Coming." Anders Nygren, *Agape and Eros*, trans. Philip Watson (London: Society for Promoting Christian Knowledge, 1953), 231, bemoans the emergence of this "compromise" theology and relates it to the accommodationism of Christian humanism throughout the ages.

Europe? Or, as I shall argue, is Constant articulating an in-between position that is consistent with the religious and moral outlook of theism?

To begin to answer these questions, and to avoid the conceptual pitfall of reductionism mentioned previously, it is worth noting that students of Western religious history have developed several conceptual distinctions that address the in-between quality of theistic thinking: that between the humanizing and secularizing of religious values; that between theocentric and anthropocentric humanism; and that which sees the seeming opposition between transcendental and immanent conceptions of God as being balanced in "dipolar" theism.[26] It is with distinctions such as these that we can begin to interpret Constant as a liberal thinker who, while turning toward the world in an anthropocentric sense, nevertheless insisted on retaining God as the measure of moral things in a theocentric sense.

To be more specific, the challenge facing us is to decide what Constant is doing – saying about the divine–human relationship – when in AML he uses a combination of religious and moral language to

---

[26] For the three distinctions, see Eric Voegelin, *The New Science of Politics* (Chicago: University of Chicago, 1952), 119; Werner Jaeger, *Humanism and Theology, under the Auspices of the Aristotelian Society of Marquette University* (Milwaukee, WI: Marquette University Press, 1943), 47; and Charles Hartshorne, *A Natural Theology for Our Time*, (LaSalle, IL: Open Court Press, 1967), 126. In addition, see the entries on "theism" and "transcendence and immanence" in the *Encyclopedia of Religion*, 2nd ed., and on "immanence," "theism," and "transcendence" in Van Austin Harvey, *Handbook of Theological Terms* (New York: Macmillan, 1964). The entries all stress the "balance" orientation of theism. Charles Trinkaus, *In Our Image and Likeness: Humanity and Divinity in Italian Humanist Thought*, vol. 1 (London: Constable 1970), 174–75, works the balance between transcendence and immanence into his interpretation of the religious views of Renaissance humanists. Also see Troeltsch's statements on the connection between immanentization as a religious process and the humanization of Christianity, in *Gesammelte Schriften*, vol. 4 (Tübingen, 1925), 293–94. For Troeltsch, however, there are degrees of immanentization. In theism, immanentization stops with humanization, recoiling from the kind of secularization of an "all-too-human humanism" mentioned previously (note 18). The recoil argument involves keeping man connected up with God. That is what theocentric humanism always maintains. R. Blutmann, "Humanism and Christianity," *The Journal of Religion*, 32 (1952), 80–81, links "genuine autonomy" to a "freedom" that finds fulfillment in God. By contrast, the kind of autonomy that "delivers" man from God produces only a "hollow" (i.e., secular) freedom. Otto Pfleiderer, "Religionless Morality," *American Journal of Theology*, 3 (1899), 250, contrasts a "godless autonomy" and a "true" one "which is bound in God."

exhort human beings to make moral perfection their "sacred" duty and "destiny" (pp. 327–28). Does the ideal of moral perfection to which Constant asks human beings to aspire entail compartmental-izing religion so that while man's dignity lies in his divine origins, that dignity is achieved in a world in which God has permitted him to be, in Cudworth's words, the "executioner" of the divine will?[27] If this is the case, then two things come into play: First, it would seem that Constant grants man relative not absolute autonomy in moral matters. And second, he seems to separate religion and morality less to uphold the moral autonomy of anthropocentric humanism than to set the terms for a divine–human cooperation in which religion and morality "supplement" each other in a Kantian sense.[28] That, it just so happens, is what philosophic theists, including Kant, had been arguing for since Plato. And it is what Constant pushes for in his religious writings from 1794 on. It is to those writings that we shall now turn to confirm this thesis.

MORAL PURPOSE AND "IMPROVED PROTESTANTISM" IN CONSTANT'S RELIGIOUS WRITINGS

Introduction: Setting an Ideological Context for the Religious Writings

As is relatively well known, Constant's *doux-commerce* liberalism holds that commerce, by providing individuals with new and expand-ing opportunities for earning a living, creates a realm of liberty – des-ignated as civil society by Hegel – in which individuals are encour-aged to pursue their interests, to enjoy the fruits of their labor, and

---

[27] Cudworth, *True System*, chap. V. In *Timaeus*, 46, 90, Plato talks this way. Accord-ing to Cicero, *On the Good Life*, trans. Michael Grant (New York: Penguin, 1971), 57, and Seneca, *Moral Letters*, 71, Socrates serves this purpose when he brings philosophy "down from the heavens." The language Seneca uses to describe how man "is stirred by a force from heaven" (*Moral Letters*, 41) can be attached to Jesus as well as to Socrates. That, of course, is the point for Christian humanists (cf. note 82).

[28] Kant, *Rational Religion*, 268, links this kind of divine–human cooperation to the idea of a "supplement" that helps men become "pleasing to God." Such cooperation is a main theme of Kant's *Religion within the Boundaries*, a text that greatly influenced Constant. See, e.g., Kant, *Rational Religion*, 106, 121, on the descent of the "divine disposition" (i.e., the principle of goodness) into the world from above.

to do so independent of the supervision of public authorities. Thus, in AML, Constant states that commercial expansion has produced the kind of "modern liberty" that citizens enjoy in a civil society – a liberty that increases the "happiness" of individuals and guarantees "the rights and enjoyment" of "individual independence" and "private pleasures," even when the independence is antisocial and the pleasures are considered "gross" (pp. 316–17, 326–27).[29] In AML, however, Constant calls into question the very idea that "personal happiness" (p. 316) should be the measure of modern liberty. His argument is twofold: (1) that the commercial process that has produced so much material prosperity and personal happiness has also led to the privatization of liberty and to the depoliticization of citizenship, and (2) that in the face of what the ancients from Solon and Plato to Sallust and Seneca termed "overmuch prosperity,"[30] modern citizens not only had abandoned moderation for acquisitiveness (*sophrosyne* for *pleonexia* for the Greeks), but had also begun to equate being civilized with indulgence in the refined pleasures of luxurious living.[31] Lacking a sense of moderation – that is, an appreciation of what A. O. Lovejoy called the ancients' "wisdom of not wanting"[32] – modern citizens had made their material possessions rather than their moral achievements the measure of happiness, with the result that self-regarding egoism rather than sacrifice for the common good defined life in civil (i.e., bourgeois) society (pp. 323–24).

In the closing paragraphs of AML, Constant argues that this measure of happiness "demean[s]" and "abase[s]" mankind (p. 327). He claims, moreover, that insofar as modern liberty identifies happiness as its "end" (p. 326), it fails to provide humanity with a higher moral purpose in life. At the same time, it squanders "a treasure of moral

---

[29] According to Ozouf, "Liberty," this is one of the two forms of liberty vying for control of the French Revolution after 1789. She works Constant into the argument on p. 726.

[30] For the Solon to Plato sequence, see Jean-Pierre Vernant, *The Origins of Greek Thought* (Ithaca, NY: Cornell University Press, 1982), chap. 6. Also see Sallust's famous opening to *The Conspiracy of Catiline* and Seneca's *Moral Letters*, 39, 91.

[31] See Voltaire, in *Commerce, Culture and Liberty: Readings on Capitalism before Adam Smith*, ed. Henry Clark (Indianapolis, IN: Liberty Fund, 2003), 265–75.

[32] Arthur Lovejoy, *Primitivism and Related Idea in Antiquity* (New York: Octagon, 1980), 11.

riches" inherited from the ancients.[33] It is here that Constant denies that happiness should be the "aim of mankind" (p. 327). To underscore the point, he uses language that contrasts the "narrow" aims of happiness with the way having a sense of moral purpose "enlarges" the human spirit (p. 327). In addition, he speaks of how moral purpose "elevates" and "ennobles" mankind and points humanity in the direction of its "destiny" and most "sacred interests" (pp. 327–28). All the more important is the fact that Constant links the moral purpose argument to what he calls the "perfectibility" of the "better part of our nature" (p. 327).[34]

At the end of AML, then, Constant can be seen separating happiness and morality in order to introduce into the discussion of modern liberty questions about man's purpose and potential for moral perfectibility. As he does this, he works the idea of perfectibility into an argument whose aim is to decouple morality from happiness. Others before him – Rousseau as well as Kant, Schiller, Herder, and Hegel – had written about the need for modern citizens to form themselves – through *Bildung* – to a higher moral end.[35] By so doing, they argued, civil society might be saved from what Schiller called the "wounds it had inflicted upon itself" and what Kant called the "glittering misery" it had produced for itself.[36] Constant, it seems to me, is writing in that tradition at the end of AML. But he had been writing this way long before 1819 and he would continue to write this way throughout the 1820s, which explains why moral perfectibility is a main topic in Constant's early (1794–1806) and later (1824–29) writings.

In what follows, I wish to demonstrate at least four things: that perfectibility is a religious idea that, for Constant, is governed by an ethical Providence; that it operates through his famous idea of "religious sentiment"; that it is the driving force behind the distinctions

---

[33] Constant makes the claim in *SCU*, 74.

[34] Fontana, *PW*, 327, uses "self-development" to translate *perfectionnement*. I prefer perfectibility.

[35] In doing this, all are trying to separate morality from happiness. Constant, as we shall see, follows them in this. See Friedrich Schiller, *Naïve and Sentimental Poetry*, trans. Julius Elias (New York: F. Ungar, 1966), 100, for an example of the "happiness" to "perfection" argument.

[36] Friedrich Schiller, *On the Aesthetic Education of Man*, ed. Elizabeth Wilkenson and L. Willoughby (Oxford: Clarendon Press, 1967), 33 (Letter #6); Immanuel Kant, *Political Writings*, ed. H. Reiss, trans. H. Nisbet (Cambridge: Cambridge University Press, 1991), 49, 231.

Constant makes between "religious form" and "religious sentiment" and between "external" and "internal" perfection; and that the former distinction provides the organizing principle for writing an "accommodationist" theology of history in which religion is a progressive force in the moral education of the human race.

Historicizing the Ideas of Religious Sentiment and Moral Perfectibility

Let us begin with a text – "On Religious Liberty" (ORL)[37] – that was published in 1815 but that existed in manuscript form as early as 1806. In this text, we see the outlines of the argument Constant makes in the closing paragraphs of AML. He begins ORL with a self-serving and deliberately "vague" definition of what he means by "religious sentiment" (pp. 279, 277). Among other things, he tells us, religion in general and religious sentiment in particular are the "most natural of our emotions." (Feelings, passions, sensations, convictions, and faculties are other terms he uses in the essay [pp. 277, 282].) He then links religious sentiment – like Rousseau and Kant had before him – to a broad range of "noble" and uplifting human activities such as "sacrifice" for others, "generosity," "courage," "love," and so on (pp. 277–78). In addition, and throughout the text, he connects religious sentiment to "moral feelings" and "moral sense," arguing that religion and morality can work together to "elevate" and promote the "dignity of the human species" (pp. 277–79, 283). His point, which pervades the argument of AML as well, is that religion is a "primitive" force in our nature, one which, when allowed freely to develop, expresses itself in "contempt for vice" and "hatred of tyranny"; directs us toward "virtuous action"; opposes "our egoism"; and exhorts us to "step beyond the narrow circle of . . . petty [and ignoble] material interests" (pp. 277–78). In this, he sees religious sentiment directing us "to detach ourselves from ourselves" as we learn the lesson that "perfection [of our moral selves] is worth more than we are [as merely physical selves]" (p. 278).[38]

---

[37] ORL is chapter 17 of Constant's PoP (1815). I use the translation in Fontana, PW, 274–89. Page references in my text are to that translation.

[38] In Western intellectual history the move from "preservation to perfection" is generally regarded as a Stoic argument. Much of the argument is organized around

Because he is so keen on connecting religious sentiment with morality (p. 283), Constant stresses how important "religious toleration" is to man's moral well-being (pp. 275–77). His argument here is that intolerance on the part of religious authorities and civil intolerance of religion on the part of "enlightened" thinkers (i.e., some of the *philosophes*) have combined to "stifle" the establishment of a cooperative nexus between religion and morality among men, with the result that religious persecution by "dogmatic religion" on the one hand and by "irreligious" philosophers on the other has produced a situation in the modern world in which "religion . . . loses its influence on morality" precisely because it is forced to "isolate" itself from public life (pp. 278–79, 285, 287).[39] Constant wishes to change that, not so much for the purpose of enlisting religion in the service of "power" or "usefulness" as for opening the way to the kind of moral elevation he called for at the end of AML (pp. 283–84). In ORL, then, Constant is seeking "a positive goal" to which religious sentiment might attach itself; and he is offering at this point the abstraction of "elevated morality" – moral "perfection", he also says – as a specific end for religion, given the deteriorating moral situation in France at the beginning of the nineteenth century (pp. 283, 278).

As Constant scholarship has recently made clear, Constant began to give his full attention to the relationship between religion and morality while studying Greek religion (through the eyes of German scholars) between 1794 and 1804.[40] And from what he tells us in ORL about the idea of religious sentiment it is apparent that by 1806 religious sentiment is playing a key role for him in turning

the idea of *oikeiosis*. That idea produces a view of man that emphasizes his double nature and stresses that human morality evolves with experience over time. Rousseau, Kant, and Schiller offer versions of the double-nature argument. I briefly discuss *oikeiosis* in "Humanitarian Values."

39 An important difference between what German scholars (e.g., Troeltsch, *Progress*, 201) call "old" and "new" Protestantism is relevant here. The latter is said to be "Enlightened" and "liberal" because it has a practical and ethical communal focus. As I have noted (Dickey, *Hegel*, [NY, 1987] and "Saint-Simon Industrialism as the End of History," in *Apocalypse Theory and the Ends of the World*, ed. Malcolm Bull [Oxford: Blackwell, 1995]), the distinction often takes the form of a "first" and "second" Reformation argument. Constant discusses the two Reformations argument in *NST*, 546. The second Reformation argument fits into the "dispositional ethic" argument discussed in note 10. The combination of the two Reformations argument produces the "religion of freedom" argument.

40 Hogue, *Constant's Books*, chap. II, has the basic information. Constant lived in Germany for extended periods of time: 1782–83, 1788–94, 1804–5, and 1811–14.

human beings away from "narrow" and "petty material interests" and toward higher moral ideals (pp. 277–78, 287). But Constant's historical sense of time and place, to which his reading of Scottish and German scholarship had contributed, impressed on him how historical circumstances as well as institutional obstacles (e.g., the priesthood) often stood in the way of religious and moral cooperation (pp. 278–83). Realizing this, Constant begins to historicize the idea of religious sentiment in two senses. On the one hand, he makes it less of an abstraction by setting it over and against positive religious institutions and dogmas at specific moments in history.[41] On the other hand, he gives it an ethicoreligious content that could only be realized gradually in history. So, given what we have seen Constant invest in religious sentiment as a force of moral progress, it cannot be surprising to see him, in the 1794–1806 period, begin to link the idea of religious sentiment to the idea of moral perfectibility – which is why Kurt Kloocke is correct when he argues that Constant's notion of religious sentiment must be understood more as a disposition – as a moral tendency – that points humanity in the direction of its moral destiny, than as a "feeling."[42] That is the move Constant makes in 1804 in order to differentiate his position from the kind of individualism we see in old Protestantism and in Romanticism.

We know, of course, that Constant had been interested in perfectibility long before the 1804–6 period.[43] And we know how important perfectibility is to the moral argument at the end of AML. Fortunately, we have a text (and some other fragments of that text) that Constant scholars date to the 1804–6 period, which helps us understand the interplay of religious sentiment, perfectibility, and moral elevation in his thinking around this time.

[41] Scholars (e.g., Lee, "Constant," and Kelly, *Comedy*) have shown how this distinction came to Constant's attention from multiple sources: Wieland, Kant, Necker, and de Staël. It is also a prominent theme in Gillis whom Constant translated in 1787.

[42] Kurt Kloocke, "Johann Gottfried Herder et Benjamin Constant," in *ABC*, 29, (2005). Although I cannot elaborate here, it should be noted that the German words *Anlage, Gefuhl, Gesinnung, Geist*, and *Gemut*, which are close in meaning to what Constant means by sentiment, all have the moral tendency argument in them. Constant's German sources, especially Kant, Herder, and Schiller, use these words with this tendency in mind. The tendency re-enforces the double-nature argument mentioned in note 38.

[43] In the early 1800s, de Staël and Villers, two of Constant's intimate friends, wrote about the Germans and the idea of perfectibility.

If this text – entitled "On the Perfection of the Human Race" (PHR)[44] – is examined closely, we discover that Constant is working in this essay with themes already familiar to us from ORL. He starts by asking two rhetorical questions: does a "tendency to perfection" exist in man, and if so, "what is the cause of this tendency" (p. 348)? To begin to answer his own questions, Constant divides human experience into two classes: "physical" sensations and "ideas" (pp. 348–49). The latter, he argues, constitutes "the thinking part of our nature" (p. 349). By means of ideas, he continues, human beings form "a world within" themselves that is "altogether independent of the external world" (p. 349). To explain the tendency toward perfectibility, he then declares, one needs to show that over time "ideas" gradually begin to "govern" or "steer" (dirigent) man toward a destiny beyond mere sense experience (pp. 352–54). For as the actions of human beings come progressively under the control of ideas, man gradually becomes "master of himself" from a point "within" his "mind" – that is, from the thinking part of his nature (pp. 353–54).[45]

For Constant, the point of establishing "the supremacy of ideas over sensations" is to give man access to his true self (le moi), something that is achieved when man awakens to, and gains insight into, his own "essence" (pp. 353–54). Even more telling, Constant introduces this claim by referring – as Herder before him had – to Socrates as the thinker who not only brought philosophy from "heaven to...earth"[46] but also assigned philosophy the task of awakening the inner self to its "moral" dignity and destiny (pp. 353–54).[47]

---

[44] References to PHR are to the translation found in Ripley, *Miscellanies*, 346–68. Page citations in my text are to that translation.

[45] Self-mastery is a Platonic idea. Charles Taylor, *Sources of the Self* (Cambridge, MA: Harvard University Press, 1989), chap. 6, explains.

[46] Herder's view of Socrates (in *Outlines of a Philosophy of the History of Man*, trans. T. Churchill (New York: Bergman Publishers, 1966), 102; in *Reflections on the Philosophy of the History of Man*, ed. Frank Manuel (Chicago: University of Chicago Press, 1968), 197–98; and in *On World History*, ed. Hans Adler and Ernest Menze, trans. Ernest Menze with Michael Palma (Armonk, NY: M. E. Sharpe, 1997), 108, which depicts him as a "pattern" for true humanity, anticipates the "axial" argument of Otto and Jaspers discussed later in this essay. Seneca, *Moral Letters*, 65, credits Plato with having linked "the idea of man," personified in Socrates, with that of "humanity."

[47] Francis Cornford, *Before and After Socrates* (Cambridge: Cambridge University Press, 1962), stresses the importance of separating Socrates's ethical view of purpose from the merely naturalistic one espoused by pre-Socratic and Sophistic thinkers.

But Constant engages in a major qualification of his argument here, for before the thinking part of man can begin to direct him toward moral perfection, man's powers of reason and reflection as well as his knowledge of the world (i.e., science) must first be improved. (Like everything else for Constant, knowledge, including the capacity for reflection, is historically conditioned [pp. 352–53, 362–63].) According to Constant, therefore, the tendency of the "human mind" toward progress unfolds on "internal and external [levels] of perfection" (p. 356). "[E]xternal perfection," he argues, has to do with the institutional, technological, and scientific advances of "civilization" (pp. 356–58). By contrast, "internal perfection" has to do with "moral perfection" and the emergence of an internal "disposition" to "sacrifice" empirical pleasures for moral ones (pp. 356, 351, 355).

In this context, PHR is noteworthy for several reasons, not the least of which has to do with Constant's identification of Socrates as the personification of an immanentizing force in history that delivers religious sentiment to humanity in the form of moral self-consciousness. In this context, Constant's main concern in PHR is with the moral implications of the movement of civilization from "sensation to ideas." Before Constant, Herder (among others) had used such a sequence to show how human history unfolded naturally and in terms of the development of humanity's capacity for rational thinking. But as Friedrich Meinecke has observed, Herder also insisted on linking the development of rationality to a divine initiative that works its way into the world through Providence, with the result that human self-realization involves rational and religious fulfillment at the same time.[48] For Constant, Socrates personified that religiophilosophical way of explaining human purpose in the world.[49]

Much in PHR mirrors aspects of Herder's earlier thinking, which, of course, is why Constant wished to translate Herder's work on perfectibility into French in 1805. But for our purposes here the sensation to idea sequence in Constant also anticipates the separation of

---

[48] For Herder, see Friedrich Meineke's wonderful chapter on him, in *Historism: the Rise of a New Historical Outlook*, trans. J. Anderson (New York: Herder and Herder, 1972).

[49] For this reason, the Germans regarded the Greek philosophical awakening as paradigmatic for Western thought. See, e.g., Herder, *Reflections*, 197–98.

happiness and morality in AML, for at a key point in PHR, Constant uses the idea of "internal" perfection to push his argument about moral perfection in a direction that moves beyond the state of civilization he has linked to merely external perfection. This suggests that PHR is historicizing perfectibility in a way that allows Constant to begin to moralize perfectibility after he has acquiesced in the external perfection of modern civilization. In both cases and in both texts, moreover, we see Constant using the idea of perfectibility to separate civilization from nature on the one hand (external perfection) and to separate moral perfection from civilization on the other (internal perfection).

As is well known, in the late eighteenth century many famous German thinkers (as well as Rousseau) discussed perfectibility this way.[50] For them, this kind of thinking was at once religious in a liberal Protestant sense and progressive in a moral sense. In the 1790s and early 1800s, Constant, as well as his intimate friends, Villers and de Staël, agreed with the Germans in this, arguing to French audiences that Protestantism was in the philosophical vanguard of religious and moral progress in Europe.[51] As Constant himself said at the time, the Germans realized that the progressive nature of the new Protestant theology lay in knowing that things religious were subject to time and, therefore, had to be studied historically and contextually. To that end, the Germans of the Aufklarung began to study religion – including a people's changing conception of gods/God – in terms of the time and place of its production. Like Fontenelle, Vico, and Hume, the Germans carried out their research within an historical framework that moved along a civilizational scale that ran from primitive to civilized. But instead of acquiescing in the elimination of religion from human life as civilization advanced – as, say, Hume thought should be the case[52] – the Germans fixated on those moments in human history when religious and moral values accommodated themselves to each other, producing the kind of

---

[50] For Rousseau, see Cassirer, Question, 75–78, 125–26. Kant, Political Writings, 49, 227–28, explicitly follows Rousseau on this. Kant writes there of man's moral destiny, of his double nature, and of how a "disposition" to moral maturity drives man toward his telos.

[51] Isbell, Romanticism, is most informative on this.

[52] David Hume, The Natural History of Religion, ed. H. Root (Stanford: Stanford University Press, 1956), esp. 70–76.

philosophical theism that Constant saw as the key to religious and moral progress in the world.

"Religious Form" and "Religious Sentiment" in the "Famous Doctrine of Accommodation"

As early as the 1820s, even before the so-called Tübingen School began to turn the study of religion in Germany and Europe in an historical direction, British Protestants had identified the Germans in general and J. S. Semler (1725–91) in particular as the scholarly force behind what they called the "famous [religious] doctrine of Accommodation."[53] Much that Constant says about religion, it turns out, especially about the notions of religious sentiment and moral perfectibility, had been shaped by this doctrine. We need to, therefore, understand how the doctrine came to Constant's attention and to why it manifests itself in his writings from the beginning to the end of his career as a religious thinker.

As students of the history of Christianity well know, accommodationism had been a technical term of biblical and historical exegesis among Christians long before eighteenth-century liberal Protestant humanists in Germany began to organize their new theism around it.[54] We have evidence that Constant had remarked on this doctrine as early as 1794 (NST, pp. 545–46, 550), which is when he began to align himself with the new theism of Protestantism and when he credited it with the breakthrough historical notion that religion, especially its doctrines, was subject to time.[55]

But, as Anthony Grafton has noted, it was not just students of Christian history who used the idea of accommodationism in their

---

[53] On this, see Thomas Arnold, *Sermons*, vol. 2 (London: B. Fellows, 1851), 383ff; Hugh Rose, *State of Protestantism in Germany Described*, 2nd ed. (London: Rivington, 1829), 74; and C. Wordsworth, "On the Interpretation of Scripture," in *Replies to 'Essays and Reviews'* (New York: Appleton, 1862), 407.

[54] Stephen Benin, *The Footprints of God: Divine Accommodation in Jewish and Christian Thought* (Albany, NY: State University of New York Press, 1993), and Amos Funkenstein, *Theology and the Scientific Imagination* (Princeton, NJ: Princeton University Press, 1986), are excellent on the history of accommodationism in pre-Christian and Christian thought. With regard to the latter, the tradition starts in the second century. Constant in 1829 states that St. Paul was an accommodationist (see Constant, in Ripley, *Miscellanies*, 345).

[55] As Overbeck and Barth will later argue, subjecting religion to time is the key flaw in liberal Protestantism.

work.[56] F. A. Wolf (1759–1824), for example, one of the key sources
Constant used in the early 1800s to understand Greek religion, used
the idea to explain how the Greeks had moralized/ethicized their
gods between Homer and Plato. To that end, Wolf showed how Xenophanes (ca. 500 B.C.E), among others, initiated an ethical rebellion
against Homer's (and the poets') "unseemly" (indecore) representations of the gods and, in the process, produced a theology organized
around the idea of what R. Otto once described as rational theism.[57]
As Wolf notes, certain educated Greeks followed Xenophanes in
accusing Homer of "impiety" because of the "absurd," "ridiculous,"
and "false" things he had said about "the nature of the gods." They
also criticized him for what he said about how the gods govern
human life. At the same time, Wolf says, these philosophers began
"to correct" Homer's false religious conceptions by "accommodat-
ing" (accommodare) his representations of the gods to "the moral
doctrines of their own [more civilized] age." For Wolf, then, accommodationism explains what happened among the Greeks when
"sacred" things (e.g., gods, books, and traditions) are found to be
"inconsistent with true wisdom and good morals" of a later age.[58]

At its core, the doctrine of accommodationism presupposes
several things that are on constant display in Constant's religious
writings. First, and as we previously saw, the doctrine operates with
the assumption that all religions are subject to time. Second, it
interprets religious representations as products of culture, history,
and the progress of human mind, which means religion is affected by
and affects forces in a society that are not strictly religious in nature.
Third, accommodationism holds that during the civilizing process
previously accepted, religious representations will begin to be – in
words Constant used in 1794 – "adapted" or "proportioned" to new
and emerging "sentiment[s]" about what constituted the "dignity
of man" (NST, pp. 544–46). Finally, the doctrine presupposes that

---

[56] Grafton, in F. A. Wolf, *Prolegomena to Homer*, ed. Anthony Grafton (Princeton,
NJ: Princeton University Press, 1985), 150n. For the references to Wolf in this
paragraph, see Wolf in Grafton's edition.

[57] Rudolf Otto, *Religious Essays*, trans. Brian Lunn (London: Oxford University Press,
1931), 98.

[58] Kant, *Rational Theology*, 267, says the same thing with regard to Christianity. Dilthey, *Works*, vol. 4, 90–94, explains what is at stake in Kant's embrace of accommodationism.

during what Constant called "epoch[s] of disproportion,"[59] religion would continually be brought – again in words Constant later used – "into a just and salutary agreement with the contemporaneous ideas of every epoch,"[60] with the result that religion can be said, as Kant also appreciated, to "keep pace with [the advance of human] intelligence" throughout history.[61] Accommodationism is, therefore, a doctrine that explains how religious sentiment as a moral tendency in the human mind influences religions that have become "positive" (NST, 546) to change for the moral betterment of humanity.

In this scheme – and it is a scheme in a Kantian sense – religious dogmas clearly arise when religious sentiments become fixed in form at particular moments in a peoples' religious history. But since sentiments change as the religious needs of a people change, there will always be moments of disproportionality between religious forms and religious sentiments in a culture. Accommodationism is a religious idea that presupposes that interplay – presupposes that religious sentiment is a force constantly pushing for a change of religious form in a culture. On these terms, however, it is not at all clear why religious sentiment should also become the source of progress (rather than mere change) in human history. And yet, that is Constant's argument, for he sees the proliferation of religious forms less as a series of unrelated mutable religious doctrines in history than as an ongoing process – "steps," he says – whereby each of the particular forms sentiment assumes in the world advances humanity toward moral perfection in history.[62] As Constant puts it in the 1820s,[63]

[Because] religious...forms are progressive, some are always better than others, and the best always appear at the suitable (opportun) moment.

[The] tendency of [religious] sentiment [is] to clothe itself in more and more perfect forms.

[Religious sentiment] tends to improve the forms in which it is clothed.

[R]eligious sentiment...always tends to a progressive development.

[59] Constant, in Ripley, *Miscellanies*, 312.
[60] Constant, in Ripley, *Miscellanies*, 315–16.
[61] Constant, in Ripley, *Miscellanies*, 302–3. For Kant, see *Rational Religion*, 143.
[62] In *NST*, 545, Constant indicates that he learned about the mutability of religious doctrine from the Germans. He frequently stresses this in the 1820s. See, e.g., Constant, in Ripley, *Miscellanies*, 292, 301, 310, 316, 344–45.
[63] For the following, see Constant, in Ripley, *Miscellanies*, 344, 306, 315, 316, respectively.

This way of thinking about the relationship between religious form and religious sentiment is already evident in NST. There, while elaborating on his own Protestant predilections for philosophical theism, many of the great themes of Constant's religious writings of the 1820s are discussed. So they deserve our full attention here.

The text[64] begins by citing the Prussian government's reactionary attempt in 1788 to stifle religious dissent in the Prussian territories following Frederick the Great's death in 1786 (pp. 543f).[65] It then links this religious persecution to a "party of dogmatists" (pp. 544, 546), who, while seeking to reverse Frederick's long-standing policy of religious toleration toward dissenters, insisted that public discussion of religious issues conform to the orthodox teachings of Lutheranism. One of the main targets of this persecution was Kant whom Constant presents in NST as a philosopher who wished to enlist philosophy in the service of an effort to elevate humanity to a higher moral level by means of religious reformation (p. 545). Taking sides in the Prussian dispute, Constant claims that religious intolerance paralyses the "human spirit" and makes it impossible for uplifting religious "sentiments" about the "destiny of man" to move humanity toward moral perfection (pp. 544–45).

With Kantianism clearly in mind,[66] Constant aligns himself with the great philosopher's highly moralized conception of God, including his explanation of how philosophy mediates between religion and morality so as to facilitate the moral perfection of humanity (p. 546). And in terms of his own emerging conception of philosophical theism, Constant states that the disposition to moral perfection was "given" to man by God in the form of "revelations" that over time educated man to his true moral destiny (pp. 545–46).[67]

At this point, much of what we said earlier about ethical Providence and about how the idea of moral perfectibility links the ideas of disposition and destiny in Constant's religious thinking can be

---

[64] Again, citations from this text NST printed in Thompson, *Constant*, 543–51.

[65] Between 1788 and 1794, Constant's friend, Mauvillon, schooled him in Prussian politics.

[66] Constant, to be sure, is reading Kant in a constructive moral way. At the time, Kant was being read in other ways as well.

[67] Constant later calls this a "gift" from heaven. See Constant, in Ripley, *Miscellanies*, 344. Following Plato, the Cambridge Platonists regarded religious sentiment itself as a "heaven-born thing." See, e.g., J. Smith, in *The Cambridge Platonists*, ed. Gerald Cragg (New York: Oxford University Press, 1968), 94.

seen taking shape in one of his earliest religious writings.[68] Even more instructive, however, is that at precisely this point in NST he inserts the idea of accommodationism into his argument (pp. 545ff). To wit, he notes how God "proportions" – "adapts" his revelations/providential directives to the level of enlightenment and moral sophistication achieved by a people at different stages of the civilizing process. And he illustrates the point by discussing the different revelations God used to educate Moses, the Greeks, the Christians, and eighteenth-century Protestants to humanity's moral destiny (pp. 546–48).

Among the more famous German thinkers, Semler, Lessing, and Kant were main theorists of accommodationism.[69] These three thinkers, moreover, stressed the educational role revelation played in the gradual moral perfection of the human race in history. This is the point Constant wishes to make in 1794, for he contends that revelation and reason, religion and intelligence, "march" toward moral perfection in tandem with each other (pp. 546–47). This means, in turn, that like the Germans before him Constant locates religious sentiment at a conceptual point in the argument that allows him to use it to mediate not only between religion and morality but also between civilization's external and religion's internal march toward perfection. True, the notes to the 1794 text reveal that Constant knows that the doctrine of accommodationism had been previously used by several non-German seventeenth-century thinkers to explain Scripture (p. 550).[70] But in this text as well as later in De la religion (DLR) Constant credits the Germans not only with having developed the accommodationist argument but also with having organized the new theology of philosophical theism around it. For having done that, he says, German Protestants put themselves in the forefront of the religious effort to create an "improved Protestantism."

The long-term importance of accommodationism for Constant is underscored in volume 1 of DLR (1824; pp. 124–134, 149). His argument there shows him using a combination of accommodationism

---

[68] He does this in Ripley, *Miscellanies*, 299.
[69] Dilthey, *Works*, vol. 4, 90–94, links Semler and Kant to accommodationism. Lessing is famous for the accommodationism of his *Education of the Human Race*.
[70] Constant also identifies Origen as an early accommodationist. Benin, *Footprints*, discusses Origen as such.

and progressive revelation to explain how useful the sentiment/form distinction is to explaining religious history. Thus, he notes that while religious forms reflect (se ressentir) the progress of civilization, they must also gradually be purified of their immoral aspects as civilization advances (pp. 149, 144). Once again, religious and moral advances in a culture are presented as correlated with each other; moments of disproportionality between religion and morality are resolved through the accommodation of the former to the latter; and most important of all, and as in the 1794 text (pp. 547–48), the coordination of religious and moral advance are linked to God through the role Providence plays in the education of the human race.

The Religion of Sentiment and Ethical Providence[71]

From early on in his career, the basic thrust of Constant's religious writing seldom deviates from the ethicoreligious and historical framework that he is paying heed to in 1794. For example, in a group of writings published between 1824 and 1829, including volumes 1–3 of DLR, Constant reproduces – sometimes verbatim – many of the themes discussed in the early writings of 1794–1806.[72] In these later writings, he again singles out the Germans as the main shaping force in his religious thinking (PDRI, 303). And once again – in DLR – he historically grounds his argument in the Prussian persecution of religion in 1788 (vol. 1, pp. 129ff). Similarly, and as a part of the effort to "make France Protestant,"[73] he juxtaposes eighteenth-century French and German philosophical responses to religious dogmatism, linking the latter to principles of religious reform and the former to the irreligious intolerance of the philosophes (vol. 1, pp. 124ff).

Although one of the reasons for proceeding this way certainly has to do with Constant's wish to incorporate the idea of religious sentiment into progressive philosophical thinking, the main theme running through the 1820s texts is accommodationism. This is especially clear in chapters 6 and 7 of volume 1 of DLR. But it is

---

[71] Constant, in Ripley, Miscellanies, 298, connects the two in unequivocal fashion.
[72] In addition to DLR, the texts under discussion here are entitled "The Progressive Development of Religious Ideas" (PDRI) and "On the Human Causes Which Have Contributed to the Establishment of Christianity" (EC). Both can be found translated in Ripley, Miscellanies, and date from 1826 and 1825, respectively.
[73] The formulation is Isbell's Romanticism, 173.

also the focus of PDRI (1826). The latter begins with a seven-page rehearsal of what we previously described as the doux-commerce argument (pp. 292–98). Here Constant claims that no area of human life is "stationary" (p. 292); that human beings are "necessarily progressive" because they have been endowed with a "progressive faculty" (pp. 292, 301); and that man "departs" from his "savage" stationary state of existence as a consequence of his inherently progressive nature (pp. 292–93). At the same time, he shows that "politics," "civil society," "government," "industry," and "social organization" are all subject to "the law of progress" (pp. 292, 296–97). As all these advances take place, the role of "ideas" in human affairs gains primacy and man's sense of his "moral worth" increases (pp. 295, 297). With this doux-commerce developmental sequence in mind, Constant asks a question: "Ought religion alone [among all cultural forces] be an exception to this law [of progress]" (p. 297), the law that drives civilization forward from its initial state of moral "infancy" to moral maturity (p. 314)?

After answering this question with an emphatic "Most assuredly not," Constant immediately begins to talk about "Providence," "the divinity of religion," the sanctity of "inward [religious] sentiment," the "destiny" of man, and the way Providence "serves as [a] guide" for religious sentiment by proportioning "its teachings to the condition of the intelligence" achieved by humans at different moments in their various "social state[s]" (pp. 298–99, 304). And over the course of the remainder of the text he repeatedly refers to God as having proportioned/adapted his plan for the education of humanity to the changing spiritual needs of people at different stages of the civilizing process (pp. 297–98, 305).

Now this is the doctrine of accommodationism, schematized (as in 1794) in the form of a progressive revelation argument. And Constant proceeds to argue that the result of the doctrine is that it enables philosophical "ideas of divine Providence" and enlightened ideas about the progressive nature of the "human mind/ spirit" (l'esprit humain) to march along parallel paths of development (p. 298). The outcome of this correlation – Kant had said "concurrence"[74] – is that as religion becomes progressively moralized/ethicized – that is, as God is transformed by way of human projection into a moral lawgiver – and as human beings become more

---

[74] Kant, *Rational Religion*, 229. Also see the striking formulation on p. 267.

civilized and enlightened, they become more or less religiously disposed. It is, therefore, natural for "religion... [to remain] in harmony with all our faculties" and for religious forms to "keep pace" with "the [most progressive] ideas of the age" (pp. 300, 302–3, 305).

As in his earlier writings, Constant recognizes that religion "ceases to be salutary" when it resists progress in the name of "inviolate" doctrine (p. 300). And as we noted earlier, he uses the word "disproportion" to indicate what happens in a society when "dogmas" and the "human spirit" fail to keep pace with each other (p. 312). In this context, he reverts to the religious form/religious sentiment distinction to make his point (p. 299), arguing that the progressive "essence" of religious sentiment is "shackled" when "existing [religious] forms and dogmas" surrender "intelligence" to "superstition" and/or the authority of the church and priesthood rather than accommodate themselves to the progressive moral "tendency" of the day (pp. 299, 304, 316).

While delineating the religious form/religious sentiment distinction, Constant turns his attention to the "tendency" argument (pp. 304–6, 316), claiming that religious sentiment has a tendency – one always resisted by the priesthood (pp. 304–6) – to present itself in "more and more perfect forms" (pp. 306, 315–16). So, when he says, "religion is progressive" (p. 313) or that "religious sentiment... tends to a progressive development" (p. 316), he means that there is a "tendency natural to man" that, in accordance with Providence and the teachings of Jesus (PDRI, 319) and Paul (EC, 344–45), pushes religious sentiment in the direction of "perfection" (p. 316). This, I think, explains why in 1825 Constant stated that the perfection of religious sentiment among human beings testifies to the "manifestation of divine goodness" in the world (EC, 344). Needless to say, that is what the ideas of ethical Providence and the "better self" are designed to articulate, for in both cases religious sentiment keeps man connected up with God while permitting him to be the agent who immanentizes divine goodness in the world through perfection of his religious sentiment.

From Polytheism to Philosophical Theism: Humanity's Tendency Toward Unity

What is intriguing about Constant's earlier and later religious work is the telling way his lifelong study of polytheism and theism fits into a threefold religiohistorical framework: into the accommodationism argument; into his understanding of religious progress among the Greeks of the fifth century B.C.E; and into his explanation of how "the progress of intelligence . . . carried [the Greek world] from polytheism to theism" (EC, 334). We know, to be sure, that his interest in polytheism dates back to the 1780s. In addition, we know that one of his main sources on religion – Hume – had written on the development of Greek polytheism.[75] And like Constant after him, Hume argued that as the civilizing process unfolded it offered human beings "leisure" time for reflection on the nature of God, with the result, Hume said, that the minds of those human beings underwent a transformation whereby religious representations based on sense gave way to ones based on reason.[76] According to Hume, these were the circumstances out of which philosophical theism emerged in Greek religious history.

With the sense to reason sequence in mind, Hume also explains how reason, as applied to religion by certain Greek philosophers (e.g., Socrates), prepared the way for the ancient world to move from polytheism to theism.[77] In this, Hume anticipates two key features of Constant's later work on theism: (1) that philosophically informed theism arises when philosophers rather than poets begin to set the terms of debate about the nature of God;[78] and (2) that philosophical theism expresses the religious outlook of an advanced civilization. True, in the end, Hume and Constant differ fundamentally about philosophical theism's long-term influence on humanity's moral development. (For Hume, theism is just a stage between polytheism and atheism, not a model for moderns to emulate.) Before reaching that point of divergence, however, Hume and Constant agreed on several things. First, they agreed that polytheism was not the result of the fragmentation and corruption of mankind's original and perfect *Urreligion*. Rather, and as the result of work they both had done in comparative religious history, which included much information about the religions of North American Indians, they saw polytheism

---

[75] Hume, *Natural History*.
[76] Hume, *Natural History*, 24. Similar formulations can be found in Gotthold Lessing, *Philosophical and Religious Writings*, ed. and trans. H. B. Nisbet (Cambridge: Cambridge University Press, 2005), 226–28; Kant, *Political Writings*, 224; and Schiller, *Aesthetic*, 179–81 (Letter #24).
[77] Hume, *Natural History*, 36, note 2.
[78] See Constant, *SCU*, 320–21, 329.

as a typical expression of the religious outlook of people living at a relatively early point on a civilizational scale (i.e., before theism but after fetishism) that ran from primitive to civilized. Thus, the two thinkers linked polytheism both with the kind of "ignorance" the eighteenth century associated with prescientific cultures and with the overly active "imaginations" of people still living in the childhood of human culture.[79] Secondly, Hume and Constant agreed that the religious movement from polytheism to theism could be correlated with advances in rationality and in humanity's understanding of its own long-term ethical purpose. Hence the philosophers' rebellion against the irrational and immoral gods of the poets was a main theme in both thinkers' work on the transition from polytheism to theism in the Greek world.[80]

But when Hume begins to distance himself from philosophical theism because it purified the gods rather than eliminated them from man's moral life, he anticipates Feuerbach more than Constant, for Constant regarded the Greek model of philosophical theism as the result of both Greek religion's accommodation to the high-minded ethical demands of an advanced civilization and humanity's recognition that God's unity was essential to what Constant called "practical religion" (EC, 328). For that reason, Constant argued, belief in one God was preferable to belief either in too many gods (i.e., polytheism) or in no gods/God at all (i.e., atheism).[81] That is what Plato had said in *Timaeus*, and that is why Constant begins DLR with an epigraph from *Timaeus*.

That Constant's lifelong fascination with the Greek moment of philosophical theism tells us much about his religious writings becomes crystal clear from the following considerations. For example, he writes that "inherent" in religious sentiment is a "tendency" toward "unity" that, among other things, expresses itself in moral terms and in the cultivation of the equally "sublime idea of universal fraternity" (PDRI, 304, 316; EC, 326; DLR, vol. 1, 142–49) – in what Herder called the ideal of "humanity." More specifically, his

---

[79] There is much thinking like this in Spinoza, Fontenelle, Vico, and the mythological school of German historical thinking.

[80] What we said earlier about *theoprepes* (note 9) applies here.

[81] There is a famous statement to this effect in Bacon's essay "Of Atheism." Constant quoted it in 1811. See Guy Dodge, *Benjamin Constant's Philosophy of Liberalism* (Chapel Hill: University of North Carolina Press, 1980), 124.

argument is that latent in the human race – in the universal "wants of the soul" – is a universal want for mankind's social, moral, and religious "unity" (EC, 326–31). Constant equates this want with "religious sentiment" and with humanity's persistent desire to "purify" religion and bring the sublime idea of unity to mankind's understanding of God (PDRI, 313, 315; EC, 326). According to Constant, theism is the natural expression of this want/sentiment/desire – which is to say, theism is at once the beginning and the end/telos of religious sentiment (EC, 326). And in keeping with what we earlier saw him say about God's ethical Providence, Constant argues that theism as a religious idea descended from "heaven to earth" when Socrates began to search within himself for purposefulness and, while so doing, discovered both his soul and man's potential for moral perfection and religious unity (PDRI, 306, 315).

The point of Constant's proceeding this way is obvious, for by linking theism to the idea of unity he can present religious sentiment as a mediating conceptual point between transcendental and immanent things. That this is his intention is evident from what he repeatedly says about the movement from polytheism to theism in the ancient world. Although he recognizes the contribution of the Jews to the development of (an inferior form of) theism in antiquity (EC, 331–33), he assigns special importance in this regard to the Greeks, especially to Plato/Socrates who used philosophy to give theism a more rational form. Focusing his attention on the time period between Homer and Plato (PDRI, 304–5, 312; DLR, vol. 1, 144), Constant notes that as many educated Greeks embraced philosophical theism they became more rational and ethical in their attitudes toward the world (PDRI, 301–4), which is to say, Constant saw a connection between the effort to moralize gods and a rise in the ethical self-consciousness of increasingly civilized human beings.

In the final analysis, then, Constant sees the inward turn of Greek philosophy playing a pivotal role in the emergence of philosophical theism among the Greeks. It is certainly true, though, that by identifying philosophical theism as an archetypal moment in Western religious history he himself presupposes that the turn inward leads to the discovery of "something" within, which is brought to mankind's attention in the form of the Greek philosophical awakening. He presupposes, moreover, that this awakening assumes that without a belief in the unity and goodness of the Godhead, and without a belief in the kinship between God and man, there can be no hope of ethical unity among human beings. Thus, the Greek ideal of religious fellowship demands that human beings uphold theocentrism as a "belief of reason" (in a Kantian sense) in order to realize the fruits of theism in a practical ethical sense – hence, Constant's statement that "religion . . . is a means" for the unity and moral perfection of man (EC, 336).

For Constant, this religious dynamics becomes operational through the idea of religious sentiment, for religious sentiment makes human beings aware of the potential ethical unity of the human race. In this respect, religious sentiment represents for Constant a special kind of knowledge that operates in two different but related ways: (1) it offers human beings insight into the providential plan set for moral perfection in the world; and (2) it contains the "sacred gift" (EC, 344) of a heaven-born capacity of moral judgment that allows human beings to discern right from wrong in the world.[82] In Plato, this capacity was discussed in terms of phronesis, and in Stoicism in the idea of a "formative *logos*"; among the Cambridge Platonists the capacity was linked to man's plastic nature; conscience serves that purpose in Rousseau; and for many of the Germans it was implicit in the words they used (e.g., Gefühl, Gesinnung, Gemüt, and Anlage) to discuss the dignity and destiny of man. What Constant says about and does with the idea of religious sentiment suggest he is working in that tradition.

CONSTANT'S AXIAL MOMENT: THE MAN-IN-MAN
THEME IN PHILOSOPHICAL THEISM

Reading Constant's religious writings the way we have draws attention to how he proposed to bring transcendental and immanent conceptions of God together, so they supplement and complete each

---

[82] It is highly significant that Constant sees this gift as being delivered by Socrates and Jesus (EC, 330, 341) as well as by revelation. As this happens, Constant says, "theism descends from heaven to earth" (PDRI, 315) – which is to say, the moral teachings of divine providence are immanentized, thus producing the balance of transcendence and immanence in what is called "dipolar" theism. That Socrates and Jesus are invoked together here is typical of a long tradition of Christian humanism that delights in merging the two figures for the purpose of supporting "ethical religion."

other without any reduction of the one to the other. Were a reduction of one to the other to occur, dipolar theism's attempt to preserve a balance between transcendence and immanence would be undermined. But if man is set at the intersection of one and the other and then allowed to live a life that participates in both the transcendent and immanent realms of experience, then man's experience of reality, although filled with tension, would register itself on human consciousness in the form of an intermediary reality – what Plato had called the *metaxy* – in which man is free to mediate between the two realms of experience – "think [the two] together" in Kant's terms.[83] Such, I would argue, is Constant's rendering of a theological anthropology that conforms to the principles of dipolar theism. And it is around theism that Constant organizes his theology of history, which, in Kantian terms, schematizes theism as a religion of freedom.

At the same time, we saw that man's telos lay at a point where a providential plan for the moral education of humanity and the awakening of man's better self to his responsibility for immanentizing goodness in the world intersected. On a still deeper religious level, Constant presented religious sentiment as the agent of that transcendent teleology, for he held that religious sentiment is connected up with an all-controlling divine Providence on the one hand and with the better self on the other. Viewed in this double perspective, religious sentiment mediates between the initiative for moral perfection that comes from above and a disposition toward moral perfection that has the appearance of being "inborn" in man. Religious sentiment, in short, is what comes into being as a force in history when man chooses to live in the intermediary reality mentioned earlier, chooses to live a life of religious freedom, that is.

A key to understanding Constant as a religious thinker arises here, for his dipolar theism, his notion of a pedagogic God who

---

[83] Again, thinking transcendent and immanent things together is central to theism in general and to the idea of ethical Providence in particular. For an appreciation of the point, see MacIntyre, *After*, 50–54. Kant is prominent in the argument MacIntyre develops there about theism. Voegelin, "Immortality," in *Harvard Theological Review*, 60 (1967), 261–63, 274–75, explains the idea of *metaxy* in Plato. G. Ladner, "The Philosophical Anthropology of Saint Gregory of Nyssa," in *Dumbarton Oaks Papers*, 12 (1958), 71–75, discusses "the Platonistic *syndesmos*-doctrine of man . . . [which is designed to depict man living] an in-between" existence in the *metaxy*.

governs humanity through an ethical Providence, and his conception of moral perfection as the telos of the better self are central
themes in a religious tradition that begins with Plato's representation of Socrates as the philosopher who, after discovering the soul
and making the soul the basis of kinship between God and man,
taught human beings that "becoming like God" in an ethical sense
(homoiosis) was the telos of the soul in a religious sense.[84] Indeed,
as the personification of philosophy and, according to Hume, one
of the first philosophical theists,[85] Plato's Socrates reminded human
beings of their divine nature (i.e., likeness to God) and asked them to
turn inward in order to gain insight (phronesis) into their connected-
ness with God and into the moral path to follow in order to ascend
to God (or achieve likeness to Him [homoiosis]).[86] While advancing
this famous argument, Plato repeatedly says that man has a "plastic"
nature[87] – a nature comprising two selves, an outer physical self (i.e.,
the body) and an inner moral/spiritual self (i.e., the soul).[88] According to Plato, the latter aspires to what is "noble," truly "human,"
"best," and "divine."[89] Achieving these things, Plato continues, is
what rational human beings do when they realize that the logos
of the soul – the archetype in it – points them in the direction of
homoiosis as man's divinely ordained end.

Students of Plato's theology often refer to the turn inward as the
moment in Western religious history when the idea of an archetypal
or ideal man was discovered in man. In the Republic, and in some

---

[84] Burkert, Greek religion, chap. VII, discusses this. For the history of homoiosis, see
Werner Jaeger, Early Christianity and Greek Paideia (Cambridge, MA: Harvard
University Press, 1961), esp. 86ff; John Dillon, The Middle Platonists: A Study
of Platonism, 80 B.C. to A.D. 220 (Ithaca, N.Y.: Cornell University Press, 1977),
122, 143–44, 193; Gerhart Ladner, The Idea of Reform (Cambridge, MA: Harvard
University Press, 1959), chap. III; and EricDodds, Pagan and Christian in an Age
of Anxiety (New York: Norton, 1970), 74–75.

[85] Hume, Natural History, 36, note 2.

[86] Taylor, Sources, chap. 6, is helpful on Plato and phronesis. Dillon, Middle, 122,
192–93, produces quotations connecting phronesis with homoiosis. Among the
Stoics, phronesis is the "moral insight" that keys moral evolution in the doctrine
of oikeiosis (note 38).

[87] Plato, Republic, 377.

[88] Constant makes the exact point in DLR, vol. 1, 146.

[89] The quotations come from the Republic, 589. From this, Cornford, Socrates, 48,
develops the notion of Socrates' and Plato's "morality of [man's] aspiration to
spiritual perfection."

of his other writings (e.g., the *Laws*), Plato talks about the "human being" who resides within the body of man.[90] Equally as important, he speaks of the need for self-mastery – that is, of the need to cultivate the inner man so as to ensure its triumph over the outer man. According to two famous twentieth-century scholars, R. Otto and K. Jaspers, this turn inward signals a transformation in the religious consciousness of the West. In Otto's words, it is the moment when the "'higher man' in man" was discovered.[91] For Jaspers, it is when the "specifically human in man" was discovered.[92] For his part, Otto relates the discussion of Plato's man-in-man theme to the emergence among the Greeks of "theism" of a rational/philosophical kind.[93] Jaspers, who sees Greek religion becoming rational and ethical as a result of the inward turn, links the man-in-man theme to an "ethical rebellion" by philosophers of the classical age against the immoral gods of the poets.[94] Hence, the "sophisticated kind of theism" that modern scholarship now associates with what Jaspers famously called the "Axial Age" of religious thinking.[95]

The tradition of rationalizing and ethicizing theism – bringing it "down to earth" as it were – starts with Plato and then works its way forward in time, in Platonizing Stoicism; Hellenistic Judaism; Middle Platonism and Neo-Platonism; in the Christian humanism of the Alexandrian and Cappadocian Fathers; in the Christian Socraticism of some of the humanists of the Middle Ages; in the Platonism of the Renaissance humanists and Erasmus; in the Cambridge Platonists; in Shaftesbury and Rousseau; and in the "new theism" of the Protestant *Aufklärung* in Germany. As it happens, then, there was something like an "axial" religious moment in late eighteenth-century

[90] Plato, *Republic*, 589; *Laws*, 644, 726, 732. Seneca, *Moral Letters*, 65, speaks of the archetypal character of Plato's thinking about "humanity." Kant, Herder, and Schiller follow him in this.

[91] Otto, *Essays*, 103.

[92] Karl Jaspers, *The Origin and Goal of History*, trans. Michael Bullock (New Haven: Yale University Press, 1953), 3.

[93] Otto, *Essays*, 98.

[94] Jaspers, *Origin*, 3. A major ancient source for the philosophers' religious rebellion against the poets can be found in Cicero, quoted to that effect in Bernard le Bovier Fontenelle, *The Achievement of Bernard le Bovier de Fontenelle*, trans. Leonard Marsak (New York: Johnson Reprint, 1970), 38.

[95] Hugh Lloyd-Jones, *The Justice of Zeus* (Berkeley, CA: University of California Press, 1971), 134. The opening chapter of Jaspers's *Origin* is entitled "The Axial Age."

German Protestant thinking, for that was the moment when Plato's ideal of man-in-man and Protestantism's demand for ethical religion versus the dogmatism of orthodoxy combined to once again move religious thinking toward theism of a philosophical kind.[96] And just as the German recovery of the Greeks helped them develop the new theism of liberal Protestantism, so did Constant's assimilation of Greek and German religious thinking help him develop the framework for an "improved Protestantism."

Our view of Constant as a philosophical theist is reinforced by another major development in the religious history of Europe in the late seventeenth and eighteenth centuries: namely, the invention of the word theism to express the ethical side of God's providential governance of the human world. As was previously noted, theism is a neologism that the Cambridge Platonists (e.g., Cudworth) began to use in the 1670s to express their philosophical belief in an ethical Providence. In Constant's era, any number of German thinkers talked about the ethical "economy" of God's Providence. And they repeatedly did so with reference to the providential education of the man in man.[97]

Among the Germans, however, Kant was the most explicit about the connection between theism and ethical Providence. As he explained throughout the 1780s and 1790s,[98] "God's providence is benevolent"; his "care for the world" expresses itself in "a plan" in which moral "purpose" in a teleological sense is communicated to man through sentiments/dispositions (*Gesinnung/Anlage/ Gefühl/Gemüt/Empfindung* in German) that providentially direct him toward the goal of moral perfection; and insofar as human beings cultivate and give objective form to these sentiments/

---

[96] Meinecke, *Historism*, chap. IX, esp. 302, makes this the focus of his great discussion of Herder's theological Platonism. Dilthey, *Works*, vol. 4, 49, puts it slightly differently, suggesting that the cooperative nexus of ethical Providence arises when religious thinkers (e.g., Erasmus and Kant) appeal to "man's [divinely inspired] moral nature" to criticize "Church dogma." Socrates, we know, was the archetype for trying "to reform religion from an ethical point of view." See A. Stavru, "Socrates," in *Encyclopedia of Religion*, vol. 12, 2nd ed., Lindsay Jones, editor in chief. (Detroit: Macmillan Reference, 2005), 8504.

[97] Two good examples: Schiller, *Aesthetic*, 17–19 (Letter #4); and Herder, *Outlines*, 439.

[98] See, e.g., Kant, *Lectures on Philosophical Theology*, trans. Allen Wood and Gertrude Clark (Ithaca, NY: Cornell University Press, 1978), 152–57.

dispositions – seeds of goodness and perfection Kant said[99] – they can be said to be partners with God in a cooperative religiomoral endeavor that is theistic.[100] Kant puts it this way: God, "who governs the world in accordance with moral laws," offers himself (perhaps in the form of a transcendental idea?) as a model of moral perfection "in order to [encourage] rational creatures [to] use their freedom in a manner agreeable to his highest will."[101]

Vital to Kant's conception of theism, which he distinguishes from deism, is the idea of a "living God."[102] For our purposes here, what is important about this idea is the way Kant contrasts it with the idea of an "idle" God. The latter, he argues, is "deistic" and "useless" with regard to explaining why moral perfection is humanity's telos. Instructively, he attaches the word "deistic" to pre-Socratic and Epicurean conceptions of God as well as to the group of eighteenth-century religious thinkers that has long been called deists, thereby creating a parallel between ancient Greek and modern German understandings of the divine–human relationship. Just as instructively, Kant singles out Socrates and Plato as the thinkers who "made God the foundation of morality." Aside from suggesting that Kant stands to deists as Socrates and Plato stood to some of their own "deistic" contemporaries, Kant's juxtaposition of theism and deism involves linking the living God in a providential sense with moral perfection in an immanent sense, which is what Kant wished to encompass with what he called "moral theism." Insofar as Kant was

---

[99] Kant, *Lectures*, 117–18.

[100] Kant, *Lectures*, 29–33, 40ff, 152–57, 165ff, on divine–human "cooperation." The same argument is evident in his *Religion within the Boundaries of Mere Reason*.

[101] Kant, *Lectures*, 170, 152, respectively. The idea of a role model God is Platonic. See the *Republic*, book II.

[102] Kant discusses the idea of a "living God" in *The Critique of Pure Reason*, trans. Norman Smith (New York: Modern Library, 1958), 525–31, and in *Lectures*, 30, 81, 166–70. In setting a "living" God versus an "idle" one, Kant is taking Cicero's side versus Epicurus in the ancient debate about divine providence. Many of Cicero's formulations (*De Natura Deorum*, trans. H. Rackham (New York: G. P. Putnam's Sons, 1933), 111–13, 181, 195–97, anticipate Kant's theism and his criticism of deism. As G. Gawlich, "Cicero and the Enlightenment," *Studies in Voltaire and the Eighteenth Century*, vol. 25 (1963), has shown, Cicero provided many resources for liberal Protestant thought during the Enlightenment. He was especially valuable for arguing that religion had to be consistent with the "moral fitness of things." This included God's revelations to man. Fontenelle, *Achievement*, 38, understood Cicero perfectly well in this regard.

one of Constant's principal German sources, the latter had access to this manner of thinking. So, when Constant speaks of the Germans as theists, when he calls them Platonists, and when he uses an epigraph from Plato's *Timaeus* – a book that argues for ethical Providence – to begin *DLR*, he is associating himself with that tradition.

But there is more, for beginning with Cudworth,[103] who uses the word theism to characterize what is, at bottom, Platonic theology, theists had been praising "a Deity moral" who used Providence to "communicate his goodness" to mankind. As distinct from "immoral theists," who believed in a "do-nothing God" – that is, in a God who knew "nothing of morality" – and as distinct from "mechanistic theists" whose nomopomorphic conception of God deprived human beings of their freedom, Cudworth anticipated Kant in celebrating the moral theism of those ancient thinkers, Socrates and Plato, when he called them "philosophic theists."

Between Cudworth and Kant, therefore, and especially in Shaftesbury and Rousseau,[104] theism developed as a philosophically informed way of discussing the role ethical Providence plays in the divine–human relationship. Constant's religious writings show him to be an heir of that tradition as well as the longer-term Platonic one to which seventeenth- and eighteenth-century theists thought they were contributing.

---

[103] See the Preface to Cudworth's *True System* and the selection from Cudworth in *Cambridge Platonists*, ed. Cragg, 204–17, for what follows.

[104] See Anthony Ashley Cooper Shaftesbury, *Characteristicks of Men, Manners, Opinions, Times*, vol. 2 (Indianapolis: Liberty Fund, 2001), 6–7, 33, 41–44, 118–19, 151–52, 201. Rousseau discusses "true theism" in *On the Social Contract*, 127–28. In *Emile*, in the section on the Savoyard Vicar, he explains how the interplay between "sentiment" and "providence" works in theism.

Conclusion

15 Eclipses and Revivals: Constant's Reception in France and America, 1830–2007

Like all great thinkers, Constant expressed ideas that would transcend his time and place. Convinced that he was living at the dawn of a new age, he addressed himself to the "modern" men and "friends of liberty" he hoped to influence, using very general, even universalizing, language. Throughout his many speeches and writings, he consistently sought to identify the broader patterns in history and the lessons that could be learned from them. Blessed not only with a keen eye for detail but with an uncommon capacity for analytical thinking, he had outstanding literary talents. All of this helps to explain why Constant's writings have continued to appeal to a broad range of readers for more than a hundred and fifty years.

Perhaps even more than other great thinkers, however, Constant has also fallen victim to superficial analyses, partial readings, and misinterpretations. Many who have read and cited him have known only a small portion of his work and have paid scant attention to its original context and intended meaning. At various points of his posthumous career, Constant's fame has therefore had little relation to his actual life, personal ambitions, and the historical purposes of his rich and multidimensional work. Instead, he appears regularly in caricature in the writings of other political theorists, who use him as a foil for their own agendas. This has resulted in there being many different "Constants," each one reflecting the context in which he is being used more than the context in which he lived and often bearing little resemblance to the man himself.

The study of Constant's reception is still in its infancy, and the goal of this essay is therefore modest. I would like to report on some preliminary findings, suggest some new avenues for research, and encourage people to pursue the topic further.

APOTHEOSIS AND DECLINE

When Constant died on December 8, 1830, he was at the height of his career and fame. By all accounts, the state funeral he received four days later was a fitting tribute. The entire Chamber of Deputies attended, and the city of Paris turned out *en masse*. On that day, the crowds honored Constant the liberal politician, the spellbinding orator, and combative journalist. They paid homage to his courageous defense of essential liberal values and freedoms, from constitutional government and the rule of law, to trial by jury, freedom of religion, and perhaps most importantly, freedom of the press. His tireless battle to uphold these principles had turned him into a national hero. Indeed, so popular had Constant become that authorities feared his funeral would trigger an uprising, and security was especially tight that day. Stirring eulogies were delivered by his graveside. Lafayette lionized him and newspapers celebrated him. According to the *Courrier français*, France owed Constant "eternal gratitude," because

no other writer has contributed as much to her political education; no other writer has been better at popularizing constitutional questions and rendering them familiar to all classes of citizens.[1]

Constant's admirers predicted that he would never be forgotten because of all the services he had rendered to France.

But forgotten he was – as his brand of liberalism failed to take root and grow. Two main reasons account for his relatively rapid eclipse. First, as is well known, French liberalism was generally weak and unable to generate much enthusiasm or support. Second, Constant's individualistic or "pure"[2] variety of liberalism had always been, and continued to be, a minority vein within French liberalism. Finally, one should not underestimate the long shadow cast by his poor personal reputation, which was exploited by his political enemies. At the very least, an almost obsessive focus on Constant's private life and personal problems deflected interest away from his political and intellectual accomplishments and helped to call into question the sincerity and seriousness of his professed ideals.

---

[1] *Courrier français*, December 9, 1830, 569. Unless otherwise indicated, all translations are my own.

[2] The word "pure" is George Armstrong Kelly's, in "Constant Commotion: Avatars of a Pure Liberal," *Journal of Modern History*, 54 (3) (September 1982), 497–518. Marcel Prélot also uses it in his *Histoire des idées politiques* (Paris: Dalloz, 1960), 441.

THE "GUIZOT MOMENT" AND THE DECLINE OF "PURE" LIBERALISM

The 1830 Revolution, which Constant had done much to prepare, brought to power François Guizot (1787–1874) and the *doctrinaires*, whose liberalism was of a more conservative, elitist, and statist variety. Guizot and his allies immediately distanced themselves from Constant, branding his liberalism as merely oppositional, "critical" or "negative," and thus *dépassé* under the new circumstances. After this so-called Guizot Moment, history would show that France preferred "a liberalism *by* the state" to the Constantian variety, mistrustful of government and focused on protecting the rights of the individual. Indeed, the dominant strain of French liberalism would be hostile to individualism and deeply suspicious of market forces.[3] Already during his lifetime, Constant's liberalism had been accused of fostering everything that post-revolutionary French thinkers feared most, from intellectual and moral anarchy to selfishness, atomization, and social dissolution. The revolutions of 1830 and 1848 only increased such anxieties. All points of the political spectrum now agreed that individualism was a serious evil undermining the social and political order. Such an atmosphere was not conducive to an appreciation of Constant, who, as late as 1829, boasted that his entire life's work had been about promoting "the triumph of individuality."[4]

Undoubtedly, anti-Protestantism also played a role in Constant's eclipse. In French history, anti-individualism has often been synonymous with anti-Protestantism.[5] During his last years, Constant repeatedly and very publicly defined himself as a Protestant. On the floor of the Chamber, he defended the cause of his coreligionists. When, in 1824, he began publishing a major work on religion, the

---

[3] Lucien Jaume, *L'Individu effacé ou le paradoxe du libéralisme français* (Paris: Fayard, 1997). On the oscillating fortunes of individualism in French history, see Alain Laurent, *L'Individu et ses ennemis* (Paris: Hachette, 1987).

[4] Constant's preface to his *Mélanges*, 623.

[5] Pierre Rosanvallon discusses this in *Le modèle politique français: la société civile contre le jacobinisme de 1789 à nos jours* (Paris: Seuil, 2004), 239–41. See Michèle Saquin, *Entre Bossuet et Maurras, l'antiprotestantisme en France* (Paris: Ecole de Chartres, 1998); Jean Baubérot and Valentine Zuber, *Une haine oubliée: L'antiprotestantisme avant le "pacte laïque" (1870–1905)* (Paris: Albin Michel, 2000); and Steven Hause, "Anti-Protestant Rhetoric in the Early Third Republic," *French Historical Studies*, 16 (1) (Spring 1989).

five-volume *De la religion considérée dans sa source, ses formes et ses développements*, it was widely recognized as Protestant in inspiration and was praised only in Protestant circles.[6] Constant also published several essays on religion, which confirmed his sympathy for liberal Protestantism. He did all this in the midst of an increasingly anti-Protestant atmosphere. Of course Catholic reactionaries, such as Joseph de Maistre (1753–1821), had for long lambasted liberalism as nothing but "political protestantism carried to the most absolute individualism."[7] But counterrevolutionaries were not alone in deploring the atomization, privatization, and selfishness supposedly caused by Protestantism. During the 1820s, the Saint-Simonians were particularly virulent. Prosper Enfantin denounced Protestants for preaching "only diversity or division, that is, individualism – or, to be frank, *egoism*."[8]

The July Monarchy (1830–48) did not help matters. Guizot, although himself a practicing Protestant, never pursued a pro-Protestant religious policy; in fact, he disappointed and even angered many French Protestants by what they interpreted as a bias toward Catholicism.[9] Ironically, however, Guizot's unpopular regime fuelled anti-Protestantism nevertheless, mainly because of its reputation for materialism and avarice. In the end, the revolution of 1848 was not only a rejection of liberalism; it was also a repudiation of the Protestant individualism that most people believed undergirded it. Once again, such an atmosphere was unlikely to encourage a revival of interest in Constant's political and religious ideas.

Finally, if Constant was forgotten, it was also because his writings did not provide much insight into the social and economic problems that were of growing concern. Indeed, there is very little about poverty or class antagonism in Constant's writings, which gives him the appearance of having been relatively unaware of or

---

[6] See Helena Rosenblatt, *Liberal Values: Benjamin Constant and the Politics of Religion* (Cambridge: Cambridge University Press, 2008).

[7] Joseph de Maistre quoted in Koenraad Swart, "'Individualism' in the Mid-Nineteenth Century (1826–1860)," *Journal of the History of Ideas*, 23 (1) (January–March 1962), 78.

[8] Prosper Enfantin as cited by Pierre Rosanvallon, *Le Modèle politique*, 240, emphasis added.

[9] On Guizot's religious views, see Douglas Johnson, *Guizot: Aspects of French History, 1787–1874* (London: Routledge & K. Paul, 1963), chap. 8.

unaffected by working-class misery and industrial unrest.[10] In justice to Constant, he died before dramatic industrial growth began in France. Economic historians locate the takeoff period of French industry between 1842 and 1847, that is, several years after Constant's death.[11] In 1830, the country remained an agrarian and rural society; the average industrial establishment was still small and there were very few factory workers. Land continued to be the main form of wealth and source of revenue for the overwhelming majority of citizens. However, by the eve of the revolution of 1848, Alexis de Tocqueville warned the Chamber of Deputies that the growing disparities between rich and poor, combined with the spread of socialist ideas, were making another revolution inevitable: "We are lulling ourselves to sleep over an active volcano."[12] Certainly, therefore, by the mid-nineteenth century, Constant's apparent insouciance about such matters, combined with his optimistic espousal of "laissez-faire, laissez-passer," seemed out of touch with the new realities of the times. After the 1848 revolution, liberals were driven even further on the defensive. On the Left, opposition divided into republicans and socialists. Neither group had much reason to revive Constant's writings, whose usefulness seemed to have run its course. His liberalism was simply too "critical," "negative," and suspicious of state power to appeal to those politicians and thinkers who saw the state as an indispensable ally and whose primary wish was to capture it in pursuit of their goals.

Moreover, Constant's writings were unlikely to appeal to the growing number of people who believed that France was in the midst of a social and spiritual crisis. All indications are that nineteenth-century France was obsessed with the fear of social decomposition. Many looked to religion to provide the cure. Right-wing thinkers were not alone in advocating a return to Catholicism in order to restore social cohesion and foster a sense of common identity. Early socialists such as Buchez, Cabet, Leroux, and Blanc all believed that

---

[10] Note, however, that in his *Commentaire sur l'ouvrage de Filangieri* (ed. Alain Laurent [Paris: Société d'édition Les Belles Lettres, 2004, 139], Constant praises Sismondi's *Nouveaux principes d'économie politique* of 1819 as being "full of good ideas and philanthropic views."

[11] David Pinkney, *Decisive Years in France. 1840–1847* (Princeton, NJ: Princeton University Press, 1986).

[12] *Recollections*, trans. George Lawrence (Garden City, NY: Doubleday, 1970), 14.

their society was sick and in need of spiritual healing; they espoused a socialism strongly impregnated with Catholicism.[13] Even a republican like Jules Michelet (1798–1874), who had admired Constant during the Restoration and who remained fiercely anticlerical after 1848, insisted on the need to combat selfishness and restore collective values to the nation. It was with a strong measure of wishful thinking that he wrote, "We all feel our individuality dying. May the sentiment of social generality [...] be born anew."[14]

Constant's poor personal reputation also contributed to his decline in stature and influence. Some accused him of opportunism and fickleness for having collaborated with Napoleon during the Hundred Days (March–June 1815). His unconventional love life was the subject of relentless gossip, as was his ruinous predilection for gambling. There is even a rumor that he was suffering from syphilis in his later years,[15] and he was most certainly in deep debt. In any case, an unrelenting aura of disrepute hovered around Constant, which played into the hands of his enemies. The witty and biting sarcasm that he heaped on his political adversaries on the floor of the Chamber only increased their animosity toward him. Indeed, his expertise in the art of ridicule was known as far away as America,[16] and may very well have kept people from taking him seriously.

Angered by Constant's continued opposition after the July Revolution, Guizot expressed deep antipathy for his liberal rival in his *Mémoires*. Venting his frustrations, Guizot described Constant as a "skeptical and mocking sophist with no convictions." Constant's soul was "blasé" and he engaged in politics only because he was

---

[13] See also Edward Berenson, *Populist Religion and Left-Wing Politics in France, 1830–1852* (Princeton, NJ: Princeton University Press 1984), for how left-wing opposition to Louis Philippe developed a critique of laissez-faire liberalism based on precepts of Catholic morality.

[14] Quoted by Pierre Rosanvallon, *The Demands of Liberty, Civil Society in France since the Revolution*, trans. Arthur Goldhammer (Cambridge, MA: Harvard University Press, 2007), 130–31.

[15] On his supposedly secret illness, see Michel Følman, *Le secret de Benjamin Constant* (Geneva: Imprimerie de la Tribune de Genève, 1959).

[16] See, for example, "Letter from Paris, March 18, 1825," *The Museum of Foreign Literature, Science and Art*, 6 (June 1, 1825), 587–88, where it is reported that "M. Benjamin Constant had the art of overwhelming with ridicule the three hundred and seventy wigged heads which decide the destiny of France" and that it is impossible to read his speeches without laughing out loud.

"bored" and in need of "amusement."[17] The literary critic Sainte-Beuve's animosity toward Constant is as venomous as it is hard to explain. Beginning around 1835, he wrote articles whose sole aim seems to have been to show that Constant was a cynic, a libertine, and a roué. In 1876, the Catholic and royalist P. Thureau-Dangin concluded that Constant had been rightly forgotten because of his many vices, his "lack of character" and "moral inconstancy." Because he was "selfish" and "corrupt," he "did not deserve glory after his death."[18] When it came to Constant's supposed immorality, both sides of the political spectrum agreed. In his *Histoire de dix ans 1830–1840* (1842–44), the early socialist thinker, Louis Blanc (1811–82), emphasized Constant's "lightweight morals," "skepticism," and moral "indifference." Constant had a "feeble temperament" and a "cold heart."[19] Not long thereafter, Karl Marx dismissed Constant as nothing more than a pathetic mouthpiece of "bourgeois society."[20]

The barrage of insults continued, making their way into scholarly texts now regarded as classic, thereby distorting the reception of Constant's political thought. According to Emile Faguet, Constant was fundamentally an "egoist," and this "was the foundation for his entire political system." Constant's egoism made his liberalism "dry" and "cold."[21] As Henry Michel wrote in his *L'idée de l'état*, there was nothing "grand" nor "generous" about Constant' liberalism. Like that of the economists, it was an essentially "negative" philosophy concerned only with the individual's calculation of self-interest.[22] Constant's Protestantism was occasionally hinted at in these appraisals, only to be dismissed in a condescending, even

---

[17] François Guizot, *Mémoires pour servir à l'histoire de mon temps*, t. II (Paris: Michel Lévy Frères, 1859).

[18] Paul Thureau-Dangin, *Le parti libéral sous la Restauration* (Paris: E. Plon Cie., 1876).

[19] Louis Blanc, *Histoire de dix ans 1830–1840* (Paris: Germer Baillière et Cie, 1877), 175–76.

[20] In *The Eighteenth Brumaire of Louis Bonaparte* (1852). This despite the fact that he had Constant's *Spirit of Conquest and Usurpation* and the *Principles of Politics* – and even *De la religion*. On this, see Patrice Higonnet, "Marx, disciple de Constant?" *ABC*, 6 (1986), 11–16.

[21] Emile Faguet, *Politiques et moralistes du dix-neuvième siècle* (Paris: Boivin & Cie, 1923), 194, 213.

[22] Henry Michel, *L'idée de l'Etat* (Paris, Hachette, 1898), reproduced by Fayard (2003), 334.

insulting, way. Faguet suggested that selfishness lay at the foundation not only of Constant's politics, but of "all of his religious ideas"
as well.[23] And yet Faguet made no attempt to come to terms with
these religious ideas or even to address them squarely. Michel went
so far as to dismiss Constant's liberalism as "lacking in metaphysical
support."[24] Was he unaware that Constant had written a five-volume
book on religion, or did he simply choose to ignore it? Anyone who
actually reads *De la religion* will find in it a sustained critique of the
ethics of self-interest, a critique that is, in fact, scattered throughout Constant's other writings as well.[25] One can only conclude that
these interpreters read him only partially and superficially, if they
read him at all.

THE AMERICAN TRANSCENDENTALISTS: CONSTANT AS RELIGIOUS REFORMER

Constant's reception in nineteenth-century America could not have
been more different. There, his Protestant and individualistic variety of liberalism was already well established, if not dominant.[26]
But in America, it was especially Constant's religious writings that
struck a positive chord. On the publication of *De la religion*, Constant quickly became a favorite among a group of liberal Protestants
who translated and disseminated his religious ideas. These were the
friends and disciples of the Unitarian minister, William Ellery Channing (1780–1842). George Ripley (1802–80), one of the more influential members of this circle, professed admiration for Constant's
services as a liberal politician, but predicted that it was, above all,
for his writings on religion that he would be remembered. These
writings were an "earnest and eloquent protest against the infidelity

---

[23] Faguet, 213.
[24] Michel, 340.
[25] Ralph Raico is particularly good on this. See his unjustly neglected "The Place
of Religion in the Liberal Philosophy of Constant, Tocqueville, and Lord Acton,"
Ph.D. dissertation, Committee on Social Thought, University of Chicago, Chicago,
IL, 1970, available online at http://www.mises.org/etexts/raico.pdf.
[26] The idea that there existed a *hegemonic* liberal consensus in America has recently
come under attack, although few people question liberalism's importance. On
this, I have found James Young, *Reconsidering American Liberalism. The Troubled Odyssey of the Liberal Idea* (Boulder, CO: Westview Press, 1996), especially
helpful.

of his day"; they attacked the "selfish and material principles" that reigned in France. In Constant, Ripley found a "cheering example of devotion to principle and of faith in humanity." Here was a man who had devoted his life to defending "the inborn rights of the soul."[27]

As early as 1827, readers of America's leading Unitarian journal, the *Christian Examiner*, learned about Constant's *De la religion*. Constant's "fine work" was said to combine "vast erudition with the most forcible thoughts."[28] In September 1834, the journal carried a full review of the book by Orestes Brownson (1803–76), who praised Constant for his "striking and important" ideas. The emanation of a "benevolent heart," Constant's *De la religion* made excellent reading for true Christians. Intended to "increase our love for mankind," it was bound "to warm the heart . . . [and] inspire us with new zeal and confidence." Of critical importance was Constant's assertion that "religious sentiment" was "a fundamental law of our nature." Equally important was his recognition that the forms that religious sentiment took over the course of history were variable and destined to improve. In short, Constant understood that man was "a progressive being" and that his religion was meant to be progressive as well. Only then could it contribute to the "noble work of setting the human race forward in the march towards perfection."[29]

Constant's *De la religion* was of more than academic interest to Brownson and his circle of friends. Brownson's writings indicate that Constant's ideas were used to lend legitimacy to their desire to break off from Unitarianism in order to found a new religious movement called Transcendentalism. In his *New Views of Christianity, Society and the Church* (1836), a key text in this project, Brownson again referred to Benjamin Constant as an authority on the idea that man was not a "stationary being"; rather, he was constantly "ascending" and thus his religious institutions should as well. "We think the

---

[27] George Ripley in *Specimens of Foreign Language Literature*. vol. I: *Philosophical Miscellanies, Translated from the French of Cousin, Jouffroy, and B. Constant*, ed. George Ripley (Boston: Hilliard, Gray, and Company, 1838), 289, 290, 259.

[28] *The Christian Examiner*, vol. I (January–February 1827), 2. See also the references to Constant in *The Unitarian Advocate* (November 5, 1830), 276; *The Christian Examiner* (July 15, 1831), 273; and *The Christian Register* (December 15, 1832), 199. Pierre Deguise compares Constant's religious views with those of the Unitarians in "La religion de Benjamin Constant et l'Unitarisme américain," *ABC*, 12 (1991), 19–27.

[29] *The Christian Examiner* (September 1834), vol. XVII, new series vol. xii, 63–77.

time has come for us to clothe the religious sentiment with a new form," wrote Brownson in his review of *De la religion*; therefore, Unitarianism should "be abandoned."[30] A later review in the *Boston Quarterly* reiterated a similar point: Constant's *De la religion* was just the work needed to "restore us to a pure, rational, and living faith."[31]

It is no wonder, then, that another leading spokesman of the Transcendentalist movement, George Ripley, translated and published three essays by Constant, encapsulating his religious philosophy. "On the Perfectibility of the Human Race," "On the Human Causes Which Have Contributed to the Establishment of Christianity," and "The Progressive Developement [sic] of Religious Ideas" appeared in Ripley's *Specimens of Foreign Language Literature* in 1838. In his introduction, Ripley paid homage to Constant's lifelong political battles. Ripley recognized Constant as a political writer, debater and "fearless advocate of constitutional freedom." But it was in Constant's religious writings that the heart of his system and its "consummate unity" could be found. Ripley read these texts as a summon to self-improvement. To him, the purpose of Constant's political system, and in particular, of his desire to limit government's power, was to allow for the maximum "freedom and improvement of the individual." Ripley celebrated Constant for his commitment to promoting "individual excellence," which he saw as clearly linked to furthering "the cause of humanity."[32]

Channing's memoirs record the sense of hope that reading Constant inspired in this American group of liberal Protestants. Constant's religious writings "[gave] promise of a better state of things."[33] He was one of the few men in France who understood that a purer, higher form of Christianity would cure society's ills. It is interesting to note that Channing, who had met that other great French liberal thinker, Alexis de Tocqueville, in October 1831,

---

[30] Ibid., 70. Ironically, Brownson later converted to Roman Catholicism.

[31] *The Boston Quarterly Review*, I (October 1838), 440.

[32] Ripley, in *Specimens*, 249, 250, 263, 264, 251.

[33] *Memoirs of Channing*, vol. III, ed. W. H. Channing (London, 1848), 396, as quoted by Pierre Deguise, "La religion," 22. See also William Girard, "Du transcendantalisme considéré essentiellement dans sa définition et ses origines françaises," *University of California Publications in Modern Philology*, 4 (3) (October 18, 1916), who writes that Channing "spoke admiringly of Benjamin Constant" (p. 421)."

disagreed with him on the topic of Christianity. When it came to religion, the great American minister had more in common with Constant.[34]

EDOUARD LABOULAYE AND THE ATTEMPT AT REVIVAL

It has often been remarked that the French liberal tradition was weak; it was fractured and riddled with contradictions. In the words of one observer, it was a "chaotic mixture."[35] By 1860, a well-known dictionary registered the problem. "Liberalism," it noted, was "vague" and "hard to define." What was clear and certain, however, was its link with individualism, and this was the cause of its doom: "according to us," the dictionary explained, "a doctrine which is nothing but individualism is nothing but an impossibility, an absurdity."[36] Liberalism's connection with individualism helps to explain why, following France's so-called republican moment[37] in the 1870s, the very term "liberalism" disappeared from the canon of the Left,[38] as even relatively sympathetic thinkers attempted to distance themselves from its pejorative connotations. As Lucien Jaume has argued, this failure of liberalism left a lasting mark on the French political tradition, which retained an admiration for strong centralized government.[39] In 1903, Emile Faguet famously remarked that "France is a republican country that has no freedom."[40]

Nevertheless, individual liberals did appear on the political horizon. One notable example is, of course, the great statesman and theorist Alexis de Tocqueville (1805–59). Curiously, however, Tocqueville never mentioned Constant, even though he took up many

---

34 George Pierson, *Tocqueville in America* (Baltimore, MD: Johns Hopkins Press, 1996), 421–23.
35 Guido de Ruggiero, *The History of European Liberalism*, trans. R. G. Collingwood (Boston, MA: Beacon Press, 1961), 203.
36 "Libéralisme," in *Dictionnaire politique* (Paris: Pagnerre, 1860), 533–34.
37 Philip Nord, *The Republican Moment. Struggles for Democracy in Nineteenth-Century France* (Cambridge, MA: Harvard University Press, 1998).
38 Tony Judt, *Past Imperfect. French Intellectuals, 1944–1956* (Berkeley, CA: University of California Press, 1992), 238, 230. Sudhir Hazareesingh speaks of its "endemic" weakness in *Political Traditions in Modern France* (Oxford: Oxford University Press, 1994), 225.
39 Lucien Jaume, *Echec au libéralisme: les Jacobins et l'Etat* (Paris: Kimé, 1990).
40 Emile Faguet, *Le Libéralisme* (Paris: Société Française d'Imprimerie et de Librairie, 1903), 113.

of the same causes. But then Tocqueville is well known for his reluctance to reveal his sources. And, in any case, as Françoise Melonio has shown, Tocqueville himself was largely forgotten after 1870.[41] A second example is the historian, liberal theorist, and statesman Edouard Laboulaye (1811–83). Laboulaye was a great admirer of both Constant and Tocqueville, whose thought he tried to revive. Cognizant of the intellectual affinity between the two men, Laboulaye expressed surprise that Tocqueville seemed unaware of Constant, at one point exclaiming,

> How much toil and fatigue that noble mind [Tocqueville] might have spared itself had he read the liberal publicist [Constant]. In all his pamphlets, of which he probably knew nothing, would he not have found his own thoughts expressed with as much finesse as force?[42]

Under Laboulaye's direction, Constant's *Cours de politique constitutionnelle*, containing his principal political works, was reissued in 1861 and again in 1872. In a long introduction to that work, as well as a biographical sketch published in the *Revue national*, Laboulaye hailed Constant as "*the* master of political science for all friends of liberty."[43]

Laboulaye read Constant primarily as a prescient advocate of small government and individual rights. Constant was someone who offered timely warnings about the dangers of state power. Laboulaye regretted deeply that Frenchmen had not heeded Constant's admonitions long ago. Sadly, they had focused on a few unfortunate details of his private life, while they had neglected the noble ideas for which he had fought. Laboulaye implored his compatriots not to ignore Constant's advice once more; his ideas were now as relevant as ever. Thirty years of history had witnessed the growth of an enormous administration in France, claiming for itself the right to regulate citizens' lives. The population had been seduced by nefarious systems

---

[41] Françoise Mélonio, *Tocqueville et les Français* (Paris: Aubier, 1993).

[42] Edouard Laboulaye, "Introduction," to his edition of *Cours de politique constitutionnelle ou collection des ouvrages publiés sur le gouvernement représentatif par Benjamin Constant* (Paris: Librairie de Guillaumin et Cie, 1872), ix. There is now proof that Tocqueville did read Constant. See Robert Gannett, Jr., *Tocqueville Unveiled. The Historian and His Sources for the Old Regime and the Revolution* (Chicago, IL: The University of Chicago Press, 2003), 32–35, 37.

[43] Edouard Laboulaye, "Avertissement de la présente édition" in the *Cours de politique constitutionnelle*, i.

of thought such as Saint-Simonianism, socialism, and communism, allowing government to balloon. To all of this, Constant's ideas were the perfect antidote. Laboulaye believed that, in some ways, France's current situation was worse than it had been under the Restoration, since its population seemed to have lost its former love of liberty. He hoped that a new edition of Constant's writings would help rekindle that love.

Laboulaye was eager to respond to criticism from both Right and Left that liberalism was an egotistic, atomistic philosophy. In stark contrast to Constant's French detractors, Laboulaye saw nothing "selfish" or "blasé" about his liberalism. On the contrary, it was precisely Constant's high-mindedness that appealed to him. More in tune with Constant's American admirers than his French critics, Laboulaye perceived that "a religious faith animates and inspires all of his politics."[44] For Constant, freedom was nothing but "the complete development of the human soul."[45]

When it came to Constant's religious writings, with which he was obviously well acquainted, Laboulaye proffered that they were integral to Constant's liberalism. His was "Protestant mind,"[46] which was also why he understood so well that "religion is the friend and necessary companion of liberty."[47] Like other liberal Protestants of his day, Constant also appreciated the fact that religious liberty was "the mother of all others."[48] Individuals must have liberty if they are to exercise and develop their faculties and thereby improve themselves intellectually and morally. Constant thus understood what so many Frenchmen had a difficulty apprehending: that liberty is "our soul in action."[49]

PROTESTANT NETWORKS, THE CAMPAIGN FOR LAÏCITÉ, AND THE SCIENTIFIC STUDY OF RELIGION

Laboulaye's attempt at revival shows that Constant was not entirely forgotten in France during the second half of the nineteenth

---

[44] *Revue nationale et étrangère, politique, scientifique et littéraire*, vol. 7 (Paris, 1861), 27.
[45] "Introduction," xii.
[46] *Revue nationale*, vol. 7, 18.
[47] Ibid., 23.
[48] "Introduction," xiii.
[49] Ibid., xii.

century. Within a minority vein of French liberalism, Constant continued to have admirers, who, from time to time, took inspiration from his political thought. His religious publications also retained an appeal to those partial to liberal Protestantism. Comments by the Protestant theologian, Alexandre Vinet, testify to the importance of Constant's religious writings for this community.[50] It is known that Edgar Quinet was an admirer of Constant and that he read *De la religion* carefully.[51] Quinet was the only one among a number of prominent French intellectuals who expressed a sympathetic interest in Protestantism during and after the Second Empire. Although more research is needed to establish exact filiations, Constant's ideas on religion and church–state relations lived on among the networks of pro-Protestant advocates of *laïcité*.[52] Ferdinand Buisson, one active member of this network, used Constant's distinction between religious "form" and religious "sentiment," as well as the idea of religious progress in his *La foi laïque* and *Le libéralisme protestant*. But it seems likely that Constant's language had by then become part of a shared vocabulary among those lobbying for the separation of church and state.

Eventually, Constant was also recognized as a pioneer in the academic or scientific study of religion. American Unitarians celebrated Constant for being among the first to recognize religion neither as a supernatural gift nor as some kind of illusion or illness, but rather "as a normal product of human nature." His big book on religion had opened a "path... [that had since] become a highway of religious

---

[50] As noted by Brian Juden, "Accueil et rayonnement de la pensée de Benjamin Constant sur la religion," in *Benjamin Constant, Madame de Staël et le Groupe de Coppet. Actes du deuxième Congrès de Lausanne*, ed. E. Hofmann (Oxford: The Voltaire Foundation, 1982), 156.

[51] Willy Aeschimann, *La Pensée d'Edgar Quinet. Etude sur la formation de ses idées avec essais de jeunesse et documents inedits* (Paris: Editions Anthropos, 1986), 277. The Protestant contribution to *laïcité* is studied by Patrick Cabanel in *Le Dieu de la République. Aux sources protestantes de la laïcité (1860–1900)* (Rennes: Presses universitaires de Rennes, 2003).

[52] Constant's connection to laïcité is understudied. Georges Weill mentions Constant briefly in *Histoire de l'idée laïque en France au xixe siècle* (Paris: Félix Alcan, 1925), 48; Jacqueline Lalouette gives him some more space in *La séparation des églises et de l'état. Genèse et développement d'une idée 1789–1905* (Paris: Editions du Seuil, 2005). See also my "On the Intellectual Sources of Laïcité. Rousseau, Constant, and the Debates about a National Religion," *French Politics, Culture & Society*, 25 (3) (Winter 2007), 1–18.

thought."[53] As a piece of cutting-edge scholarship, *De la religion* drew the attention not just of Protestants: it is known, for example, that Jules Michelet read it carefully,[54] as did Karl Marx.[55] Ernest Renan (1823–92) was accused of plagiarizing from it in his *Etudes d'histoire religieuse*.[56] In 1879, the Collège de France established a chair in the history of religion.[57] In his inaugural address, the first holder of that chair, Albert Réville, paid homage to Constant's "remarkable book," full of "wise and penetrating perceptions."[58] Tzvetan Todorov's essay in this *Cambridge Companion* argues that what distinguished Constant from previous writers on the subject of religion was his effort to work with facts alone and to relate religion closely to its historical context. Constant "proposed not to be for or against religion, but simply to study it" and he should therefore be regarded a founder of religious anthropology.[59] Many features of Constant's methodology were adopted by his successors and are now regarded as standard in the study of religion. However, the scholarship itself, based, as it was, on available published sources, was soon out of date, surpassed by other, more specialized studies. Moreover, Constant's main thesis, that of "religious perfectibility," was quickly outmoded, at least in academic circles. Not until 1999 did a new edition call attention to this remarkable work.[60]

CONSTANT, AUTHOR OF *ADOLPHE*

While Constant's political and religious writings were largely eclipsed by the end of the nineteenth century, the same period saw his rise as the author of *Adolphe*. The first edition of the novel came out in both England and France in 1816 to a mixed reception, and

---

53 *The Unitarian Review and Religious Magazine* (February 1882), 135.
54 Juden, 152, 158.
55 Patrice Higonnet, "Marx, disciple de Constant?"
56 Juden, 159.
57 Patrick Cabanel, "L'institutionnalisation des 'sciences religieuses' en France (1879–1908) Une entreprise protestante?" *Bulletin de la Société de l'histoire du protestantisme français* (January–February–March 1994), 34.
58 Albert Réville, *Prolégomènes de l'histoire des religions* (Paris: G. Fischbacher, 1881), 45.
59 See this volume, p. 276.
60 *De la religion, considérée dans sa source, ses formes et ses développements*, ed. Tzvetan Todorov and Etienne Hofmann (Arles, France: Actes Sud, 1999).

during Constant's lifetime, it failed to gain the recognition it deserved. As Paul Delbouille writes, "too romantic in 1816, [*Adolphe*] was not romantic enough in 1830."[61] It took more than seventy years for the book to become a recognized classic. In the meantime, it was read not so much as literature or as philosophy, but as thinly disguised autobiography. Readers focused on how true and sincere the novel was, and on whether it was honorable for someone to write such a book. Many assumed that the story was about Madame de Staël and thought it an ungentlemanly way for Constant to treat her. This way of reading *Adolphe* did not enhance Constant's reputation.

Throughout the nineteenth century, the reception of *Adolphe* remained tied to speculations about Constant's personal life, as a steady stream of intimate revelations, some more authentic than others, became available to the public. In 1887, Constant's private journal was published, followed a year later by a collection of his personal letters. After this, new editions of his journals came out, accompanied by collections of private correspondence. All of this fed further speculations about Constant's private life and the various perceived or real flaws in his character. One of the most frequently cited sentences from Constant's journals reads, "I am not entirely a real person. There are within me two people, one who observes the other."[62] Combined with what else was known about Constant's life and character, it seems to have kept many from taking Constant's work seriously.

By the end of the century people still read *Adolphe* less as a work of art or literature than as an exercise in psychological self-analysis. It became fairly common not just to assimilate Constant to his main character, but to see them both as symptoms of a more general illness of the age. Eventually, however, the rise of psychology as a respectable discipline helped the book to rise in the public's esteem. Over the course of the twentieth century, readers increasingly admired Constant's sincerity and willingness to bare his soul. But this only intensified the tendency toward psychologically oriented analyses of Constant's work. It took a long time before *Adolphe*

---

[61] Paul Delbouille, *Genèse, structure et destin d'Adolphe* (Paris: Les Belles Lettres, 1971).

[62] *Journaux intimes (1804–1807)*, in *OCBC/Œuvres*, VI (April 11, 1804), 104.

was regarded as a work of literary art,[63] and only very recently has the novel been seen in relation to Constant's larger intellectual and political commitments.[64]

Feminists were among the first to place *Adolphe* in a broader political context, but they did so in order to expose what they saw as Constant's hypocrisy and limitations as a thinker. Margaret Waller is a pioneer in this domain. Despite Constant's relatively progressive depiction of the relations between the sexes in *Adolphe*, Waller stresses the novel's "objectification of women and its androcentric bias." In her opinion, Adolphe's "duplicitous attempts at self-exoneration" help prove that far from promoting freedom for all, Constant "merely modernized male dominance" over women.[65] Recent work has complicated and added considerable nuance to this picture. The essays of P. Coleman, J. Izenberg, and S. Vincent in this *Companion* are important examples of this new trend.

THE RISE OF THE WELFARE STATE: CONSTANT THE LIBERTARIAN

If Constant's individualistic brand of liberalism was widely accepted in early nineteenth-century America, the situation had changed dramatically by the middle of the twentieth century. Under the impact of important social and economic changes, and two World Wars, America had lost much of its faith in laissez-faire capitalism and the individualistic principles undergirding it. What was now increasingly referred to as "classical" liberalism was in retreat, replaced by new versions of liberalism more concerned with social inequalities and more favorable to state intervention. As Friedrich von Hayek remarked in *The Road to Serfdom* (1944), "individualism has a bad name today... [it] has come to be connected with egotism and selfishness."[66] It was in an effort to correct this state of affairs, and to revive classical liberalism, that Hayek recommended Constant,

---

[63] Paul Bowman, "Nouvelles lectures d'*Adolphe*," in *ABC*, 1 (1980), provides an overview of scholarship from the perspective of 1980.

[64] For an excellent example, see Patrick Coleman's essay in this volume.

[65] Margaret Waller, *The Male Malady. Fictions of Impotence in the French Romantic Novel* (New Brunswick: Rutgers University Press, 1993), 6, 96.

[66] Friedrich Hayek, *The Road to Serfdom* (Chicago: University of Chicago Press, 1944), 14.

whom he described as one of the great political philosophers and "intellectual leaders" of nineteenth-century liberalism.[67] To Hayek, reading Constant was an excellent antidote to the creeping socialism he saw all around him. In 1960, Hayek moved from the London School of Economics to the University of Chicago, where he continued to teach and recommend Constant among other classically liberal theorists.

Some years later, one of Hayek's American disciples showcased Constant in his newly founded libertarian journal, the New Individualist Review (1961–68).[68] Along with Hayek, the economist Milton Friedman served as an editorial advisor on this journal. According to Friedman, belief in classical liberalism was then at a low ebb in America. Nevertheless, a small group of students and faculty at the University of Chicago sensed a change in the intellectual climate. They felt a growing reaction against collectivism and a resurgence of belief in individualism.[69] Attempting both to capitalize on and to contribute to this change in atmosphere, the New Individualist Review was launched in 1961. In its winter 1964 issue, its editor in chief, Ralph Raico, published a ten-page précis of Constant's life and thought.

Identifying Constant as one of the "great individualists of the past," Raico was eager to refute the reigning notion that individualists are just egotists in disguise. He wrote of the "elevated foundation" of Constant's liberalism and its "ethical ends." Raico highlighted Constant's commitment to "the development and enrichment of personality," to people's self-development and self-improvement.[70] Raico painted a well-rounded portrait of Constant. He called attention to Constant's work as both a writer and a politician, his authorship of an important novel, and his devotion to the study of religion.

It is hard to know how many people read Raico's article. The subscription list of the New Individualist Review never numbered more

---

[67] Friedrich Hayek, The Constitution of Liberty (Chicago: University of Chicago Press, 1960), 68.

[68] On this periodical, see Ronald Hamowy, "The Libertarian Press," in The Conservative Press in Twentieth-Century America, ed. Ronald Lora and William Henry Longton (Westport, CT: Greenwood Press, 1999), 339–47.

[69] Milton Friedman, "Introduction," in New Individualist Review (Indianapolis: A Periodical Reprint of Liberty Fund, 1981), ix–xiv.

[70] "Benjamin Constant," in New Individualist Review, 499, 501.

than eight hundred, but it included the editors of several prestigious magazines and newspapers, many university and college libraries, as well as prominent academics throughout the United States and Western Europe.[71] And evidence shows that groups of American libertarians continue to take interest in, and inspiration from, Constant, as can be seen on the pages of *The Freeman* and the *Journal of Libertarian Studies*.[72]

THE DANGERS OF MODERN DEMOCRACY: CONSTANT THE ANTITOTALITARIAN

Undoubtedly more important for Constant's twentieth-century reputation was Isaiah Berlin's famous essay "Two Concepts of Liberty" (1958). Driven by his fear of twentieth-century dictatorships and, in particular, the threat of Stalinist Communism, Berlin showcased Constant as one of the first writers in history to warn of the tendencies modern democracies have to become totalitarian. The genius of Constant was that he endorsed a "negative" rather than a "positive" idea of freedom. In contrast to theorists like Rousseau, to whom freedom meant the possession of a share of public power, Constant viewed freedom as "noninterference" or lack of coercion. Having witnessed the French Revolution firsthand, Constant understood that liberty in the Rousseauian, "positive" sense could easily end up destroying many of the "negative" liberties that Berlin held sacred. Constant understood the need to protect the individual from the state. This is what made him one of "the most eloquent of all defenders of freedom and privacy."[73] Berlin's distinction between negative and positive liberty, and his reading of Constant, would be enormously influential, structuring discussions for years to come.

But Berlin was not the first to interpret Constant through an antitotalitarian lens. In 1941, Helen Byrne Lippman, wife of the noted

---

[71] Hamoway, 343.

[72] See, for example, articles and reviews by Jim Powell and Sheldon Richard in *The Freeman*, June and October 1997, January 2004, and July 2007. See also Richard Ebeling's "Beware Democracy without Liberty," in *The Freeman* (April 2005) and the review of Etienne Hofmann's translation of Constant's *Principles of Politics* in the *Journal of Libertarian Studies*, 19 (1) (Winter 2005), 97–104.

[73] Isaiah Berlin, "Two Concepts of Liberty," in *Four Essays on Liberty* (New York: Oxford University Press, 1969), 126.

political commentator and journalist, Walter Lippman, published an abridged and translated version of Constant's anti-Napoleonic tract, *The Spirit of Conquest and Usurpation*. In her introduction, Lippman explained that she had been urged to read Constant in Paris in 1939 by an international group of friends who wished to revive the "forgotten classics of resistance to dictatorship and aggression." Lippman hoped that making available Constant's remarkable "prophecy from the past" would help shore up resistance to Hitler. She noted that despite the dark moment France was traversing when Constant wrote his pamphlet, he offered words of encouragement that were relevant to twentieth-century democracies as well.[74]

Nevertheless it was Isaiah Berlin's anti-Rousseauian and essentially antidemocratic reading of Constant that would have the greatest longevity and influence. It is a perspective that received strong support from other influential theorists and scholars around the same time. For Jacob Talmon, Benjamin Constant's value lay in his early realization that the true enemy of individual freedom was "totalitarian democracy."[75] John Plamenatz described Constant as someone who "feared" and "disliked" democracy.[76] Twenty years later, Guy Dodge was still admiring Constant for having understood that "the idea of popular sovereignty is the taproot of totalitarianism."[77] It should be noted, however, that this interpretation of Constant was based on a highly selective reading of his texts. It paid no attention to the many times Constant in fact defended popular sovereignty, or the repeated instances when he spoke optimistically about human "perfectibility" and the "tendency toward equality" manifest in history.[78]

---

[74] *Prophecy from the Past. Benjamin Constant on Conquest and Usurpation*, ed. and trans. Helen Byrne Lippmann (New York, 1941).

[75] Jacob L. Talmon, *Political Messianism: The Romantic Phase* (New York: Praeger, 1960), 317–22.

[76] John Plamenatz, "Liberalism," in *Dictionary of the History of Ideas*, vol. III, ed. Philip Wiener (New York: Charles Scribner's Sons, 1973), 36–61.

[77] Guy Dodge, *Benjamin Constant's Philosophy of Liberalism* (Chapel Hill, NC: University of North Carolina Press, 1980), 145, quoting Alfred Cobban.

[78] See Beatrice Fink, "Benjamin Constant on Equality" on Constant's notion of perfectibility; see also Etienne Hofmann in this volume; Florence Lotterie, *Progrès et perfectibilité: un dilemme des Lumières françaises* (1755–1814) (Oxford: Voltaire Foundation, 2006); "Le progrès désenchanté: la perfectibilité selon Constant ou

Although the liberal and antitotalitarian turn came later to France, when it did, it also led to a renewed interest in the political writings of Benjamin Constant. The then reigning Marxist and Marxist-inspired interpretations of French political history dismissed Constant's liberalism as the mere expression of bourgeois-class interest. "In no other writer are the preoccupations of the bourgeoisie more evident," wrote Jacques Droz, adding that this is what made Constant's liberalism an entirely "negative" doctrine.[79] Roger Soltau's influential survey *French Political Thought in the Nineteenth Century* makes passing reference to Constant's supposed "fickleness" as a person and regrets that he was "a liberal, not a democrat." Soltou then describes French nineteenth-century liberalism in general as just an "opportunist and class policy" designed to "make the middle class safe from democracy."[80] In Jean Touchard's survey, French liberalism is also described as a "negative" and "critical" doctrine, whose historical role was only to justify the political domination of the bourgeoisie.[81]

During the 1970 and 1980s, however, an intellectual sea change[82] occurred within the French academic community, as intellectuals abandoned the Marxist paradigm and began to reassess France's political tradition. Liberalism now emerged as an attractive alternative to Marxism, and the period of the Restoration, when Constant was at the height of his powers, became seen as a "golden age of political reflection."[83] Central to this shift in perspective was

le malaise libéral," in *Le Groupe de Coppet et le monde moderne. Conceptions-Images-Débats*, ed. Françoise Tilkin (Geneva: Droz, 1998); Ghislain Waterlot, "Perfectibilité et vérité de la religion chez Benjamin Constant," in *L'homme perfectible*, ed. Bertrand Binoche (Seyssel: Champ Vallon, 2004); and Jean Starobinski, "Benjamin Constant: la pensée du progrès et l'analyse des réactions," *ABC*, 23–24 (2000), 39–62.

[79] Jacques Droz, *Histoire des doctrines politiques en France* (Paris: Presses universitaires de France, 1948), 69–73; see also Jean Touchard, *Histoire des idées politiques*, vol. 2 (Paris: Presses Universitaire de France, 1959).

[80] Roger Soltau, *French Political Thought in the Nineteenth Century* (New York: Russel & Russel, 1959), 47. A similar characterization Constant can be found in Maxime Leroy, *Histoire des idées sociales en France*, vol. 2: *De Babeuf à Tocqueville* (Paris: Gallimard, 1950), 178–79.

[81] Jean Touchard, *Histoire des idées politiques*, vol. 2 (Paris: Presses Universitaires de France, 1959), p. xx.

[82] Mark Lilla, "The Other Velvet Revolution: Continental Liberalism and Its Discontents," *Daedalus*, 123 (2) (Spring 1994), 148.

[83] Pierre Rosanvallon, *Le moment Guizot* (Paris: Gallimard, 1985), 75.

François Furet's reevaluation of the French Revolution, *Penser la Révolution française* (1978).[84] Rejecting Marxist-inspired interpretations that he believed were more commemorative than they were analytical, Furet highlighted the Revolution's negative, even pathological, aspects. For inspiration, he turned to the ideas of French nineteenth-century liberals, who had for long been ignored, if not disdained, by Marxists.[85] In Furet's rendering, Constant emerged as one of the first to understand the pathology of the French Revolution, in other words, its proto-totalitarian nature. According to Furet, Constant's entire political thought revolved around the problem of explaining the Terror.[86] Following Furet, other French scholars took a renewed interest in Constant, admiring him mainly as an historian, interpreter, and perhaps above all, a critic of the Revolution. In his pathbreaking essay "The Lucid Illusion" (1980), reproduced in abridged form in this *Companion*, Marcel Gauchet praises Constant for having understood the Revolution's various failures, problems, and even "evils."[87]

From all of this renewed attention, Constant gained considerable stature as a founding thinker of a newly rediscovered French liberal tradition.[88] Notably, however, this Constant renaissance was based on an incomplete reading of his work. Curiously, when it came to his supposed fear or disdain for the democratic masses, the revisionists essentially agreed with the Marxists. The Constant they revived was a pessimistic, skeptical, and critical author, who had deep anxieties about democracy and the future.[89] According to Marcel Gauchet, Constant's writings were to be admired for shedding light on the "devastating contradictions of modernity"[90] and

---

[84] Michael Scott Christofferson, "An Antitotalitarian History of the French Revolution: François Furet's *Penser la Revolution française* in the Intellectual Politics of the Late 1970s," *French Historical Studies*, 22 (4) (Fall 1999), 557–611. See also Sunil Khilnani, *The Intellectual Left in Postwar France* (New Haven: Yale University Press, 1993).

[85] Another important book in this revival was undoubtedly Paul Benichou's *Le Temps des prophètes. Doctrines de l'âge romantique* (Paris: Gallimard, 1977).

[86] François Furet, "La Révolution sans la Terreur? Le débat des historiens du XIXe siècle," *Le Débat*, 13 (June 1981), 41.

[87] Ibid., 959.

[88] See, for example, Louis Girard, *Les libéraux français* (Paris: Aubier, 1985), and André Jardin, *Histoire du libéralisme politique* (Paris: Hachette, 1985).

[89] Jacques Droz, *Histoire des doctrines*, 70, 73.

[90] Ibid., 28.

the so-called democratic problem [*le mal démocratique*].[91] Pierre Rosanvallon described Constant's philosophy as one of "suspicion" and "mistrust" of popular sovereignty. While Pierre Manent and Philippe Raynaud stand out among recent French scholars for recognizing that Constant believed in and defended the idea of popular sovereignty, they too use words such as "suspicion," "nostalgia," "dissatisfaction," and "anxiety" to characterize his thought. A main reason for this pessimistic and negative reading of Constant is that the readers themselves are pessimistic.[92] They read Constant selectively, for confirmation of their own views.

THE COMMUNITARIAN CRITIQUE: CONSTANT THE LIBERAL DEMOCRAT

In America, John Rawls's landmark book of 1971, *A Theory of Justice*, caused a major revival of interest in liberalism. It also inspired much criticism and triggered a heated debate about liberalism's effects on America's moral and civic culture. What came to be known as the "communitarian" critique accused liberalism of undermining notions of citizenship and community and of thereby contributing to America's moral decline. Liberalism came under heavy attack for being too individualistic. It was said to operate with a defective notion of the self, which ignored the social constitution of individuals and the importance of communal bonds. For all these reasons, liberalism was accused of contributing to the growing sense of selfishness, rootlessness, loneliness, and alienation gripping America. Indeed, during the 1970s "liberal" became widely used as a pejorative label.

Although Locke, Kant, and Mill featured more regularly in the debates about liberalism, Constant made occasional appearances. Notably, however, whenever he did appear, it was in caricature. Constant was repeatedly cited as an unambiguous advocate of "modern" as opposed to "ancient" liberty, the proponent, in other

---

[91] Ibid., 45.

[92] Andrew Jainchill and Sam Moyn, "French Democracy between Totalitarianism and Solidarity: Pierre Rosanvallon and Revisionist Historiography," *Journal of Modern History*, 76 (1) (March 2004), 107–54, and Helena Rosenblatt, "Why Constant? A Critical Analysis of the Constant Revival," *Modern Intellectual History*, 1 (3) (2004), 439–53.

words, of Isaiah Berlin's "negative" liberty. Rawls himself referred to Constant this way, but only in order to "bypass" and "leave aside" the issue.[93] In Anthony Arblaster's polemical book, *The Rise and Decline of Western Liberalism* (1984), Constant is used to illustrate the "dark side of liberalism" – its "typically bourgeois fear of 'the masses'"[94] and deeply flawed individualistic core. Arblaster describes liberalism's "emphasis on the asocial egoism of the individual" as a "defective and inadequate way of conceiving of human beings."[95] Invariably, during these debates, a reference to Constant's liberalism was reduced to a nod to his distinction between modern and ancient liberty, and a reference to his supposed preference for modern liberty defined as "privacy." This depiction was often accompanied by a comment suggesting that Constant was a liberal and not a democrat.[96]

In 1984, Stephen Holmes used a book-length examination of Constant to defend his own version of democratic liberalism against its American critics.[97] Particularly irritated by attempts to paint Constant as an antidemocratic and necessarily antistatist thinker, Holmes argued that Constant should more accurately be described as an advocate of efficient government at the service of both liberal *and* democratic values. According to Holmes, a careful reading of Constant proved precisely that there is no fundamental opposition between these values. Holmes accused liberalism's critics of painting a "distressingly flat and unconvincing" portrait of both liberalism and Constant; he called attention to the "underlying egalitarianism of Constant's liberalism,"[98] his *critique* of negative freedom, his mistrust of the ethics of self-interest, and his commitment

[93] John Rawls, *A Theory of Justice* (Cambridge, MA: Harvard University Press, 2003).

[94] Anthony Arblaster, *The Rise and Decline of Western Liberalism* (Oxford: Basil Blackwell, 1984), 347.

[95] Ibid., 43.

[96] See, for example, *Western Liberalism. A History in Documents from Locke to Croce*, ed. E. K. Bramsted and K. J. Melhuish (New York: Longman, 1978).

[97] Holmes' political commitments are most evident in *The Anatomy of Antiliberalism* (Cambridge, MA: Harvard University Press, 1993), but see also his *Passions and Constraint: On the Theory of Liberal Democracy* (Chicago: University of Chicago Press, 1995).

[98] Stephen Holmes, *Benjamin Constant and the Making of Modern Liberalism* (New Haven: Yale University Press, 1984), 9.

to encouraging political participation and civic involvement in France.[99] Holmes arrived at this much richer and more historically accurate view of Constant by paying attention not only to a broader range of Constant's political commitments, but also to his novel *Adolphe* and, crucially, to his writings on religion.

Constant's present reputation in America remains closely tied to readings of his essay, "The Liberty of the Ancients Compared with That of the Moderns," which continues to focus political debate. Recently, however, even this essay is being read in new, more constructive ways. In *Active Liberty: Interpreting Our Democratic Constitution*, Justice Stephen Breyer of the U.S. Supreme Court takes inspiration from Constant to maintain that that in a democracy, citizens must participate constantly and actively. Breyer urges American courts to take greater account of this when they interpret constitutional and statutory texts. Sounding more like Stephen Holmes than Isaiah Berlin, Breyer reminds us that Constant never in fact called for the abandonment of ancient liberty in favor of modern liberty, but rather for a proper combination of both.[100] In a different reading of Constant, Harvard Law professor Charles Fried insists that Constant nevertheless did not think of the two types of liberty as equivalent. Unapologetically asserting his belief in the principle that "individuals come first," Fried defines liberty as "individuality made normative." What Constant really meant to promote, according to Fried, was the "power of choice": responsible judgments, self-determination, and the "triumph of individuality." At a time when Americans face "kinder, gentler, less obvious" threats to liberty than Fascism and Marxism, Fried hopes that by propagating his "Constantian" view of liberty, he might update Friedrich Hayek's message in *The Road to Serfdom*.[101]

French theorists at the turn of the twenty-first century also began correcting the image previously circulated of Constant as a primarily negative, critical, and antidemocratic thinker. They did so by taking a more comprehensive and inclusive approach to the various sides of Constant's life and work, and by paying attention to his

---

[99] Holmes, *Benjamin Constant*, 20.
[100] Stephen Breyer, *Active Liberty: Interpreting Our Democratic Constitution* (New York: Random House, 2005).
[101] Charles Fried, *Modern Liberty and the Limits of Government* (New York: W. W. Norton & Co., 2007).

historical context. Lucien Jaume has shed light on Constant's many positive contributions to legal and constitutional thought.[102] More provocatively, given the long reigning image of Constant, Jaume has highlighted his profound interest in "moral cultivation,"[103] in other words, the promotion of an ethics of responsibility. In a novel and sympathetic reading of both Constant's personal life and his works, Todorov has celebrated Constant not only as "the first French theorist of liberal democracy," but also as a great "humanist."[104] Recently, Alain Laurent has urged people to take a closer look at Constant's economic thought, a relatively underexplored subject.[105] All of this is giving us a much richer, more nuanced, and historically accurate picture of Constant.[106]

Finally, recent years have witnessed a growing interest in Constant's religious writings. At various points of his career, Constant himself called his *De la religion* his life's work, "the only interest, the only consolation of my life."[107] As we have seen, this dimension of Constant's thought was neglected if not ignored for a long time. In 1989, however, the Swiss literary critic and theorist Jean Starobinski called attention to what he referred to as Constant's "desire for re-Christianization."[108] A few years later, the American

---

[102] See for example, *Coppet, creuset de l'esprit libéral. Les idées politiques et constitutionnelles du groupe de Mme de Staël*, ed. Lucien Jaume (Paris: Economica, 1999); Lucien Jaume, "Droit, Etat et obligation selon Benjamin Constant," *Commentaire*, 22 (87) (Fall 1999), and "Le concept de responsabilité des ministres chez Benjamin Constant," *Revue française de droit constitutionnel*, 42 (2000).

[103] Lucien Jaume, "Coppet, creuset du libéralisme comme 'culture morale',' in *Coppet, Creuset de l'esprit libéral*, 225–39, and "Le problème de l'intérêt général dans la pensée de Benjamin Constant," in *Le Groupe de Coppet et le monde moderne: Conception-Images-Débats*, ed. Françoise Tilkin (Liège: Bibliothèque de la Faculté de Philosophie et Lettres de l'Université de Liège, 1998).

[104] Tzvetan Todorov, *Passion for Democracy. On the Life, the Women He Loved and the Thought of Benjamin Constant* (New York: Algora, 1999), 83, 85.

[105] Alain Laurent, *La philosophie libérale. Histoire et actualite d'une tradition intellectuelle* (Paris: Les Belles Lettres, 2002), chapter 17; see also his edition of Constant's *Commentaire sur l'ouvrage de Filangieri* (Paris: Les Belles Lettres, 2004).

[106] Nevertheless, in the works of those interested in defending and promoting republicanism as an alternative to liberalism, Constant continues to be caricatured as a simple exponent of "negative" liberty. See for example Sudhir Hazareesingh, *Intellectual Founders of the Republic*, 283; Quentin Skinner, *Liberty before Liberalism*; and Philip Pettit, *Republicanism*.

[107] *Journaux intimes*, in *OCBC/Œuvres*, VI (April 8, 1804), 102.

[108] Jean Starobinski, *Blessings in Disguise; or, the Morality of Evil*, trans. A. Goldhammer (Cambridge, MA: Harvard University Press, 1993). Originally published as *Le remède dans le mal* (Paris: Gallimard, 1989), 25.

political theorist George Amstrong Kelly suggested that Constant's ambition, above all, was to "respiritualize" liberalism.[109] Both responding and contributing to this renewed interest in Constant's religious thought, in 1999, Tzvetan Todorov and Etienne Hofmann brought out a paperback edition of Constant's *De la religion*, which Todorov celebrates in his essay for this *Cambridge Companion* as a forgotten masterpiece.[110] The essays by Bryan Garsten and Laurence Dickey approach Constant's religious texts from different perspectives, shedding new light on a subject that Constant himself thought to be crucial.

No doubt Constant will continue to be cited without being read. Like those of all great thinkers, his writings will find new contexts and applications far beyond what he could have imagined. However, it is hoped that this *Cambridge Companion* will help raise awareness of the richness, breadth, and depth of his work , so that future uses of his ideas might be better informed.

ACKNOWLEDGMENTS

I thank Bryan Garsten, Charles Fried, Jeremy Jennings, Steven Vincent, and Marvin Rosenblatt for reading and offering their comments on this essay. I am also grateful for input from Bruce Caldwell, Charles Capper, and David Robertson.

---

[109] George A. Kelly, *The Humane Comedy: Constant, Tocqueville and French Liberalism* (Cambridge: Cambridge University Press, 1992), 1, 35.

[110] Essay in this *Cambridge Companion*. Mention should be made of Pierre Deguise's important book. Constant's evolving views on religion are the topic of my *Liberal Values*.

BIBLIOGRAPHY

WORKS BY CONSTANT

Adolphe. Translated by Margaret Mauldon. Edited by Patrick Coleman. Oxford: Oxford University Press, 2001.

Adolphe, in *OCBC/Œuvres,* III, 1, Ecrits littéraires *(1800–1813),* 97–203.

"Alger et les élections," in Constant, *Positions de combat à la veille de juillet 1830: articles publiés dans le Temps, 1829–1830.* Edited by Ephraïm Harpaz. Paris: Champion, 1989, 190–92.

Amélie et Germaine, in *OCBC/Œuvres,* III, 1, Ecrits littéraires *(1800–1813),* 37–80.

Cécile, in *OCBC/Œuvres,* III, 1, Ecrits littéraires *(1800–1813),* 241–293.

Cécile, in *Œuvres,* 135–85.

Commentaire sur l'ouvrage de Filangieri. Paris: P. Dufart, 1822–24.

Commentaire sur l'ouvrage de Filangieri. Paris: Les Belles Lettres, 2004.

Cours de politique constitutionnelle. Paris: Guillaumin, 1872.

De la force du gouvernement actuel et de la nécessité de s'y rallier, in *OCBC/Œuvres,* I, Ecrits de jeunesse *(1774–1799)* (1998), 319–80.

De la justice politique par W. Godwin. Traduction très abrégée, in *OCBC/Œuvres,* II, 1, De la justice politique *(1798–1800) d'après l' "Enquiry concerning Political Justice" de William Godwin* (1998), 57–365.

De la perfectibilité de l'espèce humaine, in *De la liberté chez les Modernes.* Paris: Hachette, 1980 (Pluriel), 580–95.

De la religion, considérée dans sa source, ses formes et ses développements. Paris: Bossange, 1824–31.

De la religion, considérée dans sa source, ses formes et ses développements. Paris: A Leroux et C. Chantpie, 1826.

De la religion, considérée dans sa source, ses formes et ses développements. Edited by Tzvetan Todorov and Etienne Hofmann. Arles, France: Actes Sud, 1999.

"De la traite des nègres au Sénégal," in *Recueil d'articles: Le Mercure, la Minerve et la Renommée*, vol. 2. Edited by Ephraïm Harpaz. Geneva: Droz, 1972, 915–26.

De l'esprit de conquête et de l'usurpation dans leurs rapports avec la civilisation européenne. Edited by Ephraïm Harpaz. Paris: Flammarion, 1986.

De M. Dunoyer et de quelques-uns de ses ouvrages, in *Mélanges*, 654–78.

Des effets de la Terreur, in *OCBC/Œuvres*, I, *Ecrits de jeunesse (1774–1799)*, 507–29.

Des réactions politiques, in *OCBC/Œuvres*, I, *Ecrits de jeunesse (1774–1799)*, 447–506.

Des suites de la contre-révolution de 1660 en Angleterre. Paris: F. Buisson, 1799.

Discours de M. Benjamin Constant à la Chambre des Députés. Paris: Ambroise Dupont, 1827–28.

Discours de M. Benjamin Constant à la Chambre de Députés. Paris: J. Pinard, 1828.

Du développement progressif des idées religieuses, in *EP*, 629–53.

Du moment actuel et de la destinée de l'espèce humaine, ou histoire abrégée de l'égalité, in *OCBC/Œuvres*, III, 1, *Ecrits littéraires (1800–1813)*, 367–68.

Du polythéisme romain considéré dans sa source, ses formes et ses développements. Paris: Béchet Ainé, 1825–31.

Ecrits politiques. Edited by Marcel Gauchet. Paris: Gallimard, 1997.

"Esquisse d'un essai sur la littérature du XVIIIe siècle," in *OCBC/Œuvres*, III, 1, *Ecrits littéraires (1800–1813)*, 527–29.

"Fragment de la copie des lectures à l'Athénée Royale sur la religion," in *Bibliothèque cantonale et universitaire de Lausanne.* Fonds Constant, Co., 3279.

"Fragments d'un essai sur la littérature dans ses rapports avec la liberté," in *OCBC/Œuvres*, III, 1, 489–519.

Journal intime de Benjamin Constant et lettres à sa famille et à ses amis. Edited by Dora Melegari. Paris: Paul Ollendorff, 1895.

"Journaux intimes, 1804–1807," in *OCBC/Œuvres*, VI, *Journaux intimes (1804–1807) suivis de Affaire de mon père (1811)*, 29–576.

Le cahier rouge, in *Œuvres*, 119–67.

Lettre à Monsieur le marquis de Latour-Maubourg. Paris: Béchet, 1820.

"Liberty of the Ancients Compared with That of the Moderns [AML]," in *PW*, 307–28.

"Ma vie (Le cahier rouge)," in *OCBC/Œuvres*, III, 1, *Ecrits littéraires (1800–1813)*, 303–58.

Mélanges de littérature et de politique. Paris: Pichon et Didier, 1829.

"Mémoires sur les Cent-Jours," in *OCBC/Œuvres*, XIV, *Mémoires sur les Cent-Jours.*

Œuvres. Edited by Alfred Roulin. Paris: Gallimard, 1957 (Bibliothèque de la Pléiade).

Political Writings. Edited and translated by Biancamaria Fontana. Cambridge: Cambridge University Press, 1988 (*PW*).

Principles of Politics Applicable to All Governments. Edited by E. Hofmann. Translated by D. O'Keeffe. Indianapolis: Liberty Fund, 2003 (*PoP* 1806).

Principles of Politics Applicable to All Representative Governments (*PoP* 1815), in *PW*, 170–305.

Prophecy from the Past. Benjamin Constant On Conquest and Usurpation. Edited and translated by Helen Byrne. New York: Lippmann, 1941.

Recueil d'articles 1820–1824, 2 vols. Edited by Ephraim Harpaz. Geneva: Droz, 1972.

Recueil d'articles 1825–1829. Edited by Ephraim Harpaz. Paris: Champion, 1992.

Receuil d'articles 1829–30. Edited by Ephraim Harpaz. Paris: Champion, 1992.

"*Réflexions sur la tragédie*," in *Œuvres*, 933–62.

"*Spirit of Conquest and Usurpation and Their Relation to European Civilization, The*" (*SCU*), in *PW*, 42–167.

"Wallstein," in *OCBC/Œuvres*, III, 2, *Ecrits littéraires (1800–1813)*, 611–751.

Wallstein. Edited by Jean-René Derré. Paris: Les Belles lettres, n.d. (1965).

CORRESPONDENCE

Charrière, Isabelle de, and Constant d'Hermenches. *There Are No Letters Like Yours: The Correspondence of Isabelle de Charrière and Constant d'Hermenches.* Translated by Janet Whatley and Malcolm Whatley. Lincoln, NE: University of Nebraska Press, 2000.

Constant, Benjamin. *Correspondance générale*, in *OCBC/CG*, I–VII, 1993–2007.

Constant, Benjamin. "Lettres à Louis-Ferdinand et à Thérèse Huber (1798–1806)." Edited by Etienne Hofmann. *Cahiers staëliens*, 29–30, 1981, 77–128.

Constant, Benjamin. *Lettres à Madame Récamier (1807–1830)*. Edited by Ephraïm Harpaz, Paris: Klincksieck, 1977.

Constant, Benjamin, and Germaine de Staël. *Lettres à un ami. Cent onze lettres inédites à Claude Hochet.* Edited by Jean Mistler. Neuchâtel: A la Baconnière, 1949.

Constant, Benjamin, Germaine de Staël, and Charles de Villers. *Correspondance.* Edited by Kurt Kloocke et al. Frankfurt am Main: Peter Lang, 1993.

Constant, Benjamin, and Goyet de la Sarthe. *Correspondance, 1818–1822.* Edited by Ephraim Harpaz. Geneva: Droz, 1973.

Constant, Benjamin, and Isabelle de Charrière. *Correspondance (1787–1805).* Edited by Jean-Daniel Candaux. Paris: Desjonquères, 1996.

Constant de Rebecque, Baronne. *L'Inconnue d'Adolphe: Correspondance de Benjamin Constant et d'Anna Lindsay.* Paris: Plon, 1933.

OTHER PRIMARY SOURCES

Arnold, Thomas. *Sermons.* London: B. Fellows, 1851.

Burke, Edmund. *Reflections on the French Revolution.* London: Dent, 1953.

Cicero, Marcus Tullius. *De Natura Deorum.* Translated by H. Rackham. Cambridge: Harvard University Press, 1933.

Cicero, Marcus Tullius. *On the Good Life.* Translated by Michael Grant. New York: Penguin, 1971.

Clarkson, Thomas. *Essai sur les désavantages politiques de la traite des nègres. . . .* Neufchâtel, 1789.

Condorcet, Jean-Antoine-Nicolas de Caritat. *Réflexions sur l'esclavage, par M. Schwartz.* Neufchâtel: Société Typographique, 1781.

Condorcet, Jean-Antoine-Nicolas de Caritat. *Tableau historique des progrès de l'esprit humain. Projets, Esquisse, Fragments et Notes (1792–1794).* Edited by Jean-Pierre Schandeler and Pierre Crépel. Paris: Institut National d'Etudes Démographiques, 2004.

Coulmann, Jean-Jacques. *Réminiscences.* Paris: Michel Lévy Frères, 1862.

Cudworth, Ralph. *The True Intellectual System of the Universe.* London: Richard Royston, 1678.

Desjobert, Amédée. *L'Algérie en 1846.* Paris: Guillaumin, 1846.

Desjobert, Amédée. *La Question d'Alger: Politique, Colonisation, Commerce.* Paris: Crapelet, 1837.

Diderot, Denis. *Political Writings.* Edited by John Hope Mason and Robert Wokler. Cambridge: Cambridge University Press, 1992.

Dilthey, Wilhelm. *Selected Works.* Edited by Rudolf Makkreel and Frithjof Rodi. Princeton, NJ: Princeton University Press, 1996.

Feuerbach, Ludwig. *The Essence of Christianity.* Translated by George Eliot. New York: Harper, 1957.

Fontenelle, Bernard le Bovier. "Sur l'histoire," in *Œuvres,* vol. 3. Paris: Fayard, 1989.

Fontenelle, Bernard le Bovier. *The Achievement of Bernard le Bovier de Fontenelle.* Translated by Leonard Marsak. New York: Johnson Reprint, 1970.

Fox, William. *An Address to the People of Great Britain, on the Propriety of Abstaining from West India Sugar and Rum.* London: Gurney and

W. Darnton & Co., 1791. Reproduced in *Slavery, Abolition and Emancipation: Writings in the British Romantic Period*, vol. 2. Edited By Peter J. Kitson. London: Pickering and Chatto, 1999, 153–65.

Gibbon, Edward. *The Decline and Fall of the Roman Empire*. Edited by Hans-Friedrich Mueller. New York: Modern Library, 2003.

Grégoire, Henri Jean-Baptiste. *De la littérature des nègres ou Recherches sur leurs facultés intellectuelles, leurs qualités morales*. Paris: Maradan, 1808.

Guizot, François. *Mémoires pour servir à l'histoire de mon temps*, t. II. Paris: Michel Lévy Frères, 1859.

Hayek, Friedrich. *The Constitution of Liberty*. Chicago: University of Chicago Press, 1960.

Hayek, Friedrich. *The Road to Serfdom*. Chicago: University of Chicago Press, 1944.

Herder, J. *Outlines of a Philosophy of the History of Man*. Translated by T. Churchill. New York: Bergman, 1966.

Herder, J. *Reflections on the Philosophy of the History of Man*. Edited by Frank Manuel. Chicago: University of Chicago Press, 1968.

Herder, J. *On World History*. Edited by Hans Adler and Ernest Menze. Translated by Ernest Menze with Micahel Palma. Armonk, NY: M. E. Sharpe, 1997.

Hume, David. *Essays, Moral, Political, and Literary*. Edited by D. Miller. Indianapolis: Liberty Classics, 1987.

Hume, David. "Populousness of Ancient Nations," in *Essays Moral, Political, and Literary*. Indianapolis, IN: Liberty Fund, 1985.

Hume, David. "Of the Jealousy of Trade (ca. 1759)," in *Essays Moral, Political and Literary*. Indianapolis, IN: Liberty Fund, 1985.

Hume, David. *The Natural History of Religion*. London: Bonner, 1889.

Hume, David. *The Natural History of Religion*. Edited by H. Root. Stanford: Stanford University Press, 1956.

Kant, Immanuel. *Critique of Pure Reason*. Translated by Norman K. Smith. New York: Modern Library, 1958.

Kant, Immanuel. *Lectures on Philosophical Theology*. Translated by A. Wood. Ithaca, NY: Cornell University Press, 1978.

Kant, Immanuel. *Kant: Political Writings*. Translated by H. B. Nisbet. Edited by H. Reiss. Cambridge: Cambridge University Press, 1991.

Kant, Immanuel. *Religion and Rational Theology*. Translated by A. Wood. Cambridge, NY: Cambridge University Press, 1996.

Khodja, Hamdan. *Aperçu historique et statistique sur la Régence d'Alger, intitulé en arabe le Miroir*. Paris: Impr. De Goetschy fils, 1833.

Lessing, Gotthold. *Philosophical and Religious Writings*. Translated and edited by H. B. Nisbet. Cambridge: Cambridge University Press, 2005.

"Letter from Paris, March 18, 1825," in *The Museum of Foreign Literature, Science and Art,* 6 (June 1, 1825), 587–88.

Lezay-Marnésia, Adrien, and Benjamin Constant. *Ordine e libertà.* Edited by Mauro Barberis. Turin: La Rosa, 1995.

Maistre, Joseph de. *Considérations sur la France.* Paris: Editions Complexe, 1988.

Marx, Karl. "The Eighteenth Brumaire of Louis Bonaparte," in *The Marx Engels Reader.* Edited by Richard Tucker. New York: W. W. Norton, 1978.

Montesquieu, Charles-Louis de Secondat, Baron de la Brède. *The Spirit of the Laws.* Edited and translated by A. M. Cohler, B. C. Miller, and H. S. Stone. Cambridge: Cambridge University Press, 1989.

Raynal, Abbé. *Histoire philosophique et politique des établissements et du commerce des Européens dans les deux Indes.* Neufchâtel and Geneva: Libraires associés, 1783–84.

Rousseau, Jean-Jacques. "Emile," in *Œuvres complètes de Jean-Jacques Rousseau,* vol. 4. Edited by Bernard Gagnebin and Marcel Raymond. Paris: Pléiade, 1970.

Rousseau, Jean-Jacques. *On the Social Contract, with Geneva Manuscript and Political Economy.* Translated by Judith Masters. Edited by Roger Masters. New York: St. Martin's Press, 1978.

Saint-Simon, Claude Henri de. "New Christianity," in *Social Organization, the Science of Man and Other Essays.* Edited and translated by Felix Marham. New York: Harper & Row, 1964.

Sainte-Beuve, C. A. *Portraits contemporains,* t. 5. Paris: Calmann Lévy, 1889.

Salaville, Jean-Baptiste. *L'homme et la société ou nouvelle théorie de la nature humaine.* Carteret, 1798–99.

Schiller, F. *Naïve and Sentimental Poetry/On the Sublime.* Translated by J. Elias. New York: Unger, 1966.

Schiller, Friedrich. *On the Aesthetic Education of Man.* Edited by Elizabeth Wilenson and L. Willoughby. Oxford: Oxford University Press, 1967.

Shaftesbury, Anthony Ashley Cooper. *Characteristicks of Men, Manners, Opinions, Times.* Indianapolis, IN: Liberty Fund, 2001.

Smith, Adam. *An Inquiry into the Nature and Causes of the Wealth of Nations.* Edited by R. H. Campbell and A. S. Skinner. Indianapolis, IN: Liberty Fund, 1981.

Smith, Adam. *Lectures on Jurisprudence.* Edited by R. L. Meek, D. D. Raphael, and P. G. Stein. Oxford: Oxford University Press, 1978/Indianapolis, IN: Liberty Fund, 1982.

Specimens of Foreign Language Literature. Edited by George Ripley, vol. I: *Philosophical Miscellanies.* Translated from the French of Cousin, Jouffroy, and B. Constant. Boston: Hilliard, Gray, and Company, 1838.

Staël, Germaine de. *Considerations on the Principal Events of the French Revolution.* London: Baldwin, Cradock, and Joy, 1818.

Staël, Germaine de. *Correspondance générale*, IV/2. Edited by Béatrice Jasinski. Paris: J.-J. Pauvert, 1978.

Staël, Germaine de. *De la littérature considérée dans ses rapports avec les institutions sociales.* Edited by Axel Blaeschke. Paris: Infomédia Communications, 1998.

Staël, Germaine de. *Lettre à Son Excellence Monseigneur le prince de Talleyrand Périgord [...]. au sujet de la traite des nègres.* London: Imprimerie de Schulze & Dean/Paris: Le Normand, 1814.

Staël, Germaine de. "Lettres de Jeunesse," in *Correspondance Generale*, t.1. Edited by B. W. Jasinski, Paris: Pauvert, 1962.

Staël, Germaine de. *Œuvres de jeunesse.* Edited by Simone Balayé and John Isbell. Paris: Desjonquères, 1997.

Staël, Germaine de. *Zulma, et trois nouvelles.* London: Colburn, 1813.

Tocqueville, Alexis de. *Recollections.* Translated by George Lawrence. Garden City, NY: Doubleday, 1970.

Wolf, F. A. *Prolegomena to Homer.* Edited by Anthony Grafton. Princeton, NJ: Princeton University Press, 1985.

SECONDARY SOURCES

Abramovici, Jean-Claude. *Obscénité et classicisme.* Paris: Presses universitaires de France, 2003.

Abrams, Meyer. *Natural Supernaturalism: Tradition and Revolution in Romantic Literature.* New York: Norton, 1971.

Aeschimann, Willy. *La Pensée d'Edgar Quinet. Etude sur la formation de ses idées avec essais de jeunesse et documents inédits.* Paris: Editions Anthropos, 1986.

Aguet, Jean-Pierre. "Benjamin Constant, députe de Strasbourg, parlementaire sous la Monarchie de Juillet (juillet-décembre 1830)," in *Autour Des "Trois Glorieuses" 1830: Strasbourg, L'Alsace et la Liberté. Actes du Colloque de Strasbourg, 16–18 Mai 1980.* Strasbourg: Palais universitaire, 1981.

Alexander, Robert S. *Napoleon.* London: Oxford University Press, 2001.

Alexander, Robert S. *Re-Writing the French Revolutionary Tradition: Liberal Opposition and the Fall of the Bourbon Monarchy.* Cambridge: Cambridge University Press, 2003.

Aner, Karl. *Die Theologie der Lessingzeit.* Halle: M. Niemeyer, 1929.

Arblaster, Anthony. *The Rise and Decline of Western Liberalism.* Oxford: Basil Blackwell, 1984.

Baczko, Bronislaw. *Comment sortir de la Terreur. Thermidor et la Révolution.* Paris: Gallimard, 1989.

Balayé, Simone. "Un article inconnu de Mme de Staël: *Tableau de la littérature française au XVIIIe siècle*, par M. de Barante," *Cahiers staëliens*, (20) (June 1976), 19–26.

Barberis, Mauro. *Benjamin Constant. Rivoluzione, costituzione, progresso*. Bologna: Il Mulino, 1988.

Barth, Karl. *Protestant Thought in the Nineteenth Century*. Valley Forge: Judson, 1973.

Bastid, Paul. *Benjamin Constant et sa doctrine*, vol. I. Paris: A. Colin, 1966.

Baubérot, Jean, and Valentine Zuber. *Une haine oubliée: L'anti-protestantisme avant le "pacte laïque" (1870–1905)*. Paris: Albin Michel, 2000.

Benichou, Paul. *Le Temps des prophètes. Doctrines de l'âge romantique*. Paris: Gallimard, 1977.

Benin, Stephen. *The Footprints of God*. Albany, NY: State University of New York Press, 1993.

Bénot, Yves, and Marcel Dorigny, eds. *1802: Rétablissement de l'esclavage dans les colonies françaises*. Paris: Maisonneuve et Larose, 2003.

Berchtold, Alfred. "Sismondi et le Groupe de Coppet face à l'esclavage et au colonialisme," in *Sismondi Européen: Actes du Colloque international tenu à Genève les 14 et 15 septembre 1973*. Geneva: Slatkine, 1976.

Berenson, Edward. *Populist Religion and Left-Wing Politics in France, 1830–1852*. Princeton, NJ: Princeton University Press 1984.

Berlin, Isaiah. "Two Concepts of Liberty," in *Four Essays on Liberty*. New York: Oxford University Press, 1969.

Binoche, Bertrand, ed., *L'homme perfectible*. Seysssel: Champ Vallon, 2004.

Blanc, Louis. *Histoire de dix ans 1830–1840*. Paris: Germer Baillière et Cie, 1877.

Bourget, Paul. *Essais de psychologie contemporaine (1883–1886)*. Paris: Plon-Nourrit, 1901.

Bowman, Frank. "Benjamin Constant, Germany, and *De La Religion*," in *Romanische Forschungen*, vol. 74 (1/2) (1962), 77–108.

Bowman, Frank Paul. "L'épisode quiétiste dans *Cécile*," in *Benjamin Constant: Actes du Congrès Benjamin Constant (Lausanne, Octobre 1967)*. Geneva: Droz, 1968.

Branda, Pierre, and Thierry Lentz. *Napoleéon, l'esclavage, et les colonies*. Paris: Fayard, 2006.

Breyer Stephen. *Active Liberty: Interpreting Our Democratic Constitution*. New York: Random House, 2005.

Burkert, Walter. *Greek Religion: Archaic and Classical*. Translated by John Raffan. Oxford: Basil Blackwell, 1985.

Cabanel, Patrick. *Le Dieu de la République. Aux sources protestantes de la laïcité (1860–1900)*. Rennes: Presses universitaires de Rennes, 2003.

Cabanel, Patrick. "L'institutionnalisation des 'sciences religieuses' en France (1879–1908) Une entreprise protestante?" *Bulletin de la Société de l'histoire du protestantisme français* (140) (January–February–March 1994), 33–80.

Cappadocia, Ezio. "The Liberals and Madame de Staël in 1818," in *Ideas in History: Essays Presented to Louis Gottschalk by his Former Students.* Edited by Richard Herr and Harold Parker. Durham, NC: Duke University Press, 1965.

Carlson, Julie A. *In the Theatre of Romanticism: Coleridge, Nationalism, Women.* Cambridge: Cambridge University Press, 1994.

Cassirer, Ernst. *Kant's Life and Thought.* Translated by James Haden. New Haven: Yale University Press, 1981.

Cassirer, Ernst. *The Question of Jean-Jacques Rousseau.* Translated by Peter Gay. Bloomington, IN: University of Indiana Press, 1963.

Chopin, Thierry. *Benjamin Constant: le libéralisme inquiet.* Paris: Michalon, 2002.

Christofferson, Michael Scott. "An Antitotalitarian History of the French Revolution: François Furet's *Penser la Revolution française* in the Intellectual Politics of the Late 1970s," *French Historical Studies*, 22 (4) (Fall 1999), 557–611.

Cofrancesco, Dino. *La democrazia liberale e le altre.* Rubbettino: Soveria Mannelli, 2003.

Coppet, creuset de l'esprit libéral. Les idées politiques et constitutionnelles du groupe de Mme de Staël. Edited by Lucien Jaume. Paris: Economica and Presses universitaires d'Aix-Marseille, 2000.

Cornford, Francis. *Before and After Socrates.* Cambridge: Cambridge University Press, 1932.

Coulmann, Jean-Jacques. *Réminiscences.* Paris: Michel Lévy Frères, 1862.

Courtney, Cecil. *Isabelle de Charrière (Belle de Zuylen): A Biography.* Oxford: Voltaire Foundation, 1993.

Cragg, G., ed. *The Cambridge Platonists.* New York: Oxford University Press, 1968.

Critical Dictionary of the French Revolution. Edited by Mona Ozouf and François Furet. Translated by Arthur Goldhammer. Cambridge, MA: Harvard University Press, 1990.

Daget, Serge. "A Model of the French Abolitionist Movement and Its Variations," in *Anti-Slavery, Religion, and Reform: Essays in Memory of Roger Anstey.* Edited by Christine Bolt and Seymour Drescher. Folkstone, Kent: Dawson, 1980.

Daget, Serge. "L'Abolition de la Traite des Noirs en France de 1814 à 1831," *Cahiers d'études africaines*, 41 (1971), 14–58.

Daget, Serge. "Les mots esclave, nègre, noir, et les jugements de valeur sur la traite nègrière dans la littérature abolitionniste française de 1770 à 1845," *Revue française d'histoire d'outre-mer*, 60 (1973), 511–48.

David, Thomas. "Le rôle de la Suisse dans le mouvement abolitionniste français (vers 1760–1840)," in *Abolir l'esclavage. Un réformisme à l'épreuve (France, Suisse, Portugal, XVIII-XIXe siècle*. Edited by Olivier Pétré-Grenouilleau. Rennes: Presses Universitaires de Rennes, 2008.

Davis, David Brion. *The Problem of Slavery in the Age of Revolution, 1770–1823*. Ithaca, NY: Cornell University Press, 1975.

Deguise, Pierre. *Benjamin Constant méconnu: le livre De la Religion*. Genève: Droz, 1966.

Deguise, Pierre. "La religion de Benjamin Constant et l'Unitarisme américain," *ABC*, 12 (1991), 19–27.

Delbouille, Paul. *Genèse, structure et destin d'"Adolphe'*. Paris: Les Belles Lettres, 1971.

Delbouille, Paul. "Le dernier procès de Juste de Constant et l'esprit de famille chez Benjamin et chez Marianne Magnin," *ABC* 26 (2002),89–101.

De Luca, Stefano. *Alle origini del liberalismo contemporaneo. Il pensiero di Benjamin Constant tra il Termidoro e l'Impero*. Cosenza: Marco Editore, 2003.

Denby, David. *Sentimental Narrative and the Social Order in France, 1760–1820*. Cambridge: Cambridge University Press, 1994.

Dickey, Laurence. "Appendix IV," in Adam Smith, *The Wealth of Nations*. Abridged and edited by Laurence Dickey. Indianapolis, IN: Hackett, 1993.

Dickey, Laurence. "*Doux-Commerce* and Humanitarian Values," in *Grotiana*, vols. 22–23 (2001–2).

Dickey, Laurence. *Hegel*. New York: Cambridge University Press, 1987.

Dickey, Laurence. "Saint-Simonian Industrialism as the End of History: August Ciezkowski on the Teleology of Universal History," in *Apocalypse Theory and the Ends of the World*. Edited by Malcolm Bull. Oxford: Blackwell, 1995.

Dillon, John. *The Middle Platonists*. Ithaca, NY: Cornell University Press, 1977.

Dodds, Eric. *Pagan and Christian in an Age of Anxiety*. New York: Norton, 1970.

Dodge, Guy. *Benjamin Constant's Philosophy of Liberalism*. Chapel Hill, NC: University of North Carolina Press, 1980.

Donato, Clorinda. "Benjamin Constant and the Italian Enlightenment in the *Commentaire sur l'ouvrage de Filangieri*: Notes for an Intercultural Reading," *Historical Reflections/Réflexions Historiques*, (28) (2003), 439–453.

Drescher, Seymour. *The Mighty Experiment*. Oxford: Oxford University Press, 2002.

Drescher, Seymour. "Two Variants of Anti-Slavery: Religious Organization and Social Mobilization in Britain and France, 1780–1870," in *Anti-Slavery, Religion and Reform: Essays in Memory of Roger Astey*. Edited by Christine Bolt and Seymour Drescher. Hamden, CT: Archon Books, 1980.

Droz, Jacques. *Histoire des doctrines politiques en France*. Paris: Presses universitaires de France, 1948.

Dubois, Laurent. *A Colony of Citizens: Revolution and Slave Emancipation in the French Caribbean, 1787–1804*. Chapel Hill: University of North Carolina Press, 2004.

Dubois, Laurent. *Avengers of the New World: The Story of the Haitian Revolution*. Cambridge, MA: Harvard University Press, 2004.

Du Bos, Charles. *Approximations (I–VI)*, 192?–1932. Reprinted by Éditions des Syrtes, 2000.

Du Bos, Charles. *Grandeur et misère de Benjamin Constant*. Paris: Corrêa, 1946.

Eltis, David. *Economic Growth and the Ending of the Transatlantic Slave Trade*. New York: Oxford University Press, 1987.

Encyclopedia of Religion. Edited by Lindsay Jones. Detroit: MacMillan, ca. 2005.

Enthusiasm and Enlightenment in Europe, 1650–1850. Edited by Anthony LaVopa and Lawrence Klein. San Marino, CA: Huntington Library, 1998.

Faguet, Emile. *Le Libéralisme*. Paris: Société Française d'Imprimerie et de Librairie, 1903.

Faguet, Emile. *Politiques et moralistes du dix-neuvième siècle*. Paris: Boivin & Cie, 1923.

Fairlie, Alison. "The Art of Constant's *Adolphe*: 1. The Stylization of Experience," in *Imagination and Language: Collected Essays on Constant, Baudelaire, Nerval and Flaubert*. Cambridge: Cambridge University Press, 1981.

Fink, Beatrice. "Benjamin Constant on Equality," *Journal of the History of Ideas*, 33 (1972),307–14.

Folman, Michel. *Le secret de Benjamin Constant*. Geneva: Imprimerie de la Tribune de Genève, 1959.

Fontana, Biancamaria. *Benjamin Constant and the Post-Revolutionary Mind*. New Haven: Yale University Press, 1991.

Fried, Charles. *Modern Liberty and the Limits of Government*. New York: W. W. Norton & Co., 2007.

Friedman, Milton. "Introduction," in *New Individualist Review*. Indianapolis: A Periodical Reprint of Liberty Fund, 1981.

Funkenstein, Amos. *Theology and the Scientific Imagination*. Princeton, NJ: Princeton University Press, 1986.

Furet, François. "La Révolution sans la Terreur? Le débat des historiens du XIXe siècle," *Le Débat*, 13 (June 1981), 40–54.

Gauchet, Marcel. "Benjamin Constant: L'illusion lucide du libéralisme," in *De la liberté chez les Modernes. Ecrits politiques*. Edited by Marcel Gauchet. Paris: Livres de Poche, 1980.

Gawlich, G. "Cicero and the Enlightenment," *Studies in Voltaire and the Eighteenth Century*, 25 (1963).

Geggus, David. "Haiti and the Abolitionists: Opinion, Propaganda, and International Politics in Britain and France, 1804–1816," in *Abolition and its Aftermath*. Edited by David Richardson. London: Frank Cass, 1985.

Girard, Louis. *Les libéraux français*. Paris: Aubier, 1985.

Godet, Philippe. *Madame de Charrière, d'après de nombreux documents inédits (1740–1805)*, 2 vols. Genève: Jullien, 1906.

Grafton, A. "Historical Thought in F. A. Wolf," in *Aufklärung und Geschichte*. Edited by Hans Erich Bödeker. Göttingen: Vandenhoeck and Ruprecht, 1986.

Grafton, Anthony, ed. *F. A. Wolf. Prolegomena to Homer*. Princeton: Princeton University Press, 1985.

Grafton, Anthony. "Prolegomena to Friedrich August Wolf," in *Defenders of the Text: The Traditions of Scholarship in an Age of Science, 1450–1800*. Cambridge, MA: Harvard University Press, 1991.

Grange, Henri. *Benjamin Constant: amoureux et républicain 1795–1799*. Paris: Les Belles Lettres, 2004.

Grange, Henri. "De Necker à Benjamin Constant ou du libéralisme ploutocratique au libéralisme démocratique," in *Le Groupe de Coppet et la Révolution française*. Edited by Etienne Hofmann and Anne-Lise Delacrétaz. Lausanne: Institut Benjamin Constant, 1988.

Grange, Henri. *Les idées de Necker*. Paris: Klincksieck, 1974.

Green, Louis. *Chronicle into History: An Essay on the Interpretation of History in Florentine Fourteenth-Century Chronicles*. Cambridge: Cambridge University Press, 1972.

Greer, Donald. *The Incidence of the Terror during the French Revolution: A Statistical Interpretation*. Cambridge, MA: Harvard University Press, 1935.

Griswold, Charles. *Adam Smith and the Virtues of Enlightenment*. Cambridge: Cambridge University Press, 1999.

Gusdorf, Georges. *L'avènement des sciences humaines au siècle des Lumières*. Paris: Payot, 1973.

Halévy, Elie. *L'Ere des tyrannies*. Gallimard: Paris, 1938.

Hamowy, Ronald. "The Libertarian Press," in *The Conservative Press in Twentieth-Century America*. Edited by Ronald Lora and William Henry Longton. Westport, CT: Greenwood Press, 1999.

Harpaz, Ephraim. "Benjamin Constant, 1820–1830: grandeur et limites de sa pensée," in *Benjamin Constant, Madame de Staël et le Groupe de Coppet: Actes du deuxième Congrès de Lausanne et du troisième Colloque de Coppet*. Edited by Etienne Hofmann. Oxford: The Voltaire Foundation and Lausanne: Institut Benjamin Constant, 1982, 89–97.

Harpaz, Ephraïm. *L'Ecole libérale sous la Restauration, le 'Mercure' et la 'Minerve', 1817–1820*. Geneva: Droz, 1968.

Hart, David M. *The Radical Liberalism of Charles Comte and Charles Dunoyer*. Available online at http://homepage.mac.com/dmhart/Comte Dunoyer/index.html.

Hartshorne, Charles. *A Natural Theology for Our Time*. LaSalle, IL: Open Court Press, 1967.

Harvey, Austin. *Handbook of Theological Terms*. New York: MacMillan, 1964.

Hauranne, Duvergier de. "Prosper," in *Histoire du gouvernement parlementaire en France*. Paris: Michel Lévy Frères, 1857–72.

Hause, Steven. "Anti-Protestant Rhetoric in the Early Third Republic," *French Historical Studies*, 16 (1) (Spring 1989), 183–201.

Hazareesingh, Sudhir. *Intellectual Founders of the Republic. Five Studies in Nineteenth-Century French Republican Thought*. Oxford: Oxford University Press, 2001.

Hazareesingh, Sudhir. *Political Traditions in Modern France*. Oxford: Oxford University Press, 1994.

Heyd, Michael. *"Be Sober and Reasonable": The Critique of Enthusiasm in the Seventeenth and Early Eighteenth Centuries*. Leiden: E. J. Brill, 1995.

Higonnet, Patrice. "Marx, disciple de Constant?" *ABC*, 6 (1986), 11–16.

Hirschman, Albert. *Rival Views of Market Society and Other Essays*. New York: Viking, 1986.

Hochschild, Adam. *Bury the Chains*. Boston: Houghton Mifflin, 2005.

Hofmann, Etienne. *Catalogue raisonné de l'œuvre manuscrite de Benjamin Constant*. Genève: Slatkine, 1992.

Hofmann, Etienne. *Les "Principes de Politique" de Benjamin Constant (1806)*, 2 vols., vol. 1, *La Genèse d'une œuvre et l'évolution de la pensée de leur auteur 1789–1806*. Geneva: Droz, 1980.

Hofstadter, Dan. *The Love Affair as a Work of Art*. New York: Farrar, Straus, and Giroux, 1996.

Hogue, Helen. *Of Changes in Benjamin Constant's Books on Religion*. Geneva: Droz, 1964.

Holmes, Stephen. *Benjamin Constant and the Making of Modern Liberalism*. New Haven: Yale University Press, 1984.

Holmes, Stephen. "Liberal Uses of Bourbon Legitimism," *Journal of the History of Ideas*, 43 (2) (April–June 1982), 229–48.

Holmes, Stephen. *Passions and Constraint: On the Theory of Liberal Democracy*. Chicago: University of Chicago Press, 1995.

Holmes, Stephen. *The Anatomy of Antiliberalism*. Cambridge, MA: Harvard University Press, 1993.

Hont, Istvan. *Jealousy of Trade*. Cambridge, MA: Harvard University Press, 2005.

Huard, Raymond. *La naissance du parti politique en France*. Paris: Presses de la Fondation nationale des sciences politiques, 1996.

Ideas in History. Essays Presented to Louis Gottschalk by his Former Students. Edited by Richard Herr and Harold Parker. Durham, NC: Duke University Press, 1965.

Isbell, John. *The Birth of European Romanticism: Truth and Propaganda in Staël's* De l'Allemagne, *1810–1813*. Cambridge: Cambridge University Press, 1994.

Izenberg, Gerald. *Impossible Individuality: Romanticism, Revolution, and the Origins of Modern Selfhood, 1787–1802*. Princeton, NJ: Princeton University Press, 1992.

Jacobs, Laurence. "'Le Moment Libéral': The Distinctive Character of Restoration Liberalism," *Historical Journal*, 31 (2) (June 1988), 479–91.

Jaeger, Werner. *Early Christianity and Greek Paideia*. Cambridge, MA: Harvard University Press, 1961.

Jaeger, Werner. *Humanism and Theology, under the Auspices of the Aristotelian Society of Marquette University*. Milwaukee, WI: Marquette University Press, 1943.

Jaeger, Werner. *The Theology of the Early Greek Philosophers*. Translated by Edward Robinson. Oxford: Clarendon, 1947.

Jainchill, Andrew, and Sam Moyn. "French Democracy between Totalitarianism and Solidarity: Pierre Rosanvallon and Revisionist Historiography," *Journal of Modern History*, 76 (1) (March 2004), 107–54.

Jardin, André. *Histoire du libéralisme politique: de la crise de l'absolutisme à la constitution de 1875*. Paris: Hachette, 1985.

Jasinski, Béatrice. *L'Engagement de Benjamin Constant: amour et politique (1794–1796)*. Paris: Minard, 1971.

Jaspers, Karl. *The Origin and Goal of History*. Translated by Michael Bullock. New Haven, CT: Yale University Press, 1953.

Jaume, Lucien. "Coppet, creuset du libéralisme comme 'culture morale'," in *Coppet, Creuset de l'esprit libéral: les idées politiques et constitutionnelles du Groupe de Madame de Staël*. Edited by Lucien Jaume. Paris and Aix en Provence: Economica et Presses universitaires d'Aix-Marseille, 2000.

Jaume, Lucien. "Droit, Etat et obligation selon Benjamin Constant," *Commentaire*, 22 (87) (Fall 1999), 711–715.

Jaume, Lucien. *Echec au libéralisme: les Jacobins et l'Etat*. Paris: Kimé, 1990.

Jaume, Lucien. *La liberté et la loi. Les origines philosophiques du libéralisme*. Paris: Fayard, 2000.

Jaume, Lucien. "Le concept de responsabilité des ministres chez Benjamin Constant," *Revue française de droit constitutionnel*, 42 (2000), 227–243.

Jaume, Lucien. "Le problème de l'intérêt général dans la pensée de Benjamin Constant," in *Le Groupe de Coppet et le monde moderne: Conception-Images-Débats*. Edited by Françoise Tilkin. Liège: Bibliothèque de la Faculté de Philosophie et Lettres de l'Université de Liège, 1998.

Jaume, Lucien. *L'individu effacé ou le paradoxe du libéralisme française*. Paris: Fayard, 1997.

Jennings, Lawrence C. *French Anti-Slavery: The Movement for the Abolition of Slavery in France, 1802–1848*. Cambridge: Cambridge University Press, 2000.

Johnson, Douglas. *Guizot. Aspects of French History, 1787–1874*. London: Routledge & K. Paul, 1963.

Juden, Brian. "Accueil et rayonnement de la pensée de Benjamin Constant sur la religion," in *Benjamin Constant, Madame de Staël et le Groupe de Coppet. Actes du deuxième Congrès de Lausanne*. Edited by Etienne Hofmann. Oxford: The Voltaire Foundation, 1982.

Judt, Tony. *Past Imperfect. French Intellectuals, 1944–1956*. Berkeley, CA: University of California Press, 1992.

Kahan, Alan S. *Liberalism in Nineteenth-Century Europe: The Political Culture of Limited Suffrage*. New York: Palgrave Macmillan, 2003.

Kalyvas, Andreas, and Ira Katznelson. "'We Are Modern Men': Benjamin Constant and the Discovery of an Immanent Liberalism," *Constellations*, 6 (4) (1999), 513–39.

Kateb, George. "The Moral Distinctiveness of Representative Democracy," *Ethics*, 91 (April 1981), 357–74.

Kelly, George. "Constant and His Interpreters: A Second Visit," *ABC*, 6 (1986), 81–89.

Kelly, George. "Constant Commotion: Avatars of a Pure Liberal," *Journal of Modern History*, 54 (3) (September 1982), 497–518.

Kelly, George. *The Human Comedy:Constant, Tocqueville and French Liberalism*. New York: Cambridge University Press, 1992.

Kent, Sherman. *The Election of 1827 in France*. Cambridge, MA: Harvard University Press, 1975.

Khilnani, Sunil. *The Intellectual Left in Postwar France*. New Haven and London: Yale University Press, 1993.

Kielstra, Paul Michael. *The Politics of Slave Trade Suppression in Britain and France, 1814–48: Diplomacy, Morality, and Economics*. London: St. Martin's Press, 2000.

Klauber, Martin, and G. Sunshine. "Jean-Alphonse Turrettini on Biblical Accommodation," *Calvin Theological Journal*, 25 (1990).

Kloocke, Kurt. *Benjamin Constant: une biographie intellectuelle*. Geneva: Droz, 1984.

Klooke, Kurt. "Johann Gottfried Herder et Benjamin Constant," *ABC*, 29 (2005), 55–72.

Ladner, G. *The Idea of Reform*. Cambridge, MA: Harvard University Press, 1959.

Ladner, G. "The Philosophical Anthropology of Saint Gregory of Nyssa," *Dumbarton Oaks Papers*, 12 (1958).

Lalande, André. *Vocabulaire technique et critique de la philosophie*. Paris: Presses Universitaires de France, 1976.

Lalouette, Jacqueline. *La séparation des Eglises et de l'Etat. Genèse et développement d'une idée 1789–1905*. Paris: Editions du Seuil, 2005.

Lamberti, Jean-Claude. *Tocqueville and the Two Democracies*. Translated by Arthur Goldhammer. Cambridge, MA: Harvard University Press, 1989.

Laurent, Alain. *La philosophie libérale. Histoire et actualité d'une tradition intellectuelle*. Paris: Les Belles Lettres, 2002.

Laurent, Alain. *L'Individu et ses ennemis*. Paris: Hachette, 1987.

Lee, James. "Benjamin Constant: The Moralization of Modern Liberty," Ph.D. thesis, History Department, University of Wisconsin, Madison, WI, 2003.

Lee, James Mitchell. "Doux Commerce, Social Organization, and Modern Liberty in the Thought of Benjamin Constant," *ABC*, 26 (2002), 117–49.

L'esclavage à la française: le Code Noir (1685 et 1724). Edited by Robert Chesnais. Paris: Nautilus, 2005.

"Libéralisme," in *Dictionnaire politique*. Paris: Pagnerre, 1860.

Lilla, Mark. "The Other Velvet Revolution: Continental Liberalism and Its Discontents," *Daedalus*, 123 (2) (Spring 1994), 129–58.

Lloyd-Jones, Hugh. *The Justice of Zeus*. Berkeley, CA: University of California Press, 1971.

Lotterie, Florence. "Le progrès désenchanté: la perfectiblité selon Constant ou le malaise libéral," in *Le Groupe de Coppet et le monde moderne. Conceptions-Images-Débats*. Edited by Françoise Tilkin. Geneva: Droz, 1998.

Lotterie, Florence. *L'idée de perfectibilité entre Lumières et Romantisme (1750–1822).* Paris: X-Nanterre, 1997.

Lotterie, Florence. *Progrès et perfectibilité: un dilemme des Lumières françaises (1755–1814).* Oxford: Voltaire Foundation, 2006.

Lovejoy, Arthur. *Primitivism and Related Ideas in Antiquity.* New York: Octagon, 1980.

Löwith, Karl. *Meaning in History. The Theological Implications of the Philosophy of History.* Chicago, IL: University of Chicago Press, 1950.

MacIntyre, Alasdair. *After Virtue: A Study of Moral Theory.* Notre Dame, IN: University of Notre Dame Press, 1981.

Manent, Pierre. *An Intellectual History of Liberalism.* Translated by Rebecca Balinski. Princeton: Princeton University Press, 1994.

Meinecke, Friedrich. *Historism: The Rise of a New Historical Outlook.* Translated by J. Anderson. London: Routledge, 1972.

Mélonio, Françoise. *Tocqueville et les Français.* Paris: Aubier, 1993.

Melzer, Arthur. "The Origin of the Counter-Enlightenment: Rousseau and the New Religion of Sincerity," *American Political Science Review,* 90 (June 1996), 344–60.

Michel, Henry. *L'idée de l'Etat.* Paris, Hachette, 1898.

Miller, Peter. *Peiresc's Europe: Learning and Virtue in the Seventeenth Century.* New Haven, CT: Yale University Press, 2000.

Mintz, Sidney. *Sweetness and Power: The Place of Sugar in Modern History.* New York: Penguin, 1986.

Mortier, Roland. "Belle and Benjamin: Political Gradations," *Eighteenth Century Life,* 13 (1) (February 1989), 16–25.

Necheles, Ruth. *The Abbé Grégoire, 1787–1831: The Odyssey of an Egalitarian.* Westport, CT: Greenwood, 1971.

Neely, Sylvia. *Lafayette and the Liberal Ideal 1814–1824.* Carbondale, IL: Southern Illinois University Press, 1991.

Neely, Sylvia. "Rural Politics in the Early Restoration: Charles Goyet and the Liberals of the Sarthe," *European History Quarterly,* 16 (3) (1986), 313–342.

Nicolson, Harold. *Benjamin Constant.* London: Constable, 1949.

Niebuhr, H. R. *Christ and Culture.* New York: Harper, 1951.

Niebuhr, H. R. "Foreword," to L. Feuerbach, *The Essence of Christianity.* Translated by G. Eliot. New York: Harper, 1957.

Nord, Philip. *The Republican Moment. Struggles for Democracy in Nineteenth-Century France.* Cambridge, MA: Harvard University Press, 1998.

Nygren, Anders. *Agape and Eros.* Translated by Philip Watson. London: S. P. C. K., 1953.

Otto, Rudolf. *Religious Essays.* Oxford: Oxford University Press, 1931.

Ozouf, Mona. "'Public opinion' at the End of the Old Regime," *Journal of Modern History*, 60 (September 1988), S1–21. Special supplement, *Rethinking French Politics in 1788*.

Ozouf, Mona. "Liberty," in *Dictionary of the French Revolution*. Translated by Arthur Goldhammer. Edited by François Furet and Mona Ozouf. Cambridge, MA: Harvard University Press, 1989.

Ozouf, Mona. *Women's Words: An Essay on French Singularity*. Translated by Jane Marie Todd. Chicago, IL: University of Chicago Press, 1997.

Panges, Comtesse Jean de. "Madame de Staël et les nègres," *Revue de France*, 5 (1934), 425–443.

Peabody, Sue. *"There Are No Slaves in France": The Political Culture of Race and Slavery in the Ancien Régime*. Oxford: Oxford University Press, 1996.

Pettit, Philip. *Republicanism: A Theory of Freedom and Government*. Oxford: Clarendon Press, 1997.

Pierson, George. *Tocqueville in America*. Baltimore, MD: Johns Hopkins Press, 1996.

Pinkney, David. *Decisive Years in France. 1840–1847*. Princeton, NJ: Princeton University Press, 1986.

Pitt, Alan. "The Religion of the Moderns: Freedom and Authenticity in Constant's *De La Religion*," *History of Political Thought*, 21 (1) (2000), 67–87.

Pitts, Jennifer. *A Turn to Empire: The Rise of Imperial Liberalism in Britain and France*. Princeton, NJ: Princeton University Press, 2005.

Plamenatz, John. "Liberalism," in *Dictionary of the History of Ideas*, vol. III. Edited by Philip Wiener. New York: Charles Scribner's Sons, 1973.

Porterfield, Todd. *The Allure of Empire: Art in the Service of French Imperialism, 1798–1836*. Princeton, NJ: Princeton University Press, 1998.

Poulet, Georges. *Benjamin Constant par lui-même*. Paris: Editions du Seuil, 1968.

Pouthas, Charles. *Guizot pendant la Restauration: préparation de l'homme d'état (1814–1830)*. Paris: Plon, 1923.

Prélot, Marcel. *Histoire des idées politiques*. Paris: Dalloz, 1960.

Prosper Duvergier de Hauranne. *Histoire du gouvernement parlementaire en France*. Paris, 1857–72.

Raico, Ralph. "Benjamin Constant," in *New Individualist Review*. Indianapolis, IN: A Periodical Reprint of Liberty Fund, 1981.

Raico, Ralph. "The Place of Religion in the Liberal Philosophy of Constant, Tocqueville, and Lord Acton," Ph.D. dissertation, Committee on Social Thought, University of Chicago, Chicago, IL, 1970. Available online at http://www.mises.org/etexts/raico.pdf.

Rawls, John. *A Theory of Justice*. Cambridge, MA: Harvard University Press, 2003.

Report of the Committee of the African Institution. London: William Phillips, 1807.

Réville, Albert. *Prolégomènes de l'histoire des religions.* Paris: G. Fischbacher, 1881.

Ripley, George. *Philosophical Miscellanies.* Boston: Hilliard, Grey, and Company, 1838.

Rosanvallon, Pierre. *Le modèle politique français: la société civile contre le jacobinisme de 1789 à nos jours.* Paris: Seuil, 2004.

Rosanvallon, Pierre. *Le moment Guizot.* Paris: Gallimard, 1985.

Rosanvallon, Pierre. *The Demands of Liberty, Civil Society in France since the Revolution.* Translated by Arthur Goldhammer. Cambridge, MA: Harvard University Press, 2007.

Rose, Hugh. *The State of Protestantism in Germany Described.* London: Rivington, 1829.

Rosenblatt, Helena. "Commerce et religion dans le libéralisme de Benjamin Constant," *Commentaire,* 26 (102) (Summer 2003), 415–26.

Rosenblatt, Helena. *Liberal Values: Benjamin Constant and the Politics of Religion.* Cambridge, UK: Cambridge University Press, 2008.

Rosenblatt, Helena. "Madame de Staël, the Protestant Reformation, and the History of 'Private Judgement'," *ABC,* 31–32 (2007), 143–54.

Rosenblatt, Helena. "Re-Evaluating Benjamin Constant's Liberalism: Industrialism, Saint-Simonianism and the Restoration Years," *History of European Ideas,* 30 (2004), 23–37.

Rosenblatt, Helena. "On the Intellectual Sources of *Laïcité.* Rousseau, Constant, and the Debates about a National Religion," *French Politics, Culture & Society,* 25 (3) (Winter 2007), 1–18.

Rosenblatt, Helena. "Why Constant? A Critical Overview of the Constant Revival," *Modern Intellectual History,* 1 (3) (2004), 439–53.

Rosenblum, Nancy. *Another Liberalism: Romanticism and the Reconstruction of Liberal Thought.* Cambridge, MA: Harvard University Press, 1987.

Rouché, Max. *La philosophie de l'histoire de Herder.* Paris: Les Belles Lettres, 1940.

Rudler, Gustave. *La Jeunesse de Benjamin Constant: 1767–1794.* Paris: Colin, 1908.

Ruggiero, Guido de. *The History of European Liberalism.* Translated by R. G. Collingwood. Boston, MA: Beacon Press, 1961.

Sacquin, Michèle. *Entre Bossuet et Maurras, l'antiprotestantisme en France.* Paris: Ecole des Chartres, 1998.

Schermerhorn, Elizabeth. *Benjamin Constant. His Private Life and His Contribution to the Cause of Liberal Government in France, 1767–1830.* London: Heinemann, 1924.

Schlobach, Jochen. "Siècle," in *Dictionnaire européen des Lumières*. Edited by Michel Delon. Paris: Presses Universitaires de France, 1997.

Schmidt, Nelly. *Abolitionnistes de l'esclavage et réformateurs des colonies, 1820–1851*. Paris: Editions Karthala, 2000.

Scott, Geoffrey. *The Portrait of Zélide*. New York: Helen Marx, 1997.

Seeber, Edward Derbyshire. *Anti-Slavery Opinion in France during the Second Half of the Eighteenth Century*. Baltimore: Johns Hopkins Press, 1937.

Seigel, Jerrold. *The Idea of the Self: Thought and Experience in Western Europe since the Seventeenth Century*. Cambridge: Cambridge University Press, 2005.

Shumway, Anna. *A Study of the* Minerve française. Philadelphia, 1934.

Simmel, Georg. *Essays on Religion*. Edited and translated by Horst Helle. New Haven, CT: Yale University Press, 1997.

Skinner, Quentin. *Liberty before Liberalism*. Cambridge: Cambridge University Press, 1998.

Skinner, Quentin. "The Idea of Negative Liberty," in *Philosophy in History*. Edited by Richard Rorty, Jerome Schneewind, and Quentin Skinner. Cambridge: Cambridge University Press, 1984.

Sorkin, David. "Geneva's 'Enlightened Orthodoxy'," *Church History*, 74 (2005), 286–305.

Spitz, Jean-Fabien. *La Liberté politique: Essai de généalogie conceptuelle*. Paris: Presses Universitaires de France, 1995.

Spitzer, Alan B. *Old Hatreds and Young Hopes: The French Carbonari against the Bourbon Restoration*. Cambridge, MA: Harvard University Press, 1971.

Spitzer, Alan B. "Restoration Political Theory and the Debate over the Law of the Double Vote," *Journal of Modern History*, 55 (1) (March 1983), 54–70.

Starobinski, Jean. "Benjamin Constant: la pensée du progrès et l'analyse des réactions," *ABC*, 23–24 (2000), 39–62.

Starobinski, Jean. *Jean-Jacques Rousseau: La transparence et l'obstacle*. Paris: Gallimard, 1971.

Starobinski, Jean. "Suicide et mélancholie chez Madame de Staël," in *Madame de Staël et l'Europe*. Paris: Klincksieck, 1970, 242–52.

Starobinski, Jean. "The Word Civilization," in *Blessings in Disguise, or, the Morality of Evil*. Translated by Arthur Goldhammer. Cambridge, MA: Harvard University Press, 1993.

Stavru, A. "Socrates," in *Encyclopedia of Religion*, vol. 12. Editor in chief Lindsay Jones. Detroit: Macmillan Reference, 2005, 8504.

Stewart, Joan Hinde. "*Adolphe*, by Benjamin Constant," in *Encyclopedia of the Novel*, vol. 1. Edited by P. Schellinger. Chicago: Fitzroy Dearborn, 1998.

Stewart, Joan Hinde. *Gynographs: French Novels by Women of the Late Eighteenth Century*. Lincoln, NE: University of Nebraska Press, 1993.

Swart, Koenraad. "'Individualism' in the Mid-Nineteenth Century (1826–1860)," *Journal of the History of Ideas*, 23 (1) (January–March 1962), 77–90.

Talmon, Jacob L. *Political Messianism: The Romantic Phase*. New York: Praeger, 1960.

Taylor, A. "Theism," in *Encyclopedia of Religion and Ethics*. Edited by J. Hastings. New York: Scribners, 1921.

Taylor, Charles. *Sources of the Self*. Cambridge, MA: Harvard University Press, 1989.

Thompson, Patrice. *La Religion de Benjamin Constant*. Pisa: Pacini editore, 1978.

Thureau-Dangin, Paul. *Le parti libéral sous la Restauration*. Paris: Plon Cie, 1876.

Todd, Margo. *Christian Humanism and the Puritan Social Order*. New York: Cambridge University Press, 1987.

Todorov, Tzvetan. *Benjamin Constant. La passion démocratique*. Paris: Hachette, 1997 (Littératures).

Todorov, Tzvetan. "Un chef-d'œuvre oublié," in *Constant, De la religion considérée dans sa source, ses formes et ses développements*. Edited by Tzvetan Todorov and Etienne Hofmann. Arles, France: Actes Sud, 1999.

Touchard, Jean. *Histoire des idées politiques*, vol. 2. Paris: Presses Universitaires de France, 1959.

Trampus, Antonio. "Filangieri et Constant: constitutionnalisme des Lumières et constitutionnalisme libéral," *ABC*, 30 (2006), 51–70.

Translating Slavery: Gender and Race in French Women's Writings, 1783–1823. Edited by Doris Y. Kadish and Françoise Massardier-Kenney. Kent: Kent State University Press, 1994.

Travers, Emeric. *Benjamin Constant, les Principes et l'Histoire*. Paris: Honoré Champion, 2005.

Trevor-Roper, Hugh. "Hugo Grotius and England," in *From Counter-Reformation to Glorious Revolution*. Chicago: University of Chicago Press, 1992.

Trinkaus, Charles. *In Our Image and Likeness: Humanity and Divinity in Italian Humanist Thought*, 2 vols. London: Constable, 1970.

Troeltsch, Ernst. *Gesammelte Schriften*, vol. 4. Tübingen: Mohr, 1925.

Troeltsch, Ernst. *Protestantism and Progress: A Historical Study of the Relation of Protestantism to the Modern World*. Translated by W. Montgomery. London: Williams and Norgate, 1912.

Troeltsch, Ernst. *Religion in History*. Translated by James Adams and Walter Bense. Minneapolis, MN: Fortress Press, 1989.

Troeltsch, Ernst. *The Social Teaching of the Christian Churches*. Translated by Olive Wyan. New York: MacMillan Company, 1931.

Trousson, Raymond. *Isabelle de Charrière: Un Destin de femme au XVIIIe siècle*. Paris: Hachette, 1994.

Vallotton, François. "Constant dans tous ses états: essai de diagnostic historiographique," in *Bibliographie analytique des écrits sur Benjamin Constant 1980–1995*. Paris: Editions Champion, 1997.

Verhoeff, Han. *"Adolphe" et Constant: une étude psychocritique*. Paris: Klincksieck, 1976.

Vernant, Jean-Pierre. *The Origins of Greek Thought*. Ithaca, NY: Cornell University Press, 1982.

Vincent, K. Steven. "Benjamin Constant, the French Revolution, and the Origins of French Romantic Liberalism," *French Historical Studies*, 23 (4) (2000), 607–37.

Vincent, K. Steven. "Benjamin Constant, the French Revolution, and the Problem of Modern Character," *History of European Ideas*, 30 (2004), 5–21.

Vincent, K. Steven. "Elite Culture in Early-Nineteenth Century France: Salons, Sociability, and the Self," *Modern Intellectual History*, 4 (2) (August 2007), 327–51.

Voegelin, E. "Immortality: Experience and Symbol," *Harvard Theological Review*, 60 (2) (1967), 235–79.

Voegelin, Eric. *The New Science of Politics*. Chicago, IL: University of Chicago Press, 1952.

Voltaire (François-Marie Arouet). "The Worldling" and "The Man of the World," in *Commerce, Culture and Liberty*. Edited by Henry Clark. Indianapolis, IN: Liberty Fund, 2003.

Waller, Margaret. *The Male Malady. Fictions of Impotence in the French Romantic Novel*. New Brunswick: Rutgers University Press, 1993.

Waterlot, Ghislain. "Perfectibilité et vérité de la religion chez Benjamin Constant," in *L'homme perfectible*. Edited by Bertrand Binoche. Seyssel: Champ Vallon, 2004.

Weill, Georges. *Histoire de l'idée laïque en France au XIXe siècle*. Paris: Félix Alcan, 1925.

Welch, Cheryl. "Jansenism and Liberalism: The Making of Citizens in Post-Revolutionary France," *History of Political Thought*, 7 (Spring 1986), 151–65.

Welch, Cheryl. *Liberty and Utility: The French Ideologues and the Transformation of Liberalism.* New York: Columbia University Press, 1984.

Western Liberalism. A History in Documents from Locke to Croce. Edited by E. K. Bramsted and K. J. Melhuish. New York: Longman, 1978.

Winkler, Markus. "De la fatalité des Anciens aux préjugés sociaux des Modernes. La présence du mythe chez August Wilhelm Schlegel, Madame de Staël et Benjamin Constant," in *Le Groupe de Coppet et l'Europe, 1789–1830. Actes du cinquième Colloque de Coppet, Tübingen, 8–10 juillet 1993.* Edited by Kurt Kloocke and Simone Balayé. Lausanne: Institut Benjamin Constant, 1994.

Wolf, F. A. *Prolegomena to Homer.* Edited by Anthony Grafton. Princeton: Princeton University Press, 1985.

Wood, Dennis. *Benjamin Constant: A Biography.* London and New York: Routledge, 1993.

Wordsworth, C. "On the Interpretation of Scripture," in *Replies to "Essays and Reviews."* New York: D. Appleton, 1862.

Young, James. *Reconsidering American Liberalism. The Troubled Odyssey of the Liberal Idea.* Boulder, CO: Westview Press, 1996.

INDEX

403